SUNSTRUCK GIANT VOLUME 1

The Sino-Japanese War of 1894–1895 Part 1

John Dong

Helion & Company

Helion & Company Limited
Unit 8 Amherst Business Centre
Budbrooke Road
Warwick
CV34 5WE
England
Tel. 01926 499 619
Email: info@helion.co.uk
Website: www.helion.co.uk
Twitter: @helionbooks
Visit our blog https://helionbooks.wordpress.com/

Published by Helion & Company 2025
Designed and typeset by Mach 3 Solutions (www.mach3solutions.co.uk)
Cover designed by Paul Hewitt, Battlefield Design (www.battlefield-design.co.uk)

Text © John Dong 2025
Photographs and illustrations as individually credited
Colour artwork by Renato Dalmaso © Helion & Company 2025

Every reasonable effort has been made to trace copyright holders and to obtain their permission for the use of copyright material. The author and publisher apologise for any errors or omissions in this work and would be grateful if notified of any corrections that should be incorporated in future reprints or editions of this book.

ISBN 978-1-804518-15-1

British Library Cataloguing-in-Publication Data.
A catalogue record for this book is available from the British Library.

All rights reserved. No part of this publication may be reproduced, stored in a retrieval system, or transmitted, in any form, or by any means, electronic, mechanical, photocopying, recording or otherwise, without the express written consent of Helion & Company Limited.

For details of other military history titles published by Helion & Company Limited contact the above address or visit our website: http://www.helion.co.uk.

We always welcome receiving book proposals from prospective authors.

Contents

Acknowledgements		iv
1	The Armies of the Qing Empire	5
2	The Navies of the Qing Empire	70
3	The Army of the Empire of Japan	101
4	The Navy of the Empire of Japan	171
5	Colour Plate Commentaries	184

Appendices

I	Chinese military ranks	211
II	Imperial Japanese Army and Navy Ranks	214
III	Imperial Japanese Army Uniform Colours	222

Bibliography	229

Acknowledgements

First of all, I would like to thank the Helion & Company team, specifically Charles Singleton, for allowing me to indulge in this great passion of mine and for being so flexible with all my delays and ramblings.

Second, Mr Ryotarou Tsutsumi for inspiring my interest in this period of history and for his tireless research into late Qing military uniforms.

Third, I would like to express my sincere gratitude to K.C.L. Hamilton, Haden Gruehn, Vivian Ji, Abdel Eduardo Ruiz Muñoz, Kian Kashayar, and Sebastian Hofmann for proofreading the manuscript and catching all the dreadful clangers I missed.

Fourth, I would like to thank He Jianye and Albert Chung of the University of California at Berkeley East Asian Library, Petra Martin and Sylvia Pereira of the Staatliche Kunstsammlungen Dresden, Misako Tomita of the Oiso Town Local History Museum, Jamie Carstairs and Colonel Leslie Addington of the University of Bristol Library, Wei Ling of the National Taiwan Museum, Stanley Zielinski of BANZAI magazine, Joseph Passman of the Belfer Center for Science and International Affairs, Antoine Hiemisch of Côte d'Azur University, Cherif Slimani of the Établissement de Communication et de Production Audiovisuelle de la Défense, Tabitha Cadbury of the Box Museum, and my classmate Briana Lopez for supplying photographs and research materials for this work. I would also like to thank my dear aunt Gao Zhu for helping me get to Weihai and Liugongdao to see the First Sino-Japanese War Museum.

Fifth, I would like to thank my excellent illustrator Renato Dalmaso, whose strict attention to detail and vivid composition has done wonders in bringing this forgotten war back to life.

Last but perhaps most importantly, I would like to dedicate this work to my dear parents, whose support has been both consistent and vigorous.

Chapter 1

The Armies of the Qing Empire

Introduction

The Empire of the Great Qing, reigning from 1644 to 1911, was the final dynasty in China governed by an emperor. Though they ruled the Chinese Empire, the Qing was and is not considered a true 'Chinese' dynasty by many, as it was founded and ruled by the Manchu people, who made up less than five percent of the population, in contrast to the overwhelming Han Chinese majority. The infamous queue, a symbol of humiliation and oppression, was enforced upon the Han population under the threat of beheading and with their segregated garrison cities and special privileges, the Manchus justified their rule with the right of conquest. Despite this unhappy origin, China experienced a golden age from 1683 to 1799, during which subjects of the Qing Dynasty enjoyed some of the highest living standards on the planet. The Qing had a largely self-sufficient economy, a prolific abundance of natural resources, and no need for colonies or international markets. China, the Middle Kingdom, remained the cultural and political leader of East Asia; no threats to its dominance existed. The Qing saw no room for improvement.

By the beginning of the nineteenth century, however, there was much room for improvement. An undermanned and inefficient bureaucracy not only overtaxed the population but also discriminated against ethnic and religious minorities. Corruption had pervaded every institution, both civilian and military. Signs of military decay were showing, even in the eighteenth century, when Qing invasions of Burma and Vietnam failed multiple times. The Qing, who justified their rule with the sword, had grown increasingly unable to cope with both internal and external military threats.[1]

But it was the forceful confiscation and destruction of British-supplied opium that began what China considers to be her 'Century of Humiliation.' During the First Opium War (1839–1842), superior British organisation, technology, and tactics easily defeated the Chinese, and an 'unequal treaty' with terms favouring British commercial interests was signed at its conclusion. The Chinese, however, did not perceive the British as a real threat, and refused

---
1   Sarah C. Paine, *The Sino-Japanese War of 1894–1895: Perceptions, Power, and Primacy* (Cambridge: Cambridge University Press, 2003), p.24.

to honour the treaty, leading to the disastrous Second Opium War, or the Arrow War (1856–1860), named after the seizure of the eponymous opium ship. China's helplessness against European warmongering would become a running trend in the Century of Humiliation.

In addition to foreign incursions, China was afflicted with a series of mid-century civil wars. Tens, if not hundreds, of millions were killed in combat or by the resulting famines and plague outbreaks. There were two categories for these civil wars, the first being civil wars aiming at regime change. The Taiping Rebellion (1851–1866) was probably the most destructive of this type, with a death toll usually put at 20–30 million people. The Nian Rebellion (1851–1868) began as groups of bandits pillaging the countryside but they eventually developed political ambitions to expel the Manchus from the Imperial throne. Other revolts by sectarian or revolutionary societies, like the Red Turban Rebellion (1854–1856) and the Small Sword Rebellion (1853–1855), aimed to restore the Ming Dynasty.[2]

The second category included the wars of secession, where disenfranchised ethnic, regional, or religious groups endeavoured to break free of the Qing yoke. The Panthay Rebellion (1856–1872) led to a multi-ethnic and multi-religious independent Sultanate in Yunnan. Likewise, the short-lived Emirate of Kashgaria (1862–1877) established a short-lived autonomous Xinjiang region, the Miao Rebellion (1854–1873) saw the ethnic group revolt for the third time in a century, the Dungan Rebellion (1862–1873) involved religious and ethnic violence in the northwest provinces, and so on. Both classes of civil wars greatly damaged the Qing's political legitimacy. Several rebel states even developed functional governments that were viable and preferable alternatives to Qing rule, while the merciless reprisals by the Imperial armies further inflamed ethnic and regional tensions. Additionally, near incessant banditry, ethnic violence, religious uprisings, and local peasant insurrections remained a constant drain on Chinese military resources. According to official records (which probably underestimated the actual number), there were 2,332 civil uprisings from 1856 to 1865; 909 from 1866 to 1875; and 314 from 1886 to 1895.[3]

It seemed likely that the mid-century rebellions would splinter the Qing into the numerous warring states so familiar in Chinese history. However, by the 1880s, regional statesmen, using locally raised armies, successfully quelled all internal rebellions and restored some sense of political stability. The lack of a unified national army meant that subsequent modernisation was carried out by independent actors only loosely affiliated with the central government. Arsenals were established, arms were purchased, and foreign instructors were invited, but their effect depended on the individual whims of their Chinese benefactors. The most important of these private armies were the Xiang Army and the Huai Army, led by Zeng Guofan and Li Hongzhang, respectively. Li was a student of Zeng, and although they did not always

---

2   Paine, *The Sino-Japanese War*, pp.25–26.
3   Tai Lan, 'Mingzhi Weixin Qian: Riben Nongmin Tudi Zhanyou Zhidu Yuan Luohou Qingchao', Fenghuang Lishi (2014), https://news.ifeng.com/history/zhongguojindaishi/special/minzhongfudan/, accessed 4 Feb. 2024.

agree, they were the primary proponents of Westernisation and agreed that a wholesale reworking of Chinese society was necessary. They, among others, were repeatedly held back by conservatives and political enemies in the Imperial Court. Furthermore, reformists were unable to change the xenophobic tendencies of other provinces or regions not under their influence, resulting in modernised, Western-trained soldiers, often fighting alongside units whose training and armament had remained stagnant since the Qianlong period. To much of the Qing Empire, there was no need to wake up.

Despite these underlying issues, on the surface level, China's military strength seemed to be growing. During the Ili Crisis (1879–1881), modernised Qing forces in Xinjiang province checked the encroachment of Russian troops into disputed territory. After a painful negotiation process, the Russians were forced to return the land they had taken, which was a surprising achievement for China. Soon afterwards, the Sino-French War (1884–1885) was fought over France's colonial ambitions in Vietnam. Chinese land forces managed to humiliate the French on multiple occasions,[4] though in the end French naval supremacy and other threats ended the war with Vietnam in French hands.

China had defeated every single mid-century rebellion and even held her ground against the French and Russians; it seemed that China's weakness was temporary. On the eve of the Sino-Japanese War, Western observers almost unanimously praised the Qing military, predicting an effortless Chinese victory over Japan. The quality of the Qing military was highly variable, but the sheer quantity of Chinese soldiers available to do battle seemed inexhaustible. There were even fears that China's large population would enable her to take European colonies and eventually conquer Europe itself. Though some of these concerns were sourced from racist alarmism, Europeans overwhelmingly believed that Japan would be crushed.[5]

This sentiment was immediately reversed after the war. The perception of China as a functional country, let alone a militarily competent one, was shattered. This led to a heightened scramble for territorial and commercial concessions by the colonial nations of Europe and Japan, to the point where the complete partition of China was considered. Even in China, there was an unprecedented sense of indignity; Japan, once a deferential pupil of Chinese civilisation, had thrown off her former teacher.[6] The Sino-Japanese War was the disgraceful acme of the Century of Humiliation.

The observant reader will notice that this chapter is entitled 'The Armies of the Qing Empire' and not 'The Army of the Qing Empire.' This is because there were several different systems of military organisation operating concurrently; most of the Empire's military strength was concentrated centrifugally in the hands of individual statesmen who frequently acted

---

4   An attempted invasion of Southern China was soundly defeated and even led to the collapse of the French government.
5   Kwang-Ching Liu, 'The Military Challenge', in Albert E. Dien and Keith N. Knapp (eds.), *The Cambridge History of China* (Cambridge: Cambridge University Press, 2019), vol. 2, pp. 268–269.
6   Qizhang Qi, *Jiawu Zhanzheng*, (Beijing: Renmin Chubanshe, 1990), p.585.

independently of one another and of the central government. It therefore is necessary to examine seriatim the various existing military institutions and organisations that served under the banner of the Qing Empire.

The Army of the Eight Banners and the Green Standard Army

The Army of the Eight Banners (Baqi Jun) was composed of the descendants of the fearsome Manchu conquerors who established the Qing Dynasty. Banner status was hereditary, with a soldier's oldest son succeeding him upon his death. Although eventually Chinese and Mongols were allowed to join, Manchu dominance was unchallenged. As the Manchus treated China as a conquered land, Bannermen were stationed throughout the Empire in garrison cities segregated from the general populace.

The Green Standard Army (Luying Jun[7]) was the leftover remains of the Ming Dynasty army, composed exclusively of Han Chinese. Initially a respectable military force, the Green Standard Army evolved into a paramilitary gendarme mainly used for keeping the peace. Green Standard soldiers were mostly hereditary, and new recruits were sourced from Green Standard households. In wartime, Green Standard units often served in auxiliary roles, such as runners, orderlies, guards and police officers.

By the 1860s, both organisations were unshakable hotbeds of corruption and useless in warfare. Many Bannermen supplemented what little income they received (that had not been embezzled) with civilian side jobs. Meanwhile, the Green Standard Army devolved into a pseudo-police force, but even then, most units were understrength or composed of non-existent, infirm or elderly soldiers who continued to draw pay. Numerous attempts were made to either reform or lay off elements of these two forces, but these saw little results. The only Green Standard and Banner forces in fighting condition were either part of provincial levies or absorbed into Trained Armies (see below).

Despite their clear martial ineptitude, there was considerable political value in the continued existence of both the Banners and Green Standard.[8] As organs of the central government, they were a political counterbalance to the growing influence of privately controlled or regional armies. Additionally, the Qing continued to fund these traditional armies to prevent disenfranchised soldiery from turning to rebellion or robbery. Thus, the Banners and Green Standard continued to weigh down considerable portions of the Chinese treasury.

---

7   The Chinese name directly translates to 'Green Battalion Army,' but 'Green Standard Army,' derived from the flags they carried into battle, is the most popular English interpretation.
8   Allen Fung, 'Testing the Self-Strengthening: The Chinese Army in the Sino-Japanese War of 1894–1895', Modern Asian Studies, 30:1 (1996), pp.1027–1028.

The Tigermen

The Tigermen are one of the most iconic units of the late Qing Dynasty, and an enduring emblem of China's military backwardness. Dressed in tiger-striped costumes and a matching hood, the Tigermen were sword and shield infantry and were tasked with launching ambushes and disrupting enemy horses with their (supposedly) terrifying attire. Soldiers wearing tiger-themed hats or clothing had existed in China since ancient times, but the 'modern' Tigerman only came to be in the 1680s during Chinese border conflicts with Russia, where they played a key role in China's victory. During these skirmishes, the acrobatics of the Tigermen were used to dodge and manoeuvre around arrows and gunfire. Primitive firearms and cold weapons could not penetrate the tough, tung oil-soaked rattan shields of the Tigermen. Additionally, the irregularity of their movement and striped pattern of their uniforms did indeed frighten enemy horses during the border war with Russia and the Dzungar Wars. The military exploits of the Tigermen elevated them to an elite unit. Unfortunately, these tactics did not stand the test of time. Contrary to popular belief, the Tigermen did not participate during the Sino-Japanese War. Near the end of the war, it was proposed to send some to terrify the Japanese, but fortunately for the Tigers this never came to fruition.[9]

A parade of the Lushunkou garrison before 1891; this would mean that the photograph depicts the forces of General Song Qing's Resolute Army. Note the similarity between the red and black vests of the men in the foreground with B4 and B5 of the colour plates; given that the Gui Army was originally part of the Resolute Army, it is probable that both forces wore identical uniforms (Image courtesy of the Staatliche Kunstsammlungen Dresden).

---

9   Alfred E.J. Cavendish, 'The Armed Strength (?) Of China', Journal of the Royal United Services Institution, 42:244 (1898), p.709.

Some misconceptions exist about the Tigermen. The so-called 'Tiger Hunting Battalion,' supposedly of Tigermen, is a misleading translation of 'Huqiang Ying,' which literally means 'Tiger Spear Battalion.' The Tiger Spear Battalion was part of the Emperor's hunting establishment and used, unsurprisingly, spears to hunt tigers, which regrettably did not involve dressing up in tiger costumes. Tigermen were locally recruited and equipped and there was never a centralised command of these exotic fighters.

The Brave and Defence Armies

After being confronted with numerous rebellions which threatened to topple the Dynasty itself, the Qing were forced to rely on regional armies known as Brave Battalions (Yong Ying). Brave Armies began as militias (Xiang Yong, or 'Village Braves') raised and led by local gentry or headmen. Unlike the Green Standard, Brave Army officers unabashedly practised nepotism by personally selecting their men from friends and family. While in wartime close personal allegiances would ensure loyalty and camaraderie, the central government had no hand in controlling or funding the Brave Armies. This meant that military power became decentralised in the hands of virtually autonomous local elites and statesmen.[10]

Initially, Brave Armies were created and disbanded as the need arose, but after government forces like the Eight Banners and Green Standard army were both proven to be useless, Brave Armies took on a more permanent role. In the early 1860s, Zeng Guofan's Xiang Army (also called the Hunan Army) composed essentially the entire Qing military; most Qing officials and generals had either served under Zeng or had been vetted by him.[11] After Zeng's death in 1872, his protégé Li Hongzhang took his place with his Huai Army, also known as the Anhui Army. However, there was no guarantee Brave Armies would be loyal to the broader interests of the Dynasty; Brave Armies were responsible to their leaders and community only. Soldiers in Brave Armies swore loyalty to their commanders, not the Qing; thanked their commanders before every meal, not the Qing; and killed and died for their commanders, not the Qing. This meant that military leaders became political leaders, whose agendas may have conflicted with that of the Qing. At its worst, one particular Brave Army in Guizhou Province switched sides between the government and rebels five times in three years; the same army even overthrew the local magistrate and fought other Brave Armies for regional dominance.[12]

---

10 Kenneth E. Folsom, *Friends, Guests, and Colleagues: The Mu-fu System in the Late Ch'ing Period* (Berkeley: University of California Press, 1968), pp.122–124.

11 Ping Xu, *Jiawu Zhanzheng Zhongri Jundui Tonglan 1894–1895* (Beijing: Zhongguo Renmin Jiefangjun Chubanshe, 2014), p.76–77.

12 Edward A. Mccord, 'Local Military Power and Elite Formation: The Liu Family of Xingyi County, Guizhou', in Joseph Esherick and Mary Rankin (eds.), Chinese Local Elites and Patterns of Dominance (Berkeley: University of California, 1990), pp.169–172.

Understandably, the Qing was uncomfortable with these privately held armies and instituted numerous reforms to counterbalance their power politically and militarily. Efforts to limit the Brave Armies failed miserably, and in the 1860s all Brave Armies were officially designated the 'Defence Army' to maintain some veneer of military centralisation. In practice of course these 'Defence Armies' continued to be privately ruled. As Defence and Brave Armies were essentially identical, in this work they will be referred to as Brave Armies for familiarity's sake. After the worst of the mid-century rebellions had been suppressed, most Brave Armies tumbled into the same pitfall of corruption, neglect and complacency that had befallen the Eight Banners and Green Standard. The Brave Armies' reliance on personal relationships for recruitment backfired and most Brave Armies ended up with an officer corps full of talentless family members and a soldiery composed of freeloaders or non-existent 'ghost soldiers.' There was no standardised unit of military organisation above a battalion (ying), so expansion was a convoluted and inefficient process.

After the Sino-Japanese War, the incompetence of the Imperial government was clear, and private armies achieved an unprecedented level of independence. During the Boxer Rebellion private armies blatantly refused explicit orders or even fought government forces with impunity.[13] After the fall of the Qing, the Brave Armies, no longer needing to pay lip service to the Qing, formed the basis of the countless warlord armies of the Warlord Era (1916–1928).

The quality of Brave Armies varied greatly and depended on the training and equipment provided to them by their commanders. Some Brave commanders were rigorous advocates for modernisation, while others were content to let their armies remain in the mediaeval era. There were no official or universally adhered to rules of military organisation, but initially most Brave Armies were organised along the lines of the Xiang Army. This meant infantry battalions (ying) were composed of about 500 men, split into squads based on weapons.[14] Each battalion had five companies (shao), labelled the front (qian), rear (hou), left (zuo), right (you), and centre (zhong), the centre also being the bodyguard company (qin bing) for the battalion commander. Each non-bodyguard company had eight squads (dui), these being divided into two jingal squads, two matchlock squads, and four sword and spear squads. The bodyguard company was composed of six squads: two light mortar (pishan pao) squads, three sword and spear squads, and one matchlock squad. Additionally, there were also 180 military labourers and supernumeraries called 'changfu' who accompanied each battalion: two per squad, three per jingal or light mortar squad, four per company commander, and 78 for the entire battalion. Cavalry battalions were composed of five

---

13 The famous quarrelling between General Ronglu's Wuwei Centre Army and General Dong Fuxiang's Gansu Braves is a good example of how Brave Armies were independent political and military entities.
14 Guofan Zeng, 'Ying Gui', in anon. (ed.), Zeng Guofan Quanji (Beijing: Zhongguo Zhigong Chubanshe, 2001), vol. 16, pp.5996–5999.

companies of five squads of 10 men each, for a total of 250 horsemen per battalion. Each individual company had five squads of 'san yong' (non-mounted auxiliaries), and each battalion had 81 non-mounted military labourers in total. Therefore, including officers, each cavalry battalion had 276 horsemen, despite having 512 men in total. In the late 1860s, the growing importance of firepower stipulated a change in Brave Army organisation, with infantry battalions set (not including officers) at 500 men, companies set at 100, and squads set at 10.[15] In theory all of these were armed with firearms, but in practice they were armed with anything available. Additionally, three military labourers were allocated to each squad, and another 40 to every battalion.[16] Cavalry battalions remained fundamentally identical to the Taiping days. This basic battalion layout was not always followed; mixed battalions of infantry and cavalry were also noted by Western visitors. Of course, battalions were almost always understrength, with the norm being less than half of full strength. There was no standardised unit above battalion level. Brigades consisted of two or more battalions, with some having up to thirty. Brigades were called 'ying' again but prefixed by a commander's name (Mingzi ying, Shengzi ying, etc.) or called 'jun' prefixed by its position in the army (front jun, left jun, etc.). A division (jun) consisted of two or more brigades and was prefixed with the name of its commanders as well (Shengzi jun, Mingzi jun, etc.). Jun could also refer to any politically or militarily independent force, regardless of size. For this text, any Chinese force labelled 'jun' will be referred to as an army, regardless of actual size. For example, the Sheng Army (a division of the Huai Army and numbering 18 battalions in 1894) and the Tenacious Army (barely even of brigade size) will both be called 'armies.'

Post-1860s Brave Army infantry unit organisation[17]

Unit name	Strength
Division (jun)	Two or more brigades, commanded by general (tongling or dashuai)
Brigade (ying, sometimes jun)	Two or more battalions, commanded by general (tongling)
Battalion (ying)	500 soldiers commanded by battalion commander (yingguan) and deputy battalion commander (fu yingguan) Five companies (one of these is a bodyguard unit for the battalion commander)
Company (shao)	100 soldiers, commanded by company commander (shaoguan or baichang) and deputy company commander (shaochang, fu shaoguan, or fu baichang) 10 squads/tents
Squad (dui) or tent (peng)	10 soldiers, commanded by squad leader (shichang) and assistant squad leader (wuchang)

---

15   Xu, *Jundui Tonglan*, pp.41.
16   Heath, *China*, p.24.
17   Xu, *Jundui Tonglan*, pp.42.

Post-1860s Brave Army cavalry unit organisation

Battalion (ying)	250 cavalrymen commanded by battalion commander (yingguan) and by deputy battalion commander (fu yingguan or bangban) 5 companies
Company (shao)	50 cavalrymen, commanded by company commander (shaoguan or zheng shaoguan) and deputy company commander (shaochang or fu shaoguan) 5 squads/tents
Squad (dui) or tent (peng)	10 cavalrymen, commanded by squad leader (shichang) and sometimes by deputy squad leader (wuchang)

The Huai Army

Founded in 1861 by Li Hongzhang as an auxiliary force to the Xiang Army, the Huai Army was the most influential Chinese military institution in the second half of the nineteenth century. Named after the Huai River, the Huai Army was exclusively recruited from Li's home province of Anhui. Li and the Huai Army made their bones in their successful (and extremely brutal) pacification of the Taiping and Nian Rebellions, and after Zeng Guofan's death the Huai Army became the strongest army in China.

Unlike many others though, Li was not satisfied with Chinese military power after the mid-century rebellions had been quelled. Li had been shocked by the tremendous disparity in technology between China and the West and believed that they represented an unprecedented change from China's historical circumstances. Though hindered by his political rivals, Li established modern factories and arsenals using foreign instructors at Shanghai, Nanjing, Suzhou and Tianjin, which he used to produce local copies of foreign weaponry. It was Li who first sanctioned the training of Chinese troops by European advisors. After the 1870s China's modernisation was almost solely advanced and funded by Li and his political allies, the specifics of which will be detailed later.

During his tenure as Viceroy[18] of Zhili, most of the armies under Li's control were stationed in northern China, giving rise to the name 'Beiyang Army' (Army of the Northern Seas). 'Beiyang Army' will be used in this work to refer collectively to the Huai Army and the other armies which were under Li Hongzhang's de facto control, like the Zhili Trained Army, Songwu Army, and so on. For decades, the Huai Army remained the most well-drilled, modernised and powerful army in China, but even then, its military performance began to decline. In the 1880s the deficiencies of Brave Army organisation began to show themselves.[19] Nepotism, corruption, and the like began to afflict the Huai Army, while the dearth of a regular system of peacetime training impeded combat effectiveness.[20] In the Sino-Japanese War, most of the best Huai Army units were crushed early on in the Korea

---

18 'Viceroy' is sometimes translated as 'governor-general.' In Qing China, a viceroy (zongdu) was responsible for the governance of one or more provinces, while a governor (xunfu) was only responsible for one. For example, both Guangxi and Guangdong Provinces had their own provincial governors while still being overall subordinate to the authority of the Viceroy of Liangguang.
19 Liu, 'The Military Challenge', pp.245–246.
20 Fung, 'Testing the Self-Strengthening', p.1022.

Campaign. The poor performance of the Huai Army (though to be fair not many Chinese units performed respectably) led to Li being ruthlessly scapegoated and hounded by his political rivals. After the war Li Hongzhang was disgraced and he was blamed for the Qing's failures, which were caused by the Qing not following the reforms that he himself had suggested. The remnants of the Huai Army were integrated into newly created modernised armies like the Pacification (Dingwu) Army and the Wuwei Army.[21]

Li Hongzhang remains a controversial figure in China today, and he himself once uttered that 'for one thousand years, people will criticise me and people will praise me, but history will have the final say.'[22] During the Maoist era, Chinese analyses of history labelled Li as a scapegoat for selling out the country and upholding the 'old' order.[23] Luckily, more recent studies have largely acquitted him of this one-dimensional pooh-poohing. Like so many other Qing-era figures in China, Li Hongzhang is now remembered as a shrewd leader whose exploits were tragically undermined by the incompetence and imbecility of his government.

The Sheng Army

In 1861, the Sheng Army had its humble beginnings as a brigade in the Huai Army led by General Zhou Shengbo. Zhou was one of six brothers who joined the Huai Army, but by 1862 only Zhou Shengbo and his younger brother Zhou Shengchuan still drew breath. After numerous achievements in suppressing the Taiping and Nian Rebellions, the Sheng Army was expanded into a true army, though still inside the Huai Army organisation. Zhou Shengbo commanded the army, while Zhou Shengchuan acted as his second-in-command.[24]

Under the Zhou brothers' command, the Sheng Army became not only a formidable military force but also a popular one.[25] While stationed in Tianjin in 1875, the Sheng Army dug a series of canals and ditches to divert the flow of a major river into an arid region. Over a period of six years, the Sheng Army helped create over 600,000 acres of cultivable land. In 1882 the Sheng Army rescued victims and rebuilt dams to combat a series of floods to the northeast of Tianjin. Much of the costs were covered personally by the Zhou brothers. Along with public works, Zhou Shengchuan also emphasised the adoption of modern weaponry and advocated for the incorporation of Western medicine, telegraph networks, and railways into the Qing military.[26] He implemented a structured training regimen, with rewards and consequences based on performance. Well-versed in Western practices and having personally authored a 12 volume treatise on European gunnery, Zhou Shengchuan even critiqued his German advisors for their lack of expertise in night-fighting and

---

21 Specifically, Nie Shicheng's Wuwei Front Army.
22 The original phrase 'zhiwo zuiwo, fuzhi qianzai' is actually a modification of the Confucius aphorism 'zhiwo zuiwo, qiwei chunqiu' which has a similar meaning.
23 Paine, *The Sino–Japanese War*, p.52.
24 Erxun Zhao et al., *Qing Shigao* (Beijing: National History Museum of the Republic of China, 1929), vol. 416, biography 23.
25 Xu, *Jundui Tonglan*, pp.56–58.
26 Liu, 'The Military Challenge', pp.244–246.

prone firing. Zhou Shengbo composed a military anthem titled 'Song of the Sheng Army Braves' and encouraged his soldiers to learn and sing it whenever possible.[27] The song's lyrics provided guidance on avoiding gambling and opium, respecting civilians, maintaining weapons, following orders, and the like. Although the Sheng Army was mobilised during the Sino-French War of 1884–1885, it did not engage in active combat.

After the deaths of Zhou Shengchuan and Shengbo in 1885 and 1888 respectively, General Wei Rugui became the commander of the Sheng Army, leading it through the Sino-Japanese War. Although the Sheng Army was still well-armed, under General Wei discipline and morale plummeted. By the outbreak of the Sino-Japanese War Sheng Army soldiers had not been paid for up to 18 months. At that time the Sheng Army, totalling 18 battalions, was the largest and theoretically one of the best, if not the best, unit of the Huai Army. Sadly, General Wei did not live up to his predecessors.[28] Ironically, the Sheng Army's reputation reversed, and they became infamous for robbing civilians. After the Battle of Pyongyang, General Wei was sentenced to death (against Li Hongzhang's objections) for desertion, embezzling of wages and allowing his men to plunder. When General Wei was beheaded in January 1895, his younger brother Wei Rucheng was called up and led the newly raised Cheng Army. Wei Rucheng was not much better and again abandoned his own men in the heat of battle. An imperial edict was sent out for his punishment, but Rucheng was never found. The Sheng Army's glorious history ended with a whimper.

However, another evaluation of General Wei Rugui exists. General Song Qing of the Resolute Army (see below) conducted a personal investigation and concluded that the charges against General Wei were exaggerated if not totally fabricated.[29] Song claimed that General Wei displayed great courage in the battle of Pyongyang. He conceded that the Sheng Army did flee Pyongyang, but only with the other forces. Additionally, Song found that while in Korea, General Wei himself had not been paid on time and in full. Therefore, Wei could not be personally blamed for his soldier's lack of pay. The rumour that General Wei had bribed Li Hongzhang's son to become head of the Sheng Army was also proven false with an audit of the Wei family's finances. According to General Song, Wei's execution was intentionally manufactured by political rivals of Li. It may never be known if Wei was truly guilty. Nevertheless, the Sheng Army survived after the Sino-Japanese War under Generals Lu Benyuan and Sun Xianyin and was absorbed into General Nie Shicheng's Tenacious Army after the war.

The Tenacious Army (Wuyi Army) and the Luyu Defence Army

In 1866, during the suppression of the Nian Rebellion, Li Hongzhang's brother, Li Zhaoqing, was given command of 19 battalions, which he named

---

27 Xu, *Jundui Tonglan*, pp.56–58.
28 Zhao et al., *Qing Shigao*, vol. 462, bio. 249.
29 Zhongguo Diyi Lishi Dang'an Guan, Qingshi Yanjiu Zhuanti Yanjiu Junshi, Song Qing's letters from September 1894 at Jiuliancheng.

the Tenacious (Wuyi) Army.[30] After many military successes, Li Zhaoqing resigned from his position in 1867 and was replaced by famous Xiang Army General Guo Songlin.[31] Guo merged his own formations into the Tenacious Army, adding up to over 30 battalions. In 1870, another 10 infantry and five cavalry battalions were recruited into the Tenacious Army from Anhui and Henan, but in 1880, the Tenacious Army had only five infantry battalions after various battalions were either transferred to different armies or disbanded to cut expenses. In 1886, this was further whittled to just one battalion each of infantry and cavalry, and in 1889, these two were absorbed into the Luyu Defence Army.

The Luyu Defence Army was formed during the Ili Crisis of 1881, when many units of the Beiyang Army were rushed northward to defend Shanhaiguan (also called Yuguan) and Lutai. Even after the crisis was resolved, Li Hongzhang saw that the defence of the northeastern coastline was important and therefore established a permanent garrison there. This garrison was split into the garrison of Shanhaiguan, which comprised five battalions of the Zhengding Trained Army under then Commander in Chief of Zhengding Ye Zhichao, and the garrison of Lutai, which comprised three battalions of the Gubeikou Trained Army and two battalions of the Tenacious Army under General Yang Yushu. In 1889, General Ye Zhichao was promoted to the Commander in Chief of Zhili Province but still retained personal command over the Shanhaiguan garrison. In 1891 General Yang Yushu was transferred to a new station in Henan Province, so General Nie Shicheng replaced him as overall commander of the Luyu Defence Army. In theory, Nie's authority only applied to the Lutai garrison, as the Shanhaiguan garrison was supposed to answer only to the Commander in Chief of Zhili Province. However, Nie and Ye were both linked together in Li Hongzhang's Beiyang Army network of patronage, so in practice the entire Luyu Defence Army was left under General Nie Shicheng's command.

Eight battalions of the Luyu Defence Army participated in the Sino-Japanese War and were among the first and best Chinese units to do so. Later on, General Nie and all eight battalions of the Luyu Defence Army were recalled back to Tianjin to defend Beijing from a potential Japanese attack. There, Nie raised another 10 fresh battalions of the Gong Army, named after his courtesy name 'Gongting.' After the war ended, the Gong Army, along with the Luyu Defence Army, the Sheng Army, Wu Hongluo's Hong Army, Zhang Gaoyuan's Songwu Army, the Zhili Huai Army, the Zhili Trained Army, and numerous other former Beiyang Army units were put under General Nie's command and collectively called the Tenacious Army. In late 1898 this conglomeration was designated the Wuwei Front Army, which fought against both the Boxers and the Western invaders during the Boxer Rebellion.

General Nie Shicheng, was arguably one of the best generals China had during the late 19th century; his Luyu Defence Army was well-equipped with Mauser repeating rifles and Krupp artillery and drilled by German

---

30 Xu, *Jundui Tonglan*, pp.118–120.
31 Unrelated to Guo Songlin of the Fengtian Clique.

military instructors. Nie himself was described by Yuan Shikai as loyal and upright, loyal to his parents, incorruptible while in office, decisive in action, courageous in adversity, and strict yet compassionate towards his subordinates.[32] Nie originally joined the military as an officer under Yuan Jiasan to combat the Nian Rebellion, and after accumulating merits, became a general.[33] Nie was then transferred to the Ming Army and given the title of 'Liyong Baturu' for outstanding achievements. He then served in Keelung during the Sino-French War with great success; afterwards, Nie helped put down a major religious insurrection in Rehe (Jehol). From 1893 until early 1894, General Nie Shicheng toured the three northeastern provinces of China, the eastern border of Russia, and all eight provinces of Korea, mapping down various geographical, military, and cultural observations. During this seven-month journey, Nie visited many locations mere months before they would become battlefields in the Sino-Japanese War. During the war, General Nie earned praise from Chinese, Japanese, and Western correspondents for being one of the few Chinese generals to have not only fought bravely and skilfully but also to have actually won engagements against the enemy. After the war ended, Nie was appointed commander of the Wuwei Front Army, one of the five best armies of all China, and entrusted to guard Beijing. Unfortunately, Nie's anti-Boxer views made him a juicy target for the pro-Boxer faction in the Qing Imperial Court, and during the Boxer Rebellion, Nie was castigated, condemned, and deprived of all military authority in front of his men. Because of this public impeachment, General Nie chose to die fighting at Tianjin to redeem his name. Although he was stripped of all titles and labelled a traitor to the nation by the imperial government, after Yuan Shikai took power in 1912, full honours were restored to Nie, and he was given a proper military burial.

The Resolute Army (Yi Army)

In 1855, a local force of 300 men in Anhui was placed under the control of General Song Qing.[34] After several successful repulses of rebel forces, Song Qing was awarded the title of Yiyong Baturu in 1861, where the Resolute Army gained its name, the 'Yi Army.' The Resolute Army assisted in pacifying several rebellions, earning General Song the honour of the yellow riding jacket. Even though the Resolute Army was independent from the Huai Army, General Song enjoyed close relations with Li Hongzhang, and in 1880 he was made assistant to Li for the defence of northern China's coastline. In 1882 the Resolute Army officially moved to Lushunkou (Port Arthur), where it was stationed until the Sino-Japanese War. General Song had previously disbanded much of the Resolute Army to lessen expenses, so in 1894 the Resolute Army consisted of one cavalry and eight infantry battalions, all of which were understrength. Nevertheless, the Resolute Army distinguished themselves as gallant fighters on multiple occasions and were respected if not feared by the Japanese.

---

32 Zuxian Shen, *Yang Shouyuan Zouyi* (Taipei City: Wenhai Chubanshe, 1966), volume 14, p.4.
33 Zhao et al., *Qing Shigao*, vol. 462, bio. 249.
34 Xu, *Jundui Tonglan*, pp.59–60.

From left to right: Generals Zuo Baogui, Liu Shengxiu and Xu Bangdao, all photographed by Liang Shitai in 1886. General Xu Bangdao was appointed Commander in Chief of Zhengding shortly before the Sino-Japanese War. When the Zhengding Trained Army departed for Korea in the early stages of the war, Xu stayed behind and founded the Gongwei Army (see Volume Two).

General Song himself gained a reputation as a personally courageous and honest, if hapless, commander. By the Sino-Japanese War, he was at the ripe old age of 75 and nicknamed the 'White-Haired General.' Despite his old age, he personally participated in several battles. But courage alone could not achieve victory; General Song made many tactical blunders and was unable to cooperate with his fellow commanders. General Ma Yukun, Song's second-in-command, was another personally fearsome warrior, and was fond of leading charges from the front.[35] The forces under Ma's command were beloved by the Korean people, and it was said that 'not a dog or chicken' was harassed when the Resolute Army was marching through.[36] A temple was even built by Korean civilians to honour General Ma in Pyongyang. In addition to Ma and Song, future big-name warlords Jiang Guiti, Zhang Zuolin, Zhang Xun,[37] and Cao Kun all gained the rudiments of military know-how in the Resolute Army. The Republican-era aphorism 'good men are few and far in between; there is only one Ma Yukun and one Jiang Guiti' embodied the popularity the Resolute Army inspired.

After the Sino-Japanese War, General Song was stripped of his honours but soon regained them after the government realised the Resolute Army

---

35   Zhao et al., *Qing Shigao*, vol. 461, bio. 248.
36   Anon., 'Ma Yukun Cengbei Chaoxian Fengwei Zhongguo Sanjie Zhiyi', Jianghuai Shibao (2013), <https://m.sohu.com/n/391746180/?pvid=000115_3w>, accessed 4 Feb. 2024.
37   Not to be confused with the General of Jilin, Gobulo Changshun, who led the Banner armies of Jilin during the Manchurian and Haicheng campaigns.

was too valuable to disband.³⁸ The Resolute Army then went through numerous expansions and reorganisations. After Song's death in 1902, his second in command General Ma Yukun took over the Resolute Army. After Ma's death in 1908, the Resolute Army was then passed down through numerous commanders, including Jiang Guiti. After the fall of the Qing, the Resolute Army operated as an independent warlord clique until it was finally disbanded in 1928 by the Nationalist government.

The Xiang Army

The Xiang Army, named after the titular river in Hunan, was the grandfather of the Brave Armies and laid the foundations for the decentralisation of late Qing military power.³⁹ Organised by Zeng Guofan in 1850, and reluctantly condoned by the Imperial Government out of desperation, the Xiang Army quickly became the only reliable army the Qing had. Zeng Guofan's tactics and military organisation would become highly influential in the following decades. After the capture of the Taiping Capital in 1864, a large part of the Xiang Army was disbanded. Many of those that remained were under the command of General Zuo Zongtang, who rebranded his offshoot the Chu Army. General Zuo was no chicken, and his Chu Army did most of the grunt work in the brutal reconquest of Xinjiang Province, but after General Zuo's death in 1885 it fell out of prominence. By the 1890s, the proper Xiang Army was a shadow of its former self. Nostalgic for the old days of campaigning against the Taiping's, many Xiang Army soldiers refused to use modern rifles and cannons and instead reverted to matchlocks, jingals, broadswords, spears, and muzzle loading light mortars. Under the overall command of Hunan Governor⁴⁰ Wu Dacheng, a few elements of the Xiang Army were sent to combat the Japanese in the final stages of the Sino-Japanese War. Though they fought with the utmost courage, their overall performance would have made Zeng Guofan and Zuo Zongtang turn in their graves.

The Guangwu Army

The Guangwu Army, originally a division of the Xiang Army, originated from the local militia of Sizhou village in Guiyang of Guizhou Province.⁴¹ Chen Shijie, who had served as an aide to the famous Zeng Guofan, returned to his hometown of Sizhou in 1854 to raise a militia to combat a series of recent bandit raids. Chen Shijie's militia launched a fierce counterattack against the bandits, killing and capturing thousands. When Sizhou was finally pacified, Zeng Guofan ordered Chen to lead his militia to Hunan Province. Thus, the Guangwu Army was born: the name roughly translates to 'warriors of

---

38   Chaoying Fang, 'Sung Ch'ing', in Arthur Hummel (ed.), Eminent Chinese of the Ch'ing Period 1644–1912 (Washington: United States Government Printing Office, 1943), vol. 2, pp.245–246.
39   Xu, *Jundui Tonglan*, pp.76–77.
40   Although Governor of Hunan Province Wu Dacheng was the de facto leader of the Xiang Army during the Sino-Japanese War, theoretically the reins of leadership belonged to the Viceroy of Huguang. This position was occupied by Zhang Zhidong until late 1894, where he was briefly replaced by Tan Jixun. In 1896 Zhang returned to his position.
41   'Guangwu Jun Jianshi', Guiyang County People's Government, <http://www.hngy.gov.cn/zwgk/zwdt/7478/7493/content_1443719.html>, accessed 12 Nov. 2024.

Huguang.' The Guangwu Army fought bravely and heroically against the Taiping rebels, and later also put a stop to the 1865 mutiny of the Ting Army, which had arisen because of the resignation of its founder Bao Chao. After the quelling of the mutiny, Chen Shijie disbanded the Guangwu Army. In 1883, on the eve of the Sino-French War, Chen rebuilt the Guangwu Army and recruited 4,000 braves from Guiyang, Hunan, Shandong, Zhejiang, and other regions. By 1884 the Guangwu Army had 3,200 men divided into Centre, Front, Left, Right, and Rear Battalions, plus an Auxiliary Centre Battalion and the Right and Left Artillery Battalions. The majority of the infantry were standardised with Hotchkiss rifles, and in total the Guangwu Army had 32 horse-drawn Krupp guns, 16 per battalion. Then, in 1885, the Yellow River overflowed and flooded over its dikes, and the Guangwu Army worked tirelessly for two years in fixing the riverbed and providing aid to those ravaged by the disaster. In 1886, Chen Shijie disbanded his army yet again and resigned from his position of Governor of Shandong, leaving only the Front Battalion, two companies of the Auxiliary Centre Battalion, and the two battalions of artillery. The last major action the Guangwu Army participated in before the Sino-Japanese War was in 1892, when they assisted in the construction of the Jiaoao Fort at Qingdao. During the Sino-Japanese War, the Guangwu Army was sent along with the Songwu and Fu Armies to the Liaodong Peninsula; although the soldiers and officers of the Guangwu Army fought braver than most, their heroism could not salvage the outcome of the war.

The Ming Army
The Ming Army was founded by Liu Mingchuan in 1862 as a battalion in the Huai Army.[42] After victorious operations against the Taiping and Nian rebels, the Ming Army became the most powerful unit in the Huai Army. During the Sino-French War, the Ming Army was transferred to Taiwan and successfully repulsed the French on multiple occasions. Afterwards, Liu Mingchuan was appointed Governor of Taiwan, and his nephew Liu Shengxiu succeeded him as commander of the Ming Army. Liu Shengxiu was a family man, appointing close relatives to high positions in the Ming Army. Said relatives were appointed based on nepotism alone and not actual military competence. Hence during the Sino-Japanese War the Ming Army under Liu Shengxiu was initially characterised by wholesale failure and cowardice. Liu, surprisingly, redeemed himself after the Battle of Ganwangzhai by inflicting the heaviest percentage of losses of the war on the enemy, but later resigned and was replaced by Jiang Guiti. Later during the Yiwei War some remnants of the Ming Army stationed in Taiwan participated in the defence of the Republic of Formosa.

The Ren Army
The Ren Army was a unit of the Xiang Army, predictably, established during the Taiping and Nian Rebellions.[43] It was founded by General Tang Renlian

---
42 Xu, *Jundui Tonglan*, pp.60–62.
43 Zhao et al., *Qing Shigao*, vol. 409, bio. 196.

and soldiers of this force were designated the 'Tiger Braves.' Three cavalry battalions and two battalions of the Ren Army were transferred to the Huai Army to combat the Nian, and when much of the Xiang Army was disbanded in the 1860s, the Ren Army remained under Huai Army control and was expanded. During the Sino-Japanese War the Ren Army was overall under the command of General Wu Yuren, but in the field led by General Jiang Zikang. Near the end of the war, General Tang Renlian himself was called out of retirement and ordered to raise twenty battalions, but the war ended before he could do so.

The Songwu Army

The Songwu Army was founded in Henan in 1866 during the Nian Rebellion and led by General Zhang Yao.[44] The Songwu Army and Song Qing's Resolute Army were collectively known as the 'Yu Army' due to their Henan provenance, and the 'Yu Army' was reputed to be the third greatest army in all China, after the Xiang and Huai Armies. Accordingly, Zhang Yao performed excellently in fighting the Nian rebels, but after one particularly decisive defeat he was labelled by one Imperial historian as being an illiterate bumpkin and unfit to lead. Zhang's past achievements saved him from censuring and execution, so he began to teach himself to read and write, even wearing a seal that read 'illiterate' on his clothing to encourage himself. Eventually, after Zhang achieved his previous level of repeated victories and also full literacy, the Imperial historian was forced to eat his words. In 1876, Zhang led over 10 battalions of the Songwu Army to aid General Zuo Zongtang in the reconquest of Xinjiang, and afterwards in 1886 the Songwu Army was transferred to Shandong. Unfortunately, Zhang Yao died of illness in 1891, and was succeeded by General Zhang Gaoyuan, the Commander in Chief of Dengzhou of Shandong Province. Zhang Gaoyuan, a Huai Army veteran, followed his patron Li Hongzhang and effectively enrolled the Songwu Army into Beiyang Army control. In the Sino-Japanese War, General Zhang Gaoyuan distinguished himself with courageous conduct in battle.

The Sui and Gong Armies

The Sui and Gong Armies were first founded by Governor of Hunan Wu Dacheng and General Dai Zongqian in 1880 to guard against Russian aggression near Jilin Region.[45] In 1883 Dai and the Sui and Gong Armies were transferred to northern Zhili (modern day Hebei Province), where Dai's commendable achievements during the suppression of the Nian Rebellion landed him a high-paying position there. In 1887 Li Hongzhang stationed them at Weihaiwei, where they would fight during the Sino-Japanese War. Although not formally part of the Huai Army, General Dai (a Huai Army veteran) and the Sui and Gong Armies nonetheless belonged to the Beiyang Army roster and were under the control of Li et al.

---

44 Xu, *Jundui Tonglan*, pp.67–68.
45 Xu, *Jundui Tonglan*, pp.73–74.

General Dai Zongqian provides a good example of extreme corruption within the Qing armies.[46] Dai stipulated that new recruits had to forfeit their first three months' pay and deposit it in the commander's fund to purchase supplies. These 'supplies' often took the form of Dai's personal indulgences. Dai was deeply unpopular among his men, and on numerous occasions they attempted to protest in demand of their pay, which was invariably in arrears. General Dai's own bodyguard battalion was at less than half its full strength at the time of the Sino-Japanese War, and he was more than happy to collect pay from his benefactors for the missing men. In the Sui and Gong Armies, drinking, prostitution, gambling, quarrelling, selling off military supplies and opium smoking were habitual; on the northern coast of Weihaiwei there were 50 to 60 brothels in close proximity to the Sui Army barracks.

Therefore, it is no surprise that during the Battle of Weihaiwei the officers and soldiers of the Sui and Gong Armies had abysmal morale. Shortly before the Battle of Weihaiwei Dai sent over 8,000 taels of silver of his men's pay to his son, who was safe back in his hometown far from the frontlines. Liu Chaopei, Dai's second in command, abandoned his post and deserted, as did entire battalions of the Sui and Gong Armies. With already understrength units simply dispersing and ceasing to exist, the fate of the Sui and Gong Armies was a testament to the sorry state of the Chinese military establishment. Dai himself would experience something of a tragic redemption with his dramatic death by suicide.

The Trained Armies

The Qing government was not ignorant of the ineptitude of the Eight Banners and Green Standard Army but was also uncomfortable with the autonomy of the Brave Armies. Thus, in the 1860s, the best Green Standard Army and Banner units were reformed into the Trained Armies (Lian Jun).[47] These forces were theoretically still part of the aforementioned two organisations, and therefore under the command of the national government, as opposed to individual statesmen of dubious allegiance. Unfortunately, as provincial officials were responsible for Trained Armies, regionalism again dominated. Additionally, many Brave commanders held high-ranking positions in provincial governments, and co-opted the Trained Armies into Brave Armies, free from central oversight. For example, the best of the Trained Armies in Zhili Province were co-opted into Li Hongzhang's force and were commanded by former Huai Army leaders. Although Trained Armies were supposed to be trained in modern warfare, in practice their military value varied greatly. The Trained Armies under Li Hongzhang's control possessed respectable fighting ability, while those of northern China called up to do battle during the later stages of the war were little more than an

---

46   Zhao et al., *Qing Shigao*, vol. 460, bio. 247.
47   Liu, 'The Military Challenge', pp.207–207.

THE ARMIES OF THE QING EMPIRE

From left to right: General Ye Zhichao, Commander in Chief of Zhili Province; Zheng Guokui, Commander in Chief of Tianjin (until his death in 1888); General Wu Yuren, commander of the Ren Army and Commander in Chief of Tongyong; and General Pan Wancai, Commander in Chief of Huaiyang, all photographed in 1886 by Liang Shitai. General Pan was a subordinate of Ye Zhichao and accompanied him to Korea. After the Sino-Japanese War, Pan quickly rose up the ranks of the Qing bureaucracy and eventually became Commander In Chief of Guizhou Province. (Public domain)

armed rabble.[48] Just like Brave Armies, Trained Army units were generally understrength and frequently afflicted with corruption.

The overlap between government and private armies meant individuals would often hold two similar but parallel ranks from different military institutions (see Appendix I). For example, General Ma Yukun was the government-appointed Commander in Chief (Zongbing) of Taiyuan, but also a General (Tongling) of the privately owned Resolute Army. General Fengsheng'a was the government-appointed Deputy Commander of the Han Bordered White Banner (Xiang Baiqi Han Jun Fu Dutong) and the Commander (Zongtong) of the Sheng Trained Army. This organisational quagmire meant that a streamlined, singular military chain of command did not exist, as many generals were of equal or similar authority to one another from different systems. To avoid burdening the reader with prodigious numbers of obscure loanwords, generic English titles will be used (i.e. Commander in Chief of Zhili Province instead of Zhili Tidu, Battalion Commander instead of Yingguan, etc.).

The Zhili Trained Army

As the flagship Trained Army, the Zhili Trained Army was formally established in 1865, and was composed of six separate forces, named after

---

48 Fung, 'Testing the Self-Strengthening', p.1018.

their founding regions.⁴⁹ These were the Baoding, Xuanhua, Gubeikou, Daming, Zhengding, and Tongyong Trained Armies. The Viceroy of Zhili at that time suggested allocating command of these to Brave Army commanders, but this attempt at decentralisation was quickly vetoed by the government. But when in 1870 Li Hongzhang became Viceroy of Zhili, the government was helpless to prevent the Zhili Trained Army from becoming another of Li's assets. The Zhili Trained Army soon became trained, paid, and equipped along Huai Army lines, and prominent Huai Army commanders began infiltrating the ranks of the Trained Armies (see section on the Tenacious Army and Luyu Defence Army). Under Li's control, the Zhili Trained Army was considered a de facto element of the Huai Army; soldiers of these two theoretically independent military organisations were even found brigaded together.⁵⁰ Additionally, General Ye Zhichao, a Huai Army veteran and favourite of Li's, was appointed Commander of the Zhengding Trained Army in 1875, and then Commander in Chief of Zhili province in 1889, thereby solidifying Li Hongzhang's control over what was originally meant to be a counterbalance against him.

General Ye Zhichao does not enjoy a positive reputation at home and abroad, as he has been condemned as the most blatant example of cowardice the Chinese army had to offer in the war. Ye's high positions have been cited as an example of Li Hongzhang's tendency towards nepotism. The truth is, however, that General Ye had earned his position. In 1862, Ye began his career as a non-combatant cook in the Huai Army and had volunteered to participate in combat.⁵¹ Ye was shot in the waist while leading a charge, but was unharmed, as the musket ball had bounced off his scabbard.⁵² Convinced of divine intervention, Ye always took the lead in charges afterwards. His resolve was legendary; he once jumped back into battle after crawling out of a literal pile of dead bodies. After being promoted, Ye also showed outstanding potential as a tactician, and his skill in putting down insurrections earned him Li Hongzhang's favour. Therefore, Ye had an excellent track record and, as it will be seen, much of Ye's poor performance came from bad luck as opposed to genuine incompetence or cowardice. Today, some Chinese scholars are attempting to exonerate Ye from his poor legacy.⁵³

The Feng Army

Sometimes called the Fengtian Trained Army, or Feng Trained Army, the Feng Army began as a division of the Zhili Gubeikou Trained Army.⁵⁴ When a section of said army remained in Fengtian in 1880, it was expanded

---

49 'Lian Jun', Qingshi Baike, <http://www.historychina.net/qsbk/bz/389134.shtml>, accessed 4 Feb. 2024.
50 Ian Heath, *Armies of the Nineteenth Century: China* (Nottingham: Foundry Books, 2009), pp.25.
51 Xu, *Jundui Tonglan*, pp.117–118.
52 Zhao et al., *Qing Shigao*, vol. 462, bio. 249.
53 Yongfu Han, 'Qingmo Jiangling Ye Zhichao Bing Sixing Bu Jianyu Kao', Lishi Dang'an (2017), <https://xueshu.baidu.com/usercenter/paper/show?paperid=1s5j0jj0gb1e0a30su160pg0jx122428&tn=SE_baiduxueshu_c1gjeupa&ie=utf-8&site=baike>, accessed 7 Feb 2024.
54 Xu, *Jundui Tonglan*, pp.68–70.

and placed under the command of General Zuo Baogui. Upon its creation, the Feng Army consisted of five battalions of cavalry and one of infantry, though expansions followed. The Feng Army was one of the best Trained Army units, being armed with repeating rifles and Krupp artillery, as well as drilling regularly. In particular, Feng Army soldiers were well-trained in trench warfare; night-fighting, digging trenches, constructing fortifications, and planting stakes were key elements of their drilling. The Feng Army even possessed its own dedicated engineering corps, which few other armies in China could boast at the time. Discipline was harshly enforced, with soldiers being beheaded for theft, rape and desertion. Less severe crimes were punished by piercing the ears, tying a string in the wound, and parading the offender around camp. Such draconian methods apparently worked, as the Feng Army was one of the most disciplined formations in the entire Empire.

A devout Hui Muslim, General Zuo Baogui was beloved by both rich and poor, foreigner and Chinese alike for his extensive philanthropic efforts.[55] Born to a poor farming family in Fei County of Shandong Province, Zuo joined the army, and soon rose through the ranks through courage and tactical ingenuity.[56] He was kind to his subordinates and, on account of his strict adherence to Islamic scruples, he did not fall victim to the hedonism, corruption and degeneracy that had befallen so many other Qing generals.[57] If one of his subordinates was killed or injured, he would use his own personal funds to support their families. During the Sino-Japanese War, his uncompromising courage in battle and dramatic manner of death cemented him as a national and folk hero. Numerous memorials were built in China to honour General Zuo; an ornate tomb was built in his hometown of Linyi, and a bronze statue of Zuo was raised in Fengtian with donations from locals. The Japanese even erected a memorial obelisk for him after the battle of Pyongyang as a sign of respect.[58]

The Zhenbian Army and the Dikai Army

The Heilongjiang armies consisted of the numerous Banner and Manchu militia units under the command of General Yiketang'a of the Zhalali (Jalari) Clan.[59] The most notable of these were the Zhenbian Army and the Dikai Army. In 1890, Yiketang'a established the Zhenbian Army to defend the Chinese border from Russia.[60] Upon its conception, it was composed of 18 battalions of cavalry, infantry, and riverine units, with 10,000 Western rifles. A Zhenbian Army force of 2,250 picked men from four battalions of infantry and one of cavalry was stationed in modern-day Tieli and were known as the 'Five Great Battalions.' In 1891, Yiketang'a and the Zhenbian Army

---

55   Isabella B. Bishop, Korea, and Her Neighbors (New York: F.H. Revell Company, 1898), p.205.
56   Zhao et al., *Qing Shigao*, vol. 460, bio. 247.
57   Anon., *Shenyang Xianzhi* (Shenyang: Chengwen Chubanshe, 1974), Zuo Baoguizhuan.
58   Bishop, *Korea*, p.316.
59   Zhao et al., *Qing Shigao*, vol. 461, bio. 248.
60   Xu, *Jundui Tonglan*, pp.72–73.

constructed a series of walls, defences and forts around modern-day Aihui, due to its very volatile border with Russia.

The Dikai Army was raised during the Sino-Japanese War and was composed mainly of local hunters and bandits. Despite being poorly armed and trained, the soldiers of the Dikai Army were still good fighters with plenty of experience in hunting (and probably banditry). The Dikai Army excelled in guerilla warfare, and during the defence of Manchuria inflicted several defeats on the Japanese. Nicknamed the Hunters of the Eastern Mountains (Dongshan Liehu), the Dikai Army became feared among the Japanese for their ability to take potshots and immediately disappear into the woods. Yiketang'a's sneaky hit-and-run tactics apparently disgusted the Japanese, who compared his men to an army of 'dogs and rats.' During the Sino-Japanese war, the Heilongjiang armies managed to prevent a Japanese attack on Fengtian but could not escape their lack of discipline and proved extremely ineffective in conventional operations. After the war ended, Yiketang'a vigorously pursued economic and military modernisation for his troops. Funded by mining revenue, Yiketang'a built forts, cracked down on corruption, raised new regiments, and purchased modern weaponry for the Heilongjiang armies.

Yiketang'a was not an archetypal inkbrush-pushing Manchu official and thus performed far better. Yiketang'a rose through the ranks during the Nian Rebellion and the border conflicts with Russia, where in 1899 he was promoted to the General of Heilongjiang, the highest military rank in the Heilongjiang Region of Manchuria.[61] Yiketang'a earned the fitting moniker of the 'Tiger General' for his formidable martial prowess, yet less often recounted are his somewhat sloppy habits. In one notable engagement during the Nian Rebellion, Yiketang'a found himself accidentally abandoned by his comrades due to taking too long to finish breakfast.[62] Rushing to catch up, he slung his unwashed cooking pot directly onto the horse's back. However, the pot was still extremely hot, and the horse ran off with Yiketang'a on it. By some miracle, he ended up behind the rebel army and led a one-man charge against their rear. His unit, taking advantage of the confusion, engaged the rebels from the front and won a decisive victory.

Total strength

Given the dismal state of record-keeping, it is impossible to accurately provide statistics for the total prewar military strength of the entire Chinese Empire. Many thousands of recorded soldiers only existed on paper or were too weak or old to fight. Furthermore, the myriads of independent armies that participated can be classified in an infinite number of ways. For example, the Sheng Trained Army was sometimes called the Fengtian Trained Army Sheng Division, making it part of the Feng Army instead of its own

---

61 Heilongjiang did not become a formal province of the Qing Empire until 1907.
62 Anon., 'Jilinshi Faxian 'Hujiangjun' Yiktang'a Mudi', Jiangcheng Wanbao (2014), <https://www.sssc.cn/a/20120629/134093472973328.shtml>, accessed 4 Feb. 2024.

organisation, while the Ji Trained Army was sometimes listed as a subsection of the Ji Army. Likewise, many armies did not have a single commander, and instead authority was shared between several different general of the same rank: for example, Jiang Xiyi and Cheng Zhiwei both commanded sections of the Datong Army, but Jiang Xiyi's unit was called the Xi Army to differentiate it from Cheng Zhiwei's. This kind of absurdly convoluted organisation makes even naming all the Chinese armies of this war basically impossible, let alone compiling accurate figures. However, a Homeric attempt at creating an exhaustive list of every army that participated in the Sino-Japanese War is included here; note that many of the armies listed here did not necessarily fight any battles but were only mobilised. They can be separated into seven main categories:

1. The Beiyang Army, or the forces under the overall command of Viceroy of Zhili Province Li Hongzhang. These include the Huai Army, the Trained Armies under Li's control, as well as several other independent Brave Armies linked to Li, such as the Resolute, Gongwei, Sui and Gong Armies.
2. The regional armies of Fengtian, under the overall command of the General of Fengtian Yulu.[63] The regional armies of Fengtian, Heilongjiang and Jilin were mainly composed of Banner or reorganised Banner units.
3. The regional armies of Heilongjiang, under the overall command of the General of Heilongjiang Yiketang'a.
4. The regional armies of Jilin, under the overall command of the General of Jilin Changshun.[64]
5. The provincial armies of Shandong, under the overall command of Governor Li Bingheng.[65]
6. The Xiang Army, under the overall command of Governor of Hunan Wu Dacheng. Governor Wu volunteered to lead the Xiang Army in the war, so the Viceroy of Huguang (Hubei and Hunan Provinces) devolved military authority to him.
7. All other armies, from a variety of provinces and commanders, such as the Jinsheng Army of Tianjin, the Dinghai Army of the Penghu Islands, and the Datong Army of Shanxi Province.

---

63 The three Manchurian 'Regions' of Fengtian, Heilongjiang, and Jilin did not become formal provinces until after the Sino-Japanese War. Consequently, the highest ranking military official in Fengtian was the General of Fengtian, for Heilongjiang the General of Heilongjiang and so on.
64 Not to be confused with the future warlord Zhang Xun.
65 Shandong Province was one of the few that did not fall under the authority of a regional viceroy.

All Chinese armies that participated or were mobilised in the Sino-Japanese War

Army name	Commander(s)	Theoretical strength	Affiliation	Notes
Sheng Army	Wei Rugui, later Lu Benyuan and Sun Xianyin	18 battalions; 9,000 men	Beiyang Army; Huai Army	
Ming Army	Liu Shengxiu, later Jiang Guiti	12 battalions; 6,000 men	Beiyang Army; Huai Army	
Qing Bodyguard Army	Huang Shilin	8 battalions; 4,000 men	Beiyang Army; Huai Army	Named after Wu Changqing; also simply called 'Qing Army' (see C3 in Chapter Five)
New Qing Army	Zhang Guangqian	5 battalions; 2,000 men	Beiyang Army; Huai Army	Named after Wu Changqing
Tenacious Army	Nie Shicheng	2 battalions; 1,000 men	Beiyang Army; Huai Army	The rest of the Luyu Defense Army strength is included with the Zhili and Tianjin Trained Armies
Gong Army	Nie Shicheng	10 battalions; 5,000 men	Beiyang Army; Huai Army	Named after Nie's courtesy name Gongting; unrelated to the Weihaiwei Gong Army
Ren Army	Wu Yuren, Jiang Zikang, and Tang Renlan	Two battalions; 1,000 men; four battalions of 2,000 men recruited in 1894 and another 30 battalions of 15,000 men recruited in 1895	Beiyang Army; Huai Army, formerly part of Xiang Army	
Chu Braves Cavalry	Unknown	Two battalions; 500 men	Beiyang Army; Huai Army	
Mingwu Army	Unknown	4 battalions; 3,000 men	Beiyang Army; Huai Army	
He Army	Cheng Yunhe	4 battalions; 2,000 men	Beiyang Army; Huai Army	
Cheng Army	Wei Rucheng	8 battalions; 3,500 men	Beiyang Army; Huai Army	
Huai Army (called Zhao Huaiye's Army in this book)	Zhao Huaiye	6 battalions; 3,000 men	Beiyang Army; Huai Army	Named after Zhao Huaiye
Xi Army	Jiang Xiyi	8 battalions; 4,000 men	Beiyang Army; Shanxi Province	Part of the Datong Army
Datong Army	Cheng Zhiwei	Unknown	Beiyang Army; Shanxi Province	
Zhili Trained Army	Ye Zhichao	35 battalions; 11,000 men	Beiyang Army	
Tianjin Trained and Defense Armies	Ye Zhichao	14 battalions; 5,000 men	Beiyang Army	
Guangwu Army	Zhang Gaoyuan and Yang Shoushan	4 battalions; 2,000 men	Beiyang Army; transferred from Xiang Army	
Resolute Army	Song Qing	9 battalions; 4,500 men; 5 battalions of 2,500 men recruited during the war	Beiyang Army	
Gui Army	Jiang Guiti	4 battalions; 2,000 men	Beiyang Army; part of Resolute Army	

THE ARMIES OF THE QING EMPIRE

Army name	Commander(s)	Theoretical strength	Affiliation	Notes
New Resolute Army	Li Yongfang, Liu Fengqing, Long Dianyang, Cheng Yun, and Li Jiachang	25 battalions; 10,000 men	Beiyang Army; expansion of Resolute Army	Cheng Yun commanded four infantry battalions while Liu Fengqing commanded five infantry battalions and one cavalry battalion; the other generals all commanded five infantry battalions each
Gongwei Army	Xu Bangdao	6 battalions; 2,000 men; later expanded to 11 battalions by merging with other former Lushunkou garrison units	Beiyang Army	
Songwu Army	Zhang Gaoyuan, Liu Shijun, Sun Jinbiao, Sun Wanling, and Xia Xinyou	12 battalions; 6,000 men; 8 battalions of 3,500 men recruited during the war	Beiyang Army	
Weijing Army	Liu Shijun	5 battalions and 3 companies; 2,800 men	Beiyang Army	
Sui Army	Liu Peichao	6 battalions; 3,000 men	Beiyang Army	
Gong Army	Dai Zongqian	6 battalions; 3,000 men	Beiyang Army	
Beiyang Guards	Zhang Wenxuan	4 battalions; 2,000 men	Beiyang Army; Huai Army	
Feng Army	Zuo Baogui, later Ma Jinxu	9 battalions; 3,000 men	Under overall command of General of Fengtian Hitara Yulu	
Sheng Trained Army	Gobulo Fengsheng'a	10 battalions; 4,500 men; four battalions of 2,000 men recruited in 1895	Under overall command of General of Fengtian Hitara Yulu	
Yingkou Daobiao Army	Qiao Minchen and Wang Deyi	2 battalions; 1,000 men	Under overall command of General of Fengtian Hitara Yulu	
Qi Yongsheng's Yingkou militia	Qi Yongsheng	3 companies; 300 men	Under overall command of General of Fengtian Hitara Yulu	
Haifang Trained Army	Qiao Gancheng	3 battalions and 1 company; 1,350 men	Under overall command of General of Fengtian Hitara Yulu	
Jiesheng Trained Army	Irgen Gioro Lianshun and Tong Maoyin	30 companies; 4,000 men	Under overall command of General of Fengtian Hitara Yulu	
Changsheng Trained Army (Fengtian detachment)	Unknown	5 battalions; 2,000 men	Under overall command of General of Fengtian Hitara Yulu	
Jing Feng Army	Unknown	5 battalions; 2,000 men	Under overall command of General of Fengtian Hitara Yulu	
Fengtian Zhenbian Army	Yi Yi	3 battalions; 1,500 men	Under overall command of General of Fengtian Hitara Yulu	
Han Dengju's Fengtian militia	Han Dengju	3 battalions; 1,500 men	Under overall command of General of Fengtian Hitara Yulu	
Zhendong Army	Xu Qingzhang	10 battalions; 4,000 men	Under overall command of General of Fengtian Hitara Yulu	

Army name	Commander(s)	Theoretical strength	Affiliation	Notes
Dingbian Army	Zhang Xiluan	2 battalions; 1,000 men; 5 battalions of 2,500 men recruited during the war	Under overall command of General of Fengtian Hitara Yulu	
Ren, Yi, Li, Zhi, Xin, Wen, Liang, Gong, Jian, and Rang militias	Jiang Tianfu, Han Yuchen, Lu Shoushan, Chu Wenyan, Fu Cai, and others	10 militias; maximum of 20,000 men but probably closer to 10,000 to 15,000 men	Under overall command of General of Fengtian Hitara Yulu	
New Feng Army	Geng Fengming	12 battalions; 6,000 men	Under overall command of General of Fengtian Hitara Yulu; expansion of Feng Army	
Jingbian Trained Army	Ding Chunxi	18 battalions and 7 companies; 9,050 men	Under overall command of General of Jilin Gobulo Changshun	Apparently also called the Jingbian Army.
Jilin Eight Banners Trained Army	Unknown	14 battalions; 4,600 men	Under overall command of General of Jilin Gobulo Changshun	
Ji Trained Army	En Xi	12 battalions; 5,000 men	Under overall command of General of Jilin Gobulo Changshun	Technically considered part of the Ji Army
Ji Army	Fu Linbu	5 battalions; 2,500 men	Under overall command of General of Jilin Gobulo Changshun	
Rehe Cavalry Detachment	Gobulo Changshun	5 battalions; 1,500 men	Under overall command of General of Jilin Gobulo Changshun	
Zhenbian Army	Unknown	17 battalions; 7,000 men	Under overall command of General of Heilongjiang Zhalali Yiketang'a	
Dikai Army	Yuan Yongshan and Yuan Shoushan	10 battalions; 4,000 men	Under overall command of General of Heilongjiang Zhalali Yiketang'a	
Qi Trained Army	Gobulo Wohenge	6 battalions; 3,000 men	Under overall command of General of Heilongjiang Zhalali Yiketang'a	
Qi New Army	Unknown	5 battalions; 1,200 men	Under overall command of General of Heilongjiang Zhalali Yiketang'a	
Jingyuan New Army	Unknown	5 battalions; 1,200 men	Under overall command of General of Heilongjiang Zhalali Yiketang'a	
Yu Elite Army	Jiang Shangjun	4 battalions; 2,000 men	Under overall command of General of Heilongjiang Zhalali Yiketang'a; recruited from Henan Province	
Jidongyu Militia	Xu Zhen	70,000–80,000 at most	Under overall command of General of Heilongjiang Zhalali Yiketang'a	

THE ARMIES OF THE QING EMPIRE

Army name	Commander(s)	Theoretical strength	Affiliation	Notes
Xing'an Army	Unknown	6 battalions and 4 companies; 2,550 men	Under overall command of General of Heilongjiang Zhalali Yiketang'a	
Shandong Trained Army	Wang Liansan	10 battalions; 3,500 men	Under overall command of Governor of Shandong Li Bingheng	
Fu Army	Feng Yide, Li Rendang, and Li Shihong	8 battalions; 3,500 men	Under overall command of Governor of Shandong Li Bingheng	
Shandong Bodyguard Army	Unknown	7 battalions; 6,500 men	Under overall command of Governor of Shandong Li Bingheng	
Dong Army	Cao Zhengbang	3 battalions; 1,500 men	Under overall command of Governor of Shandong Li Bingheng	
Ding Army	Unknown	5 battalions 2,000 men	Under overall command of Governor of Shandong Li Bingheng	
Xinkuiqian Braves	Unknown	5 battalions; 2,000 men	Under overall command of Governor of Shandong Li Bingheng	
Jikang Army	Unknown	4 battalions; 2,000 men	Under overall command of Governor of Shandong Li Bingheng	
He Defence Army	Yan Desheng	5 battalions; 2,500 men	Under overall command of Governor of Shandong Li Bingheng	
Xiang Army	Cao Fengyi	3 battalions; 1,500 men	Under overall command of Governor of Shandong Li Bingheng	Unrelated to the Hunan Xiang Army
Deng Trained Army	Initially Li Zhengrong; probably replaced by Li Ying	1 battalion; 500 men	Under overall command of Governor of Shandong Li Bingheng	
Dengzhou Defense Army	Xia Xinyou	3 battalions; 1,500 men	Under overall command of Governor of Shandong Li Bingheng	
Qing Defence Army	Li Bingheng	2 battalions; 1,000 men	Under overall command of Governor of Shandong Li Bingheng	
Yantai Trained Army	Sun Jinbiao	1 battalion; 500 men	Under overall command of Governor of Shandong Li Bingheng	
Yantai Fubiao New Army	Li Bingheng	1 battalion; 500 men	Under overall command of Governor of Shandong Li Bingheng	
Rong Trained Army	Li Zhengrong, later Li Ying	1 battalion; 500 men	Under overall command of Governor of Shandong Li Bingheng	
Laibian Artillery	He Minggao	4 battalions; 2,000 men	Under overall command of Governor of Shandong Li Bingheng	
Xing Army	He Minggao	4 battalions; 2,000 men	Under overall command of Governor of Shandong Li Bingheng	

Army name	Commander(s)	Theoretical strength	Affiliation	Notes
Qingdao Artillery	Unknown	1 battalion and 1 company; 600 men	Under overall command of Governor of Shandong Li Bingheng	
Song Army Cavalry	Unknown	1 battalion; 500 men	Under overall command of Governor of Shandong Li Bingheng	
Ji Auxiliary Centre Battalion	Huang Jinde	1 battalion; 500 men	Under overall command of Governor of Shandong Li Bingheng	
Feng Army	Wu Fengzhu	7 battalions; 2,750 men	Xiang Army (Hubei)	Unrelated to the Fengtian Feng Army
Tie Army	Xiong Tiesheng	10 battalions; 5,000 men	Xiang Army (Hubei)	
Kai Army	Wu Yuankai	4 battalions; 2,000 men	Xiang Army (Hubei)	Unrelated to Cheng Xueqi's Kai Battalion
Zhen Army	Yu Hu'en	5 battalions; 2,500 men, later expanded to 13 battalions	Xiang Army (Hubei)	
Fubiao Bodyguard Army	Liu Shuyuan	6 battalions; 3,000 men	Xiang Army	
Fushou Army	Chen Shi	10 battalions; 5,000 men	Xiang Army	
Jiangnan Defense Army	Chen Shi and Li Guangjiu	6 battalions; 3,000 men, later expanded to 10 battalions	Xiang Army	
Wuwei Army	Wei Guangtao	10 battalions; 5,000 men	Xiang Army	Also called the New Xiang Army; unrelated to the Wuwei Army that participated in the Boxer Rebellion
Wan Army	Cheng Wenbing	20 battalions; 10,000 men	Xiang Army	Also called the Wujing Army
Zhongxin Army	Zuo Xiaotong	5 battalions; 2,500 men	Xiang Army	
Old Xiang Army	Li Guangjiu	5 battalions; 2,500 men	Xiang Army	
Dubiao Bodyguard Army	Liu Guangcai	7 battalions; 3,500 men	Xiang Army	
Changsheng Army	Wan Benhua	5 battalions; 2,500 men	Jiangnan Region	
Miao Army	Ding Huai	5 battalions; 2,500 men	Jiangnan Region	
Ming Army Cavalry Detachment	Chen Fenglou	3 battalions; 750 men	Jiangnan Region	
Qinghuai Cavalry Detachment	Chen Fenglou	2 battalions; 500 men	Jiangnan Region	
Guosheng Army	Li Zhanchun	5 battalions; 2,500 men	Jiangnan Region	
Jiansheng Army	Zhang Guolin and Yang Wenbiao	5 battalions; 2,500 men	Jiangnan Region	
Jinsheng Army	Cao Kezhong	15 battalions; 30,000 men	Tianjin	
Gan Army	Dong Fuxiang	30 battalions; 12,000 men	Gansu Province	Better known as the Kansu Braves
Hong Army	Wu Hongluo and Zhou Zhenbang	11 battalions and 1 company; 5,600 men	Penghu Islands	
Guoyi Trained Army	Unknown	1 battalion; 500 men	Penghu Islands	
Penghu Torpedo Battalion	Unknown	3 companies; 300 men	Penghu Islands	
Penghu Defense Army	Guo Runxin	4 battalion; 2,000 men	Penghu Islands	
Dinghai Army	Zhu Shangpan	3 battalions; 1,500 men	Penghu Islands	

Military culture

After the First Opium War, the famous scholar Feng Guifen[66] declared that China had 'nothing to learn from the barbarians, besides strong ships and powerful guns.' At the beginning of the Sino-Japanese War, China did indeed possess strong ships and powerful guns. And yet, regardless of whether or not they were armed with modern weaponry or pitchforks, Chinese armies almost invariably faced defeat. Military affairs cannot be examined in a vacuum; China faced unique cultural, social, and political factors that undermined its war effort and jeopardised its transition into modernity.

Military philosophy

Qing China was a peace-loving nation, perhaps to an excessive degree. The dominant intellectual tradition of the late Qing despised the soldiering profession and believed war to be an unprofitable and immoral venture.[67] The popular aphorism 'good iron is not wasted to make nails as good men are not wasted to make soldiers' summarised this anti-military tradition. Even worse, soldiers themselves were despised by the population, for good reason. The almost non-existent state of logistics forced armies to live off the land at the expense of its original inhabitants.[68] Public support for war was therefore based on which side plundered the least. Though more politicised accounts describe the First Sino-Japanese War as a united anti-imperialist struggle of the Chinese nation, it must be admitted that Chinese civilians frequently got along better with the Japanese than with their own army. During the early stage of the war, the Sheng Trained Army behaved so poorly that some residents of Manchuria actually hoped for a Japanese occupation to restore order.[69] The military profession being so abhorred and miserable, it is small wonder that the Chinese deserted in such numbers during the Sino-Japanese War.

Blind arrogance, an unfortunate result of the belief that Chinese civilisation was inherently superior to anything else, was also a recurring trend amongst Chinese military leaders. Suicidal overconfidence and a psychological inability to accept defeat were two key symptoms of this mindset, both of which were still present in considerable amounts during the Sino-Japanese War. The 1894 Chinese declaration of war labelled the Japanese as a barbarian nation of midgets, pirates and thieves. The idea that the Japanese were equals, let alone superiors, to the Chinese in anything was inconceivable. Torture, beheading and mutilation of prisoners were also gruesome manifestations of this superiority complex. Captured Japanese soldiers could expect to be mutilated in any number of creative ways. A

---

66 In reality Feng's proposals for reform were far more extensive than what this quote would imply. However, the phrase does represent authentically the narrow-minded attitude many Chinese leaders had towards modernisation.
67 Paine, *The Sino-Japanese War,* p.147.
68 Stewart Lone, *Japan's First Modern War: Army and Society in the Conflict with China, 1894–1895* (London: St. Martin's Press, 1994), p.58.
69 Bishop, *Korea*, p.212. This is not to say that the Japanese soldier was always a pious and perfect creature; atrocities like the Lushunkou Massacre and the killing of wounded Chinese are good reminders of the brutality both sides were capable of.

A line of Chinese soldiers during the 1888 Junliangcheng manoeuvres. The ostentatious love of showing off as many flags as could be carried was more often than not a liability for the Chinese in the Sino-Japanese War. Photographed by Captain Albert d'Amade. (Image courtesy of ECPAD/Albert d'Amade funds)

probable explanation for these unpleasant habits would be the traditional Chinese view of rebellion, considered to be one of the worst crimes an individual could commit, so terrible that its punishment warranted such methods of mutilation.[70] The Qing viewed the Japanese as an inferior vassal state 'rebelling' against established Chinese hegemony. Moreover, Confucianism strongly emphasised that altering the body in any way was abominable.[71] Cutting off hair or getting a tattoo was bad enough, but having one's reproductive organs removed, hearts extracted or eyes gouged out (as some luckless Japanese experienced) ensured that they would find absolutely no peace in the afterlife. Unsurprisingly, this behaviour failed to endear the Chinese army to the international world, and it only bolstered the resolve of the Japanese to defeat their cruel and inhuman enemy.

Although an increasing number of officials and officers were trained in Western ways and understood the need for reform, it was clear that many remained just as stubborn and arrogant as before. In 1894 General Wu Dacheng of the Xiang Army allegedly claimed that he only needed 10 men with guns per battalion; all they had to do was shoot the Japanese officers and that was enough to win the war.[72] He also reasoned that soldiers would fight best in shifts of two hours, so those not in active combat could eat a leisurely dinner. Another general was assigned to defend the coast against the Japanese. To accomplish this, he hired a few coolies and instructed them to report back if the Japanese were sighted. He also (allegedly) issued his

---

70 Guy Boulais, *Manuel du Code Chinois* (Shanghai: Imprimerie de la Mission Catholique, 1924), p.28.
71 David Henley and Nathan Porath, 'Body Modification in East Asia: History and Debates', *Asian Studies Review*, 45:2, pp.198–216.
72 Cavendish, 'Armed Strength', pp.721–722.

men with bags of pepper to throw at the Japanese. While the vile foe was busy sneezing, spearmen would rush up and impale them. Other fanciful plans included hiring American mercenaries to invade Japan from the East, and persuading fishermen to rush Japanese warships en masse. These stories of the Chinese as ridiculous, exotic fighters with delusional tactics were no doubt exaggerated by the racist condescension of their European reporters, but their partial truth does indicate that Chinese military modernisation was very unevenly affected.

The cultural perceptions surrounding military leadership in China also affords great insight into the mindset of the late Qing military establishment. The archetype of the beloved war hero was not a mature tradition in Qing China and was even discouraged; there were precious few Gordons or Kitcheners in the Chinese public consciousness. Charismatic, popular war heroes had proven themselves time and time again in China's long history to be catalysts of dynastic change, and the Qing had no intent to repeat this. Military leaders, especially ethnic Chinese, were treated as disposable or scapegoats by the government, and their veneration was heavily discouraged. In the event of failure, otherwise loyal or successful commanders would be beheaded in front of their men. This did not affect the morale of Chinese armies positively, and also (understandably) incentivised Chinese commanders to report glorious victories when the opposite had actually occurred. Chinese commanders rarely favoured the offensive unless directly ordered to, since if their initiative failed, they would be held personally responsible.[73] These norms limited the options of military leaders and ensured that passive defence was the only real option.

Some sources have claimed that the Chinese had a philosophical indifference to the act of fleeing in combat.[74] Certainly there is no shortage of evidence proving that cowardice and desertions were common in the Chinese armies, but the aforementioned claim necessitates qualification. Throughout the Sino-Japanese War, numerous examples showed that the act of 'headlong flight' was condemned in Chinese military culture. The act of dying in battle against overwhelming odds was perhaps viewed more positively in Western cultural perceptions of heroism, but this does not mean that it did not exist at all in China.[75] There are numerous examples of Chinese soldiers choosing to die instead of retreat; one of the first conflicts of the war, the Battle of Pungdo, saw a Chinese officer give a morale-boosting speech about fighting to the death, even when victory was literally impossible. Captain Deng Shichang and General Zuo Baogui were both honoured by millions for their courageous deaths in combat. Contrariwise, Ye Zhichao and Wei Rugui were sentenced to death for their ignominious flight. General Yiketang'a was given flak by the Imperial Court for his 'dishonourable' hit and run tactics and ordered to go on the offensive. After the disastrous battle of Weihaiwei, several Chinese officers, though they had survived the battle, committed

---

73 Paine, *The Sino-Japanese War,* p.161.
74 Heath, *China*, p.30.
75 Jane E. Elliott, *Some Did It for Civilization, Some Did It for Their Country*, (Hong Kong: The Chinese University Press, 2002), p.393.

suicide out of shame. Admiral Ding Ruchang was offered political asylum by the Japanese, but his choice to take poison was seen as supremely honourable in both China and Japan.[76] Therefore it is excessive to claim that Chinese military culture condoned or even encouraged running away in combat.

Nationalism and regionalism

At the time of the Sino-Japanese War in 1894, a sense of unified Chinese nationalism was still embryonic. This is not the time nor place to debate the semantics and nuances of what defines the Chinese 'nation.' However, it is not controversial to say that before and during the war, regional loyalties superseded loyalties to the Qing Emperor and government.[77] Armies from different provinces did not get along, and the regional nature of Brave Armies codified these intense cleavages. Any kind of mutual cooperation was absent between soldiers and commanders of different regions, leading to a total lack of coordination among armies.

Beyond the military level, the idea of a unified nation was generally not present. Rivalries between provinces, regions, ethnic groups, religions and so on marred cooperation, military or otherwise. Most Chinese considered the Sino-Japanese War to be the concern of the northern provinces only and paid little more than passing interest to it. The northern Chinese had had a similar reaction to the Sino-French War. During the Sino-French War, Li Hongzhang's Beiyang Navy refused to help the Nanyang Navy (the southern Chinese navy) against the French, resulting in defeat. During the Sino-Japanese War, the Nanyang Navy was overjoyed to repay him. There is no shortage of examples on regionalism and its effects on the Chinese war effort. During the Battle of Weihaiwei, the southern sailors of Admiral Ding Ruchang, an Anhui native, mutinied and threatened him with knives. When a southern warship was captured by the Japanese during the same battle, it requested to return home as it was technically not a participant in the war. Feng Zicai, a native of southern Guangxi and hero of the Sino-French War, was called up to fight in 1894 but he dilly-dallied so much that the war ended before he got anywhere close to the frontlines.[78] The Sino-Japanese War was not a war between China and Japan; it was a war between some elements of Northern China and Japan.[79]

Even more detrimental than regional tensions were Chinese-Manchu tensions. Quarrelling between Manchu and Chinese soldiers was often violent and lethal and of course did not improve coordination between units. On a broader level, the Manchu Qing Dynasty's claim to legitimacy was growing increasingly shaky, and ethnic Chinese soldiers had no desire to sacrifice themselves for a cruel alien dynasty, nor did military officials have any inclination to help a dynasty which they viewed as infirm and ailing.[80]

---

76 James A. Scherer, *Japan To-day* (Philadelphia: J.B. Lippincott, 1904), p.46.
77 'The China-Japanese War,' The Pall Mall Gazette (London), 4 September 1894, p.7.
78 Momose Hirose and Chao-ying Fang, 'Feng Tzu-Ts'ai', in Arthur Hummel (ed.), Eminent Chinese of the Ch'ing Period 1644–1912 (Washington: United States Government Printing Office, 1943), vol. 2, pp. 687–688.
79 'A Divided House,' The North-China Herald (Shanghai), 29 March 1895, p.472.
80 'Says Chinese Don't Care,' The New York Times, 16 May 1895, p.1.

The Manchus knew this, and constrained the power of ethnic Chinese leaders and armies with checks and balances, a practice that handicapped their only competent fighting forces (see below). The Manchus had justified their brutal rule over China with military force, but time and time again they had shown they had lost their monopoly on violence. From the view of the Han, the failure of the Sino-Japanese War was but the last croak of a doomed dynasty. For many Chinese, there was no saving the Qing.

Corruption

Anyone with the most elementary understanding of late Qing military history will not be surprised at the inclusion of a description of corruption. Corruption was omnipresent within virtually every Chinese institution and was a major factor in the dismal outcome of the Sino-Japanese War. The prevalence of corruption seems to stem from the aforementioned lack of national unity or identity. Though today such practices are condemned as shameful and traitorous, Qing officials not unreasonably felt they owed nothing to their ruling Dynasty. Officials used prebendalism to benefit themselves, their families, their friends, and political cliques, at the cost of national interest.[81]

This of course compromised military effectiveness. Both civil and military officials often appointed large numbers of unqualified friends and relatives in high positions. In Brave Armies this initially improved esprit de corps but eventually degenerated into sinecure offices. In military arsenals, the gunpowder used in making shells could be replaced with charcoal, concrete or sand and the difference pocketed.[82] The purchase of foreign materials with third parties had plenty of potential for embezzling funds, which of course was exploited. Commanders could simply deduct wages from their men with no repercussions or draw money from the government to pay hundreds or even thousands of non-existent 'ghost soldiers.' Poor recordkeeping meant soldiers and their families could also collect salaries even when retired, infirm, elderly, or even deceased. Manchu Bannermen could record their newborn children as having enlisted and receive wages, and during times of war could pay a substitute to fight (or desert) in their place. The terrible morale and high desertion rate of the Chinese armies during the Sino-Japanese War was mostly due to a lack of pay. These practices resulted in a large theoretical strength of the Chinese armies, but a much less impressive praxis.

Checks and balances

Frequently analysed is the failure of the Chinese military to adapt to new military technology. While the tragic image of Chinese soldiers charging into battle with swords and spears against state of the art rifles and artillery is iconic, the weaknesses of Chinese military organisation must also be examined in detail.

---

81 Chun-ming Chang, 'The Chinese Standards of Good Government: Being a Study of the "Biographies of Model Officials" in Dynastic Histories', *Nankai Social & Economic Quarterly*, 8:2, (1935), pp.226–227.
82 Paine, *The Sino-Japanese War,* p.156.

First and foremost, the Qing proved the old biblical adage true: a house divided cannot stand. The Chinese military consisted of several separate institutions operating independently and at times at odds with one another. The Eight Banners was theoretically the 'official' army of the Qing Dynasty, but by the 1860s it was ineffectual in all fields save for embezzling funds and drug addiction. The other traditional system, the Green Standard, was purposely kept weak and divided, as a strong ethnic Han army could potentially threaten the Manchu government. The Brave Army system, which dominated from the 1860s onwards, was one of privately raised armies loyal only to their founders. The Trained Armies were a bizarre mixture of all of the above, organisationally and functionally. Even worse, civil and administrative officials and the soldiers under their authority were thrown into the mix, resulting in a truly convoluted series of different but parallel hierarchies of ranks. For example, in 1894 General Song Qing, Commander in Chief of Sichuan Province (Sichuan Tidu) and Commander of the Resolute Army (Yijun Zongtong), was given the lead role in organising the defence of the Yalu River against the Japanese. He was meant to collaborate with Yiketang'a, who was the General of Heilongjiang Province (Heilongjiang Jiangjun) and Commander of the Han Bordered Yellow Banner Army (Xiang Huangqi Han Jun Dutong). General Song, being a Han Chinese, held both a Green Standard Army rank as well as a non-government assigned rank in his Resolute Army, while General Yiketang'a held ranks in the Eight Banners system, so it was unclear who held supreme authority. Their friendship having failed to blossom, they each established independent defence sectors. Neither lifted a finger to aid the other when the Japanese attacked. A similar example occurred at the pivotal Battle of Lushunkou, where all of the Chinese commanders had the same ranks of 'tongling' and 'zongbing' and failed to agree on any single course of action. The coexistence of several different military systems precluded properly coordinated military action.

Unfortunately, the Qing government saw these divisions as a necessary evil. Even more fearful of internal insurrections than foreign threats, the Qing took great lengths to prevent military strongmen from uniting or getting too powerful. Ergo, military organisation contained a torturous system of checks and balances. These policies ensured the painfully long survival of the Manchu government at the cost of military performance. In the Green Standard Army, solely manned by Han Chinese, military officers and men were rotated periodically to bar personal bonds from forming.[83] As most units were therefore made of virtual strangers from disparate provinces, military command was paralysed. When it became necessary to counterbalance the private Brave Armies and reform the feeble Green Standard and Eight Banners, the new Trained Armies were formed. When the best of the Trained Armies were then co-opted by private actors, the Qing essentially sabotaged their own army.

---

83   Heath, *China*, p.19.

In the field, the Great Qing Legal Code strictly restricted armies based on predetermined schedules and movement. Deviation from these inflexible conventions could mean death, exile or beheading. Orders from superiors were to be obeyed step-by-step without question, even when it took days or even weeks for said orders to be conveyed.[84] Furthermore, capital punishment was threatened for abandoning one's designated deployment to aid faraway comrades. Individual responsibility was encouraged for military commanders, as collaboration resulted in rewards being split.[85] All this was done to ensure that the Qing controlled the gun, and that the gun never controlled the Qing. Against domestic rebellions these shortcomings had been manageable, but against a modern and mobile army like Japan's, Chinese commanders were completely unable to adapt to changing circumstances, nor cooperate well.[86] The outcome was a disparate collection of strategically inflexible armies, incapable of collaborating properly or making independent decisions.

Tactics and strategy

Chinese military tactics during the Sino-Japanese War were primarily defensive. These stemmed from the celebrated exploits of Zeng Guofan during the Taiping Rebellion. As most Chinese commanders had gained their experience in the mid-century rebellions, Zeng's tactics were almost universally used. Zeng reasoned that the attacker, the 'guest,' was always disadvantaged to the defender, or the 'host.' Therefore, unless the guest had overwhelming numerical superiority, it was preferable to be the host.[87] Even while on the offensive, host position was obtained by baiting the enemy into killzones to be mowed down, and cities were taken by building fortifications around to besiege them into submission. Every night when encamped, special care would be taken in choosing advantageous terrain for the encampment, and fortifications like mud redoubts, trenches with firing holes and steps, underground shelters from artillery, stakes, and abatis were erected.[88] The Chinese also made extensive use of booby traps, such as explosive charges planted below piles of pebbles as substitute for shrapnel, deep holes with punji stakes, and rigging various objects to explode or discharge poison upon touch. More permanent city defences were no less impressive. Typically, Chinese cities were protected by tall, crenelated stone walls and overwatched with artillery forts. The defences of Lushunkou (Port Arthur) were even considered superior to those of Hong Kong. Chinese fortifications were generally considered formidable, the loss of the battle typically being the fault of the defenders as opposed to the defences themselves.

---

84 Boulais, *Manuel*, pp.415–420.
85 Heath, *Armies*, p.70.
86 Paine, *The Sino-Japanese War*, p.145.
87 Guofan Zeng, 'Bing', in anon. (ed.), Zeng Guofan Quanji (Beijing: Zhongguo Zhigong Chubanshe, 2001), vol. 16, pp.5992–5993.
88 John Lamprey, 'The Economy of the Chinese Army', Journal of the Royal United Services Institution, 11:43 (1867), p.409.

Strategically, the Chinese forces focused on defending key cities and regions instead of counterattacking. In theory, this would have been perfect for the Chinese during the war. Almost interminably, Japan was the 'guest' and China the 'host' during the Sino-Japanese War. Japan was the invader and relied on quick, decisive victories to maintain adequate morale and supplies. Contrariwise, China could handle a long war of attrition on its home turf, in which inadequate Japanese logistics would eventually fail. Japanese financial and public support was finite, and if China simply stalled, eventually the Japanese would have to sue for peace.[89] Furthermore, the immobility of Chinese armies favoured defence as the only viable option anyway. Although China's lack of initiative did cost them opportunities to strike at vulnerable Japanese forces,[90] the oft-criticised defensive strategy utilised by the Chinese did possess military value.

Modernisation

It is a commonly held stereotype that the Chinese army made little to no efforts to modernise due to blind arrogance and traditionalism. This is a reductive interpretation; although ultimately modernisation was undermined by reactionary elements, it cannot be ignored that substantial elements of the Qing made extensive and impressive achievements in modernising the military.

It is far beyond the scope of this work to do justice to the complexities of this particular topic, but a brief summary will be detailed. The military modernisation process in China generally operated on the assumption that Chinese culture was superior in all regards except military. Traditionally, the Chinese believed themselves to be the nucleus of all civilisation, surrounded concentrically by barbarians of increasing depravity. During the eighteenth century, no real military threat to Chinese hegemony had materialised, and the prosperity of the era essentially dismissed any thought of social, political or military reform.

When the threat of the mid-nineteenth century rebellions and the Opium Wars arose, many of the more conservative officials believed that superficially improving certain aspects of the military and government was enough. They believed that Chinese institutions, civilian and military, were already fine, save for a few specific deficiencies. In effect, the Chinese civilisation suffered from success: the 5,000 years of unchallenged superiority China faced gave the modernisation effort a sense of conceit and complacency. The idea of technological or social 'progress' did not exist. The Chinese view of history was cyclical: dynasties would rise, prosper, stagnate, and fall. Thus, the aim of reform was not to move 'forward,' but instead to return to an idealised Confucian tradition. These reactionary officials had no intention of joining the modern world; they instead wanted to expel the modern world from

---

89　Fung, 'Testing the Self-Strengthening', 1019.
90　Paine, *The Sino-Japanese War*, pp.157–158.

their own cloistered, idealised worldview. With such a parochial attitude, modernisation could only be surface level.[91]

The Qing was not blind to its weakness, or at least certain factions of the Qing were not. The principal failing of China's modernisation was the fact that most reforms and modernisation programmes were carried out piecemeal by individual statesmen and their political cliques. Local officials who did not want to modernise did not. For those who did, funding for modernising ventures was irregular and often came from personal coffers.[92] The rigid traditionalism of the aforementioned conservatives, who held important positions in government meant that ambitious proposals for reform were more likely than not to be vetoed.[93] Thus, the modernisation process in China was uneven, superficial, and undermined from within; the political disorganisation in the Qing Empire was one of the principal failures of China's modernisation.

The assumption that the wholesale refusal to adopt modern technology is what doomed the Chinese army can be proven false with the First Opium War, the beginning of the Qing's unhappy history of foreign conflicts. Even while the war was still going on, ships and cannons were built with strong influence from British examples.[94] Just after the Opium War's conclusion, a memorial was written to the emperor recommending the acquisition and production of European weaponry. In the 1850s and 60s, Zeng Guofan founded arsenals in Jiangxi, Anqing, and Jiangnan for this exact reason. The influential Chinese scholar Feng Guifen famously proclaimed that China had to learn 'strong ships and powerful cannons' from the West. Therefore, the belief that the Chinese simply refused to acquire modern weaponry is false. What is true, however, is that after the worst of the mid-century rebellions had subsided, there was no immediate need to further modernise the armed forces. This once again led the Qing government into the pitfall of apathy. They did not see modernisation as a continuous and ongoing process, and those officials that did realise did what little they could.

Training and military academies

The training of Chinese soldiers by European instructors first began during the Taiping Rebellion. After the mid-century rebellions, Li Hongzhang in 1872 and 1876 sent several Chinese officers to Germany to study Europe's strongest military power. Upon their return, Li was so impressed that he invited German officers to train his men, and a German-officered corps was established of three battalions of infantry, two squadrons of cavalry and two batteries of artillery.[95] Li Hongzhang knew how quickly the mighty army of France had been worsted by the Germans in the Franco-Prussian War, and from that point on German military influence prevailed.

---

91 Paine, *The Sino-Japanese War*, p.340.
92 Folsom, *Friends*, p.151–152.
93 'Responsibility', The North-China Herald (Shanghai), 28 December 1894, p.1043.
94 Elliott, *Some Did It*, p.400.
95 Heath, *China*, p.26.

Tianjin Military Academy weekly schedule[96]

	Monday	Tuesday	Wednesday	Thursday	Friday	Saturday
Mornings	Land warfare	Tactics	Coastal Warfare	Land warfare	Tactics	Fortification Warfare
	Weapons study	Mathematics	Fortifications	Weapons study	Mathematics	Fortifications
	Photography	Physics	Terrain study	Astronomy	Photography	Chemistry
Afternoons	Drafting	Wargames	Mathematics	Wargames	Wargames	Mathematics

The traditional military examination for officers was graded based on the ability to recite verses from ancient poetry, skill in archery and throwing around an oversized halberd. These skills were not really applicable for the proper command of war in the modern era. In response, Li Hongzhang established several schools teaching the Western art of war, the first being the Tianjin Military Academy, founded in 1885.[97] Taught by German officers, the Tianjin Military Academy's curriculum obviously consisted of Western tactics and strategy, but also Western scientific concepts and 'political education' taught by Chinese officers. The first class of around 50 students graduated in 1888, and the skill that these cadets demonstrated encouraged Li to set up another military academy based in Kaiping, which was moved to Shanhaiguan in 1889. In 1889, five Chinese students were sent to study at an overseas German military academy for half a year, and then to the Krupp artillery factory for another half year. When they returned to China, they were hired to teach at the newly established Weihaiwei Military Academy. These Western-trained officers, though relatively few in number, formed the backbone of the Beiyang Army officer corps.

In 1882, a French military officer inspected Li Hongzhang's German-trained bodyguard and was impressed by the precision of their Prussian discipline. Trained by Krupp technician Theodore Schnell, they were equipped with Mauser magazine rifles and Krupp artillery. The same French officer also reviewed an English-trained unit armed with Martini-Henry rifles and Armstrong guns; he again found them the equals of any European force.[98] In 1886, a French military report claimed that a body of around 18,000–19,000 English-trained soldiers was present in Beijing, along with 40 German-trained artillery batteries. Another 40 batteries were due to finish training in two years.[99] A different French report from 1888 claimed that out of the fourteen infantry, cavalry and artillery units observed in Zhili

---

96   Joseph Passman, *Schools of Violence: Military Academies in the Fight for Modern China* (Berkeley: University of California at Berkeley, 2024), p.17. My sincere gratitude to Dr. Passman for providing me with a copy of his dissertation.

97   Chaoying Lu, 'Tianjin Wubei Xuetang', Tianjin Dang'an (2004), <https://xueshu.baidu.com/usercenter/paper/show?paperid=82f07a5e1a032b73e9c0657b5b6f0d00&tn=SE_baiduxueshu_c1gjeupa&ie=utf-8&site=baike>, accessed 7 Feb 2024. Zhou Shengbo and Zhou Shengchuan of the Sheng Army originally proposed the idea to Li Hongzhang.

98   Archives Militaires de l'Armee de Terre, Series 7N1665, Report by Captain Chambry to the Minister of War from 29th November 1882.

99   Archives Militaires de l'Armee de Terre, Series 7N1665, Report No. 21 by General Chanoine on a mission to China from 12th April 1886.

Province, twelve were Western trained with Western weaponry.[100] It must be remembered, however, that these descriptions were limited only to the slight minority of Li Hongzhang's Beiyang Army; the rest of the Chinese armies received very limited modern training.

Even Li's efforts in improving military leadership and training faced several insurmountable obstacles. The Huai Army had not participated in war since 1885 and even then, the units that fought were stationed in the South which was untouched by the Sino-Japanese War. Many Beiyang Army officers felt that being instructed by foreign barbarians was degrading and refused to listen to advice.[101] The talents of foreign advisors were then squandered by appointing them as drill instructors with minimal influence. Ultimately, a wholesale reform of the officer corp was not carried out due to financial and political difficulties. Officers, resentful of foreign methods, frequently regressed into leading traditional drills involving archery, spear and sword practice.[102] By the outbreak of the Sino-Japanese War, most Chinese generals did not know what the Japanese army was. For centuries, the Japanese had been midget pirates scrounging on the outskirts of Chinese civilisation, and the thought of them offering any resistance to the army of the Celestial Empire, let alone being superior to them, was ridiculous.

The best trained Chinese units were shattered early on during the campaign in Korea; much of the remaining troops were inexperienced levies and partially modernised armies. Chinese soldiers equipped with modern weapons were not necessarily well-trained in these weapons. The issuing of repeating rifles was totally useless in the hands of these men who had been trained with spears. Target practice, if done at all, was customarily at a maximum distance of 60 metres away, the usual being around 15 metres. More often was simply 'handling' foreign weapons; loading and firing them was enough, regardless of where the projectile went. These untrained armies, either raw recruits or even drafted beggars given a couple days' drill, lacked the knowledge or discipline to keep their weapons in working order.[103] Bent breeches and barrels filled with dirt and mud were but a few of the abuses suffered by their rifles. Without proper training, Chinese soldiers had no idea what the purpose of a firearm was. It was a (not totally unfounded) stereotype that Chinese military tactics involved making loud noises, shooting in the general direction of the enemy, and then routing if the slightest inconvenience materialised. Some soldiers cut the sights off their rifles, believing they prevented proper aiming, or set them to maximum range under the impression they controlled bullet velocity, both of which resulted in subpar accuracy. Even the best Chinese armies were not spared from this issue. General Song Qing complained that many soldiers, even when armed with the excellent Mauser magazine rifle, had dismal marksmanship or did not know how to use the weapon altogether.[104] During

---

100 Archives Militaires de l'Armee de Terre, Series 7N1665, Report by Captain d'Amade on the Chinese forces in Zhili in winter 1888.
101 Liu, 'The Military Challenge', pp.266–269.
102 Cavendish, 'The Armed Strength', pp.720–721.
103 Fung, 'Testing the Self-Strengthening', pp.1022–1024.
104 Fung, 'Testing the Self-Strengthening', pp.1017–1018.

the Sino-Japanese War, Governor of Hunan Wu Dacheng very enthusiastically attempted to institute a programme of daily rifle practice for new recruits, but this was cancelled due to insufficient and incompatible ammunition.[105] It is impossible to say with certainty how many armies were trained, untrained or well-trained, but the failure to modernise the officer corps and institute a regular programme of training certainly played a key role in China's dismal failure in the Sino-Japanese War.

Moreover, most units lacked the support functions and logistics critical in Western armies. Better disciplined armies like the Feng Army had supply caravans of camels and horse carts supplying food and ammunition, but more often the corruption and inefficiency of the commissariats meant Chinese soldiers had to plunder or loot whoever and whatever they could find, even eating their own beasts of burden.[106] Hired labourers, or even civilians impressed at gunpoint, were usually the main method of transporting supplies. Ironically, the frequent retreating of Chinese armies routinely involved leaving behind copious stocks of food and ammunition for the Japanese to use. Thus, the Qing armies, though numerically superior to Japanese forces, lacked the ability to exploit this advantage, and were in fact frequently outnumbered on the field. There were no established medical corps, the custom being to strip the wounded; depressing stories of wounded Qing soldiers abandoned or even robbed by their comrades, begging their way back towards China surfaced. Chinese hospitals were almost always established by charitable Westerners or wealthy philanthropists, and the scope and scale of their contributions was severely limited by the lack of government support.

Military industry
The early 1860s saw the establishment of modern arsenals at Jiangnan (Shanghai), Tianjin and Nanjing by Zeng Guofan and Li Hongzhang. The immediate aim of these was to produce copies of Western firearms to suppress the ongoing rebellions, but Li envisioned an eventual integration of Western industrial machinery into Chinese society as a whole.[107] By 1875 the Jiangnan, Tianjin and Nanjing had entered full production of Western small-arms, ammunition and cannon.[108] Further expansions and additions to China's budding military industry would follow. In less than a decade, the Industrial Revolution had been introduced to the Middle Kingdom.

The development and expansion of Chinese military industry was not at all a smooth path. Firstly, corruption and favouritism-based hiring practices drained the budget and decreased productivity. For example, most of the directors at the Jiangnan Arsenal were Hunanese, and almost exclusively hired their provincial compatriots.[109] An investigation conducted after the Sino-Japanese War concluded that many of these directors brought in 30–40

---

105 Xu, *Jundui Tonglan*, p.153.
106 Cavendish, 'The Armed Strength', p.717.
107 Thomas L. Kennedy, *The Arms of Kiangnan: Modernisation in the Chinese Ordnance Industry 1860–1895*, (Colorado: Westview Press, 1978), p.76.
108 Kennedy, *The Arms of Kiangnan*, pp.47–48.
109 Kennedy, *The Arms of Kiangnan*, pp.125–127.

freeloading friends and relatives whose only contribution was collecting pay. There were attempts to address this; the Tianjin Arsenal was run smoothly and what little corruption there was, was quickly stamped out. However, there was still no systematic or objective method for selecting arsenal workers. In the 1880s, one particularly stingy director of the Jiangnan Arsenal fired a Chinese technician for riding a carriage to work instead of walking. The same technician, gifted in mathematics and mechanical drawing, subsequently signed on with a foreign firm. The poor management of human resources sapped the military industry of productivity and already sparse funds. Chinese arsenals also remained heavily reliant on foreign instructors. When the Nanjing Arsenal let go of its foreign advisors prematurely, production backslid into antiquated jingals, muskets and smoothbore cannon.[110] In 1896, a Chinese scientist visiting Germany noted that Chinese machinery was on-par or in some cases even more advanced than that of Europe, but also that Chinese technicians lacked the expertise to continue updating and refining the manufacturing process.[111] The scientific and technical education provided to Chinese staff was unable to produce scientists of sufficient quality or quantity to develop a self-sufficient military industry, but this problem is outside the scope of this work.

Second, the absence of domestic coal and steel industries in China necessitated the costly importation of these materials from overseas. At the Jiangnan Arsenal, insurance for imported materials ate up over half of all funds spent prior to 1875.[112] Of course, whenever compradors were involved, corruption was also present; one official at the Jiangnan Arsenal was reported to have first purchased raw materials at low prices and then resold them at an exorbitant cost. Dependence on foreign supply greatly concerned Li Hongzhang, and he sarcastically remarked that the Jiangnan Arsenal was just buying weapons from foreigners with extra steps. To remedy this, he advocated utilising Western machinery to extract raw material domestically. In 1874, the Tianjin Arsenal began using domestically mined coal, but in 1879 around 59% of the Tianjin Arsenal's annual expenditures were still for imported material.[113] The Chinese military industry never achieved self-sufficiency, despite Li's efforts.

Third, there was no central authority governing the operation, funding or expansion of arsenals. This resulted in a disjointed and confused modernisation process. For example, in the 1860s Zeng Guofan intended to turn the Jiangnan Arsenal into a steamship factory, against the wishes of his student Li Hongzhang and the central government. Zeng went through with the plan anyway and ended up producing a series of functional but extremely expensive vessels. Furthermore, the steamships did not conform to any commercial standards and were useless to China's military needs.[114] Li Hongzhang ended up terminating steamship making after Zeng's death, and the whole ordeal resulted in not

---

110 Kennedy, *The Arms of Kiangnan*, p.115.
111 Elliott, *Some Did It*, p.418.
112 Kennedy, *The Arms of Kiangnan*, p.65.
113 Kennedy, *The Arms of Kiangnan*, p.118.
114 Kennedy, *The Arms of Kiangnan*, p.93.

much more than hundreds of thousands of taels in waste. Even worse, funding for arsenals was irregular and generally not permanent. Money came from a miscellany of sources, such as the sale of scrap metal, personal funds, loans from third parties, customs income, and government grants.[115] To be fair to the Qing, the Imperial treasury was already drained from addressing the mid-century rebellions and the slew of natural disasters in the 1870s and 1880s. Regardless of the cause, funding for Chinese military industry was limited, miscellaneous and often squandered through mismanagement. Moreover, the diverse needs of Chinese armies strained production; manufacturing several different types of ammunition, small arms and guns overstretched industrial capacities. By 1885, the Jiangnan Arsenal was making ammunition for Mauser, Lee, Snider, and Remington rifles, resulting in increased expenditure for specialised machinery. By the end of the Sino-Japanese War, the Jiangnan Arsenal had produced six different types of cartridges and percussion caps.[116]

Confronted by these problems, the expansion of Chinese military industry continued slowly in the 1870s and early 1880s. The Chinese arsenals did not have the required machinery or technicians to produce the most modern weaponry, and consequently their products lagged considerably behind those of the West in modernity and quality. In 1874, the Jiangnan Arsenal began producing 12 pound muzzleloading, rifled Armstrong guns, but a year later two of these Chinese-made guns burst, killing their operators. Following this incident, Chinese-made artillery prioritised barrel thickness overall, resulting in inordinately heavy and clumsy Armstrong guns that could only be used for coastal defence. These obsolete muzzle-loading pieces remained in production by the Jiangnan Arsenal at least until 1889. During the Sino-French War, these Armstrong guns were found to be totally immobile in land warfare, and production had to revert to smoothbore guns.[117] In the late 1870s jingals and Gatling guns of dubious military worth continued to be manufactured in great numbers, notably by the Nanjing Arsenal.[118] The Chinese copy of the Remington centre-fire rifle, which began production at the Jiangnan Arsenal in 1884, had a dangerous manufacturing defect in the breech mechanism and Huai Army units refused to accept them. Although a solution was suggested in 1890, by then the Remington was already outmoded and nearly 15,000 rifles had to be discarded.[119] Even by 1893, some guns were still partially handmade.

The Sino-French War exposed the Chinese military industry's shortcomings, and major programmes of modernisation were taken. New machinery was installed and old machinery was modified to facilitate the copying and manufacturing of more advanced foreign weaponry. At the Jiangnan Arsenal, Remington rifle machinery purchased in 1871, was updated to produce centre-fire rifles in 1884, and magazine rifles in 1890. Higher quality gunpowder began production at newly established powder plants at Tianjin in 1887, and at Jiangnan in 1894. In 1887, the Tianjin

---

115 Kennedy, *The Arms of Kiangnan*, p.124.
116 Kennedy, *The Arms of Kiangnan*, p.134.
117 Kennedy, *The Arms of Kiangnan*, pp.108–109.
118 Kennedy, *The Arms of Kiangnan*, p.119.
119 Kennedy, *The Arms of Kiangnan*, pp.109–110.

Arsenal established what many foreign observers deemed the largest and highest quality gunpowder factories in the entire world.[120] Chinese-made heavy artillery experienced a great leap forward in 1878, with the production of the first steel barrels. In 1886, an English technician well-versed in the latest Armstrong guns was hired by the Jiangnan Arsenal such that by 1889, production of these was proceeding full-time. In 1892 Hotchkiss, Maxim and Nordenfelt machine guns were being produced at the Nanjing Arsenal, and in the same year a French military observer claimed that the Chinese could copy any Western weapon they wanted, no matter how complex.[121] There were moves to lessen reliance on imported materials, and in the 1880s China's first steel refinery was established near Shanghai in 1892, and another in Tianjin in 1893. In 1895, smokeless powder began production in the Jiangnan Arsenal. By 1896 (though too late to impact the Sino-Japanese War), the Tianjin Arsenal was able to manufacture Maxim machine guns, Nordenfelt cannon, Krupp guns and suitable ammunition for all of these.

A few good examples prove that Chinese military industry was not totally imitative. For example, prototypes of naval mines, percussion caps and iron-moulded cannon were actually invented in the 1840s and 1850s, independently of European designs, but they were not widely adopted until decades later. A slightly modified copy of the British Lee-Metford rifle, designated the M1890 Xinli, was briefly produced and tested, but was scrapped by Li Hongzhang in favour of another domestically designed magazine rifle.[122] This model, called the Jiangnan Rifle (officially the M1891 Kuaili; sometimes Jiangnan is written as Kiangnan), was a heavily modified version of a M1888 Mannlicher, and began test production in 1891 at the eponymous arsenal. The Jiangnan Rifle was a promising weapon, and shortly before the Sino-Japanese War a visiting Japanese general was so impressed he requested to take home two to serve as samples. Unfortunately, poor performance due to inferior steel, powder quality and the relative ease of acquiring foreign weaponry precluded the Jiangnan Rifle from being adopted on a larger scale. A total of 11,608 Jiangnan Rifles were produced from its invention in 1890 to its discontinuation in 1901, with a theoretical yearly output of 1,055 rifles per year.[123]

A remotely detonated electric naval mine was developed and tested in the 1880s by the Jiangsu Arsenal. These weapons were deployed during the Sino-Japanese War, but their failure to impact the war was entirely the fault of their operators. In 1896 (though the weapon was probably developed earlier) a visiting French Captain reported seeing very light 40mm mountain guns of an unknown type at the Hankou arsenal.[124] These could be carried easily by small pack animals, suggesting they were likely designed to be fast-moving and used against highly mobile bandits or small-scale rebellions.[125]

---

120 Kennedy, *The Arms of Kiangnan*, p.142.
121 Elliott, *Some Did It*, pp.409–410.
122 Kennedy, *The Arms of Kiangnan*, pp.133–134.
123 Bin Shih, Lin Xu, Stanley Zielinski, 'The Chinese Kuaili Rifle', *BANZAI: The Japanese Militaria Collector's Bulletin*, (2014), accessed 28 Feb. 2024. My sincerest gratitude to Stan for lending me a copy of this invaluable article.
124 Archives Militaires de l'Armee de Terre, Series 7N1664, Report by Captain Meillet in China 1900.
125 Elliott, *Some Did It*, p.412.

Despite these impressive results, the Chinese military industry was simply unable to equip the Empire's enormous and overextended armed forces. The heavy guns produced at the Jiangnan Arsenal in the 1890s were equal in quality to those of the West, but only twelve 50 pounders, or six 100 pounders could be produced annually. Chinese arsenals were capable of producing at most several thousand small arms a year, meaning most units still relied on imported weaponry. Qing-era industrialisation ultimately never expanded past a handful of privately owned experimental arsenals. The aforementioned systemic issues (corruption and poor hiring practices, reliance on expensive imported materials, and lack of centralised coordination) were never fully resolved. The Sino-Japanese War caught the Chinese military industry in an embryonic stage, where the journey to modernisation had only begun.

Major arsenals established in China from 1860 to 1895[126]

Year established	Name	Location	Establishing official	Products	Comments
1861	Anqing Arsenal	Anqing, Anhui Province	Zeng Guofan	Small guns, explosive shells	
1863	Shanghai Arsenal	Shanghai, Jiangsu Province	Li Hongzhang	Small guns, explosive shells	Merged with Jiangnan Arsenal in 1865
1863	Songjiang Arsenal; later Suzhou Arsenal	Shanghai, Jiangsu Province; later Suzhou, Jiangsu Province	Li Hongzhang	Explosive shells	Moved to Suzhou in 1863; merged with Nanjing Arsenal in 1865
1865	Jiangnan Arsenal	Shanghai, Jiangsu Province	Li Hongzhang and Zeng Guofan	Rifles, coastal defence ordnance quick firing guns, gunpowder, cartridges, mines, steel machine tools, steamships	Rocket plant established in 1867; gunpowder plant established in 1871–1874
1865	Nanjing Arsenal (also called Jinling Arsenal)	Nanjing, Jiangsu Province	Li Hongzhang	Iron ordnance and ammunition	Wulong Shan Arsenal established in 1874; merged with Nanjing Arsenal in 1879
1866	Unknown	Tianjin, Zhili Province	Liu Zhangyu and Chonghou	Traditional weaponry	Ceased operations in 1868
1866	Tianjin East Arsenal	Tianjin, Zhili Province	Chong Hou	Gunpowder, cartridges, naval ammunition, steel	
1867	Tianjin West Arsenal	Tianjin, Zhili Province	Chong Hou	Small guns, machinery	
1869	Fuzhou Arsenal	Fuzhou, Fujian Province	Ying Gui	Ammunition and gunpowder	Ceased operations in 1872; resumed in 1875
1869	Xi'an Arsenal; later Lanzhou Arsenal	Xi'an, Shaanxi Province; later Lanzhou, Gansu Province	Zuo Zongtang	Ammunition and gunpowder	Moved to Lanzhou, Gansu Province in 1872; ceased operations in 1882

---

126 Kennedy, *The Arms of Kiangnan*, Appendix II.

Year established	Name	Location	Establishing official	Products	Comments
1870	Tianjin Mobile Arsenal	Tianjin, Zhili Province	Li Hongzhang	Ammunition	Subordinate to Huai Army
1872	Yunnan Arsenal	Kunming, Yunnan Province	Unknown	Ordnance, ammunition and gunpowder	Ceased production sometime before 1880; resumed production in 1880–1881; resumed production again in 1885
1873	Guangdong Arsenal	Guangzhou, Guangdong (Canton) Province	Rui Lin	Steamships, ammunition and mines	Merged with Guangdown Powder Plant in 1885
1875	Shandong Arsenal	Ji'nan, Shandong Province	Ding Baozhen	Rifles, ammunition and gunpowder	
1875	Hunan Arsenal	Changsha, Hunan Province	Wang Wenshao	Unknown	
1875	Guangdong Powder Plant	Guangzhou, Guangdong (Canton) Province	Zhang Zhaodong	Gunpowder	
1877	Sichuan Arsenal	Chengdu, Sichuan Province	Ding Baozhen	Rifles, guns, ammunition and gunpowder	Sichuan Powder Plant established nearby in 1880
1881	Jilin Arsenal	Jilin City, Jilin Province	Wu Dacheng	Ammunition and Gunpowder	
1881	Nanjing Powder Plant	Nanjing, Jiangsu Province	Liu Kunyi	Ammunition and gunpowder	
1882	Zhejiang Powder Plant	Hangzhou, Zhejiang Province	Unknown	Gunpowder	Merged with Zhejiang Arsenal in 1885
1882–1884	Shanxi Arsenal	Taiyuan, Shanxi Province	Zhang Zhidong	Ammunition	
1883	Beijing Field Forces Arsenal	Beijing, Zhili Province	Prince Chun	Unknown; probably ammunition	Destroyed by fire in 1890
1883	Zhejiang Arsenal	Hangzhou, Zhejiang Province	Liu Bingzhang	Ammunition and gunpowder	
1885	Guangdong Cartridge Plant	Guangzhou, Guangdong Province	Zhang Zhidong	Cartridges	
1885	Taiwan Arsenal	Taipei, Taiwan Province/Prefecture[127]	Liu Mingchuan	Ammunition and gunpowder	
1890	Hanyang Arsenal	Hanyang, Hubei Province	Zhang Zhidong	Rifles, artillery, ammunition and gunpowder	Entered production 1895
1894	Shaanxi Arsenal	Xi'an, Shaanxi Province	Lu Chuanlin	Ammunition	

---

127 Taiwan was a prefecture of Fujian Province until 1887.

Uniforms

Unfortunately, very few Chinese uniform regulations from before 1905 are readily available today, and any kind of information about specific armies or units comes from surviving examples, eyewitness records, contemporary prints, and other such sources (see Chapter Five).

Several participants in an 1888 military exercise of Beiyang Army troops in Junliangcheng, Tianjin. The soldiers are dressed in turbans, hao yi, zhan qun, and Tartar boots, accompanied by their officer in a warm hat, a ma gua, and a xing pao. Most Chinese who fought in the Sino-Japanese War were dressed similarly. Photographed by Captain Albert d'Amade. (Image courtesy of ECPAD/Albert d'Amade funds)

Military jackets (hao yi, ma gua, and ma jia)

The most commonly issued item of dress was the military jacket, the 'hao yi' (livery jacket).[128] The hao yi was a loose-fitting, waist-length cotton or linen jacket which had slits at the front, sometimes the back, right and left for ease of movement. A hao yi's edges would conventionally have facings in a contrasting colour, often with piping. Virtually any combination of colours could be used for hao yi, but the most common colours were blue edged in red, followed by red edged in black. Purple edged in black, brown edged in pink, green edged in red, blue edged in black, magenta edged in pink, black edged in white, yellow edged in red and black and white edged in green and red were also observed combinations. Piping was typically white or yellow. Tragically very little about the specifics of unit colours is known, besides

---

128 Xu, *Jundui Tonglan*, pp.333–334.

surviving examples. The facings of hao yi often featured spade-shaped designs known as 'cloud heads' (yun tou) or 'ru yi' (named after a type of Chinese ceremonial sceptre). This artistic motif symbolised power and control and was a common design of civilian clothing as well. Underneath hao yi civilian clothing was usually worn. Qing soldiers therefore could seamlessly blend into the civilian population by taking their uniforms off, a very handy trick for deserting.

There were several different variations of the hao yi. Sleeveless hao yi were called 'ma jia' style, while hao yi with sleeves were 'ma gua' style. The hao yi could also sport different styles of lapel.[129] The first was the Manchu-styled 'great lapel' (da jin) which featured a slanted opening with a lapel that closed on the right side. The 'double lapel' (dui jin) opened down the front like a European military tunic. These two styles were the predominant lapel styles; less popular was the 'one lapel' (yizi jin) style. The one lapel style opened horizontally on the front chest, resembling the Chinese character for 'one.' The one lapel design was exclusive to sleeveless vests, known as the 'warrior vest' (batulu kanjian) or 'vest of the 13 officials' (shisan taibao kanjian), named after the thirteen sons of a renowned official from the Tang era. This style was originally associated with the warrior tradition of the Eight Banners, but modernised versions were adopted in the 1860s and onward, most notably by troops on the southern frontier and bodyguard units of the Beiyang Navy. Some warrior vests were stuffed with cotton to make them bulletproof, but obviously this practice fell out of favour after the introduction of Western firearms. By far the rarest variety worn was the 'pipa lapel' (pipa jin),[130] which was similar to a front-opening double lapel except a portion of the left placket was significantly longer and overlapped onto the right side of the jacket.

The most iconic feature of Chinese military jackets was the identification patch (buzi), most often circular, attached to the breast and back of the jacket in contrasting colours. These cloth or paper discs, often treated in a waterproof oil that rendered it a dark yellow colour, would show details about the wearer's military unit. The amount of information inscribed varied greatly; at most the disc could show a soldier's name, rank, squad, company, division, army division, army and commander's name, and at least it would simply indicate the wearer as a soldier. Identification patches were customarily yellow or white with characters in red and black, though other combinations existed. They also gave the enemy an excellent bull's eye for aiming, so painting or embroidering Chinese characters directly onto uniforms became increasingly commonplace as time went on.

The hao yi, though worn throughout the entire century, went through several modernisations, though these revisions were not universally applied. In some armies, the baggy sleeves of the hao yi were reduced in

---

129 Li Du, Yan Chen and Jingqiong Zhang, 'Jindai Fuzhuangmen Jinyukou Pande Xingzhi Zuhe Yu Shenmei Biaoda', *Zhuangshi*, 12:6 (2012), pp.74–75.
130 Pipa lapels are today often called 'pian jin' (slanted lapel) or 'xie jin' (oblique lapel). The precise definitions of these two words are nebulous, as depending on the context or period they sometimes refer to any slanted lapel (i.e. da jin) or might refer to specific types of lapels (xie jin for Y-shaped cross over designs for pre-Qing times, and pian jin for rounder lapels).

The uniform of this Chinese soldier is typical of those that participated in the Sino-Japanese War. He wears a brightly coloured hao yi with contrasting borders, a dark blue turban with queue coiled inside, a detailed identification patch and decorated zhan qun. Photographed in 1882 by John Thomson. (Public domain)

either length or width to facilitate handling of weapons, and some were given loops and buttons on the sleeves to shorten their width. Sleeveless hao yi were similarly adopted on a grander scale. Units clothed in foreign style wore jackets of Western cut with Chinese buttons and decorations. In winter, the Chinese military solution to the cold was to simply wear up to twelve quilted or animal skin jackets on top of each other at a time, giving off a comical balloon-like appearance. This was apparently very effective in defending against the elements.

Trousers, footwear, and zhan qun

In tropical regions, trousers were knee-length, the lower leg being covered either by white Chinese stockings or coloured puttees from the ankle to the knee. In colder areas puffy cotton-stuffed trousers were worn, often tightened near the ankle with puttees. In northern China, padded leggings that reached from the ankle to the upper thighs called 'tao ku' were worn. Footwear could include leather Mongol boots with projecting nails to prevent slipping and traditional Chinese slippers, though in warmer climates soldiers could go barefoot or don straw or rope sandals.

A uniquely Chinese article of dress was the 'zhan qun' (battle skirt). The zhan qun was a long, oblong waist apron split down the middle into two separate cloth panels hanging over the outer side of each leg. In the centre was sometimes a semicircle shaped pocket, resembling a groin guard. Zhan qun were not perfectly rectangular, as the outer edges were usually rounded. Zhan qun were almost always worn with hao yi and were usually in complementing colours. Zhan qun could also be highly decorated with edges in contrasting colours, cloud head decorations, and sometimes embroidered emblems or symbols. The most popular zhan qun symbol was the circular copper coin pattern (tongqian wen), designed to resemble its namesake and representing wealth and prosperity. Other designs included stylised bats, the Chinese character for 'shou' meaning longevity, and three halberds rising out of a vase (pingsheng sanji, a homophone for 'promoted three ranks'). See colour plates for more information. The zhan qun evolved from the xing shang (travelling skirt), an almost identical traditional Manchu garment. The xing shang in turn evolved from traditional Manchu armour, which featured two armoured side skirts to protect the sides of the legs while mounted. However, the zhan qun, being worn by both infantry and cavalry, seems to have been primarily for decoration or marginal defence against the elements.

Headwear

Chinese soldiers enjoyed a wide selection of headwear. The most iconic was the velvet or silk Manchu hat with overturned brim, sometimes called a 'pork pie' or 'pillbox' cap by Westerners. This hat was colloquially referred to as the 'great hat' (da mao) or 'official hat' (guan mao), but its official name was the 'warm hat' (nuan mao).[131] Warm hat crowns were almost always red in colour and topped with a button, sometimes with crimson

---

131 'Great hat' formally refers to a category of Qing official headwear, which includes the 'warm hat' and the 'cool hat' mentioned below.

cloth tassels arranged around. Warm hats of Bannermen always, regardless of rank, had two sable tails attached to the button in a V-shape. Lower rank officers simply wore Banner-style sable tails, while mandarins grades six to nine wore blue pheasant tails, and mandarins of grades one to five wore a peacock feather, the number of eyes on the feather denoting past achievements. Non-banner units began to phase out warm hats in the latter half of the 19th century, and by the Sino-Japanese War mostly officers and Bannermen wore warm hats.

Instead, turbans (variously called pa shou, pa tou, tou jin, tou bao, chan tou, and other regional names) became increasingly commonly worn in the 19th century, and by the Sino-Japanese War they were almost universally adopted by infantrymen, the reason for their popularity being the fact that queues[132] (around ninety centimetres long) could be conveniently coiled inside. Turbans were wrapped in a near-infinite number of styles. Simpler styles like cloth strips or bandannas woven around the head were more associated with local militias or rebels, while more complex arrangements were worn by regular units. Turbans were worn in every conceivable colour, the most common being black or dark blue. According to contemporary photographic and eyewitness evidence, Sino-Japanese War-era turbans seem to have been almost exclusively black or dark blue.[133]

Though the turban was the most popular, a whole slew of official and unofficial military headgear could be worn. Wide-brimmed sun hats of various patterns are portrayed frequently in Japanese prints; these were usually the colour of their material or dyed black or red, and made of straw, paper or cloth. An imitation of the British straw sennett or 'boater' hat began to be adopted in increasing numbers from the 1880s onwards. A cloth band with unit colours or details was wrapped around the crown, which could also hold the wearer's queue inside. These sennett hats were primarily worn by modernised units like the Sheng Army and Zhili Trained Army. Chinese skull caps, consisting of six flaps arranged in a dome shape and topped with a ball of cord, were called 'melon skin hats' (guapi mao) or 'lesser hats' (xiao mao), and were worn by lower ranking officers. The conical straw hat, known as the 'cool hat' (liang mao) was rarely seen worn during the Sino-Japanese War; it was ill-suited to the cold climate of Northern China, where most of the fighting took place. When it was, it was mainly the tasselled version for officers. Finally, fur hats of varying pattern and design were worn to combat the cold, though these were habitually acquired individually by soldiers so within the same unit several different styles could coexist.

---

132 Some evidence from Japanese descriptions of Chinese prisoners suggests that some Chinese soldiers cut off their queues and wore turbans or other hats to hide the fact.

133 Strangely, Japanese woodblock prints most frequently depict Chinese soldiers wearing white turbans. This is probably a result of said prints being a child of public imagination as opposed to accurate depictions of war; most woodblock print artists did not actually participate in the conflict. Though many captured Chinese uniforms were displayed in Japan as novelties, it seems likely that plain strips of cloth were not the ideal candidates for war souvenirs. As such, Japanese woodblock prints portray some aspects of Chinese military dress with considerable authenticity, but unfortunately this did not extend to turbans.

Officer dress
The dress of officers in the field was the ma gua (horse/riding jacket), a front-opening waist-length jacket with short, baggy sleeves.[134] Ma gua had slits in the front, sides and back just like hao yi. Yellow ma guas were awarded to officers for meritorious service. A sleeveless version of the ma gua called the ma jia was occasionally worn. Ma gua and ma jia invariably had five buttons, symbolising the five elements of ancient China. Hao yi and ma gua were both commonly paired with a plain garment worn underneath; this garment usually had long, horseshoe shaped cuffs (mati xiu) as a sign of steadfast loyalty to the Emperor, as the officer was likened to a loyal warhorse. Underneath the ma gua some kind of long robe split in the middle and extending down to the ankles was worn, called xing pao but also generically known as chang shan, chang yi, chang pao, or zhan pao. Officers could also wear zhan qun, though these were undecorated. Officer zhan qun usually had detachable sections called que jin, which could be secured or discarded by means of buttons. Officers apparently had considerable freedom in choosing the particulars of their outfit; according to Japanese documents regarding captured Chinese officers, General Tan Qingyuan wore a (probably yellow/gold) ginkgo-patterned ma gua with a green chang shan and a blue sash, General Wang Futing wore a white ma gua with yellow chang shan, General Kang Yuankai wore a blue ma gua with white chang shan, an unidentified Zhili native wore a black ma gua with purple silk trousers, and General Li Shouheng wore a gold patterned ma gua with a blue sash.[135]

Equipment

According to Japanese records, a total of 10,344 breech loading single shot and repeating rifles of various types; 7,193 muzzleloading, matchlock or jingal guns; and 11,764 cold weapons were captured during the entirety of the Sino-Japanese War.[136] It would appear that only a dismal 35 percent of Qing soldiers were armed with breech loading rifles of any kind during the war, while 25 percent had obsolescent muzzle loaders and 40% cold weapons. To be fair, some of these cold weapons may have been ceremonial weapons, but there is no doubt many were used by the rank and file. When viewing these dismal figures, it must be recalled nevertheless that most of China's best units were shattered early on in the war, owing to deficient leadership, sheer bad luck and low morale, not poor weaponry. The high incidence of antiquated weapons therefore came from the later stages of the war, when less than modernised units were called up to fight.[137] The contrast between

---
134 'Tangzhuang' is a somewhat Westernised variant of ma gua which was introduced in the 20th century; the two items of clothing are not the same despite visual similarities.
135 Shunyodo, *Nisshin Kosen Roku* (Tokyo: Shunyodo, 1894), pp.48–49.
136 Buchende Jingyuan, 'Jiawu Zhanzhengshi, Qingjunde Zhuangbei Zongti Shangruoyu Rijun, Dui Zhanzheng Jieguo Youbuxiaode Yingxiang', Toutiao (2019), <https://www.toutiao.com/article/6770525340583330311/>, accessed 7 Feb. 2024. These figures do not include the Yiwei War. It is also not stated how many of the jingals captured were breech or muzzle loading.
137 Fung, Testing the Self-Strengthening, p.1018.

the armament of different Chinese armies is difficult to overstate. The Huai Army was equipped with magazine rifles which even the Japanese envied, while the Dian Army of Yunnan did not have a single firearm of any sort among its thousands of men.[138]

Cold weapons

It is not even possible to list all of the cold weapons used by the Qing army; as there is no shortage of information on this topic, very basic summaries will be provided. Swords were classified either as 'dao' (single-edged used for cutting) or 'jian' (double-edged or pointed used for stabbing),[139] and scabbards either 'fangshi' (angular) or 'yuanshi' (round).[140] Jian were more associated with the refined scholar-gentleman class, while dao were the crude, unpretentious killing tools of the rugged soldiery. European style swords began to be increasingly imported from the 1870s onwards, but they were only issued to officers.[141]

The most common type of sword was broadly categorised as the 'yao dao' or 'pei dao,' both names referring to the fact that it was frequently worn at the waist from a belt or sash.[142] Yao dao could be divided into many more groups. These included the 'yanling/yanmao dao' (goose quill sabre), named for its curved tip; the 'miao/liuye dao' (sprout/willow leaf sabre), with curvature for the entire blade; the 'pian dao' (slicing sabre), with the entire blade being deeply curved; the 'niuwei dao' (oxtail sabre), with the tip widely flared; the 'zhanma dao' (horse-cutting sword), a two-handed sword used against horses; the 'changren dadao' (long-edged great sabre),[143] a two handed sword similar to zhanma dao; the 'wo dao' (Japanese pirate sword), a short, heavy sword inspired by Japanese designs; and so on. Dao with straight blades were generally uncommon and only found in the hands of ethnic minorities or frontier garrisons.

Polearms were even more diverse. Most polearms had a tuft of red-dyed yak or horsehair attached below the tip, meant to distract the enemy's eyes during a duel. Spears were called either 'mao' or 'qiang,' with mao being more 'conventionally' shaped, while qiang blades could be any variety of fantastical shapes like crosses, spades, etc.[144] Spears could be bamboo shafted (zhu gan) or wood shafted (mu gan). Notable varieties included the 'goulian qiang' or 'shuang goulian qiang' (hook spear or double hook spear), which

---

138 The Dian Army was sent from Yunnan to Shandong in the late stages of the war, but luckily the fighting ended before they saw any action.
139 Tom Philip, 'Military Sabers of the Qing Dynasty', Mandarin Mansion (2009), <https://www.mandarinmansion.com/article/military-sabers-qing-dynasty>, accessed 7 Feb. 2024.
140 Peter Dekker, 'Qing Dynasty Saber Mounts, Fangshi & Yuanshi', Mandarin Mansion (2016), <https://www.mandarinmansion.com/article/qing-dynasty-saber-mounts-fangshi-yuanshi>, accessed 7 Feb. 2024.
141 Heath, *China*, p.45.
142 Peter Dekker, 'A Typology of Chinese Sabers', Mandarin Mansion (2016), <https://www.mandarinmansion.com/article/typology-chinese-sabers>, accessed 7 Feb. 2024.
143 Peter Dekker, 'Chinese Long Sabers of the Qing Dynasty', Mandarin Mansion (2016), <https://www.mandarinmansion.com/article/chinese-long-sabers-qing-dynasty>, accessed 7 Feb. 2024.
144 Peter Dekker, 'Spears of the Qing Dynasty', Mandarin Mansion (2016), <https://www.mandarinmansion.com/article/spears-qing-dynasty>, accessed 7 Feb. 2024.

A line of captured swords from the Battle of Pyongyang. From left to right: a sheathed sword of unknown type, possibly a southern style double edged dao; a southern style sword resembling the 'nan dao' (contemporary wushu term meaning 'southern sword'); a niuwei dao with the popular cup guard developed around the time of the mid-century rebellions; a southern style double-edged dao; a heavy-bladed da dao; a Western style sabre, probably imported; another niuwei dao with cup guard; the snapped off head of a podao, with a dragon head design at the ricasso; another niuweidao with a better view of the cup guard; another nan dao, and a single hudie dao (meaning 'butterfly sword', typically used in a pair but sometimes alone with a shield). Strangely enough, many southern styles of sword are seen, even though the Battle of Pyongyang was fought by northern Chinese armies. Photographed by Georges Ferdinand Bigot. (Public domain)

had a distinctive hook next to the tip used the pull away an enemy's shield or to catch fleeing criminals; the 'shou qiang' (hand spear), used for close quarters thrusting; the 'Luying mao' (Green Standard Spear); and so on and so forth. Cavalry lances and infantry spears were not differentiated in Chinese terminology.

Glaives are somewhat confusingly classified, as the aforementioned 'dao' could actually refer to any one-sided blade, not just swords.[145] The most iconic is the 'Guan dao' (referring to legendary hero Guan Yu's weapon), also called the 'yanyue dao' or 'chunqiu dadao' (reclining moon glaive or spring and autumn glaive), which featured a smaller, secondary blade on the back of the curved larger one, sometimes with serration. Less fancy versions included the 'po dao' (plain glaive), which had a generally featureless blade and shared the alternate name of 'zhanma dao' with the sabre, and the

---

145 Peter Dekker, 'Edged Weapons of the Green Standard Army', Mandarin Mansion (2016), <https://www.mandarinmansion.com/article/edged-weapons-green-standard-army>, accessed 7 Feb. 2024.

A collection of captured Chinese items from the Battle of Pyongyang; on the bench are two bugles and a drum, all in Western style. The three polearms in the centre, from left to right, are a po dao, an unknown variety with a straight and narrow blade, and a tang pa trident. The trident may also possibly be the Korean equivalent dang pa, as it was still popular among Korean levies at this time. On the right side is a long lapa trumpet. Photographed by Georges Ferdinand Bigot. (Public domain)

'shuangshou dao' or 'huya dao' (double-handed glaive or tiger tooth glaive), a type of po dao with 1:1 shaft-blade ratio.[146] Tridents were similarly common, including the 'tang pa' (trident rake) or 'tongtian pa' (sky-connecting rake), a three-pronged polearm with the outer prongs pointing slightly outward; the 'hu cha' (tiger fork), an iconic and widely used trident designed for keeping tigers at bay; the 'she lian qiang' (snake-sickle spear), a trident with zigzagged outer prongs; and many more. Tridents were apparently carried mostly by non-commissioned officers.

Shields, uncommonly unused in the Sino-Japanese War, were usually made of rattan, round, and able to deflect blows from a sword or spear. They were not effective against rifle fire. Some kind of hideous face, of a stylised tiger or demon, was typically painted on the front with the character 'wang,' meaning 'king.' Bows had been generally phased out during the Sino-Japanese War; at most, Manchu irregulars or hunters would have used them. Prowess in archery was still required on the military examination as late as 1901, and most Chinese officers regardless of Western training were still excellent archers. For example, General Ma Yukun of the fairly modernised Resolute Army gained the nickname 'Ma Sanyuan' for hitting three coins with bow

---

146 Chunqiu Zhanguo, 'Telling Apart Chinese Polearms: A Quick Visual Guide', Great Ming Military (2019), <https://greatmingmilitary.blogspot.com/2019/03/telling-apart-chinese-polearms-quick.html>, accessed 7 Feb. 2024.

and arrow.[147] However, it is extremely unlikely that bows were actually used in combat by Chinese soldiers during the Sino-Japanese War.

Traditional firearms

The standard traditional firearm was a smoothbore matchlock called the 'bird gun' ('niao qiang' or 'niao chong'). The name has sometimes caused confusion about the purpose of the bird gun. Bird guns were not exclusively for hunting; the name was coined in reference to the downwards 'pecking' movement of the matchlock's serpentine.[148] Bird guns used an unguarded trigger whose serpentine contained a burning hemp cord or stick of dried manure. The trigger was not always used, and Chinese bird gunners were seen on multiple occasions simply touching the match to the priming pan to fire the weapon. Though the bird gun is most often described with an orthogonal pistol grip, straight grips could also be found, especially for cavalry matchlocks.

Powder was carried in either individually measured bamboo cartridges or in a single metallic container. Bird gun bullets were notoriously ill-fitting, owing to their substandard manufacture and standardisation, and to make the bullet stay in the barrel it was common practice to first put the bullet in the mouth, coat it with saliva and then spit it down the barrel. The poor quality of Chinese powder often meant that the weapon was completely useless; the projectile frequently failed to penetrate clothing and, even at close range, the impact only caused bruising. Likewise, bird guns were as a rule poorly and improperly maintained. Firing and loading the bird gun was not a pleasant ordeal. No rammers were used in loading, and if the bullet did not go down the soldier would simply smack the butt of the weapon on the ground. Wadding was similarly neglected, meaning the bullet might simply slide out if aimed at a lower angle. The alternative was shooting over the heads of the enemy, and both unfortunate scenarios were known to have occurred. Aiming the pistol grip variation was theoretically supposed to be taken with the grip against the cheek, but the considerable recoil being inexpedient to proper dental health, most Chinese soldiers fired from the hip with poor accuracy.

The elderly matchlock remained in considerable use during the Sino-Japanese War, especially in the hands of backwards Manchu Banner units and the Xiang Army, which felt nostalgic for its Taiping Rebellion days. According to Japanese records of captured weapons, around 24.5 percent of all Chinese soldiers were equipped with matchlocks, jingals or muzzleloaders of all kinds. Around 300 matchlocks were captured during the Battle of Pyongyang. Surely the incidence of these anachronistic weapons was even higher during the later stages of the war.

---

147   Another story maintains he got that nickname from being the third child of the Ma family; these stories are part of local folklore and it is difficult to verify them.
148   Peter Dekker, 'Niaoqiang', Mandarin Mansion (2019), <https://www.mandarinmansion.com/glossary/niaoqiang>, accessed 7 Feb. 2024.

Jingals

The iconic jingal, known as 'taiqiang' or 'taifu,' saw some use during the Sino-Japanese War.[149] The jingal, essentially a long-barrelled wall gun, ranged from two to six metres in length, with a calibre typically exceeding 28 mm. The smaller varieties required up to four men for operation: one for firing and aiming, one for carrying the long barrel on his back, and the last two for either loading or spotting. Sometimes a fork rest or tripod was employed in place of human bipods.

Earlier versions were muzzle-loading matchlocks that fired either solid slugs or numerous smaller projectiles, including pebbles or bits of metal. As China's fledgling military industry developed, breechloading editions of the jingal also appeared. Long-barrelled Remington, Mauser, Spencer, and Lee rifles began appearing in Chinese arsenals from the 1880s and onwards. These modernised jingals were not spared from the Chinese lack of standardisation: the Jiangnan Arsenal produced breech loading jingals with a 15.9mm calibre and a total length of 2.5 metres, the Shanxi Arsenal 25 mm calibre and 2.2 metres, the Shaanxi Arsenal 41.3 mm and 1.6 metres, and so on.[150]

Despite often being improperly sighted or loaded with an improper charge size, jingals theoretically had a greater range than standard-sized firearms. Furthermore, the sheer size and noise of the piece was often enough to scare away less determined enemies like rebels or bandits. During the mid-century rebellions, where unfavourable terrain frequently hindered the use of field artillery, jingals served as a (relatively) portable form of light artillery. While their military value was questionable, jingals continued to be manufactured and utilised by non-modernised or partially modernised armies.

The jingal saw only limited use during the Sino-Japanese War, primarily by less technologically advanced Qing Armies. Modernised units like the Huai Army and Zhili Trained Army did not employ jingals, breech loading or otherwise. Japanese records indicate that numerous jingals were captured during the war, though the exact number remains unclear. However, when the non-jingal using modern units were routed during the early stages of the war, the jingal experienced a resurgence in popularity among the less technologically knowledgeable generals of the Chinese Army.[151] At the end of the Sino-Japanese War, China's various arsenals were manufacturing around 120,000 jingals of all types.[152] Breech loading jingals continued to be used during the Boxer Rebellion and the early Warlord Era.

Western firearms

Since the 1850s, Western firearms had been imported and, since the 1860s, copies of said firearms were manufactured in Chinese arsenals. The quantity and quality of Chinese-produced weapons never reached sufficient levels,

---

149 Matchlock jingals were called 'nine-headed bird guns' during the late Ming Dynasty; the author has seen no usage of this term during the Qing period.
150 'Tai Qiang', Wuqi Daquan, <http://www.wuqidaquan.com/index.php?doc-view-14932>, accessed 7 Feb. 2024.
151 'The Army of the Chinese Troops', The North-China Herald (Shanghai), 8 February 1895, pp.202–203.
152 Cavendish, 'Armed Strength', p.713.

and consequently large numbers of weapons continued to be imported from Europe. Regrettably, the inadequate technical knowledge of many officials meant China however made the fatal mistake of buying every kind of rifle possible. Models imported included Enfields, Boxers, Mannlichers, Hotchkisses, Martini-Henrys, Peabody-Henrys, Lees, Berdans, Spencers, Remingtons, Winchesters, Gras, Chassepots, and Mausers (1871, 1871/1884, and 1888 models). These were the better purchases. Some less knowledgeable officials imported second or even third hand 'weapons' from Europe, including Napolenic era museum pieces or defective firearms that literally could not hit the side of a barn from 90 metres.[153] In 1876, a purchase was made of 26,000 Mauser M1871 single shot rifles and, in 1882, the decision was made to standardise on the German 11mm cartridge. This of course was never achieved, though the Mauser M1871 rifle and later on the M1871/1884 eight shot[154] magazine rifle would see continuous and copious usage in the Qing armies.

Distributing ammunition for this assortment of weapons was a logistical nightmare. On multiple occasions during the Sino-Japanese War, ammunition was issued by heaping out piles of bullets of every make and manufacture on the floor. Soldiers would take individual rounds based on what fit in their guns. It could take up to 10 tries before a single suitable round was found. A few soldiers even whittled or mutilated cartridges to get them to fit. The quality of ammunition was also questionable, as some bullets were up to 27 years old or defective, being only enough to tear the clothing of the enemy.[155] The haphazard coexistence of so many types of rifle and ammunition was problematic, but some officers understood this. As a workaround, they standardised every battalion to use a different type of rifle, and strictly segregated ammunition supplies. Less enlightened officers, who still occupied a considerable proportion of the Chinese army, continued to indiscriminately distribute weapons and ammunition.

The Beiyang Army, under the command of Viceroy of Zhili Li Hongzhang, was the best armed and trained in the entire empire. Li Hongzhang developed a highly efficient and specific system for purchasing weapons abroad. Li ensured that the weapons purchased abroad were only weapons that the Chinese arsenals could make ammunition for, such as Mausers, Remingtons, and Spencers. Li's progress in standardising the armament of his men was impressive in its speed and thoroughness. In the Ili Crisis of 1881, out of the 85,000 men Li mobilised against the Russians, 59 percent were armed with Enfields; 12 percent had Remingtons; nine percent Chassepots; seven percent Mausers; seven percent Winchesters, Sniders or Albinis; and six percent some other kind of firearm.[156] A year later, a Japanese report estimated that 60 percent of the modernised units were equipped with modern weapons. By 1884, all Huai Army infantry units were equipped with magazine rifles

---

153 Heath, *China,* p.49.
154 A ninth cartridge could be loaded in the chamber, thereby giving the M1871/1884 rifle the nickname 'nine bullet Mauser' (jiuzi Maose) in China.
155 Cavendish, 'Armed Strength', p.718.
156 Heath, *China,* p.49.

of some kind, while cavalry was standardised with Winchester repeaters.[157] In the same year, Li Hongzhang issued an order banning the distribution of Mauser rifles to units that had already received Hotchkiss rifles. An 1888 series of French military reports on the Chinese forces present in Tianjin and Shanhaiguan noted that out of the fourteen units surveyed, only two were equipped with outdated weaponry, and only three not yet Western-trained. Only one unit was armed with a pell-mell mixture of firearms: Mausers, Berdans, Winchesters and some muzzle loaders.[158] In 1892, a French military captain wrote anxiously that the troops of Zhili Province were to receive 30,000 new Mauser rifles.[159] By the Sino-Japanese War most Huai Army and Zhili-based armies, like the Sheng and Ming Army, were mostly equipped with M1871/1884 Mauser magazine rifles and Krupp cannon, which were the most advanced in the world. At least one unit of the Sheng Army had Hotchkiss rifles, and Sheng Army cavalry used Winchester and Spencer repeaters. Also common in Huai Army units were Mannlichers, a handful of China's own Jiangnan Rifles, and Winchester repeaters.

Huai Army armament[160]

Gun name	Date first used by Huai Army
Winchester rifle	1873
Gatling gun	1873
Remington rolling block rifle	1873/1874
Snider-Enfield rifle	1873/1874
Martini-Henry rifle	1873/1874
Berdan rifle	1874
M1871 Mauser rifle	1875/1876
Lee rifle	1879
M1886 Lebel rifle	1888
Maxim gun	1885
M1888 Mauser rifle	1895

The armament of the other armies that participated in the Sino-Japanese War is not as well documented. In the 1880s Zuo Baogui's Feng Army was equipped with an assortment of both single shot and magazine rifles, with two Gatling guns and six mountain guns for artillery. Sometime before the Sino-Japanese War, Li Hongzhang allocated 500 Mauser repeating rifles, 100,000 rounds of ammunition, and 20 new Krupp 75mm guns to the Feng Army. The Feng Army was armed well and did have a number of magazine rifles before Li's generous donation, but it is unclear how many. The Resolute Army was similarly armed with repeating rifles of various kinds PLUS Krupp guns. In contrast, Fengsheng'a's Sheng Trained Army was miserably equipped with

---

157 Tai Lan, 'Zouxiang Jindai Hua: Taipingtianguo Zhanzheng Hou Qing Lujun Jiji Xuexi Xifang', Fenghuang Lishi (2014), <https://news.ifeng.com/history/zhongguojindaishi/special/wuqizhuangbei/>, accessed 28 Feb. 2024.
158 Archives Militaires de l'Armee de Terre, Series 7N1665, Report by Captain d'Amade on the Chinese forces in Zhili in winter 1888.
159 Elliott, *Some Did It*, p.422.
160 Lan, 'Zouxiang Jindai Hua'.

smoothbore muzzleloaders, matchlocks, jingals, bayonets fixed on poles, and other such impedimenta, all of which were rusty and poorly maintained.[161] The Chinese armies in Shandong Province were comparable. Governor of Shandong Province Li Bingheng reported that there were only a thousand or so breechloader's of all kinds in the coastal regions of Shandong Province, so most of his soldiers had to make do with muzzleloaders or matchlocks.[162] In Jilin the situation was somewhat better: in 1894 General of Jilin Changshun reported that at least a majority of the men were armed with rifles, both single-shot and repeating, but the rest only had mediaeval implements of war. General Yiketang'a's Heilongjiang armies seemed to have been much better armed. A 3,000 man unit of Yiketang'a's Heilongjiang armies present at the Battle of Jiuliancheng was reportedly equipped with 3,800 repeating rifles of various types, with more than one rifle per man. In October 1894, Yiketang'a was allocated a further 6,000 imported rifles of unspecified manufacture, and by the end of the war one, again unspecified, unit of the Heilongjiang armies had 10,264 rifles of various types on the field. Some of these weapons were outdated, but a solid majority were still modern repeating rifles, though probably different kinds.

In 1892 Wu Dacheng, Governor of Hunan Province and de facto leader of the ageing Xiang Army, memorialised that the atmosphere of modernity had not yet settled in Hunan yet, and that their foreign weapons had been poorly maintained and unfit for service. In September 1894, General Wei Guangtao of the Wuwei Army complained that the Xiang Army had only a few hundred Remingtons without enough ammunition. Wu Dacheng at the end of the year again reemphasised that the Xiang Army was inadequately armed and had no modern artillery and estimated that they only had 4,600 rifles of every type, age and make to arm around 10,000 men from 23 battalions. To remedy this, Governor Wu ordered 10 heavy guns, hundreds of smaller pieces, 8,000 Mannlichers and one million rounds of ammunition from abroad. In November 1894, Guangdong Province coughed up from their stockpiles 16,000 foreign rifles of various types and 3.6 million bullets to the Xiang Army. Despite this, the Xiang Army was not given proper training in these weapons, and much of this excellent hardware was wasted. Additionally, many Xiang Army soldiers found the recoil of their foreign rifles annoying and much preferred their older and trustier matchlocks.

As the Japanese invasion of northern China continued unopposed, Li Hongzhang and others attempted to purchase as much modern weaponry and ammunition as possible. In October 1894, Li successively ordered 56 Western quick-firing cannons, over 28,300 repeating rifles, and more than 15 million cartridges of various sizes. In December 1894 Li placed another order of 23,300 repeating rifles, 6.22 million bullets, and several light artillery pieces with German, American and British ministers. Another prominent reformist and Viceroy of Huguang, Zhang Zhidong, reported in late 1894 that he had instructed his ministers abroad to purchase 9,250 new repeating rifles, 30 artillery pieces, seven million bullets, and 14,400 shells. Liu Kunyi,

---

161 Bishop, *Korea*, pp.209–210.
162 Lan, 'Zouxiang Jindai Hua'.

Viceroy of Liangjiang (the Provinces of Jiangnan and Jiangxi), bought 15,000 rifles and 2.8 million rounds of ammunition, and made plans to purchase another 10,000 repeating rifles with 500 cartridges apiece. Liu Kunyi also used his overseas connections to secure 14,000 breechloaders for various Northern armies. Over 110,000 rifles were imported overall during the entire war; of these, about 52,000 were ordered by Li Hongzhang alone. 57,250 were Mausers; 24,000 were Martini-Henry rifles; 10,000 were M1883 Winchester-Hotchkiss rifles; and 8,000 were Mannlichers. These costly purchases did little to remedy the situation. By late 1894, most Qing soldiers on the field were untrained conscripts who gave even less consideration to properly using their expensive equipment than to actually fighting the Japanese.

As Chairman Mao later noted with relish, the weapons factor was not the decisive element in the Sino-Japanese War for the Qing armies. In the early war, Chinese armies were armed with superior magazine rifles, which the Japanese did not have ready access to. Still, they failed. In mid-1894, the gazetteer Zeng Guangjun attempted to systematically examine China's arms stock.[163] He divided them into three different grades of quality, the first being Mausers, Hotchkiss, Lees, Martinis, the Chinese Jiangnan Rifles, and other comparable weapons. He claimed that even excluding the lower two grades, China had enough high-quality rifles to arm the bulk of the frontline army. Zeng was confident that Japan could be defeated if these modern rifles were distributed in a coordinated manner to men who were well-trained in their use, which did not occur. Zeng Guangjun's assessment confirms that the Qing armies' lack of suitable weaponry was not the primary factor in their defeat.

The Jiangnan Rifle

In 1891, Liu Qixiang, the director of the Jiangnan Arsenal, reported that he and his staff had created several prototypes of a new magazine rifle officially designated the M1891 Kuaili. Featuring a fixed vertical feed magazine capable of holding five rounds, the 'Jiangnan Rifle' was based on the M1888 Mannlicher rifle, the 'Nanxia rifle,' and the M1890 Xinli (the Chinese modification of the Lee-Metford).[164] The Jiangnan Rifle's bolt, receiver, safety, and bayonet were directly lifted from the Mannlicher, while the barrel was from the Xinli and the feed mechanism from the Nanxia. Apparently, the Jiangnan Rifle could be loaded from both the breech and the muzzle, though the details of this peculiar mechanic are unclear. Earlier versions of the Jiangnan Rifle were prone to rapid overheating after firing 15 shots due to the poor quality of steel used; it is unclear if this issue was ever resolved.[165] In 1892, the weapon underwent limited testing by soldiers in Tianjin. During a visit by General Kawakami Soroku of the Imperial Japanese Army to Tianjin in 1893, he was impressed by the Jiangnan Rifle and asserted its superiority over the Japanese Murata magazine rifle. He even took home two samples of the Jiangnan Rifle to act as samples for Japanese weapons development

---

163 Lan, 'Zouxiang Jindai Hua'.
164 Xu, *Jundui Tonglan*, pp.257–258. The identity of the "Nanxia rifle" is a bit of a mystery and its name is probably a strangely translated or transliterated Western term.
165 Shih, Xu, Zielinski, 'The Chinese Kuaili Rifle'.

(this was before open hostilities broke out between China and Japan, so the Jiangnan Arsenal staff did not have a protective sense of confidentiality).

Jiangnan Rifle specifications[166]

Specification	1897 report	Existing rifle
Total length	129.6 centimetres	128 centimetres
Barrel length	77.3 centimetres	77.0 centimetres
Cartridge	7.62x55 mmR	7.62x55 mmR
Weight	4.25 kilograms	4.14 kilograms

Jiangnan Rifle production numbers

Year	Number produced
1890	3 rifles, 2 carbines
1891	6 rifles
1892	460 rifles
1893	578 rifles
1894	1,224 rifles
1895	1,106 rifles
1896	1,396 rifles
1897	1,473 rifles
1898	1,980 rifles
1899	1,800 rifles
1900	1,504 rifles
1901	78 rifles
Total	11,608 rifles, 2 carbines

Not all was well with this new firearm, however. After the Sino-Japanese War, the Jiangnan was in close competition with the Type 88 Hanyang rifle to be the standardised rifle of the Chinese armies, and the latter won. The Jiangnan was meant to use smokeless powder, but due to supply shortages soldiers often had to substitute black powder, which produced inferior results. Using black powder, the Jiangnan Rifle bullets could not even pierce a cowhide from 30 feet. In 1897, Viceroy of Huguang Zhang Zhidong also reported that the wedge mechanism used to lock the breech in the Jiangnan Rifle was prone to getting stuck due to overheating or accumulation of dirt.[167] He also complained that the Jiangnan Rifle's bayonet was too narrow. The final nail in the coffin for the Jiangnan Rifle was a 1900 report from one General Dai Yi, who found that most of the 2,000 Jiangnan Rifles issued to his men were defective, to the point of being injurious to the operators. In 1902 Viceroy Zhang Zhidong finally scrapped all remaining 2,000 Jiangnan Rifles, and the Hanyang 88 officially became the standard issue service weapon of the Chinese armies.

---

166 Shih, Xu, Zielinski, 'The Chinese Kuaili Rifle'. The existing rifle measurements are taken from an existing Jiangnan Rifle from Lin Xu's private collection.
167 Shih, Xu, Zielinski, 'The Chinese Kuaili Rifle'.

Artillery

In general, it seems the artillery of the Qing armies was of a much higher standard than infantry weapons. Whether or not the Chinese could use them, well, that was another question. Li Hongzhang's Beiyang Army, again, was equipped with first-rate artillery guns. In 1872, Li Hongzhang placed an order for two 4 pounder Krupp guns and was satisfied enough to standardise the Beiyang Army with Krupp cannon.[168] In 1874, 50 Krupp cannons were purchased, to be stationed in various locations around Zhili Province. By 1877, the Huai Army had 19 new German-trained artillery battalions, each with six Krupp pieces. In 1880 alone Krupp sent 150 siege and fortress guns and 275 field guns to Li. A report from 1881 described the Beiyang Army as having ten batteries of American and French machine guns, with Armstrong, Bokhoum, Broadwell, Krupp, and Vavassern 9 and 12 pounders.[169] In 1884, a secret Russian report listed the artillery available in Zhili Province as consisting of 586 Krupp guns of various calibres as well as a handful of Armstrong, Bokhoum and Vavassern guns.[170] An 1886 French military report claimed that forty German-trained artillery battalions were present in Beijing with another forty still in training, all doubtlessly furnished with Krupp guns. In 1888 alone 370 artillery pieces were purchased, the majority being Krupp with a smattering of Armstrong and German-made Gruson guns. Limited testing was also done with the German Fahrpanzer movable turret, and by the end of 1889 the Beiyang Navy owned a small number of them.[171] An 1892 French report on Zhili Province reported that most Chinese artillery consisted of Krupp guns of calibres 120 mm to 210 mm, with a handful of Armstrong 120 pounders. The report additionally noted the presence of modern naval mines and torpedoes in ports and Gatling guns and Maxim guns in land armies.[172] The Jiangnan Arsenal had also produced a total of 145 breech loading Armstrong guns before the Sino-Japanese War, most of these being sent to the Huai Army. By the beginning of the Sino-Japanese War, most of the Beiyang Army artillery was German-trained and using Krupp guns; between 1870 and 1895, 1,933 Krupp guns of all types were delivered to China, not including those acquired indirectly or second-hand from other sources. Some English-trained units continued using Armstrongs, and at least a few Gruson guns were in service. Machine guns used included Gatling, Gardiner, Nordenfeldt, and Maxim guns, though many of these were not actively used in battle.

The artillery of the other armies was not as pretty. Guns of every type and age were deployed alongside one another, making it difficult to coordinate

---

168 Lan, 'Zouxiang Jindai Hua'.
169 Heath, *China*, p.55.
170 Archives Militaires de l'Armee de Terre, Series 7N1679, Confidential report translated from Russian from 1884.
171 Sun Lie, 'The Emergence of Appropriate Technology: The Localization of German Krupp Artillery Technology in China (1866–1932)', Chinese Annals of History of Science and Technology, 7:1.
172 Archives Militaires de l'Armee de Terre, Series 7N1666, Report by Captain de Fleurac on mines and torpedoes in the ports of Zhili.

and deploy artillery effectively on the battlefield.[173] Traditional artillery was mounted on crude wooden wedges or carts without effective mechanisms for elevations or depressions. Due to the poor quality of casting methods, traditional Chinese artillery used inordinate amounts of metal to prevent their barrels from bursting. The Xiang Army used mainly domestically manufactured artillery of this type, including bronze muzzleloaders, jingals of various sizes, and light mortars called 'mountain splitting guns' (pishan pao) that were in vogue during the mid-century rebellions. Foreign muzzleloaders, imported during the 1860s, were never scrapped, and continued to be used under the philosophy that old guns were better than no guns. This philosophy was taken to an extreme with the Heilongjiang armies, whose 172 cannons included only 12 Western imports with the rest being vintage from the Kangxi (r. 1662–1722) and Qianlong (r. 1736–1795) periods. Many of the artillery shells supplied to Chinese armies were also defective, owing to poor or corrupt manufacture. By far the oldest cannon used in the Sino-Japanese War was the Zhenhai Hou, or the 'Marquis of Suppressing the Sea,' in Dengzhou (now Penglai), Shandong.[174] This venerable piece was cast during the time of the Ming Dynasty hero Qi Jiguang, who died in 1588. Thus, besides the Beiyang Army, the situation of artillery was almost always quite poor.

Accouterments
Since most supplies were carried on the baggage train, Chinese soldiers carried very little on their person. In addition to more conventional cross belts, slinged bags, and sashes, the traditional xingfu dai (travelling belt) was frequently worn.[175] Two thin strips of cloth were attached to each side of the xingfu dai, and to these pouches, purses, containers, scabbards and other such things would be connected by a set of strings. A combined knife and chopsticks sheath, a fan case, pouches containing money, bags for dice and other personal necessities were typical passengers of xingfu dai, and these would dangle awkwardly along the wearer's thighs as he walked. At least one European eyewitness mentioned that xingfu dai were basically ubiquitous,[176] although they do not appear in most photographs. Backpacks were very rarely used; only Nie Shicheng's Gong Army, which was raised near the end of the war and did not participate

Ammunition was held in bandoliers or cartridge boxes, the former being more common. Other miscellany customarily carried included pipes, umbrellas and fans. These became unfortunate symbols of the incapacity of the Qing armies. Pipes were of course associated with the opium addiction rampant in the ranks of the Chinese armies. Another addiction was to fan themselves excessively, even during combat and inspection. During the Battle

---

173 Heath, *China*, pp.52–54.
174 Xunzheng Shao (ed.) et al., Zhongri Zhanzheng (Shanghai: Shanghai Renmin Chubanshe, 1961), volume 1, p.56.
175 Junshi Jilu, Weiguan Zhanchang: Jiawu Zhanzheng, Jinlu Zhizhan, CCTV, (2012).
176 Arthur Cunningham, *The Chinese Soldier and Other Sketches With A Description of the Capture of Manila* (London: Sampson Low, Marston and Company Ltd, 1899), p.25.

of Pyongyang, some soldiers were observed 'aiming' their rifles in one hand while blocking the rain with their umbrellas in the other.[177] Both umbrellas and fans were of the traditional Chinese kind made of bamboo and brightly coloured paper.

Though Western bugles, horns and drums were seen in increasing numbers from the 1860s on in modernised units, Chinese military musicians at the time of the Sino-Japanese War did not abandon their traditional arsenal of instruments. Qing-era military music was heavily derived from the music style of 'chui da,' literally translating to 'blowing and beating.' Unsurprisingly, chui da music heavily involves the blowing of extremely loud horns and the beating of drums and gongs of infinitely many sizes, shapes and sounds were employed.

There were three main types of Chinese military trumpet.[178] The first, called 'la pa,' 'chang hao' or 'xiao tongjiao,' was a brass horn around 1.5 to 2 metres in length, and remained in vogue both during and after the Sino-Japanese War. Larger la pa had to be supported by a second man, who bore the shaft on his shoulders jingal-style. The sound was described as deep, hoarse and bassoon-like, and owing to its continued use in some Chinese festivals one can find recordings of this instrument online. A curved version of the la pa, known as 'zha jiao,' was used somewhat less frequently but a few sources record its use. The final type of military horn was the 'hao tong' or 'da tongjiao.' The hao tong had a long, barrel-like mouth, and the other end could fold inside like a telescope.[179] La pa was more frequently used for field signals, while the latter two types seem to have only been seen in noncombatant military bands.

Flags

For details regarding specific flags used during the Sino-Japanese War, consult the colour illustrations. Chinese armies were known for their extravagant love of flags; typically, 10 percent of soldiers were responsible for carrying a flag. Up to 20 percent or more could be given this task, however, during the Haicheng campaign, the Japanese observed the ratio of five men to a small flag and 10 to every large flag.[180] The purpose of these wonderful displays was to give the impression of overwhelming numbers to shock and awe the enemy into surrendering. All this usually achieved was giving the enemy precise details of Chinese movements. During a few battles of the Sino-Japanese War, crafty commanders like General Nie Shicheng used the abundance of flags to their advantage and used deceptive placement to misdirect enemy intelligence. Spear points or trident heads usually topped Chinese flag poles, as standard bearers rarely had any other weapons besides their standard. Up to three tufts of red or black yak or horsehair were placed

---

177 Heath, *China*, p.41.
178 Jules A. van Aalst, *Chinese Music* (Shanghai: Statistical Dept. of the Inspectorate General of Customs, 1884), pp.58–59.
179 A.C. Moule, 'A List of the Musical & Other Sound-producing Instruments of the Chinese', *Journal of the North China Branch of the Royal Asiatic Society,* 115:39 (1908), pp.99–101.
180 Kawamura Ue et al., *Nisshin Senso Jikki* (Tokyo: Hakubunkan, 1894–1896), pp.2–3.

above some flags, as were coloured pennants or streamers. The tufts of hair were supposedly individually bestowed upon each flag by the Emperor for exceptional merit, but by the Sino-Japanese War most were handed out for the successful completion of basic tasks.

Like with uniforms, there was a total lack of standardisation regarding Qing military flags. Generally, each battalion had its own unique triangular ensign, and the battalion commander had his own rectangular standard. Chinese company (shao) flags were denoted by different colours after the five elements of traditional Chinese philosophy: front (red), back (black), left (blue), right (white), and centre (yellow).[181] This same colour structure, though not universally in service of course, was reused for battalions, brigades and armies, with borders indicating units larger than a company. Another system was using different Chinese trigram arrangements; for example, one army manual assigned the trigram for 'wind' for the right wing, first battalion and the trigram for 'fire' for the right wing, second battalion. More often, however, there was no coherent system of flags corresponding to unit organisation and in practice flags were designed and flown according to individual commanders' wishes.

Chinese flags were brightly coloured and frequently had borders, either plain or serrated, in contrasting colours. Most were triangular, but rectangular (or square) ones became almost just as common by the time of the Sino-Japanese War. The flags of commanders often featured a single character of the commander's surname. Unit flags could feature any number of traditional Chinese symbols, characters, phrases or designs. Common motifs included unit mottos, yin and yang symbols, the eight trigrams (ba gua), concentric squares, cloud heads (yun tou, see Uniforms), the Chinese dragon, the Big Dipper constellation, and various patterns involving lightning and clouds. Chinese flags could also be decorated using simple striped arrangements; these could be of only two colours (most often red and white), or of red, black, blue, white, and yellow, though not always in that order.

---

181 Cavendish, 'Armed Strength', p.714.

Chapter 2

The Navies of the Qing Empire

Introduction

Like her armies, China's navies were divided asymmetrically among four regions of the Empire: under Li Hongzhang's control was the Beiyang Navy (Navy of the Northern Seas),[1] headquartered in Shanghai was the Nanyang Navy (Navy of the Southern Seas), and based in Guangzhou and Fuzhou were the Guangdong Navy and Fujian Navy, respectively. These navies were, unsurprisingly, controlled by provincial leaders or cliques instead of any centralised authority, and therefore only cooperated when their commanders found it advantageous to do so. The Beiyang Navy was the only one to participate meaningfully in the Sino-Japanese War; the others, though they may have contributed a ship or two (unenthusiastically), took every precaution to stay out of the way of the war.

The modernisation of the Chinese navy began during, not after, the First Opium War. The celebrated statesman Lin Zexu noted that while British warships were unbeatable, this was only the case in deep waters. In shallower waters, the British had in fact used native junks fitted with foreign guns.[2] While the war was still ongoing, Lin authorised the purchase of a British schooner, HMS *Cambridge*, the first foreign-built ship in Qing service.[3] He then commissioned Chinese shipbuilders to build copies of the *Cambridge* down to the tiniest detail. This reverse-engineering effort ultimately failed, as the *Cambridge* was later captured and burnt by the British in 1841. Lin did not desist however, and in 1842 a steamship was built in Guangzhou with much help from a foreign engineer.[4] Despite being crudely constructed,

---

1   In Chinese, the term 'Beiyang Fleet' (Beiyang Shuishi) was used before 1888, but when the Beiyang Navy became an official navy theoretically under central control it was formally rechristened as the 'Beiyang Navy' (Beiyang Haijun). 'Beiyang Squadron' (Beiyang Jiandui) is a general term that can refer to both stages of the Beiyang Navy. For accuracy's sake 'Beiyang Navy' will be used in lieu of the more familiar 'Beiyang Fleet.' The same terminology rules also apply for the other three navies.
2   Elliott, *Some Did It*, p.142.
3   Bruce Elleman, *A History of the Modern Chinese Navy, 1840–2020* (London: Routledge, 2021), pp.79–80.
4   Elleman, *Modern Chinese Navy*, pp.81–83.

this steamship was the first Chinese-owned steamship, and an undeniable milestone. Regrettably, the decision to pursue naval modernisation was rejected by the Imperial government. Instead of further tinkering with Western designs, paddle-wheel boats dating from the Song Dynasty began appearing. Bizarre methods to defeat the foreign devils were considered, such as catapulting trained monkeys with firecrackers onto enemy vessels, using 'water devil' fishermen who could allegedly hold their breath for the entire day underwater to drill holes in ships, and using an entire city's worth of chamber pots to asphyxiate British sailors; these ideas were not particularly successful.[5] The fateful choice to reject modernity and embrace tradition sent the Chinese navy a great leap backwards and playing catch-up for the rest of the century.

The next major flirtation with foreign vessels occurred during the Taiping Rebellion, when the value of modern European weaponry began to be more widely understood by Chinese authorities. In 1861, the Qing government attempted to purchase a fleet of British steamers for use against the rebels.[6] This fleet, called the Lay-Osborn Flotilla, was composed of seven gunboats and a support vessel.[7] However, because of disagreements regarding fleet command and the transmission of orders, the fleet was disbanded. Foreign purchases continued: in 1867, the Viceroy of Liangguang (the Provinces of Guangdong and Guangxi) ordered seven steamers from France and Britain to combat piracy.[8]

China also attempted to begin manufacturing its own ships. In 1865, Zeng Guofan kickstarted an indigenous shipbuilding programme, and in the same year China's first indigenously built steamship, the *Huanghu*, finished construction at the Anqing Arsenal. The Jiangnan Arsenal, under Zeng's blessings, completed its first steamship, the *Tianji*, in 1868.[9] One year later, the Fuzhou Dockyard launched its own steamship, the *Wannian Qing*.[10] As lovely as this all was, Li Hongzhang came to the conclusion that simply purchasing foreign-built ships was cheaper, more effective and more efficient than developing indigenous shipbuilding programmes. Chinese-built ships simply could not compare to those of the West, in both quantity and quality.

But it was not Western incursions that spurred further Chinese naval development; in 1874, Japan launched a punitive expedition against the Aboriginal tribes in Western Taiwan, which was mostly uncontrolled by the Chinese government.[11] The justification was ostensibly the murder of 54 shipwrecked Ryukyuan fishermen three years earlier. The Kingdom of Ryukyu was lawfully under Chinese suzerainty and Japan, by 'representing' the Ryukyuan sailors, challenged this. As early as 1867, Chinese statesmen had warned against the potential threat of a quickly rising Japanese navy, and

---

5   Elleman, *Modern Chinese Navy*, p.86.
6   Elleman, *Modern Chinese Navy*, p.103.
7   Richard Wright, *The Chinese Steam Navy 1862–1945* (Annapolis: Naval Institute Press, 2001), pp.17–18.
8   Wright, *Chinese Steam Navy*, p.20.
9   Wright, *Chinese Steam Navy*, p.33.
10 Wright, *Chinese Steam Navy*, p.37.
11 Elleman, *Modern Chinese Navy*, pp.106–107.

in 1874, China's few modern steamships and wooden warships appeared to be no match for the Japanese ironclads.[12] Hoping to avoid conflict, the Qing paid a hefty indemnity for the sailors to effect the Japanese withdrawal from Taiwan. This admission of weakness quietly conceded the Ryukyu Islands to de facto Japanese control, and they were officially annexed five years later.

Unable to contest Japanese aggression, China's ineptitude at sea had been humiliatingly exposed, but yet another pressing concern arose from the northwest. In 1874, what is today Xinjiang Province was under the control of the Emirate of Kashgaria (1862–1877). The Emirate had received status as an Ottoman vassal state in 1873, and its legitimacy was humoured by diplomatic delegations from both the Russians and British. It seemed likely Xinjiang would permanently detach itself from Chinese rule. By 1874, the worst of the mid-century rebellions had ceased, so General Zuo Zongtang's forces in the northwest were in a favourable position to reconquer Xinjiang.[13] Despite some dissent, notably from Li Hongzhang, the Imperial government funded the inordinately expensive task of reconquering and rebuilding Xinjiang, which lasted from 1875 to 1881 and set Imperial coffers back some 51 million taels. This extremely costly decision ensured that Xinjiang remained in Chinese hands but severely limited the finances and prospects of naval modernisation.

Nevertheless, shortly after the debacle with Japan, the Imperial government allocated two million taels each to the newly appointed Beiyang Commissioner, Li Hongzhang and Nanyang Commissioner, Shen Baozhen, to develop modern naval capabilities in their respective commands. The government edict of 1875 proclaimed the creation of three regional navies, a northern navy, a southern navy, and a central navy.[14] However, by the late 1870s the Southern navy had split into two, so in total there were four navies: the Beiyang Navy, the Nanyang Navy, the Guangdong Navy, and the Fujian Navy. The Beiyang Navy was responsible for patrolling from the Liaodong Peninsula to the Shandong Peninsula, while the Nanyang Navy took care of the East China Sea in central China, especially the Changjiang River (better known as the Yangtze). The Fujian Navy, unsurprisingly, operated in the waters of Fujian and the Strait of Taiwan, while the Guangdong Navy guarded the South China Sea. The Qing purposely discouraged the four navies from working together for fear of a centralised fleet mutinying, reinforcing the regionalist thinking so detrimental to military interests.[15] The four navies developed independently of one another and at different speeds; by 1894 the Beiyang Navy was considered the best in Asia, while the Guangdong Navy still retained numerous obsolescent wooden gunboats.

---

12   Whether this is true or not is not as one-sided. In reality the Japanese ironclads and military industry were not much ahead of China's, if at all,
13   Liu, 'The Military Challenge', p.255.
14   Elleman, *Modern Chinese Navy*, p.110.
15   Elleman, *Modern Chinese Navy*, p.111.

THE NAVIES OF THE QING EMPIRE

The Beiyang Navy

During the Taiping Rebellion, Li Hongzhang had worked with a shallow water fleet of junks, sampans, and other traditional Chinese craft, which the Huai Army mainly used for transportation along China's rivers.[16] But during the rebellion, Li was exposed to the awe-inspiring capabilities of Western seafaring steamships, and strongly felt that China had to adopt these new technologies or be defeated again. However, Li's vision of a strong Chinese navy was limited to defensive purposes only. Li continued to view China as a land power and saw little utility in expanding or projecting power overseas.[17] Thus, coastal defence was the primary directive of the Beiyang Navy, not open battle on the high seas.[18]

The official start of the Beiyang Navy's modernisation was in 1872, when two steamships from the Nanyang Navy were transferred to the Beiyang Navy: the wooden gunboats *Caojiang* and *Zhenhai*.[19] At some point in the early 1870s, the 515 ton wooden gunboat *Meiyun* was also donated to the Beiyang Navy. Li also arranged for the Jiangnan-built 195 ton ironclad *Jinou* to be sent to him in 1875, but this wish appears to have never been carried out.[20] Quite early on, Li concluded that the Chinese shipyards at Jiangnan, Fuzhou, and Guangdong were unable to produce ships of a satisfactory standard and turned his attention to purchasing ships abroad.

Yet, it was not until after the Japanese incursion of 1874 that Li Hongzhang began to seriously expand the Beiyang Navy. Thanks to the ongoing Xinjiang Campaign, the financial situation was extremely cramped, and both the Beiyang and Nanyang Fleet did not receive all of their promised two million taels. Thus, the Beiyang Navy had to look for affordable but still usable warships. The answer seemed to lie in the Rendel flat-iron gunboats, which were designed to encircle and outmanoeuvre the larger ironclad warships with their great speed.[21] During the Japanese aggression of 1874 they had shown off their fancy new ironclads in stark contrast to China's wooden steam navy; the flat-iron gunboats appeared to be an inexpensive counter.[22]

Initially, Li ordered ships from abroad with Robert Hart, Inspector-General of China's Imperial Maritime Custom Service, as his middleman, which presented some issues of rivalry, as both Li and Hart bought and fulfilled orders from and for different sources and officials. Nevertheless, in 1876 the *Longxiang* and the *Huwei*, two 320 ton flat-iron gunboats that Li had purchased a year earlier, sailed from Britain to China. The second pair, the 440 ton flat-iron gunboats *Feiting* and *Cedian*, arrived a year later. These four gunboats formed the core of the early Beiyang Navy's steamship fleet. Then, in 1878 Shen Baozhen, the Nanyang Commissioner, ordered four British-built 440 ton flat-iron gunboats: the *Zhendong*, *Zhenxi*, *Zhennan*, and

---

16   Liu, 'The Military Challenge', p.312.
17   Liu, 'The Military Challenge', pp.314–315.
18   Elleman, *Modern Chinese Navy*, p.122.
19   Liu, 'The Military Challenge', pp.315–316.
20   Wright, *Chinese Steam Navy*, p.37.
21   Liu, 'The Military Challenge', pp.316–317.
22   Wright, *Chinese Steam Navy*, pp.43–44.

Zhenbei. Li Hongzhang saw that they were much newer and more advanced than his, and, around the time of Shen Baozhen's death in 1879, 'swapped' the four *Zhen* ships for his own outmoded and less capable quartet.[23] This action was not particularly considerate, and would precipitate a generally uncooperative relationship between the four regional navies. A final pair of 440 ton flat-iron gunboats, the *Zhenzhong* and *Zhenbian*, arrived for the Beiyang Navy in 1881. Despite the purpose of these gunboats being to attack and destroy ironclads, they were mostly employed as coastal defence or inland patrol ships.[24] Perhaps this was for the best, as their main guns were too heavy and unwieldy, causing the ships to be unstable on the high seas. Li eventually came to believe that purchasing them at all was a grave mistake.

Now that the Beiyang Navy actually had ships, it was time to choose who would command and staff the Navy. In 1879, Li appointed three English captains to supervise and teach the infant Beiyang Navy officer corps, but this proved to be futile, as they had only commanded civilian commercial vessels before.[25] Li replaced them with Captain William M. Lang, who had served in the Royal Navy previously, and sailed the *Zhen* gunboats from Britain to China. Lang was an excellent advisor, and his guidance was responsible for the heyday of the Beiyang Navy. He worked so hard that it was claimed that he waved signal flags and shouted orders even when using the toilet.[26] With regards to Lang's maintenance of discipline, a saying developed among Beiyang Navy officers: 'even those that do not fear Admiral Ding still fear Captain Lang.'

With the establishment of Chinese diplomatic legations in London and Berlin in 1877, Li was provided a direct line of communication with Western shipbuilders. In 1880, an order was quickly placed for two English cruisers, the Chaoyong and Yangwei.[27] At 1,350 tons, they were meant to be a larger and faster upgrade of the flat-iron gunboats. In 1881, Ding Ruchang travelled to Britain to bring back the *Chaoyong*, *Yangwei*, *Zhenzhong*, and *Zhenbian* with their English-trained Chinese crew, and upon his return Li was so pleased with the new acquisitions that he made Ding Admiral of the Beiyang Navy. Nonetheless, the two cruisers quickly became outdated by international standards, and Li set his sights on acquiring ironclad warships. Britain was reluctant to supply China with such vessels for fear of upsetting Russia, but Germany had no such concerns. With the help of the newly appointed Chinese envoy to Berlin, Li toyed with the idea of purchasing up to a dozen German-made warships, but thanks to the uncertain state of the Beiyang Navy's budget only two ironclad warships, the *Dingyuan* and *Zhenyuan*, and one protected cruiser, the *Jiyuan*, were purchased in 1880.[28] The Beiyang Navy also acquired 10 torpedo boats from Vulcan in Germany

---

23 Wright, *Chinese Steam Navy*, p.46.
24 Liu, 'The Military Challenge', p.317.
25 Liu, 'The Military Challenge', p.319.
26 Anon., 'Long Qi Piaoyang de Jiandui Jiexuan-Cong Lang Weili Kan Yang Guwen', *Jianchuan Zhishi Wangluo Ban* (2003), <https://mil.news.sina.com.cn/2003-01-14/102544.html>, accessed 6 Feb. 2024.
27 Wright, *Chinese Steam Navy*, pp.48–49.
28 Wright, *Chinese Steam Navy*, p.51.

in the early 1880s: two of them for the *Dingyuan*, two for the *Zhenyuan*, another four to become *Boats One* through *Four*, and the final two *Zhongjia* and *Zhongyi*. Li Hongzhang also began fortifying and building dockyards in certain ports to maintain and protect the Beiyang Navy. The Beiyang Navy's area of responsibility had numerous ports, such as Qingdao (Tsingtao), Zhifu (Chefoo), Weihaiwei, Dalian, Lushunkou (Port Arthur), Yingkou, Shanhaiguan, and Tanggu (Dagu was the name of the mouth of the Peiho [Baihe] River).[29] Due to budgetary restrictions only Weihaiwei, Lushunkou, and Dagu were substantially fortified and subsequently upgraded through the years.

The outbreak of the Sino-French War complicated matters greatly; initially, it fell on the Fujian Navy to defeat the French, with the Nanyang, Beiyang, and Guangdong Navies content to spectate. In fact, shortly after the Sino-French War began, a few ships of the Beiyang Navy ran into two armoured cruisers and a sloop of the French Navy at Zhifu, where they provided a demonstration of their total firepower superiority. This unabashed exhibition of gunboat diplomacy did not encourage Li to participate in the conflict on behalf of his southern countrymen.[30] When the Fujian Navy was devastated, owing to a lack of a coherent command system, the Nanyang Navy was then given the undesirable task of expelling the French. The Beiyang Navy was not particularly eager to assist, although they could not do much; France had pressed Germany into delaying the delivery of the *Dingyuan*, *Zhenyuan*, and *Jiyuan* until 1885, even though they had been finished up to two years earlier. Nonetheless, in 1884 the *Chaoyong* and *Yangwei* sailed to Shanghai to join forces with the Nanyang Navy in preparation of the war against France. At the last minute, however, Li ordered the two cruisers back with the rationale of guarding Korea against Japanese aggression. The result was a complete trouncing of the Nanyang Navy by the French, epitomising the defects of a regionalist navy. Li Hongzhang did send a few Western military advisors to the Fujian and Nanyang Navies, but beyond that he steered his forces well out of harm's way. In truth, Li had good reasons to keep the Beiyang Navy away from the French, as they had considered making an attack in northern China and possibly even on Beijing, and the pulling back of the Beiyang Navy may very well have prevented this.[31] Furthermore, Russia and Japan were indeed both making risky moves in Korea, and the last thing China needed was a two-front war. Regardless of intent, Li's action was perceived as skulduggery by the Nanyang Navy and would be joyfully reciprocated during the Sino-Japanese War.

After the war, the Imperial government attempted to create a centralised Navy Yamen in 1888, which is when the 'Beiyang Fleet' became the 'Beiyang Navy.'[32] Despite the name-change, of course the regional navies continued to be regional and fragmented. With the arrival of the *Dingyuan* and *Zhenyuan* in 1885, the Beiyang Navy was considered the strongest in Asia and a serious

---

29 Liu, 'The Military Challenge', pp.321–322.
30 Wright, *Chinese Steam Navy*, pp.60–61.
31 Liu, 'The Military Challenge', p.252.
32 Liu, 'The Military Challenge', p.319.

threat even to Western powers. Even then, Li Hongzhang remained hard at work in improving the Beiyang Navy. Aware of the theoretical debates occurring in Europe at the time over the relative merits of armoured or protected cruisers, Li purchased two of each kind in 1885.[33] In 1886 a representative of Li's ordered a first-class, high-seas torpedo boat of the most modern manufacture from, which would be uncreatively named the *Left Fleet Boat One* (*Zuo Yi*).[34] The other *Left* and *Right Fleet* torpedo boats were purchased the same year, but from Germany.

In 1886, the Beiyang Navy visited Nagasaki Harbor, and around 500 Chinese sailors went ashore on leave to drink and womanise.[35] When a brothel they were intending to patronise had a waiting list, the sailors began rioting, damaging property, and even sexually harassing Japanese civilians. The Japanese police were sent in, and after a few violent clashes, during which one Japanese police officer was stabbed, the unruliest sailors were taken into custody. The remaining sailors, armed with cudgels, sticks, and even swords purchased or shoplifted from Japanese antique shops, brutally attacked the police to rescue their comrades. The next day, the Chinese prisoners were handed over to the Beiyang Navy authorities, with the promise that sailors would only go ashore with strict supervision from their superiors. The very next day, seeking revenge, several hundred Chinese belligerently surrounded a police station, and some began urinating on the walls. This escalated into a massive street brawl involving hundreds of sailors, policemen, and Japanese civilians, which ended with eight Chinese dead and 42 injured, and two Japanese dead and 29 injured.

The Japanese government and public were understandably outraged, but the Qing government refused to apologise. Li Hongzhang thought the 'Nagasaki Incident' was a silly little affair whose importance was blown out of proportion, but the Japanese did not concur and continued to complain. The Beiyang Navy responded by aiming the *Dingyuan*'s guns at the heart of Nagasaki. Captain Lang advised withdrawing the diplomatic envoy from Japan, breaking off diplomatic contact, and even destroying the infant Japanese navy. At this time, the newly arrived *Dingyuan* and *Zhenyuan* were far superior to anything the Japanese had in their navy, and if China had warred with Japan in 1886 the Japanese navy would have been destroyed and involved in irretrievable ruin. However, just coming out of the Sino-French War, the Qing government showed restraint and did not fight. In particular, Admiral Ding Ruchang felt that such an action would be immoral, as it was the Chinese sailors' fault for the whole affair. Instead, both sides agreed to pay each other compensation for the damages; the peaceful nature of this resolution masked the intense anger and humiliation felt by the Japanese. Japan paid more in compensation than China did, so in point of fact Japan had paid an indemnity. Li had intended this show of force to serve as a deterrent for any Japanese ambitions, but in reality, it only inflamed Sinophobic sentiments and Japanese

---

33   Wright, *Chinese Steam Navy*, p.73.
34   Wright, *Chinese Steam Navy*, pp.183–184.
35   Songce Xiong, 'Qingmo "Changqi Shijian" Shimo', Gejie (2012), volume 180.

determination to humble the Chinese Empire. Though the Beiyang Navy had asserted its dominance, one seemingly minor detail of the Nagasaki Incident would lead to grave consequences in the Sino-Japanese War. After the street fight, a Japanese picked up a booklet dropped earlier by a Chinese sailor, which turned out to be the manual to deciphering coded Chinese telegram messages. Shortly before the Sino-Japanese War broke out, the Japanese cracked the code, allowing them to analyse, predict, and respond accordingly to Chinese movements.

The Beiyang Navy acted as a trump card during the subsequent great game between China and Japan in Korea, where it reasserted Chinese dominance over the Peninsula after the failed Gapsin Coup of 1884. Regrettably, shortly before the Sino-Japanese War, the Beiyang Navy entered a period of steep decline.[36] First, there was the omnipresent issue of funding. The 1875 decision allocated two million taels annually to the Beiyang Navy, but by 1889, only 1.3 million made their way into Beiyang Navy coffers each year. Thus, after 1889, the Beiyang Navy could barely afford to maintain their ships and facilities, much less purchase newer models. To make things even worse between 1889 and 1894, the Empress Dowager Cixi elected to spend upwards of several million taels to renovate the (new) Summer Palace to celebrate her 60th birthday; some sources claim that this money came from the funds of the Beiyang Navy.[37] Estimates of the amount embezzled ranges from six million to 22 million taels. Some scholars, however, have challenged this assertion, and instead claimed that factional rivals of Li Hongzhang were the ones to blame for the Beiyang budget cuts. Some of these rivals did not believe Japan to be a legitimate threat to China, and decided, not totally unreasonably, to spend government monies on addressing the various natural disasters at the time.[38] Whatever the cause, the budget for the Beiyang Navy was drastically slashed, with predictable results for the fleet's efficacy. Before budget cuts, the Beiyang Navy developed standard procedures for naval exercises in 1888, with emphasis on a regular schedule of such training with rewards and punishments being doled out based on performance, but after the budget cuts, the scale and regularity of these exercises was greatly reduced.[39]

Moreover, Li was not able to make any substantial purchases of weaponry, machinery or vessels during this time.[40] The Beiyang ships began to show their age; the main ships were between seven and 13 years old and mainly used old breech loading guns that typically could only fire once every minute. In 1893, Admiral Ding Ruchang attended several demonstrations of German and British quick loading guns in Shanghai, but the already strained budget was instead diverted to purchase coastal guns for the defence of Taiwan. Additionally, the boilers of the Beiyang Navy ships were old and decaying; Admiral Ding requested repairs innumerable times, but was shut down every

---

36 Wright, *Chinese Steam Navy*, p.84.
37 Elleman, *Modern Chinese Navy*, p.122.
38 Chang, Jung (2013). The Concubine Who Launched Modern China: Empress Dowager Cixi. New York: Anchor Books. pp.182–184. The curious reader is encouraged to read this work for a revisionist look at the 'Old Buddha.'
39 Liu, 'The Military Challenge', p.320.
40 Liu, 'The Military Challenge', pp.323–324.

time due to lack of funds.[41] Similarly, the quality of coal was questionable, leading to poor fuel efficiency and voluminous clouds of black smoke being produced.[42] The Beiyang Navy's coal was sourced mainly from the Kaiping coal mine, whose corrupt manager was not obligated to uphold any standards of quality. Even if he was not corrupt, the Beiyang Navy simply did not have the funds to purchase higher quality coal. The omnipresent plague of corruption also found its way into the Beiyang Navy. Many Chinese-made artillery shells were filled with sand or cement instead of gunpowder, making them completely useless.[43] These 'shells,' even if they hit, simply bounced off the enemy ships harmlessly. All the usual crimes – captains stealing funds meant for the maintenance of their ships, mandarins stealing the funds that the captains would have stolen, and so on – flourished. Another issue was the fact that Li Hongzhang was human. As a moderniser, a diplomat, a politician, a general, and a viceroy, the ageing Li, now in his seventies, did not have the same vigour and energy as he did during the mid-century rebellions to scrutinise every detail of the Beiyang Navy. His inattention to the affairs of the Beiyang Navy naturally meant that authority was seceded to Admiral Ding. Admiral Ding, though a good and upright man, had no formal education in modern naval affairs, and was not liked by his officers.[44] This precluded him from properly leading his men and making the proper decisions in the expansion, operation, and modernisation of the Beiyang Navy.

Finally, there were tensions between foreign and Chinese officers. Many foreign officers were extremely arrogant and intolerant of Chinese customs. Likewise, many Chinese officers felt humiliated listening to the instructions of foreign barbarians. Especially spiteful was the Commodore of the Beiyang Navy, Liu Buchan, who despised Captain Lang's presence.[45] Liu was the Captain of the Dingyuan, and fancied himself the senior naval officer to Captain Lang.[46] In 1890, during the Dingyuan's visit to Hong Kong, Lang flew the admiral's flag to indicate that he represented the authority of Admiral Ding, who was not present.[47] Liu ordered it to be lowered and replaced with the captain's flag, a gesture which meant that Liu, not Lang, was the highest ranking officer aboard. Liu was technically correct, since Lang claimed the officially non-existent rank of 'deputy admiral,' but a bitter quarrel broke out.[48] The animosity between Lang and Liu had not started with the flag-raising incident, and Lang finally had enough and resigned. With the Beiyang Navy's helmsman gone, the decline of the Beiyang Navy was cemented. Even worse, Lang told everyone who would listen about how he was mistreated by the Beiyang Navy officers, which led to a ban on all

---

41 Anon., 'Daodi Shi Shui Nuoyong Le Beiyang Jiandui Junfei? Weng Tonghe Zhishi Diaonan, Zuikui Huoshou Lingyou Qiren', Redian Xinjian (2024), <https://kan.china.com/qd/mkan/article/1170376_4.html?qudao=mkan>, accessed 6 Feb. 2024.
42 Gi-yun Kim et. al, *Taimullain M Je 2 Ho* (Seoul: Doseo Chulpan Gilchajgi, 2023), pp.50–51.
43 Elleman, *Modern Chinese Navy*, p.131.
44 Liu, 'The Military Challenge', p.323.
45 Xu, *Jundui Tonglan*, pp.152–153.
46 Two interpretations of this incident will be given below in the section on 'Naval Academies.'
47 Wright, *Chinese Steam Navy*, p.83.
48 See Appendix I for a list of all Beiyang Navy ranks.

Chinese students from attending British naval schools. After this debacle, Li hired more foreign advisors, two from Britain, two from America, and four from Germany. More were hired, but none of them were as talented as Lang.

The highest ranking foreign advisor at the time of the Sino-Japanese War was Constantin von Hanneken, a German expert in gunnery.[49] First appointed in the late 1870s, Hanneken had designed the defences of Lushunkou and Weihaiwei. On the eve of the war, Hanneken was present onboard the Gaosheng (Kowshing) and managed to escape the unhappy fate that befell most of its crew. After making his way to Beijing, he was eventually appointed the 'co-admiral' of the Beiyang Navy. Hanneken, however, was a soldier and not a sailor, so he was assisted by his second-in-command William Ferdinand Tyler, who had served in the Royal Navy Reserves and in the Imperial Chinese Maritime Customs previously. Hanneken and Tyler both served onboard the Chinese flagship *Dingyuan*, along with a British artillery instructor and a German engineer. Onboard the *Zhenyuan* was Philo Norton McGiffin, a graduate of the US Naval Academy. Initially, he was employed as an instructor at the Tianjin Naval Academy but later became superintendent of a smaller naval college at Weihaiwei. During the Sino-Japanese War, McGiffin served onboard the *Zhenyuan*, along with a German gunnery expert. There were also a number of other European personnel working at the naval bases of Lushunkou and Weihaiwei. Despite their numbers, these foreign advisors did not match up to Lang's talent, and even if they did, they were given insufficient authority to rectify the growing list of problems with the Beiyang Navy.

After Lang's departure, the recruitment, discipline, training, and education of Beiyang Navy officers plunged into freefall. The curriculum provided by Chinese naval academies was already considered very bare-bones, and many Beiyang Navy officers were only in their position because of connections or for the pay and were apathetic to their actual duties. Admiral Ding Ruchang, even if a bit ignorant in naval warfare, was at least courageous and honest; during the Battle of the Yalu, many officers hid below decks and made no attempt to lead or encourage their men.[50] It is sometimes alleged that Liu Buchan intentionally injured Admiral Ding during the Battle of the Yalu and/or sabotaged the Beiyang Navy formation to position his ship further away from Japanese fire. This is not to say that there were no heroes, like Captain Deng Shichang of the *Zhiyuan*, but heroism only occurred in isolated, individual cases, instead of in a coordinated and coherent structure.

With the budget being jettisoned, Li's watchful eye weakening, and the fleet's father-figure having disappeared, the Beiyang Navy's training, maintenance, and modernisation all stagnated. Perhaps the most damning record of the Beiyang Navy's decline occurred in 1891 during a visit to Yokohama in Japan.[51] The Japanese were well wary of the Beiyang Navy's fearsome reputation before, but this visit changed everything. The then-Captain Togo Heihachiro, during his inspection of the *Dingyuan*, found the

---

49 Elleman, *Modern Chinese Navy*, pp.119–120.
50 Elleman, *Modern Chinese Navy*, p.131.
51 Wright, *Chinese Steam Navy*, p.84.

Portrait of Admiral Ding Ruchang, photographed in 1886 by Liang Shitai. (Public domain)

sailors of the Beiyang Navy to be utterly incompetent, addicted to opium, and prone to gambling and drinking below decks. The officers had not the slightest notion of their duties, clotheslines were hung from the machinery, and the ships were filthy and poorly maintained. Some of the officers lived and dallied with their teenage concubines inside their quarters. When Togo poked his finger into the barrel of a gun, he found that his white glove had been dirtied from all the dust and grime inside. Togo deduced that with such an ineffective crew and command system the Beiyang Navy was useless. This incident gave Japan the confidence to challenge China on the high seas.

After the Sino-Japanese War, the Beiyang Navy was almost totally destroyed and was formally abolished. As damaged as its reputation was, it was revived in 1899 with Ye Zugui as Admiral. In 1896, Wang Wenshao replaced Li Hongzhang as Beiyang Commissioner and set about rebuilding and replacing the Beiyang Navy, purchasing a number of protected cruisers and destroyers. If they did not flee to the South to avoid conflict, the ships of the Beiyang Navy were mostly defenceless victims during the Boxer Rebellion, as several warships and torpedo boats were captured during the Battle at the Dagu Forts and even incorporated into the navies of the Eight Nation Alliance.[52] The Beiyang Navy's miserable existence was finally put to an end in 1909, where it, along with the other three navies, was reorganised into a single national navy divided into the Cruiser Squadron and the Changjiang (Yangtze) River Squadron.

Naval Academies and Training

Li Hongzhang understood that a modern navy without a modern crew was completely useless and spared no expense in providing naval education to the officers of the Beiyang Navy. China's first naval academy was established in the late 1860s at the Fuzhou Dockyard, before the Dockyard itself even finished construction.[53] The Fuzhou Naval Academy was split into two schools: one for navigation and seamanship taught by Englishmen, and one for engineering and ship construction taught by Frenchmen. Under English supervision, the Fuzhou Naval Academy acquired several training ships for the students such as the *Qianwei*, ex-*Mattadore*, in 1869. The curriculum took five years, and after this period students were sent abroad to further refine their craft, with officers and sailors sent to Britain and shipbuilders and engineers to France.

Beginning in 1872, 120 Chinese students were sent to America and studied Western engineering, society and science as part of the Chinese Educational Mission.[54] The Mission ended prematurely in 1881 due to a variety of extenuating circumstances, such as xenophobic racism from both sides, but despite this a good number of its Western-trained students contributed substantially to China's modernisation. For example, the Mission student Cai

---

52 Wright, *Chinese Steam Navy*, pp.116–119.
53 Wright, *Chinese Steam Navy*, pp.30–31.
54 John Benjamin Powell, *Who's who in China; containing the pictures and biographies of China's best known political, financial, business and professional men* (Shanghai: The China Weekly Review, 1925), p.728.

Tinggan studied electrical engineering at a machine shop in Massachusetts, then minelaying, torpedo engineering and surveying at the Tianjin Naval Academy. During the Sino-Japanese War, he served as the Captain of the *Fulong* torpedo boat.

In 1877, 12 students from the Fuzhou Naval Academy were sent to Britain to study at the Royal Naval Academy at Greenwich and serve onboard British vessels.[55] Many of these students would later find high-ranking positions within the Beiyang Navy. Commodore Liu Buchan became the second-in-command of the Beiyang Navy, Ye Zugui served as the Captain of the *Jingyuan* protected cruiser during the Sino-Japanese War and later as Admiral of the Beiyang Navy in 1899, and Sa Zhenbing became an instructor at the Tianjin Naval Academy in 1894.

In 1881, the Tianjin Naval Academy (sometimes called the Beiyang Naval Academy) was finally opened with Li Hongzhang's efforts, ending northern China's estrangement from naval education.[56] Both Chinese and foreign teachers were present at the Tianjin Naval Academy, though most classes were taught in English. The curriculum lasted five years and focused on various naval concepts such as tactics, torpedo engineering, surveying, and navigation, but also included the basics of Western engineering like algebra, geometry, astronomy, and mechanical drawing. Chinese classics were taught two days a week in order to develop a strong sense of national identity, ethical principles, and rules of conduct. After the five years were completed, students were to study abroad in Western countries and put their skills to the test. Unfortunately, one year after the grand opening, the results were unimpressive. The number of students was far from maximum capacity, and those that were enrolled were not at all enthusiastic. After Li Hongzhang increased the monthly stipend and encouraged good behaviour with a more thorough system of rewards and punishments, this problem was rectified. By the Sino-Japanese War, around 300 students had graduated from the Tianjin Naval Academy.[57] At the same time, more than double had graduated from the Fuzhou Naval Academy in the South. Between 1877 and 1890, 35 students were sent to Britain to study abroad; of these 31 were from the Fuzhou Naval Academy. The other four were from the Tianjin Naval Academy, but one of these was a native of Guangdong Province. Southern Chinese officers and sailors, therefore, comprised the majority of the Beiyang Navy's staff. This inevitably fermented regional tensions between navy staff and Admiral Ding Ruchang, who was from Northern China.

Some see fit to view the officers of the Beiyang Navy as being HMS Pinafore-esque twits who only rose to their position through nepotism, bribery, and mismanagement as opposed to military skill. Admiral Ding Ruchang is often singled out as a scapegoat for the Beiyang Navy's shortcomings. Traditionally, Ding's background as a cavalry officer is cited as evidence for his poor fit as a naval admiral.[58] It is true that Ding Ruchang

---

55 Wright, *Chinese Steam Navy*, p.31.
56 Wright, *Chinese Steam Navy*, p.30.
57 Liu, 'The Military Challenge', pp.317–318.
58 Wright, *Chinese Steam Navy*, p.46.

Beiyang Navy and army officers pose in front of a German Fahrpanzer during a Krupp weapons exhibition in 1890. The Beiyang Navy officers are all wearing the customised Manchu warm hat with a steeper edge, while the army officers wear traditional ma gua with xing pao and cool hats. The chubby fellow to the right of the Fahrpanzer is General Ye Zhichao, who apparently gained some weight after his last photograph in 1886. Probably photographed by a Krupp technician. (Image courtesy of the Staatliche Kunstsammlungen Dresden)

did not have much formal naval education, but he self-studied navy strategy. From the letters and written documents he left behind, it is clear that Ding was well-versed in naval terminology, but beyond that he usually devolved authority to his foreign advisors. This decision initially fared well, but after 1890, when the quality of foreign instruction greatly declined, this proved problematic. During the Battle of the Yalu, some sources, not unreasonably, even listed Hanneken as the Admiral of the Beiyang Navy, not Ding.[59]

More devastating was the fact that Admiral Ding's lack of a formal education allowed his subordinates to look down on him and disregard his commands. Without their respect, Admiral Ding was unable to command his own Navy, much less mediate between the foreign advisors and the Chinese officers. Ding's popularity was not improved by his regional provenance. Ding, a native of Anhui Province, was neither trusted nor liked by the majority of his officers or sailors, who were mostly Southern Chinese: 123 out of 206 officers and 15 of the 18 captains were all Fujianese, who had originally been trained at Zuo Zongtang's Fuzhou Naval Academy. Commodore Liu Buchan, who enjoyed support from his fellow Fujianese, was the chief instigator of these regional tensions.[60] Ding had to spend much of his energy fighting the insubordination of Liu's Fujian 'clique' instead of actively improving or maintaining the navy. At the Battle of Weihaiwei, this culminated in Ding being physically threatened by Fujianese sailors, who

---

59 Elleman, *Modern Chinese Navy*, p.129.
60 Bo Tang, '"Cheqi Shijian" yu Beiyang Jiandui Zhihui Quan Zhizheng', HistoryChina.net (2019), <http://www.qinghistory.cn/qsjj/qsjj_dwgx/387856.shtml>, accessed 29 Feb. 2024.

mutinied and refused to carry out his orders. It appears that Ding's greatest shortcomings lay not in his lack of knowledge of or skill in naval warfare, but rather his inability to properly lead and coordinate the officers of the Beiyang Navy. Despite his unimpressive performance, Ding did not lack courage or honesty. Even though he was offered political asylum in Japan, Ding chose to commit suicide out of shame after the Battle of Weihaiwei. This act was seen as heroic in both China and Japan. One particular incident sets Ding out as a man of honest persuasion and stalwart bearing; sometime in the 1880s, a coal shipment was recorded to be 10 tons short. Admiral Ding refused to accept this and exchanged five strongly worded letters demanding the rectification of this error.

Praised as a national hero in China and reviled as an incompetent coward in the West, Commodore Liu Buchan is also a difficult figure to evaluate. More nationalistic Chinese sources tend to portray the flag-raising incident between Liu and Lang as an important matter of national sovereignty, as Liu symbolically declared that the Beiyang Navy was Chinese, and not a foreign puppet.[61] This interpretation claims that Liu was fearful of Lang acting as an agent of the British government to control the Chinese navy. Contrariwise, Western sources regard the whole affair as unnecessary and extremely damaging to the Beiyang Navy's functionality, and Liu as an insubordinate and conceited individual. Neither interpretation is intended to be represented as definitive. Some scholars have blamed the Chinese disorganisation during the Battle of Yalu on Liu, claiming that he disobeyed orders to minimise the risk to his own life.[62] Originally, the Chinese formation had the *Dingyuan* in the lead, and Liu, not wanting to be in the front line, selfishly changed it to the ill-fated wedge formation. It is also alleged that he intentionally injured Admiral Ding for the same cowardly reasons. But this condemnation was written by a foreign officer onboard the *Dingyuan* who himself did not enjoy a positive relationship with Liu, so the account should be viewed with some scepticism. Moreover, despite his resentment against Lang's tutelage, Commodore Liu was not blindly conceited; after the 1891 visit to Japan, Liu figured that the Beiyang Navy was falling behind Japan's and urged Li Hongzhang to expand and modernise.[63] During the same visit the high-ranking Beiyang Navy officers were invited to a lavish banquet, but Liu stayed behind to supervise the Chinese ships and prevent any potential Japanese sabotage. Furthermore, the characterisation of Liu as a coward seeking to save his own skin does not make sense when considering the fact that his performance during the Battle of the Yalu River was both courageous and commendable.[64] Finally, Liu committed suicide with Admiral Ding after the scuttling of the *Dingyuan* at the Battle of Weihaiwei, after vowing that the death of the ship must be followed by that of the Captain.[65]

---

61 Bo Tang, 'Cheqi Shijian'.
62 Elleman, *Modern Chinese Navy*, p.129.
63 Zhongguo Diyi Lishi Dang'an Guan, Chi, Liu Junmen Zixiang Shilue, Haijun Shiji, Jiawu, Zhenwang Sinan, Qungong Shilue.
64 Qi, *Jiawu*, pp.139–140.
65 Zhongguo Diyi Lishi Dang'an Guan, Taile, Zai Zhongguo Qianxian.

THE NAVIES OF THE QING EMPIRE

Total strength

In 1888 the Beiyang Navy was divided into a front and a rear squadron.[66] The front squadron was to serve as the main fighting force of the Navy and was split into the centre, right, and left wings. The rear squadron was the logistics and support fleet, and included training ships, tugboats, and dispatch ships. Most of these auxiliary ships were extremely outdated by the time of the Sino-Japanese War, so foreign vessels had to be chartered for transport purposes.

Beiyang Navy Front Squadron Ships, 1894[67]

Name	Type	Tonnage	Horsepower	Maximum speed (knots)	Commander	Organisation	Complement	Construction information
Dingyuan	Ironclad	7,220	6,200	14.5	Admiral Ding Ruchang; Commodore Liu Buchan, Commander of Right Wing	Right wing, centre ship	363	1881–1883; Vulcan, Germany
Zhenyuan	Ironclad	7,220	7,200	15.4	Captain Lin Taizeng, Commander of Left Wing	Left wing, centre ship	363	1882–1884; Vulcan, Germany
Zhiyuan	Protected Cruiser	2,300	6,850	18.5	Captain Deng Shichang	Centre, centre ship	204–260	1885–1887; Armstrong, England
Jingyuan (PC), also known as the *Ching-Yuen*	Protected Cruiser	2,300	6,850	18.5	Captain Ye Zugui	Centre, right ship	204–260	1885–1887; Armstrong, England
Jingyuan (AC), also known as the *King-Yuen*	Armoured Cruiser	2,900	4,400	15.5	Captain Lin Yongsheng	Left wing, left ship	202–270	1885–1887; Vulcan, Germany
Laiyuan	Armoured Cruiser	2,900	4,400	15.5	Captain Qiu Baoren	Right wing, left ship	202–270	1885–1887; Vulcan, Germany
Jiyuan	Protected Cruiser	2,355	2,800	16.5	Captain Fang Boqian	Centre, left ship	180	1883–1884; Vulcan, Germany
Chaoyong	Cruiser	1,380	2,800	16.5	Captain Huang Jianxun	Left wing, right ship	140	1880–1881; Mitchell & Company, England
Yangwei	Cruiser	1,380	2,700	16	Captain Lin Luzhong	Right wing, right ship	140	1880–1881; Mitchell & Company, England
Pingyuan	Ironclad	2,150	2,400	10.5	Captain Li He	Unassigned	204	1886–1889; Fuzhou Dockyard, China

---

66   Xu, *Jundui Tonglan*, p.381.
67   Yue Chen, *Zhongguo Junjian Tuzhi* (Shanghai: Shanghai Shudian Chubanshe, 2015).

Beiyang Navy Ship Armament, 1894[68]

Name	Armament	Torpedoes
Dingyuan	Four 305 mm Krupp breech loading guns, two 150 mm Krupp breech loading guns, four 75 mm Krupp guns, two 57 mm Hotchkiss guns, two 47 mm Hotchkiss guns, eight 37 mm Hotchkiss guns	Three 356 mm torpedo tubes
Zhenyuan	Four 305 mm Krupp breech loading guns, two 150 mm Krupp breech loading guns, four 75 mm Krupp guns, two 57 mm Hotchkiss guns, two 47 mm Hotchkiss guns, eight 37 mm Hotchkiss guns	Three 356 mm torpedo tubes
Zhiyuan	Three 210 mm Krupp breech loading guns, two 152 mm Armstrong breech loading guns, eight 57 mm Hotchkiss guns, six 37 mm Hotchkiss guns, six 11 mm Gatling guns	Four 356 mm torpedo tubes
Jingyuan (PC), also called *Ching-Yuen*	Three 210 mm Krupp breech loading guns, two 152 mm Armstrong breech loading guns, eight 57 mm Hotchkiss guns, six 37 mm Hotchkiss guns, six 11 mm Gatling guns	Four 356 mm torpedo tubes
Jingyuan (AC), also called *King-Yuen*	Two 210 mm Krupp breech loading guns, two 150 mm Krupp breech loading guns, two 75 mm Krupp guns, two 47 mm Hotchkiss guns, one 40 mm Hotchkiss gun, five 37 mm Hotchkiss guns	Four 356 mm torpedo tubes
Laiyuan	Two 210 mm Krupp breech loading guns, two 150 mm Krupp breech loading guns, two 75 mm Krupp guns, two 47 mm Hotchkiss guns, one 40 mm Hotchkiss gun, five 37 mm Hotchkiss guns	Four 356 mm torpedo tubes
Jiyuan	Two 210 mm Krupp breech loading guns, one 150 mm Krupp breech loading gun, four 70 mm Jinling guns, two 47 mm Hotchkiss guns, nine 37 mm Hotchkiss guns	Four 381 mm torpedo tubes
Chaoyong	Two 254 mm Armstrong breech loading guns, four 120 mm Armstrong breech loading guns, two 9 pounder Armstrong guns, two 25 mm Nordenfelt guns, four 11 mm Gatling guns	None
Yangwei	Two 254 mm Armstrong breech loading guns, four 120 mm Armstrong breech loading guns, two 9 pounder Armstrong guns, two 25 mm Nordenfelt guns, four 11 mm Gatling guns	None
Pingyuan	One 260 mm Krupp breech loading gun, two 150 mm Krupp breech loading guns, two 57 mm Hotchkiss guns, two 47 mm Hotchkiss guns, four 37 mm Hotchkiss guns	Three 457 mm torpedo tubes

Beiyang Navy Gunboats, 1894

Name	Tonnage	Horsepower	Maximum speed (knots)	Armament	Complement	Construction information
Zhendong	440	472	10	One 279 mm Armstrong muzzle loading gun, two 76 mm Armstrong guns, two 11 mm Gatling guns	28	1878–1879; Mitchell & Company, England
Zhenxi	440	472	10	One 279 mm Armstrong muzzle loading gun, two 76 mm Armstrong guns, two 11 mm Gatling guns	28	1878–1879; Mitchell & Company, England
Zhennan	440	472	10	One 279 mm Armstrong muzzle loading gun, two 76 mm Armstrong guns, two 11 mm Gatling guns	28	1878–1879; Mitchell & Company, England
Zhenbei	440	472	10	One 279 mm Armstrong muzzle loading gun, two 76 mm Armstrong guns, two 11 mm Gatling guns	28	1878–1879; Mitchell & Company, England
Zhenzhong	440	455	10.3	One 279 mm muzzle loading Armstrong gun, two 76 mm Armstrong guns, two 11 mm Gatling guns, two Nordenfelt guns	28	1880–1881; Mitchell & Company, England
Zhenbian	440	455	10.3	One 279 mm muzzle loading Armstrong gun, two 76 mm Armstrong guns, two 11 mm Gatling guns, two Nordenfelt guns	28	1880–1881; Mitchell & Company, England

---

68   Chen, *Junjian*.

Beiyang Navy Torpedo Boats, 1894

Name	Tonnage	Horsepower	Maximum speed (knots)	Armament	Torpedoes	Complement	Construction information
Left Fleet Boat One (Zuo Yi)	90	1,000	23.8	One 47 mm Hotchkiss gun, two 11 mm Gatling guns	Three 356 mm torpedo tubes	28	1886; Yarrow, England
Left Fleet Boat Two (Zuo Er), Left Fleet Boat Three (Zuo San)	66	600	20	Two 37 mm Hotchkiss guns	Two 356 mm torpedo tubes	28	1882–1883; Vulcan, Germany
Right Fleet Boat One (You Yi)	74	900	20	Two 37 mm Hotchkiss guns	Two 356 mm torpedo tubes	28	1884; Vulcan, Germany
Right Fleet Boat Two (You Er), Right Fleet Boat Three (You San)	66	597	20	Two 37 mm Hotchkiss guns	Two 356 mm torpedo tubes	28	1882–1883; Vulcan, Germany
Dingyuan Boat One, Dingyuan Boat Two	15.7	200	15	None	Two 356 mm torpedo tubes	7	1883; Vulcan, Germany
Zhenyuan Boat One, Zhenyuan Boat Two	15.7	200	15	None	Two 356 mm torpedo tubes	7	1883; Vulcan, Germany
Centre Ship (Zhonghao)	Unknown	Unknown	15	One cannon	Unknown	Unknown	Unknown
Centre Fleet Boat A (Zhongjia), Centre Fleet Boat B (Zhongyi)	Unknown	15.7	16	None	One 356 mm torpedo tube	Unknown	Probably 1881–1882; Vulcan, Germany
Boat One, Boat Two, Boat Three, Boat Four[69]	28	650	13.2	One gun	One torpedo tube	16	1881; Vulcan, Germany
Fulong[70]	120	1,597	24.2	One Hotchkiss 47 mm gun, one Hotchkiss 37 mm gun, two 11 mm Gatling guns	Three 356 mm torpedo tubes	20	1885; Schichau, Germany
Hanlei[71]	Unknown	Unknown	6	One gun, probably Hotchkiss	Unknown	7	Unknown
Kan Yi, Kan Er[72]	28	650	18.2	One 37 mm Hotchkiss gun	One 356 mm torpedo tube, four spar torpedoes	7	1881–1882; Vulcan, Germany

---

69 These four ships are only found listed in Beiyang Navy records.
70 Chen, *Junjian*, p.133.
71 This is another strange ship that is listed in Beiyang Navy and Japanese records but not Professor Chen's work. This suggests it may have been an auxiliary vessel during the war.
72 Chen, *Junjian*, p.12. Kan Yi and Kan Er were used as tugboats during the construction of the fortress of Lushunkou and renamed 'Lushunkou Construction Boat One' and 'Two." Their fate after this is unknown.

Beiyang Navy Rear Squadron, 1894

Name	Type	Tonnage	Horse-power	Maximum speed (knots)	Number of guns	Torpedo tubes	Comp-lement	Construction information
Meiyun	Gunboat/Training ship	515	320	9	5	None	70	1869–1870; Fujian Dockyard
Kangji	Gunboat/Training ship	1,268	750	12	15	2	180	1878–1879; Fujian Dockyard
Weiyuan	Training ship	1,268	750	12	7	None	180	1876–1877; Fujian Dockyard
Minjie	Training ship	700	Unknown	Unknown	Unknown	None	60	1888; England
Caojiang	Gunboat/Transport ship	640	425	10	8	None	91	1869; Jiangnan Arsenal
Tai'an	Gunboat/Transport ship	1,258	500	10	None	None	100	1876; Fujian Dockyard
Haijing	Transport ship	1,258	600	10	None	None	100	1873; Fujian Dockyard
Liyun	Transport ship	1,080	110	Unknown	None	None	57	Unknown
Xizhao	Transport ship	Unknown	60	9	Unknown	None	Unknown	1888
Zhenhai	Gunboat/Transport ship	572	350	9	5	None	70	1871; Fujian Dockyard
Feifu	Transport ship	Unknown	Unknown	Unknown	Unknown	None	Unknown	Unknown
Tielong	Transport ship	Unknown	Unknown	Unknown	Unknown	None	Unknown	Unknown
Feilong	Transport ship	Unknown	Unknown	Unknown	Unknown	None	Unknown	Unknown
Kuaishun	Transport ship	Unknown	Unknown	Unknown	Unknown	None	Unknown	Unknown
Lishun	Transport ship	Unknown	Unknown	Unknown	Unknown	None	Unknown	Unknown
Jieshun	Transport ship	160	Unknown	Unknown	Unknown	None	15	1891; Tianjin Arsenal
Haima	Transport ship	Unknown	Unknown	Unknown	Unknown	None	Unknown	Unknown
Kuaima	Transport ship	Unknown	Unknown	Unknown	Unknown	None	25	Unknown
Feiting	Transport ship	Unknown	Unknown	Unknown	Unknown	None	18	Unknown
Baofa	Minelayer	Unknown	Unknown	Unknown	Unknown	None	Unknown	1890; Tianjin Arsenal
Shoulei	Minelayer	Unknown	Unknown	Unknown	Unknown	None	16	1888; Tianjin Arsenal
Xialei	Minelayer	Unknown	Unknown	Unknown	Unknown	None	16	1888; Tianjin Arsenal
Xunlei	Minelayer	Unknown	Unknown	Unknown	Unknown	None	4	Unknown
Ganlei	Minelayer	Unknown	Unknown	Unknown	Unknown	None	Unknown	Unknown
Lishui	Small steamship	Unknown	Unknown	Unknown	Unknown	None	20	Unknown
Chaohai	Small steamship	Unknown	Unknown	Unknown	Unknown	None	Unknown	Unknown
Yushun	Tugboat, capable of conversion to gunboat or minelayer	Unknown	350–420	12	Unknown	None	20	1886; Tianjin Arsenal
Dongli	Small steamship	Unknown	Unknown	Unknown	Unknown	None	Unknown	Unknown
Ganhai	Small steamship	Unknown	Unknown	Unknown	Unknown	None	Unknown	Unknown
Daohai	Dredger	500	400	Unknown	Unknown	None	164	1883; Vulcan, Germany
Daohe	Dredger	Unknown	Unknown	Unknown	Unknown	Unknown	Unknown	Unknown
Feihu	Dispatch ship	Unknown	Unknown	Unknown	Unknown	None	Unknown	Unknown
Fuping	Coal ship	Unknown	Unknown	Unknown	Unknown	None	Unknown	Unknown
Yongping	Coal ship	Unknown	Unknown	Unknown	Unknown	None	Unknown	Unknown
Kaiping	Coal ship	Unknown	Unknown	Unknown	Unknown	None	Unknown	Unknown
Beiping	Coal ship	Unknown	Unknown	Unknown	Unknown	None	Unknown	Unknown

THE NAVIES OF THE QING EMPIRE

Uniforms

Before 1882, the uniforms of Beiyang Navy sailors and officers were not at all standardised. In theory, they were meant to wear hao yi more or less identically to their army compatriots, but in practice they seem to have worn a variety of different jackets. However, in 1882, Admiral Ding Ruchang sanctioned the drafting of a new set of standardised naval uniforms for the Beiyang Navy.[73] The 1882 Uniform Regulations would be worn until 1888.

The Model 1882 Regulations divided uniforms into three categories: officers, marines and sailors. These were further separated into spring, summer, autumn, and winter variations. Interestingly, none of the 1882 uniforms had identification discs like in the army. The dress of officers and non-commissioned officers consisted of a double lapelled hao yi with white pants and black Chinese boots. The hao yi was dark blue, and made of heavy wool in winter and fall, while in summer and spring it was white and made of a lighter thread, though the dark blue uniform was usually worn with white pants in summer and spring. In both seasons, the hao yi was edged and highlighted in black and adorned with cloud-head symbols. There did not appear to be collar insignia present on officers' uniforms. The sleeve insignia of officers' uniforms had three cloud-head symbols on it, and inside these cloud-heads would be various symbols denoting rank. For example, an admiral would have nine 'shou' characters, meaning longevity, on each sleeve,

Several Beiyang Navy officers loafing about, dressed in blue and black winter uniforms and skull caps. Their cuff insignia comprises two bands, with two dragon heads and an orb on the upper band. Thus, their rank is either dusi (lieutenant commander) or shoubi (lieutenant), depending on if the orb is blue or white respectively. (Public domain)

---

73 Xu, *Jundui Tonglan*, pp.350–355.

while the captain would have seven, the first mate six, and so on. Medical officers had a complex sleeve design of a ganoderma lucidum mushroom, a longevity peach, and a bat, overlaid on one another. The ship scribe had an arrangement of a brush and rice paper, the gunnery officer a halberd and gun, the navigation officer a Chinese knot, and et cetera.

In the summer, officers wore straw sennett hats to offer some protection from the sun, while in the other seasons a simple black Chinese skull cap was worn. The summer Sennett hats had a black ribbon around the crown, with yellow text listing the ship and rank of the wearer. The skull caps were apparently plain and without any decoration. Before 1882, on ceremonial occasions, standard Manchu cool or warm hats were assumed depending on the season. However, these hats were extremely cumbersome to wear when working inside the ship, and at some point, an officer of the *Zhenhai* went to a hat shop to commission a custom-made warm hat with a steeper edge such that it resembled a brimless bell-boy hat. This more practical customisation was much more suited to shipboard activities, and Admiral Ding included this modified version into the 1882 Regulations. The custom warm hat became the new standard-issue for ceremonial occasions and was worn regardless of season.

In summer, Beiyang Navy sailors wore a simple white hao yi with blue edging and a pointed 'sword-head' (jian tou) design down the collar, black Chinese boots and a Sennett hat. In the other three seasons sailors wore a blue hao yi edged in black and a black turban, but the other items of dress remained identical. 1882 sailor hao had arm patches with yellow symbols denoting rank and specialisation and had 'Beiyang' and the name of their ship (e.g. Beiyang *Zhiyuan*) embroidered in yellow on both their collars. It appears that these regulations were not really well adhered to, as a good number of surviving examples contradict them. One sailor uniform of the Laiyuan consisted of a blue hao yi edged in red and piped in white with text embroidered on the chest, not the collars. Another of the *Zhiyuan* consisted of a white hao yi edged in yellow with an identification disk reading '*Zhiyuan* Steel Ship' and 'Beiyang Fleet' (Beiyang Shuishi) on them. Some sailors also apparently wore plain jackets with no edging or other decorations at all. In the 1882 Regulations, non-commissioned officer uniforms were almost identical to those of officers. The main difference was that non-commissioned officers wore the same headgear as sailors (sennett hats in the summer and black turbans in the other three seasons) and did not have sleeve rank insignia. Instead, like sailors, they wore arm patches.

According to the 1882 Regulations, Beiyang Navy marines wore red (possibly magenta?) hao yi edged and highlighted in black, red trousers, black Chinese boots, and straw sennett hats in summer and black turbans in winter. Unit information was embroidered in red on the collars and in yellow around the black crown ribbons on the sennett hats. Marine officers had a similar system of cloud-head patterns on the cuffs to indicate rank; squad leaders would have a traditional Chinese symbol of three halberds rising from a vase (see plate commentary for A2 for more details on this symbol) with two Chinese knots on each side, while the deputy squad leader's cuff was identical sans the Chinese knots.

In 1888, the Beiyang Navy uniforms went through another round of revisions. The 1888 Regulations uniforms were the ones worn during the Sino-Japanese War, and they would only be retired in the late 1900s. The 1888 Regulations were generally quite similar to those of 1882, but with a few notable differences. First, the 1888 Regulations reworked officers' sleeve insignia and completely removed the symbol and cloud-head cuff insignia. In its place was a system of bars, dragons, and orbs. The 1888 sleeve insignia featured a design of two dragons facing a coloured orb; the long bodies of the dragon would wrap around the sleeve to become a rank bar of sorts. The orb appeared, disappeared, and changed colours based on the rank of the wearer. For example, Admiral Ding's sleeves had his dragons facing a red orb, with four bars below them; a captain would have two dragons facing a red orb with two bar below them; a first class naval cadet would have two small dragons facing a white orb with no bars below; and so on. Specialised officers had a system of symbols comparable to their 1882 version: torpedo boat captains had a sleeve design of two crossed torpedoes, engineers a design of a Buddhist swastika, and so on.

Unfortunately, there is total disagreement on the 1888 redesign of the sailor uniforms. The photos that exist frequently show the coexistence of several different uniforms in use together. The 1888 Regulations added a square identification patch on the chest for sailor uniforms; this was black for winter dress and white for summer dress, and the text was yellow for summer dress and either red or yellow for winter dress. There is no consensus on the precise details of this identification patch. Some contemporary recreations show 'Beiyang Navy' (Beiyang Haijun) on one side and the ship name on the other (e.g. *Zhiyuan* tiejian, meaning *Zhiyuan* steel ship); sources do not agree on whether each inscription was on the left or right side of the patch. Other recreations[74] claim that the identification patch only contained the name of the ship (e.g. *Zhiyuan* tiejian) and that the inscription was red for winter dress. A photo from the 1900s shows the name-only arrangement for the patch but also shows sailors wearing plain uniforms with no patches at all.

The arm patch symbols for sailors were also all redesigned to varying degrees; these would be yellow in summer and red in winter. For example, the 1882 arm patch design for the first mate (three bars) remained untouched in 1888. The 1882 design for the head carpenter (two crossed axes) was only slightly changed in 1888 and became two crossed axes with a slightly different design and angle surrounded by some decorative bordering. However, the 1882 design for a stoker (a four and three bladed propeller for a regular and an assistant stoker respectively) was changed to chevrons (three for the head stoker, two for the second class stoker, and one for the third class stoker) in 1888. Some designs were done away with altogether; in 1882 the torpedo engineer patch design was of a stylised fish with a wrench underneath for the head engineer and without for the assistant engineer, but in 1888 torpedo engineers did not have their own unique arm patch insignia. In addition, the 1888 Regulations introduced special uniforms for the bodyguards of high

---

74　Chen, *Junjian*, p.518.

ranking officers. This uniform consisted of a blue warrior vest edged in black with white buttons, blue trousers, a black turban, and black Chinese boots. The warrior vest was plain and featured no text or insignia anywhere. The marine uniform did not change perceptibly, though the cuff insignia was probably changed.

Flags

Before 1890, there were only three flags in use: the Qing national flag, the admiral's flag, and the captain's flag.[75] The Qing national flag was the only triangular flag of the three and had a familiar yellow background with a blue dragon. The admiral's flag was flown when the admiral was on board and had a red anchor design in the canton and was striped, yellow, white, black, green and red in that order, with yellow on top and red on bottom. The captain's flag was flown when the highest ranking officer aboard was the captain and had the red anchor in the canton but was only striped, black, green, and red, in that order with black on top. These designs were the ones used during the flag-raising incident of 1890; Lang had raised the admiral's flag, while Liu had replaced it with the captain's flag.

A new set of flag regulations were put into action in late 1890. The Qing national flag was made into a rectangular standard to conform with Western standards. The admiral's standard changed its canton design from an anchor to a forward facing blue dragon with the same stripe and colour arrangement. The captain's flag was replaced with the officer flag, which had five coloured stripes (red, green, yellow, black and white, from top to bottom) without any special canton design. The 1890 regulations also introduced the swallow tailed 'squad leader' flag, which was swallow tailed and had four coloured stripes (red, yellow, green and white, from top to bottom). The captain of torpedo boats received a new flag as well, which followed the familiar five striped pattern but with green, red, yellow, white and black stripes, and the Daoist hexagram for 'peace' in the upper canton. A plain yellow triangular pennant with a central red circle was flown by all ships while on duty, and during mealtimes this was replaced with a plain white pennant with a central red circle. A plain red flag with the inscription 'Tianshang Shengmu,' meaning 'celestial holy mother' and referring to the Chinese goddess of the sea, Mazu, was flown on the first and 15th day of each month and during religious ceremonies and festivals.

The Nanyang Navy

Despite its namesake, the Nanyang Navy was responsible for the protection of central China and the East China Sea. Headquartered in Shanghai, the Nanyang Navy was the largest and most powerful of the four Chinese modern fleets before the disastrous Sino-French War. The Nanyang Navy had its beginnings with the very first steamship built at the Jiangnan Arsenal, the

---

75   Chen, *Junjian*, pp.287–291.

Tianji.[76] From that point on, the Nanyang Navy would mainly be composed of Chinese-built ships from the Jiangnan Arsenal and the Fuzhou Dockyard. After the success of the *Tianji*, the Nanyang Navy received four Jiangnan-built wooden gunboats, *Caojiang*, *Zehai*, *Weijing*, and *Haian* in 1869, 1869, 1870, and 1872, respectively.[77] The wooden frigate *Hai'an* was the largest Chinese-built ship until the 1930s, and in 1873 her sister ship *Yuyuan* joined the Nanyang Navy. Unfortunately, despite their large size, they were built from poor quality imported Oregon and Vancouver wood. Already showing signs of decay after a trip from Shanghai to Nanjing and generally clumsy at sea, the *Hai'an* was used as a training ship, while the *Yuyuan* was left idle as a guardship and storeship.[78] The Fuzhou Dockyard also contributed the wooden gunboat *Jingyuan* (named identically to the Beiyang Navy protected cruiser) in 1872, the wooden frigate *Yuankai* in 1875, and the wooden transport *Dengyingzhou* in 1876.[79]

Jiangnan Arsenal Shipbuilding[80]

Name	Type	Year completed
Tianji, later *Huiji*	Wooden hull, paddle wheel	1868
Caojiang	Wooden hull, propeller	1869
Zehai	Wooden hull, propeller	1869
Weijing	Wooden hull, propeller	1870
Zhen'an, later *Hai'an*	Wooden hull, propeller	1872
Unknown	Armour plated, twin propeller	1872
Unknown	Armour plated, twin propeller	1872
Unknown	Armour plated, twin propeller	1874
Yuyuan	Wooden hull, propeller	1873
Jinou	Ironclad (monitor class)	1875
Unknown	Armour plated, twin propeller	1874–1875
Unknown	Armour plated, twin propeller	1874–1875
Unknown	Motorised sampan	1874–1875
Unknown	Foreign style sailing vessel	1874–1875
Unknown	Twin propeller	1881
Baomin	Steel armoured	1885

The Nanyang Navy's first ironclad was the *Jinou*, built at the Jiangnan Arsenal in 1876.[81] Named after a golden ceremonial cup that symbolised the harmony of the Qing Empire, the 195 ton *Jinou* was the first Chinese-built ironclad, but this did not stop her from being ironically nicknamed the 'Terror of the Western World.' In 1878, Nanyang Commissioner Shen Baozhen ordered four flat-iron gunboats *Zhendong*, *Zhenxi*, *Zhennan*, and *Zhenbei* from the English Mitchell & Company.[82] Li Hongzhang finagled

---

76 The Tianji is often misspelt as 'Tianqi' and was later renamed the 'Huiji'.
77 Wright, *Chinese Steam Navy*, p.34.
78 Wright, *Chinese Steam Navy*, pp.34–35.
79 Wright, *Chinese Steam Navy*, p.38.
80 Kennedy, *The Arms of Kiangnan*, p.161.
81 Wright, *Chinese Steam Navy*, p.36.
82 Wright, *Chinese Steam Navy*, pp.44–46.

these four modern gunboats and switched them with four older ships from his own fleet. The Fuzhou Dockyard constructed several composite sloops, which made their way to the Nanyang Navy in the late 1870s and early 1880s. In 1883, the Nanyang Commissioner ordered the *Nanchen* and *Nanrui* 2,200 ton steel cruisers from the German Howaldt company.[83] Some rumours surfaced that copies of these two ships were being built in China, but these were false, and a product of their somewhat undeserved reputation as fancy German ironclads. Despite finishing construction in March 1884 on the eve of the Sino-French War, the French did not consider them a threat (or because they were unarmed) and made no attempt to delay their arrival, unlike the Beiyang Navy's *Dingyuan*, *Zhenyuan*, and *Jiyuan*.

During the Sino-French War, the Nanyang Navy initially held back its vessels to defend Shanghai and Nanjing, where the abundance of foreign nationals and commercial connections saved the two cities from French attack. The French, after wrecking the Fujian Navy, initiated a blockade of the island of Taiwan.[84] A Nanyang Navy squadron was tasked with breaking this blockade, made up of the composite cruiser *Kaiji*, the ironclads *Nanrui* and *Nanchen*, the composite sloop Chengqing, and the wooden frigate *Yuyuan*. The Beiyang Navy's *Chaoyong* and *Yangwei* were initially meant to go with them, but Li Hongzhang's famously unscrupulous act meant that the Nanyang Navy fought alone. The Nanyang Navy's five ship squadron was very poorly manned, as only one officer had any kind of formal naval training. Most of the best Southern Chinese officers had been sent North to study at the Tianjin Naval Academy or enlist with the Beiyang Navy, leaving the Nanyang Navy with untrained recruits that had never been to sea before. Consequently, this five-ship Nanyang squadron was in no hurry to meet the French, and even hoped they wouldn't encounter the French at all.[85] When they did meet the French in combat, the Chinese saw that they were outgunned and attempted to withdraw, but the two slowest ships, the *Yuyuan* and *Chengqing*, were left behind.[86] The *Yuyuan* was torpedoed and the *Chengqing* scuttled after being mistakenly hit by Chinese coastal batteries. The other three ships hid in Zhenhai Bay along with two Fujian vessels and were blockaded by the French for the rest of the war. The French made plans to attack the bay and sink as many of the Chinese ships as possible, but after an exchange of shelling, the assault was cancelled. The French viewed this as a minor skirmish but the Chinese saw it as a major victory. The end of the so-called Battle of Zhenhai marked the end of the naval combat of the Sino-French War. Nevertheless, the Chinese continued to run equipment, supplies, and even soldiers into Taiwan past the French naval blockade, leading to a convincing French defeat on the island.[87]

After the catastrophe of the Sino-French War, the Nanyang Navy's superiority over the Beiyang Navy was disintegrated, especially with the arrival of the *Dingyuan* and *Zhenyuan*. A few notable additions were made regardless.

---

83   Wright, *Chinese Steam Navy*, pp.56–57.
84   Liu, 'The Military Challenge', p.251.
85   Elleman, *Modern Chinese Navy*, p.114.
86   Wright, *Chinese Steam Navy*, p.65.
87   Eliott, *Some Did It*, pp.197–198.

The 1,477 ton steel cruiser *Baomin*, ordered in 1883, finished construction in the Jiangnan Arsenal in late 1885, almost immediately after the end of the Sino-French War.[88] The Fuzhou Dockyard also contributed two 2,100 ton composite cruisers, the *Jingqing* and *Huantai*, in 1886 and 1887, respectively. In 1891, the newly appointed Viceroy of Liangjiang, Liu Kunyi, inspected the Nanyang Navy and found that only six ships were capable of fighting at all, with two barely even being seaworthy. In the Imperial Court, there was talk about disbanding the Nanyang Navy altogether so more funds could be allocated to the Beiyang Navy. In the end, the Nanyang Navy was saved from total abolition but was relegated to a coastal defence force. This, of course, meant that the Nanyang Navy's funding was drastically pared to make way for the Beiyang Navy, which became the Imperial government's main focus after the Sino-French War.

The Nanyang Navy's refusal to help the Beiyang Navy during the Sino-Japanese War became legendary as an example of Chinese regionalism. Initially, Li did not even want the help of the Nanyang Navy, bluntly stating, 'the ships of the Southern Provinces are totally useless; how can they scare the Rising Sun?'[89] But after the Battle of the Yalu and when Japanese forces were fast converging on Lushunkou, Li finally relented and requested help from the other regional navies. The Imperial government asked Liu Kunyi to send three warships northward to assist Li's Beiyang Navy. Liu however delivered poetic justice to the Beiyang Navy. He claimed that if the Nanyang Navy sent ships to the North, the East China Sea would be left undefended and vulnerable to attack. Liu was not completely unreasonable; there was concern that the Japanese would attack Shanghai and target the Jiangnan Arsenal. The attack on Shanghai never occurred, but the parallels with the Beiyang Navy's snub during the Sino-French War were obvious.

When Liu Kunyi was deployed in Northern China to manage troops and logistics in late 1894, the Viceroy of Huguang Zhang Zhidong was appointed interim Viceroy of Liangjiang and therefore held the authority of directing the Nanyang Navy. Li, once again, asked the Nanyang Navy to send help, but Zhang, again not unreasonably, claimed that the Nanyang Navy had no experienced officers and would be of no use.[90] He proposed that Li send some of his own Beiyang Navy officers to first train the Nanyang Navy ships and then sail north afterwards. When Li rejected this proposal, Zhang attempted to recruit talent from the Guangdong and Fujian Navies, but after the fall of Lushunkou, Zhang saw that the direction of the war was irreversible and did not make any serious attempt to aid his northern compatriots. Only after the Sino-Japanese War were ships of the Nanyang Navy sent north to patrol.

---

88 Wright, *Chinese Steam Navy*, pp.67–68.
89 Qingfeng Wenshi, 'Jiawu zhanzheng zhong, Nanyang shuishi weihe bu beishang canzhan? Qishi shi bu xiang qu "song rentou"', Qingfeng Wenshi (2022), <https://www.163.com/dy/article/HINND4040552XHZR.html>, accessed Feb. 29, 2024.
90 Qihao Shuo Sanguo, 'Jiawu Haizhan shi, weihe Nanyang Shuishi kanzhe Beiyang Shuishi quanjun fumie, ye bu beishang bangzhu ta?', Qihao Shuo Sanguo (2020), <https://www.sohu.com/a/399050670_120174872#:~:text=%E7%94%B2%E5%8D%88%E4%B8%AD%E6%97%A5%E6%88%98%E4%BA%89%E7%88%86%E5%8F%91,%E6%89%80%E4%BB%A5%E5%8E%8B%E6%A0%B9%E4%B8%8D%E6%95%A2%E5%8C%97%E4%B8%8A%E3%80%82>, accessed Feb. 29, 2024.

Total prewar strength

Nanyang Navy Ships, 1894

Name	Type	Tonnage	Horsepower	Maximum speed (knots)	Number of guns	Number of torpedo tubes	Complement	Construction information
Huantai	Cruiser	2,200	2,400	18	13	2	213	1884–1887; Fuzhou Dockyard
Jingqing	Cruiser	2,200	2,400	17	13	2	213	1884–1886; Fuzhou Dockyard
Kaiji	Cruiser	2,200	2,400	16	10	None	300	1881–1884; Fuzhou Dockyard
Nanchen	Cruiser	2,200	2,400	14.5	12	None	250	1883; Howaldt, Germany
Nanrui	Cruiser	2,200	2,400	14.5	12	None	250	1884; Howaldt, Germany
Baomin	Cruiser	1,480	1,900	13	8	None	260	1883–1885; Jiangnan Arsenal
Cedian	Gunboat	400	270	9.5	4	None	30	1875–1876; Mitchell & Company, England
Feiting	Gunboat	400	270	9.5	4	None	30	1875–1876; Mitchell & Company, England
Longxiang	Gunboat	320	235	10	4	None	30	1875–1876; Mitchell & Company, England
Huwei	Gunboat	320	235	10	4	None	30	1875–1876; Mitchell & Company, England
Weijing	Gunboat	1,000	605	12.5	12	None	145	1870; Jiangnan Arsenal
Zehai	Gunboat	600	431	12.5	8	None	117	1869; Jiangnan Arsenal
Jinou	Gunboat	195	340	10	1	None	53	1875; Jiangnan Arsenal
Dengyizngzhou	Gunboat	1,258	500	10	7	None	100	1875–1876; Fujian Dockyard
Junhe	Gunboat	Unknown	Unknown	Unknown	5	None	Unknown	1882

The Fujian Navy

The Fujian Navy had its beginnings as a provincial Green Standard Army fleet in 1650 composed of wooden junks, mainly used for anti-piracy purposes, but its modernisation only began in the late 1860s. Financed by General Zuo Zongtang and with French assistance, the Fuzhou Dockyard and naval academy finished construction in 1867; the French were afraid of potential Japanese or British expansion in Southern China.[91] The *Wannian Qing*, the Fuzhou Dockyard's first steamship, was launched in 1869. Virtually all of

---

91   Elleman, *Modern Chinese Navy*, pp.108–109.

the Fujian Navy's ships were Chinese-built and either wooden or composite; the two exceptions were two 256 ton flat-iron gunboats, the *Jiansheng* and *Fusheng*, ordered in 1875 from the Laird shipbuilding company of Britain.[92]

On the eve of the Sino-French War, most of the Fujian Navy's ships were around a decade old. Furthermore, they were incompetently crewed. One source claims that only eight of the 14 ship captains that fought in the Sino-French War had modern training of any kind and quality.[93] When war became inevitable, the French made plans to destroy the Fuzhou Dockyard, which lay near the city of Mawei down the Min River.[94] Ironically enough, the Fuzhou Dockyard had been constructed with much French assistance, and was now slated to quite literally meet its maker. After hostilities were effected, the French informed the Fujian Navy of their intentions to attack. The Chinese failed to prepare in any meaningful way, since neither side had formally declared war, and they did not believe the French would attack without a formal declaration. They were sorely disappointed. The result was a three hour turkey shoot where the Chinese ships, most of them completely dwarfed by French ironclads, were hopelessly outgunned by the French's quick firing guns and torpedo boats.[95] The night after, the Chinese attempted to attack the French with fireships, torpedo boats, and war junks but these were unsuccessful. The next morning the French launched a bombardment on the Fuzhou Dockyard, managing to cause some damage but not enough to disable it. The dockyard was situated in shallow water that the heavier French ships could not traverse, so they were only able to send a few smaller ships with less firepower. Even the French felt somewhat disappointed at the results of this bombardment; the Dockyard was able to resume operations after only minor repairs. The composite sloop *Henghai*, still under construction at the Dockyard at the time of the battle, was left mostly intact by the French shelling and even launched the following year.

Besides the Fuzhou Dockyard's miraculous survival, the Fujian Navy was devastated. The French attack had destroyed nine of the 11 Fujian warships, sunk 19 transport ships and caused the scuttling of another two. After the war, the Fujian Navy was crippled and became the smallest and weakest fleet of the four regional navies. Despite some half-hearted attempts to rebuild, only the 1,000 ton torpedo boat *Fujing* (formerly the *Guangding*), built in 1893, could claim to have any fighting capacity at all.[96] The remaining ships could only be used as transport, auxiliary or merchant escort ships. The 144 ton torpedo boat *Fulong*, ordered in 1885, was transferred to the Beiyang Navy only six years after its arrival in 1886.[97]

---

92 Wright, *Chinese Steam Navy*, p.42.
93 Elleman, *Modern Chinese Navy*, p.111.
94 Wright, *Chinese Steam Navy*, pp.62–63.
95 Liu, 'The Military Challenge', p.251.
96 Wright, *Chinese Steam Navy*, p.70. The Armstrong gunboat Fu'an, supposedly built in 1894, appears to never have existed as it does not appear in manufacturer or government records.
97 Wright, *Chinese Steam Navy*, p.184.

Total prewar strength

Fujian Navy Ships, 1894

Name	Type	Tonnage	Horse-power	Maximum speed (knots)	Number of guns	Number of torpedo tubes	Complement	Construction information
Fujing	Torpedo Cruiser	1,000	2,400	16.5	7	4	110	1893; Fujian Dockyard
Jingyuan	Gunboat/training ship	572	350	9	5	None	118	1872; Fujian Dockyard
Chenhang	Transport ship	1,450	600	10	8	None	107	1874
Jinghai	Gunboat	578	480	Unknown	7	None	Unknown	1873
Yixin	Gunboat	245	200	10	5	None	58	1875–1876; Fujian Dockyard
Changsheng	Gunboat	195	340	10	1	None	Unknown	1875
Yuankai	Dispatch ship	1,258	600	10	5	None	84	1874–1875; Fujian Dockyard
Chaowu	Dispatch ship	1,268	750	12	Unknown, probably 7	None	84	1877–1878; Fujian Dockyard
Fubo	Transport and dispatch ship	1,258	600	10	7	None	Unknown	1870; Fujian Dockyard
Feiyun	Transport and dispatch ship	1,258	600	10	7	None	Unknown	1872; Fujian Dockyard
Feijie	Unknown	1,033	110	Unknown	Unknown	None	Unknown	1890

The Guangdong Navy

Having faced the fearsome effects of Western firepower during the First Opium War, the provincial Guangdong Navy was the grandfather of the modern Chinese navy. The earliest reverse-engineering of a British sloop was built in Guangdong Province, while the first Chinese-built steamship was constructed in Guangzhou in 1842.[98] After the kerfuffle of the Lay-Osborn flotilla, the Viceroy of Liangguang purchased seven steamers for anti-piracy purposes in 1867. By 1875 the Guangdong Navy had 12 men-of-war: seven steamers, three converted junks, and two British gunboats. Further additions continued, mainly of composite and steel gunboats.[99] The Guangdong Navy remained a green water defence force however and did not intend to openly contest sea power.

The Guangdong Navy did not participate at all during the Sino-French War. In 1882, the Imperial government ordered the Guangdong Navy to patrol the Gulf of Tonkin to counter French aggression, and two ships from the Fujian Navy, the *Feiyun* and *Ji'an*, were temporarily assigned to the Guangdong Navy. They were quickly returned in 1884 when confrontation with the French was imminent and were destroyed during the Battle of

---

98 Elleman, *Modern Chinese Navy*, pp.81–83.
99 Wright, *Chinese Steam Navy*, p.20.

Fuzhou.[100] The Guangdong Navy did nothing, even when the French blockaded the Guangxi port of Beihai (Bakhoi in Cantonese).

After the Sino-French War the Guangdong Navy experienced a period of significant growth in size and quality. These new vessels were a mix of Chinese-built and foreign-built ships. Two 64 ton torpedo boats, the *Leihu* and *Leilong*, had finished construction in 1884, but since they were built by the German Vulcan company their delivery was delayed by French chicanery until 1885.[101] In 1886, four composite 300 ton gunboats, the *Guangheng, Guangli, Guangyuan,* and *Guangzhen*, finished construction at the Whampoa Dockyard.[102] Then a whopping nine 26 torpedo boats were ordered from the Schichau shipbuilding company of Germany, all arriving in 1886.[103] Four 320 ton Fuzhou-built wooden gunboats, the *Guanggeng, Guangxing, Guangzhen* and *Guangkui*, were sent to the Guangdong Navy in 1887.[104] In the same year, the Fuzhou Dockyard also built the 1,296 ton composite cruiser *Guangjia* and in 1893 three 1000 ton torpedo boats, the *Guangyi, Guangbing,* and *Guangding*.[105]

During the Sino-Japanese War, three ships of the Guangdong Navy participated in combat: the *Guangjia, Guangyi* and *Guangbing*. The *Guangyi* was destroyed at the Battle of Pungdo early on, while the *Guangjia* attempted to flee the Battle of Yalu but ran aground near Dalian Bay. The *Guangbing* was holed up at Weihaiwei during the battle, and her captain politely requested to the Japanese that she be let go, reasoning that the war was an entirely northern affair and that the Guangdong Navy was not an active participant in the war. The Japanese rejected this modest proposal and took the *Guangbing* into their own navy as the *Kohei-go*.

Total prewar strength

Guangdong Navy Ships, 1894

Name	Type	Tonnage	Horsepower	Maximum speed (knots)	Number of guns	Number of torpedo tubes	Complement	Construction information
Guangjia	Cruiser	1,300	1,600	14	11	4	145	1885–1887; Fujian Dockyard
Guangyi	Torpedo Cruiser	1,000	2,400	16.5	7	4	56	1888–1892; Fujian Dockyard
Guangbing	Torpedo Cruiser	1,000	2,400	16.5	7	4	56	1891–1893; Fujian Dockyard
Zhendong	Gunboat	170	170	Unknown	3	None	Unknown	1867
Guangwu	Gunboat	Unknown; probably around 400	400	Unknown	6	None	Unknown	1886; Guangdong Dockyard
Guangji	Gunboat	Unknown; probably around 400	400	Unknown	6	None	Unknown	1886; Guangdong Dockyard
Guanggeng	Gunboat	320	400	12	4	None	Unknown	1888–1889; Fujian Dockyard
Guangkui	Gunboat	320	400	11	5	None	Unknown	1887; Fujian Dockyard

---

100 Wright, *Chinese Steam Navy*, p.38.
101 Wright, *Chinese Steam Navy*, p.181.
102 Wright, *Chinese Steam Navy*, p.69.
103 Wright, *Chinese Steam Navy*, pp.179–182.
104 Wright, *Chinese Steam Navy*, p.71.
105 Wright, *Chinese Steam Navy*, p.70.

Name	Type	Tonnage	Horsepower	Maximum speed (knots)	Number of guns	Number of torpedo tubes	Complement	Construction information
Guangzhen	Gunboat	320	400	11	5	None	Unknown	1887; Fujian Dockyard
Guangxing	Gunboat	320	400	11	5	None	Unknown	1887; Fujian Dockyard
Guangxin	Gunboat	400	Unknown	11	2	None	Unknown	Unknown
Guangyu	Gunboat	320	500	9	5	None	Unknown	1889–1890; Guangdong Dockyard
Guangjin	Gunboat	320	500	9	5	None	Unknown	1889–1890; Guangdong Dockyard
Guangyuan	Gunboat	Unknown	78	10	5	None	Unknown	1885–1886; Guangdong Dockyard
Guangzhen	Gunboat	Unknown	78	10	5	None	Unknown	1885–1886; Guangdong Dockyard
Guangheng	Gunboat	Unknown	65	9	5	None	Unknown	1885–1886; Guangdong Dockyard
Guangli	Gunboat	Unknown	65	9	5	None	Unknown	1885–1886; Guangdong Dockyard
Guangde	Gunboat	Unknown	Unknown	Unknown	Unknown	None	Unknown	Unknown
Guangjing	Gunboat	Unknown	Unknown	Unknown	Unknown	None	Unknown	Unknown
Pengzhouhai	Unknown	800	500	Unknown	6	None	Unknown	1889
Zhizhong	Unknown	500	300	Unknown	6	None	Unknown	1879
Haijingqing	Gunboat	440	455	10.3	7	None	Unknown	1880; Mitchell & Company, England
Zhentao	Unknown	450	265	7	7	None	Unknown	1867
Anlan	Gunboat	1258	600	10	7	None	Unknown	1871; Fujian Dockyard
Haidongxiong	Gunboat	430	200	7.5	3	None	Unknown	1879; Guangdong Dockyard
Haichangqing	Gunboat	320	200	Unknown	4	None	Unknown	1872
Jixi	Unknown	320	200	Unknown	6	None	Unknown	1872
Lianji	Unknown	200	180	Unknown	4	None	Unknown	1883
Guang'an	Gunboat	150	150	Unknown	7	None	Unknown	1867
Chengbo	Gunboat	150	100	6	2	None	Unknown	Unknown
Shenji	Gunboat	150	Unknown	Unknown	3	None	Unknown	1867
Jingbo	Unknown	150	100	6.5	Unknown	None	Unknown	Unknown
Jing'an	Unknown	150	100	6	2	None	Unknown	Unknown

Chapter 3

The Army of the Empire of Japan

Introduction

The Empire of Japan (1868–1947) had technically existed since 660 BC with the first Emperor of Japan, thereby making Japan an 'empire.' Though technically the Emperor had always had supreme authority, a dynastic series of military strongmen called 'Shogun' from the Tokugawa clan actually held the power since their unification of Japan in 1603, with the Emperor as a figurehead. The period of Tokugawa Shogunate rule is often called the Edo period, for its capital in the eponymous city, while the Shogunate itself was labelled the 'bakufu', meaning 'tent government' in reference to its military authority and origins.

For various sociopolitical reasons, in 1639 the Tokugawa Shogunate effected a strict isolationist policy called Sakoku, meaning 'locked up country.'[1] The only exceptions were trade with China, Korea and other immediate neighbours, as well as a Dutch enclave on a small island called Dejima near Nagasaki. Contact with European colonial powers did not shake Japan's determination until the fateful arrival of American Commodore Matthew Perry's 'black ships' in 1853. Commodore Perry provided a textbook example of 'gunboat diplomacy' with his fleet, leading to a helpless Japan repealing Sakoku and establishing several treaty ports with America, Britain, Russia, Holland, and France in the 1850s.

The full title of the Shogun was 'Sei-i Tai Shogun,' meaning 'Great General, Conqueror of the Barbarians.' However, Japan's total vulnerability at the hands of Western military might had severely damaged the Shogun's legitimacy as de facto ruler since the barbarians were clearly capable of conquering Japan and not the other way around. The Emperor Osahito (posthumously styled Emperor Komei) himself attempted to challenge the authority of the Shogun and issued an edict with the pithy slogan 'Sonno Joi,' meaning 'Honour the Emperor and Expel the Barbarians.' The Shogunate could not veto this, but at

---

1   Ian Heath, *Armies of the Nineteenth Century: Japan and Korea* (Nottingham: Foundry Books, 2009), pp.10–12.

the same time refused to enforce it in consideration of the barbarians' superior weaponry. Two factions in Japan began to develop: first, the Tokugawa Shogunate and their allied feudal domains, and second, the Imperial Court and a coalition of south-western domains led by the Satsuma and Choshu. Satsuma and Choshu had opposed the Tokugawa Shogunate's ascendancy in 1600, and their resentment had not dissipated even after centuries. The Imperial faction sought to depose the Shogun, return to Sakoku, and restore the full authority of the Emperor. Their preferred methodology was initially that of terrorism. European merchants, sailors, diplomats and pro-foreign Japanese were repeatedly murdered, both clandestinely and not. Choshu and Satsuma in particular attempted to take pot-shots at foreign vessels, leading to reprisals that finally convinced the Imperial faction of Western military superiority. Learning their lesson, the Imperial faction began to reform their armies based on modern models of training and armament.

Domestic political developments were also concerning; a failed coup by Choshu led to a civil war with the Shogunate. By then, the Choshu had already adopted the European art of war and handily thrashed the Shogun's disjointed and poorly armed forces; the death of the Shogun forced his successor to humiliatingly sue for peace with their own vassal. The death-spiral of the Shogunate was now irreversible. Emperor Osahito died in 1867, and his teenage son Mutsuhito took his place, who would be crowned the Meiji Emperor within a year. The Tokugawa Shogunate made some desperate last-ditch attempts to reform, but an 1867 uprising led by the Satsuma and Choshu domains forced the Shogun himself to abdicate. The Imperial Court then declared the full authority of the Emperor and demanded the Tokugawa clan cede its properties to the revitalised Imperial Government. The Tokugawa clan and their pro-Shogun allies did not find this proposition attractive, and marched on Kyoto with 30,000 men, but were intercepted and defeated by the Satsuma General Saigo Takamori. This signalled the beginning of the Boshin War, named for the Year of Boshin. At this point, both the Shogunate and Imperial faction saw the value of Western military equipment and training. Although the armies of Choshu and Satsuma had long been trained in the ways of the foreign barbarians, the Shogunate worked hard to close the gap. Nevertheless, the bulk of Shogunate forces had been defeated by 1868 and that same year Emperor Meiji was victoriously escorted into the former Shogunate capital of Edo, now renamed Tokyo, and proclaimed Emperor of all Japan. The Empire of Japan, having existed only in name for hundreds of years, had truly gained its title. The so-called Meiji Restoration of 1868 did not end the Shogunate resistance, and the last holdouts were finally defeated in mid to late 1869. Fortunately for Japan, the Boshin War was surprisingly bloodless: less than 10,000 soldiers were killed overall.

Emperor Meiji had little time to rest on his laurels however, and he quickly embraced a series of sweeping reforms aimed at modernising Japan. Ironically, even though the Imperial faction had been the most anti-foreign, they now switched their policy and began to reshape the Japanese government and society along Western lines. In 1869, the feudal domains were confiscated by the government and enrolled into a centralised Imperial administration.[2] Basic schooling became compulsory for all children in 1872, and a year later enlistment in the Imperial Japanese Army (IJA) became a patriotic duty for each and every Japanese man. In 1887, a meritocratic civil service examination was designed and implemented, and in 1889 the Meiji constitution established a limited monarchy government with a veneer of Western-style democracy.

These reforms were not universally accepted by the Japanese population, and they responded with a series of rebellions and civil uprisings. The Meiji government, as a rule, refused to budge or compromise, and instead massacred the rebels, regardless of the legitimacy of their cause.

The most famous of these rebellions was Saigo Takamori's 1877 Satsuma Rebellion (called the Southwest War in Japanese, or 'Seinan Senso'), caused mainly by the disenfranchisement of the samurai feudal class.[3] One year later, the supposedly loyal Imperial Guard, who had put down the Satsuma Rebellion, also rebelled. Land reform policies caused a sharp skyrocketing of animosity in landlord-tenant relationships, leading to various riots and peasant rebellions. Although these fortunately did not reach the horrifically large size and scale of China's, they proved to be substantial and expensive obstacles to the Meiji reforms.

After the quelling of the domestic unrest and the successful implementation of the reforms, the Meiji government considered itself a fully modernised society equal to the European powers, both socially and technologically. The Japanese believed that the only way to stave off foreign imperialism was to participate in imperialism themselves, and for this, Korea was the prime option. Having been under Chinese suzerainty, the Korean peninsula could be used as a staging point for an invasion of the Japanese home islands by either China, Russia, or some other unfriendly power. Therefore, Japanese control over Korea became critical to national defence; to achieve this, Japan would have to wage war against Korea's suzerain, China. The Chinese made themselves a very easy enemy to rally the public against. Traditionally, the Chinese had regarded themselves as the only civilisation in the entire world and still called the Japanese 'midgets' (wo) in official dispatches and letters. The profound humiliation Japan experienced during the 1886 Nagasaki Incident led to Japanese schoolchildren making models of Chinese warships and pretending to sink them with stones and virtually unanimous calls for the avenging of Japan's honour. The gruesome acts of torture and mutilation inflicted upon Japanese soldiery during the war continued to fuel public support for the war. Japan, modernised and rejuvenated, felt that the time of China's backwards arrogance had to come to an end. The Empire of Japan called itself an Empire to assert that she was equal to China; she was not a tributary 'Kingdom' like Korea. Now the time came to show Japan's strength, and to earn the respect and fear of the whole world.

As the Japanese won virtually every battle they participated in, the Empire of Japan is frequently presented as the ultimate contrast to the Qing Empire. Dynamic, vigorous, and above all modern-minded, the Imperial Japanese

---

2 Paine, *The Sino-Japanese War*, p.87.
3 Heath, *Japan*, p.13.

Army (IJA) delivered decisive victory after victory over the poorly led, poorly armed, and poorly motivated Chinese forces. But Japan's success in creating a loyal and patriotic centralised army is often taken for granted, and the fact that the road was a long and tortuous one is often glossed over. Even during the Sino-Japanese War, the Imperial Japanese Army was not the immaculate, perfectly organised, and fully 'modernised' army it is often reputed to be and suffered its own fair share of problems and defects.

Organisation

At the time of the Sino-Japanese War, the Imperial Army was organised into the six Line military divisions (shidan) of Tokyo, Sendai, Nagoya, Osaka, Hiroshima, and Kumamoto.[4] Each Line military division was a self-sufficient military force and theoretically composed of two brigades (each of two regiments) of infantry, one cavalry battalion, one field and mountain artillery regiment, one engineer battalion, and one commissariat battalion in peacetime, and when fully mobilised a field hospital, seven ammunition trains, two companies of medical attendants, as well as various administrative and noncombatant support functions. In practice, there were minor differences in the strengths of the artillery, cavalry, engineer and commissariat detachments for each division. The Tokyo and Kumamoto divisions also included fortress artillery units for coastal defence. Divisional strength in peacetime was around 9,000 men, which could be increased to 17,000–18,000 in wartime. Two divisions could be pieced together to form an army (gundan), and Japan was capable of forming three armies, each composed of two divisions. In addition to these six Line divisions, there also existed the Imperial Guard Division (Konoe Shidan) for the protection of the Imperial Family, the Kempeitai (Military Police) as a gendarme that also acted as a secret police, the Tondenhei settler militia that was responsible for guarding and developing Hokkaido and other northern colonial possessions, a first and second Reserve, and finally a militia that acted as a de facto third reserve.[5]

The general structure of the IJA's ranking system was determined with Imperial Decree 28 on 20 March 1891 (Meiji 24).[6] A few changes did come after, mainly involving the matching of military officer ranks with parallel civilian official grades. There were a few notable exceptions though: Imperial Decree 104 on 16 July 1894 (Meiji 27)[7] added 'special sergeants' (Tokumu Socho) under the rank of second lieutenants (and above the rank of superior supervisors for engineers and artillery) for all branches. After the Treaty of Shimonoseki (and during the Yiwei War) Imperial Decree

---

4 Heath, *Japan*, pp.40–41.
5 Zenone Volpicelli, *The China-Japan War Compiled from Japanese, Chinese, and Foreign Sources* (London: S. Low, Marston Limited, 1896), p.82.
6 Kokuritsu Kobunshokan, Naikaku Sorifu, Ref.A15112245000.
7 Kokuritsu Kobunshokan, Naikaku Sorifu, Ref.A15112771400.

111 of 15 July 1895 (Meiji 28)[8] declared that Kempeitai superior privates would be considered commissioned officers; after this, no changes would be made until May 1896. See Appendix II for a list of all Imperial Japanese Army ranks.

The Imperial Japanese Army (including the Imperial Guard and Tondenhei) was split into five main branches of service: infantry, artillery, engineers, commissariat, and cavalry. As of 20 March 1891 (Meiji 24) Regulations, these branches of the IJA used a generally identical but parallel rank system, up to the rank of colonel. For example, the ranks of Tondenhei Infantry Colonel, Line Commissariat Colonel, and Imperial Guard Artillery Colonel all existed, but a Major General was called just that. Army non-commissioned officer (NCO) and officer titles were customarily prefixed by 'army' (rikugun) and their branch name to distinguish them from the similarly titled Imperial Japanese Navy (IJN) officers (i.e. Rikugun Taisho, meaning Army General, versus Haigun Taisho, meaning Navy Admiral) and also other arms of service (Hohei Shosa, meaning Infantry Major, versus Kihei Shosa, meaning Cavalry Major). Technically, according to regulations, the rear echelon ranks of chief, assistant chief and enlisted gunsmiths, blacksmiths, carpenters, saddlers, and metal casters only existed in the artillery service branch, but they could be assigned to other units as well (for example, each infantry regiment had six gunsmiths). In addition to the five service branches, there was a military band, a Sanitation Department, the Kempeitai and the Tondenhei, that all had their unique rank systems. See Appendix II for a full list of all IJA ranks at the time of the Sino-Japanese War.

The Imperial Ordinance No. 267 of 1 November 1890 (Meiji 23)[9] set peacetime regulations for infantry, artillery, engineers, commissariat, cavalry, and Tondenhei unit sizes and organisation for units including and above the size of a company. Platoons and squads were a mere formality and did not exist in practice during peacetime. Unfortunately, Japanese units were typically understrength, and wartime regulations were not clearly defined so various estimates exist for wartime unit organisation and strength. Furthermore, estimates sometimes included or excluded the various noncombatant support functions attached to each unit.

Infantry

Discipline and unwavering courage were the bread and butter of the IJA infantry, who were predominantly drawn from the rugged peasant class.[10] The fact that soldiering was a glorious privilege and that they were serving a living god was repeatedly drummed into the heads of every Japanese infantryman, and saving the nation's 'face' was considered more important than individual self-preservation. Desertion and occasional breaches in discipline were not impossible, but they were negligible compared to that of their Chinese foes. Infantrymen were trained in

---

8   Kokuritsu Kobunshokan, Naikaku Sorifu, Ref.A15112957900.
9   Xu, *Jundui Tonglan*, pp.50–51.
10 Heath, *Japan*, pp.50–52.

Two smartly dressed privates second class on the eve of the Sino-Japanese War. Both men are armed with the Type 18 Murata rifle, plus a M1892 haversack and the M1887 backpack with horseshoe shaped blanket roll, spare boots, and a feldspaten shovel. A cartridge box is probably attached to their belt on the back, while the 1892 canteen is almost certainly stored in their haversack. (Public domain)

harsh physical education, in which they were forced to march 100 or so kilometres in 25 hours and run for long distances with minimal food and water. Thus, the Japanese peasants were not only proud to be soldiers, but also used to simple living, deferring to authority, and enduring great physical and mental burdens. The average Japanese infantryman's tough agrarian background helped them cope with the hardships of military life, to the point where some farmers even considered Japanese soldiers to be spoiled and pampered.

In addition to their patriotic brainwashing, Japanese infantrymen were also taught that self-preservation and cowardice were not only shameful, but also tactically inept. The Japanese system of infantry tactics was based on the theories of Major Klemens Meckel, a German military advisor who believed that close-order advances of three and four deep formations with one yard between each man was the best method for attack. Japanese infantrymen were instructed that any display of weakness or wavering among their ranks would lead to a total rout and crushing defeat. For the most part, the Japanese were correct: Chinese officers frequently cited the sight of an advancing Japanese line, calm and collected under heavy fire, as completely shattering Chinese morale. This is not to suggest that the Japanese infantry relied on human wave 'banzai charges' without regard for life or cover. The Japanese made great use of reconnaissance and made every effort to utilise favourable terrain, attack the enemy from the rear or flanks, and avoid obstacles and traps.

During the Sino-Japanese War, the Chinese were still fond of using tightly packed volley firing lines, which resulted in voluminous clouds of black powder smoke that obscured sight and therefore muddled accuracy.[11] The Japanese circumvented this by dividing the firing line into an overlapping series of company sections and half-companies. These subunits were small enough to preclude the gun smoke from accumulating too excessively. Each company section would operate independently, seeking cover and favourable terrain while other sections provided suppressing fire, and then furnishing the same service when the other sections were ready to advance. These infantry manoeuvres allowed the Japanese to minimise casualties and maximise individual firepower and accuracy. Volley fire was used, but only at long distances. Japanese infantrymen were also partial to the use of the bayonet; at around 40 or 50 paces from the enemy, a bayonet charge would be launched, either by hand, verbal, or bugle signals.

---

11 Junshi Jilu, Weiguan Zhanchang: Jiawu Zhanzheng, Pingrang Zhizhan, CCTV, (2012).

Peacetime Infantry unit organisation

Unit name	Strength
Brigade (Ryodan)	Two regiments
Regiment (Rendan)	1,730 men; three battalions
Battalion (Daitai)	560 men; four companies
Company (Chutai)	136 men; four platoons
Platoon (Shotai)	Strength varies; four squads
Squad (Buntai)	Strength varies

Peacetime Infantry Regiment Strength

Rank	Strength
Colonel (or Lieutenant Colonel)	1
Majors	4
Captains	13
Lieutenants	27
Second Lieutenants	25
Special Sergeants	12
Sergeant Majors	12
Sergeants	130
Privates	1,440
Medical Officer (Regimental Surgeon)	1
Military Doctors	5
Chief Medical Attendants	3
Medical Attendants	12
Accountants/Administrative Staff	7
Gunsmiths	6
Tailors	21
Cobblers	11
Total	1,730 (1,664 combatants, 55 non-combatants)

Artillery

Artillery regiments were composed of two field artillery battalions and one mountain artillery battalion, although all artillerymen were trained to use both field and mountain guns in case of one or the other being unavailable.[12] Field artillery batteries were equipped with 142 rounds per gun and mountain artillery batteries with 144 rounds, with a further 144 rounds (for both field and mountain guns) stored in the commissariat ammunition train in the rear. In addition to the regular artillery, there also existed a corps of fortress artillery for the defence of Japan's coastlines along with fortifications on Taiwan and Tsushima. Regulations required each fortress artillery regiment to have three battalions, but in practice each regiment could disobey this standard on an ad-hoc basis. For example, the 1st Division was recorded as having a single regiment of fortress artillery despite only having two battalions. Likewise, fortress artillery battalions could have three companies instead of their mandated four.

Japanese batteries had a maximum speed of 8–9.5 kilometres per hour and, whenever in action, almost always entrenched themselves 22 paces apart per gun, with emphasis on concealing their position with earthworks. Battalions preferred to fight together in groups of two or three companies, and isolated battery actions were greatly shunned. The accuracy of Japanese artillery was considered to be decent, if not exceptional. One defect was the fact that Japanese doctrine discouraged moving batteries in broad daylight, mainly due to the poor quality of artillery horses. As a result, once entrenched they seldom followed the infantry advance and could not affect the battle much once out of range. Luckily, this was mostly mitigated by the Chinese preference of hiding behind stationary fortifications, but the artillery's static nature certainly did create difficulties on several occasions during the Sino-Japanese War.

Compared to the Chinese, the Japanese artillery had two advantages, the first being that they were present to begin with. Too often, the Chinese simply did not have any or enough guns available, and they were left without much-needed artillery support. The Japanese, on the other hand, almost always complemented their infantry charge with fierce bombardments from their guns. The second major advantage of the Japanese artillery was the use of shrapnel, a kind of shell that was still unfamiliar to most Chinese military men. Shrapnel shells burst in mid-air and therefore did not need direct hits to inflict horrific casualties upon the Chinese. In virtually every battle of the war where Japanese artillery was involved, shrapnel shells played a significant role in slaughtering large numbers of the enemy and demoralising those that remained.

---

12 Heath, *Japan*, p.75.

Peacetime Artillery unit organisation

Unit name	Strength
Regiment (Ryodan)	737 men; two field artillery battalions and one mountain artillery battalion
Battalion (Daitai)	270 men; two companies/batteries of mo; 12 guns
Company/Battery (Chutai)	112 men; three platoons; six guns
Platoon (Shotai)	Strength varies; two guns

Peacetime Artillery Regiment Strength

Rank	Strength
Colonel (or Lieutenant Colonel)	1
Majors	3
Captains	9
Lieutenants	15
Second Lieutenants	12
Special Sergeants	6
Sergeant Majors	7
Sergeants	64
Privates	576
Military Doctors	3
Chief Medical Attendants	1
Medical Attendants	6
Veterinarians	2
Accountants/Administrative Staff	8
Farriers	2
Saddlers	2
Blacksmiths	2
Tailors	10
Cobblers	6
Carpenters	2
Total	737 (693 combatants, 44 noncombatants)

Peacetime Fortress Artillery unit organisation

Unit name	Strength
Regiment (Ryodan)	1,697 men; three battalions
Battalion (Daitai)	542 men; four companies; 12 guns
Company/Battery (Chutai)	134 men

Peacetime Fortress Artillery Regiment Strength[13]

Rank	Strength
Colonel (or Lieutenant Colonel)	1
Majors	3
Captains	15
Lieutenants	27
Ensigns	24
Special Sergeants	11
Sergeant Majors	13

---

13   Volpicelli, *China-Japan War*, p.83.

Rank	Strength
Sergeants	136
Privates	1,404
Medical Officer (Regimental Chief Surgeon)	1
Military Doctors	2
Chief Medical Attendants	3
Medical Attendants	12
Accountants/Administrative Staff	7
Gunsmiths	2
Saddlers	11
Blacksmiths	2
Tailors	21
Carpenters	2
Total	1,697 (1,404 combatants, 63 noncombatants)

Engineers

Although they were only named an official service branch in 1872, an engineering corps had existed in some form in Japan since 1861.[14] Each engineering battalion had three companies; two served as field companies with the last as a bridging and telegraph company.

Typically, IJA engineers would be attached to artillery units for maintenance, erect earthwork fortifications, repairing or building roads, and such tasks. In combat, engineers were expected to locate and destroy booby traps, demolish obstacles and gates, dig trenches, and build bridges, often under direct enemy fire. Japanese engineers took a far more active role in war than those of their European counterparts; during the Battle of Pyongyang, Japanese engineers were able to quickly dig three lines of trenches for the infantry even as the Chinese were shooting at them with magazine rifles. After the victory in said battle, Japanese engineers constructed almost 64 kilometres of telegraph wires in less than 10 hours. During the Battle of Jiuliancheng, the Japanese engineers rapidly built a pontoon bridge over the freezing Yalu River without the Chinese even noticing.

Peacetime Engineers unit organisation

Unit name	Strength
Battalion (Daitai)	410 men; three companies
Company (Chutai)	126 men

Peacetime Engineers Battalion Strength[15]

Rank	Strength
Colonel (or Lieutenant Colonel)	1
Majors	1
Captains	4
Lieutenants	7
Second Lieutenants	6
Special Sergeants	3
Sergeant Majors	3

---

14 Heath, *Japan*, pp.45–46.
15 Volpicelli, *China-Japan War*, p.83.

Rank	Strength
Sergeants	32
Privates	330
Military Doctors	1
Chief Medical Attendants	1
Medical Attendants	3
Accountants/Administrative Staff	2
Gunsmiths	2
Blacksmith	1
Tailors	7
Cobblers	5
Carpenters	2
Total	410 (386 combatants, 24 noncombatants)

The Commissariat

The commissariat arm of service has been variously translated as the transportation corps, the military train, and so on; the Japanese name (shicho) roughly translates to 'military supplies'. Unsurprisingly, the commissariat dealt with managing the baggage train, transporting supplies, and distributing food and ammunition to the frontline troops. Similar to the engineers, the commissariat was only formally established as a branch in 1872 but had existed since 1869.[16]

Peacetime Commissariat unit organisation

Unit name	Strength
Battalion (Daitai)	614 men; two companies
Company (Chutai)	290 men

Peacetime Commissariat Battalion Strength

Rank	Strength
Majors	1
Captains	3
Lieutenants	5
Second Lieutenants	4
Special Sergeants	2
Sergeant Majors	3
Sergeants	31
Privates	360
Military Doctors	2
Chief Medical Attendants	1
Medical Attendants	2
Veterinarians	2
Accountants/Administrative Staff	2
Gunsmiths	1
Farriers	3
Tailors	7
Cobblers	5
Total	614 (589 combatants, 25 non-combatants)

---

16 Heath, *Japan,* pp.46–47.

In wartime, commissariat battalions were split between different functions, including regimental transportation, divisional supply columns, divisional ammunition columns and such. Each division had three supply columns and five ammunition columns; these took the form of either pack ponies or traditional Japanese two-wheeled handcarts pulled either by a single pony or three men. Wagons, either requisitioned or purchased from locals, were also used and drawn by beasts of burden (sometimes of different kinds). As they were not really needed during peacetime, the commissariat battalions were extremely understrength but maintained a large reserve to be recruited as labourers in wartime. The commissariat was also responsible for hiring, paying and organising Chinese, Japanese and Korean labourers as needed.

Each Japanese soldier was expected to carry one day's food supply and two days' emergency rations on his person, while the regimental train was meant to carry a day or more's worth of food, followed by the divisional train which had four or more days' rations. Additionally, infantrymen stored 100 rounds on their person, while the battalion commissariat had 30 rounds per rifle and the divisional column 50 rounds per rifle. Since their equipment did not allow them to cook themselves (see Accoutrements), individual soldiers were wholly dependent on the commissariat for their rations.

Although the Japanese military leadership understood the importance of a strong logistics system, their implementation left much to be desired, and the many horrendous failures experienced during the Sino-Japanese War would prove a tremendous learning experience. For example, early in the war the Wonsan Detachment did have commissariat troops for the exact purpose of moving supplies, but they were so understaffed that they had to order an entire infantry battalion to act as a noncombatant transportation unit.[17] Another particularly dismal incident revolved around the mobilisation of General Oshima's 9th Brigade. When mobilisation was announced the commissariat attempted to hire military labourers in Japan instead of pack horses because of the poor state of Korean roads. This would not be so easy; the commissariat failed to recruit enough men out of bureaucratic incompetence as opposed to a genuine lack of suitable reservists. For example, in one unit, only 130 men had been recruited of the required 640. This understrength force was sent to Korea anyway. The 9th Brigade's commissariat then attempted to recruit local Japanese residents to fill up the remaining vacancies. Still, this failed, so 2,000 Korean labourers and 700 pack horses were hired from various nearby villages. The Koreans did not find the idea of assisting an invading force appealing and, before the march even began, fled into the countryside, along with the supplies they were meant to carry. The Japanese battalion commander, Major Koshi Masatuna, felt himself personally responsible and committed suicide. This unhappy series of events was not an isolated incident; deserting Korean and, later, Chinese porters would become a running trend.

---

17   More on these incidents will be expounded in Volume Two.

A group of Japanese military labourers receiving rations of rice and dried fish at roll call. Note the bizarre mix of Western and Japanese hats worn; also note the small patch on the left arm denoting battalion affiliation. Drawn by Georges Ferdinand Bigot. (Public domain)

In the harsh Manchurian winter, the horror stories of commissariat underperformance became even more deadly. Soldiers frequently had to endure freezing temperatures in socks and sandals instead of winter boots or in summer uniforms without cotton undershirts or greatcoats. These items were usually supplied to the soldiers via donations from family, friends, or patriotic Japanese civilians as opposed to being distributed on a systematic and uniform basis. One of the most famous Japanese military songs, 'Yuki no Shingun,' or 'Marching in the Snow,' was written by a disgruntled Japanese soldier, Nagai Kenshi during the Battle of Weihaiwei. This was no heroic ballad extolling the virtues of persevering through hardship; rather, it was a cynical depiction of the average Japanese soldier suffering from inadequate winter clothing, chronic shortages of fuel, and meagre food rations. The final line 'we weren't meant to come home alive anyway' is a flagrant jab at the callousness of the IJA high command; it is no surprise that this song was banned during the Showa period. The popularity of this song among the Japanese soldiery suggests the prevalence of the conditions described.

Yuki no Shingun, with English translation[18]

Stanza	Original Japanese	Translated lyrics
One	Yuki no shingun koori wo funde	Marching in snow, stepping in ice
	Dore ga kawa yara michi sae shirezu	Rivers and roads can't be told apart
	Uma wa taoreru sutete mo okezu	The horses are dying, but we can't just abandon them
	Koko wa izuku zo mina teki no kuni	What kind of place is this? All around us is enemy soil
	Mama yo daitan ippuku yareba	It is what it is, so I take a cigarette break
	Tanomi sukunaya tabako ga nihon	Why are there two of them frozen together again?
Two	Yakanu himono ni han nie meshi ni	Uncooked dried fish and half-boiled rice
	Namaji inochi no aru sono uchi wa	We survive on these things, only half-alive
	Korae kirenai samusa no takibi	To fend off the cold, we made a bonfire
	Kemui hazu da yo namaki ga iburu	How the green wood smokes!
	Shibui kao shite komyo banashi	I put on a 'sour' face and try to tell heroic tales
	Sui to iu no wa umeboshi hitotsu	The only 'sour' thing here is a pickled plum
Three	Ki nomi ki no mama kiraku na fushido	We sleep freely without changing clothes
	Haino makura ni gaito kaburya	My backpack as a pillow and my coat as a blanket
	Sena no nukumi de yuki doke kakaru	The warmth of my back melts the snow
	Yagu no kibigara shippori nurete	Soaking my millet-husk bedding from top to bottom
	Musubi kanetaru roei no yume wo	In this dreamless shelter with neither roof nor wall
	Tsuki wa tsumetaku kao nozokikomu	The cold hearted moon shines over our faces
Four	Inochi sasagete detekita mi yue	We have come here prepared to die
	Shinuru kakugo de tokkan suredo	Ready to give our lives, we charge yelling
	Buun tsutanaku uchiji ni seneba	But if fortune is cruel and does not grant us death
	Giri ni karameta juppei mawata	Our donated cotton clothing, woven with duty
	Sorori to kubi shime kakaru	Slowly but surely will tighten around our necks
	Dose ikashite kaesanu tsumori	For we weren't meant to return home alive anyway

Therefore, although the Japanese logistics system actually existed and was therefore superior by default to the Chinese one, the IJA won in spite of it, not because of it. One reason for the Japanese success was pure Chinese ineptitude. For example, the failure to destroy vital food supplies during the Battles of Pyongyang and Jiuliancheng and so on compensated for the lacklustre Japanese logistic system and quite literally saved them from starvation. The Chinese logistics system ironically failed to provide for its own men but managed to consistently supply the Japanese with ample food, fuel, ammunition, and shelter. If the Chinese had managed to destroy, poison, or transport their substantial food reserves at the aforementioned locations, the Japanese would have been extremely hard-pressed to survive the bitter Manchurian winter. Chinese incompetence must not be mistaken for Japanese competence.

---

18   The author expresses his humble gratitude to his good friend Akeiko Sumeragi for her invaluable help in translating the linguistic nuances of this song.

Cavalry

The cavalry of the Imperial Japanese Army was no doubt the weakest service branch.[19] During the Edo Period, the Shogunate had forbidden commoners from riding horses and Japanese animal husbandry suffered a great decline in standards. Moreover, with the transition of the samurai from mounted warriors into sedentary bureaucrats, the art of cavalry warfare was neglected. As a result, Japanese horses were poorly bred, rarely gelded, and described as small, aggressive, sickly and inadequately trained.[20] This issue had been realised during the last years of the Shogunate, and attempts were made to crossbreed foreign stock to improve the genetic pool. In 1861, 15 Arab stallions and 11 mares were presented to the Shogun by the French government, while in 1868, the Japanese acquired 265 more foreign stallions from America and French North Africa. By the 1880s and 1890s, foreign horse imports were typically from Hungary, America, or Australia as opposed to North Africa. However, the results of these efforts left much to be desired, and in 1892 an observer noted that only officers could afford to ride crossbreeds. At the beginning of the Sino-Japanese War, around 40,000 horses were required for the army, but this was far too ambitious a number. Even of those that could be requisitioned, many were too sickly, weak or aggressive for service. For example, one divisional district managed to scrape together 11,000 horses, of which 6,000 were unsuitable for military use. Thus, many Japanese cavalrymen had to purchase or replace their horses in Korea and China.

The terminology in describing Japanese cavalry units is often very confusing in English documents, as 'battalion,' 'regiment,' 'company,' and 'squadron' all have different definitions depending on the writer. This was not a problem in the Japanese language, as the IJA simply used the same terminology for cavalry as with the other branches: battalions, or 'daitai'; companies, or 'chutai'; and platoons, or 'shotai.' Cavalry regiments would not come about until after the Sino-Japanese War. Peacetime regulations set battalion strength at 514 men including officers and support personnel, company strength at 159, while platoon strength had no specific regulations and thus varied in wartime. Supposedly, each of the Line army's six divisions were to have a full battalion of three companies, but virtually all (except the First Division) could only muster a full company or two at the beginning of the Sino-Japanese War.

Given that military horses were of a dubious quality and quantity, the Japanese cavalry was typically used for scouting, screening, or escort duty as opposed to charges and shock action. Japanese cavalrymen were trained to fight on foot and frequently served as mounted infantry as opposed to true cavalry. Japanese cavalry also accompanied screening detachments at the vanguard of any marching force. Despite the unsuitability of their mounts, Japanese cavalrymen still distinguished themselves by their courage in combat, and sometimes even in the charge.

---

19   Heath, *Japan*, p.43.
20   Heath, *Japan*, p.94.

A. Chinese military uniforms of the Sino-Japanese War
See Colour Plate Commentaries for further information.

B. **Chinese military uniforms of the Sino-Japanese War**
See Colour Plate Commentaries for further information.

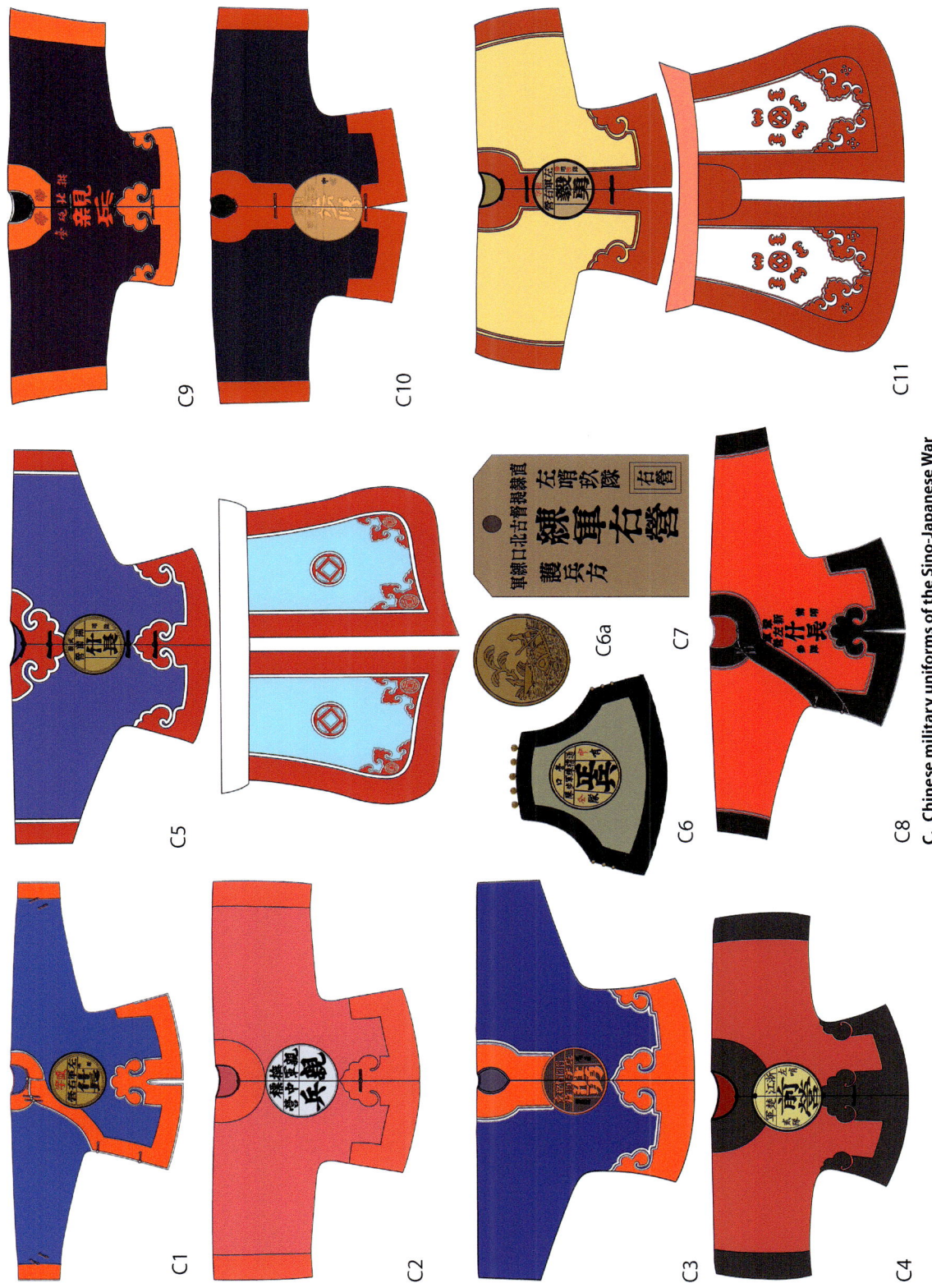

C. Chinese military uniforms of the Sino-Japanese War
See Colour Plate Commentaries for further information.

iii

D. Chinese military flags of the Sino-Japanese War
See Colour Plate Commentaries for further information.

1. Sheng Trained Army Cavalryman
(Illustration by Renato Dalmaso © Helion & Company)
See Colour Plate Commentaries for further information.

2. Resolute Army soldier
(Illustration by Renato Dalmaso © Helion & Company)
See Colour Plate Commentaries for further information.

3. Baoding Trained Army Bodyguard
(Illustration by Renato Dalmaso © Helion & Company)
See Colour Plate Commentaries for further information.

4. Sui Army bodyguard
(Illustration by Renato Dalmaso © Helion & Company)
See Colour Plate Commentaries for further information.

5. Japanese infantryman (front)
(Illustration by Renato Dalmaso © Helion & Company)
See Colour Plate Commentaries for further information.

6. Japanese infantryman (back) (Illustration by Renato Dalmaso © Helion & Company) *See Colour Plate Commentaries for further information.*

7 Japanese infantry captain
(Illustration by Renato Dalmaso © Helion & Company)
See Colour Plate Commentaries for further information.

8. Japanese cavalryman
(Illustration by Renato Dalmaso © Helion & Company)
See Colour Plate Commentaries for further information.

Peacetime Cavalry unit organisation

Unit name	Strength[21]
Battalion (Daitai)	514 men; three companies
Company/squadron (Chutai)	159 men; four platoons
Platoon/troop (Shotai)	Strength varies; four squads
Squad/section	Strength varies

Peacetime Cavalry Battalion Strength[22]

Rank	Strength
Colonel (or Lieutenant Colonel)	1
Majors	1
Captains	4
Lieutenants	7
Second Lieutenants	6
Special Sergeants	3
Sergeant Majors	3
Sergeants	35
Privates	426
Military Doctors	2
Chief Medical Attendants	1
Medical Attendants	3
Veterinarians	2
Accountants/Administrative Staff	2
Farriers	4
Saddler	1
Tailors	7
Cobblers	5
Total	514 (485 combatants, 29 non-combatants)

The Imperial Guard

The Imperial Guard, tasked with protecting the Emperor and the Imperial Family, had its beginnings in the Goshinpei (Honourable Guard Army), which was established in 1863 but disbanded, reestablished, and renamed several times after.[23] The latest rendition of the Goshinpei of 1871 was established before universal conscription was implemented, and was exclusively drawn from men of the Imperial faction domains of Satsuma, Choshu, and Tosa. At this time, many Shogunate feudal lords were still grumbling over their defeat in the Boshin War, and total loyalty could not be expected of them. Thus, the Goshinpei began as a pro-Imperial factional army, safe from the resentments that the former Shogunate-supporting domains cultivated. The Goshinpei was renamed to the Imperial Guard Bureau (Konoe Kyoku) in 1872 but remained organisationally identical to before. But with the gradual

---

21 Xu, *Jundui Tonglan*, p.5.
22 Volpicelli, *China-Japan War*, p.83.
23 'Konoe Shidan', Weblio, <https://www.weblio.jp/wkpja/content/%E8%BF%91%E8%A1%9B%E5%B8%AB%E5%9B%A3_%E8%BF%91%E8%A1%9B%E5%B8%AB%E5%9B%A3%E3%81%AE%E6%A6%82%E8%A6%81>, accessed 7 Feb 2024.

Japanese cavalry scouts in Korea, carrying short carbines and dressed in Attila jackets. Drawn by Georges Ferdinand Bigot. (Public domain)

disbanding of feudal loyalties and the promotion of a unified Japan, the Meiji government felt safe enough to disband the Guard's more feudally organised units and transfer many others to Line units by the end of 1873.[24] The Imperial Guard was then reshaped into a crack force of elite soldiers from all over Japan, as opposed to its original purpose as a pro-Imperial military monopoly.

Unfortunately, the Imperial Guard was not as loyal as had been hoped. In 1878, after the Satsuma Rebellion, Imperial Guardsmen, though liberated from feudal loyalties, were dissatisfied with the poor pay and rewards they received for their service in the war and rebelled, intending to burn down the estate of the Crown Prince. This was, of course, put down, but the fact that the supposedly zealous Imperial Guard had revolted at all was unfathomably embarrassing. The 1878 incident was heavily censored and few even knew of its existence until after World War Two. The 1878 revolt led to the establishment of the Kempeitai Military Police in 1881 and the Imperial Palace Police (Kogu Keisatsu) in 1886 as further safety nets for the Emperor in case the Imperial Guard were to prove disloyal again. The Imperial Palace Police was specifically charged with protecting the Imperial family and was independent from the Japanese military and was instead under civilian police jurisdiction. In 1885, the military Imperial Guard's name was again changed to just the Imperial Guard (Konoe). After 1888, when the IJA organisation

---

24   Heath, *Japan*, pp.42–43.

replaced the garrison (chindai) system with the division (shidan) system, the Imperial Guard was fittingly renamed to the Imperial Guard Division (Konoe Shidan) three years later in 1891. The Imperial Guard would retain that name until it was disbanded in 1945 after World War Two. Today, the men responsible for protecting the Japanese Imperial family are part of the civilian Imperial Palace Police, even though they might be called the 'Imperial Guard.'

The Imperial Guard, at its beginning, was a purely infantry force but eventually included counterparts of all five service branches. Unit organisation for these differed slightly from Line units. The Imperial Guard also received different weapons; the infantry were armed with the Type 22 Murata rifles long before any Line units were, and all Guard artillery units used mountain guns instead of field guns. Eligible recruits for the Imperial Guard had to have six months of Line experience under their belts. Once accepted, Imperial Guardsmen were to serve three years; afterwards, they would serve three and a half years in the Guard reserves, for a total of seven years of service. When the duration of service was increased to 10, 12 and 12 years and four months later in the century, Imperial Guardsmen were to serve in local Line units as substitute for their Second Reserve.

Peacetime Imperial Guard Infantry unit organisation

Unit name	Strength
Regiment (Rendan)	1,608 men; two battalions
Battalion (Daitai)	800 men; four companies
Company (Chutai)	198 men; four platoons
Platoon (Shotai)	Strength varies; four squads
Squad (Buntai)	Strength varies

Peacetime Imperial Guard Artillery Organisation

Unit name	Strength
Regiment (Ryodan)	465 men; two mountain artillery battalions
Battalion (Daitai)	228 men; two companies/batteries; 12 guns
Company/Battery (Chutai)	112 men; three platoons; six guns
Platoon (Shotai)	Strength varies; two guns

Peacetime Imperial Guard Engineers unit organisation

Unit name	Strength
Battalion (Daitai)	260 men; two companies
Company (Chutai)	126 men;

Peacetime Imperial Guard Commissariat unit organisation

Unit name	Strength
Battalion (Daitai)	449 men; two companies
Company (Chutai)	220 men

Peacetime Imperial Guard Cavalry unit organisation

Unit name	Strength
Battalion (Daitai)	485 men; three companies

Company (Chutai)	159 men; four platoons
Platoon (Shotai)	Strength varies; four squads
Squad (Buntai)	Strength varies

The Military Band

The history of Western military music in Japan began in 1853, when Commodore Matthew Perry brought two military bands with his black ships. In the 1850s, the Nagasaki Naval Academy introduced Dutch drum signals to Japanese military men, which was very popular thanks to the traditional use of drums in Japanese warfare. In 1866, when the Satsuma Domain reorganised its army based on the British model, it brought with it the drum and fife. The Shogunate was not far behind but instead had copied French bugle calls into its military by 1867. Upon the arrival of the first French military mission to Japan, both sides gradually began to eschew drum signals in favour of bugles.[25] When the Imperial Japanese Army and Navy were both officially established in 1871, the Army used French bugle signals while the Satsuma-dominated Navy used British ones. This lasted until 1885, when the Emperor forced them to adopt a unified set of bugle calls.[26] Japan's first Western-style military march, 'Miya-san, Miya-san' came in 1868 and although it was originally played by Japanese flutes and drums its purpose as a rhythmic marching song was indubitably European. For decades, this song would serve as the sole musical representative of Japan for the Western world, even being immortalised in the celebrated operetta *The Mikado*.

Full Western-style military bands in Japan took a little longer to develop. They first began in September 1869, when 30 young Satsuma men formed the aptly named Satsuma Band, led by British conductor John William Fenton, who also composed the first version of Japan's national anthem 'Kimigayo.' In 1871, upon the establishment of the Imperial Japanese Army and Navy, these 30 musicians would form the first official military band of the Empire of Japan.

In 1872, the second French military mission to Japan saw the arrival of the French bandmaster Gustave Charles Dragon, and he helped organise the first military music school at the Toyama Military Academy. In 1873, this new military band, conducted by Dragon, performed in front of the Meiji Emperor. The Japanese military authorities were enthralled and invited foreign musicians from abroad, most notably Charles Edouard Gabriel Leroux, who composed many of Japan's most celebrated military marches such as 'Battotai' and 'Fusoka.' Leroux, who had studied at the Paris Conservatory and was a student of Antoine Marmontel, arrived in Japan in 1884 and succeeded Dragon as the head of the military music school. Dragon brought his talents to the navy military band instead. Also noteworthy was the arrival of the German bandmaster Franz Eckert in 1882, who composed the modern melody for the Japanese anthem 'Kimigayo.' Eckert was an old-school authoritarian music teacher, who pushed his Japanese students so

---

25 Masanori Tsujida, *Nihon no Gunka: Kokumin Teki Ongaku no Rekishi*, (Tokyo: Gentosha, 2014), pp.85–91.
26 Tsujida, *Gunka*, pp.85–91.

hard that some of them would collapse from sheer exhaustion.[27] In the 1890s, however, the Japanese military band began to move away from both German and French influence and slowly replaced foreign conductors and composers with Japanese ones, albeit trained in Europe.[28] The Minister of Education, Toyama Shoichi, who wrote the words to Battotai march, encouraged this move, and worked hard to endear the concept of military music, or 'gunka,' into mainstream Japanese society.[29] Popular marches from this period of musical independence include Setoguchi Tokichi's 'Warship March' (Gunkan Koshinkyoku), 'Marching in the Snow' (Yuki no Shingun) by Nagai Kenshi, and 'Thousands of Enemies' (Teki wa Ikuman) by Sakunosuke Koyama. During the Sino-Japanese War, Japanese newspapers solicited submissions from the masses for military songs as a patriotic home front campaign. Interestingly, a majority of these were about battles and events as they happened, making them a kind of news source when performed publicly.[30] The artistic merit of many of these songs was disappointing, however; most were hastily composed, childishly written propaganda pieces written for a cheap buck and have since been forgotten. During the entire Sino-Japanese War around 1,300 military songs were written.[31]

By 1888, there were three full Western-style military bands: one for the IJA military academies, one for the Imperial Guard, and the last for the Fourth Division in Osaka.[32] This situation did not change until the end of the century. In 1891, the military academy band was relocated to the Toyama Military Academy, being renamed to the Toyama Military Academy Military Band. During the Sino-Japanese War, all three bands accompanied the Japanese military to mainland Asia.

The Sanitation Department

The IJA Sanitation Department was the medical service of the IJA. Originally called the 'Gun-i Bu' (Military Medicine Department), its official name was changed to 'Eisei Bu' (Sanitation Department) in 1888.[33] Despite the name change, the Sanitation Department was responsible for more than just maintaining sanitary conditions, and was divided into three branches: military medicine, pharmaceutical medicine, and veterinary medicine. Military doctors, pharmacists, and veterinarians were all considered officers. Managing them were medical officers and medical superintendents, who could serve as head surgeons or hospital directors. The highest ranking pharmaceutical and veterinarian positions were equivalent to that of a second rank medical officer. The surgeon general, officially known as the medical superintendent-general, was in charge of the entire Sanitation Department. The NCOs of the Sanitation Department were the chief medical and pharmaceutical attendants, each of three possible classes. Below them

---

27 Tsujida, *Gunka*, pp.92–101.
28 Tsujida, *Gunka*, pp.92–101.
29 Tsujida, *Gunka*, p.16.
30 Tsujida, *Gunka*, p.61.
31 Tsujida, *Gunka*, p.50.
32 Heath, *Japan*, p.97.
33 Kokuritsu Kobunshokan, Naikaku Sorifu, A15111512100.

were the medical attendants, who essentially served as orderlies, stretcher bearers, caretakers, and custodians in field hospitals. One medical attendant was assigned to each infantry company. Veterinarian attendants did not exist by the time of the Sino-Japanese War; the two positions of horse trainers and veterinary attendants were both abolished in 1886 and their duties reallocated to farriers.

In addition to the medical staff attached to combatant units (see other sections), each IJA division also had its own individual medical department, consisting of a central unit of 11 officers, 93 medical attendants, and 49 horses; a field hospital of eight officers, 108 attendants and 44 horses; and two stretcher-bearer companies of one officer, 155 medical attendants and 48 stretchers (120 in the Imperial Guard).[34] Field hospitals were divided into three types, the first being triage stations which were in charge of receiving and forwarding patients, the second being operating stations for more serious maladies, and finally dressing stations.

On the field, each infantry company had four privates trained in first aid, who could provide some basic treatment to the wounded until the stretcher bearers (also infantry privates) could take them to the rear. These four privates were marked with a special plain red armband on the left upper arm. The stretcher bearer privates were attached at the regimental level; apparently, they were reservists led by combatant officers. Note that stretcher bearers and first aid privates were still considered infantry soldiers and not dedicated medical attendants, and therefore they were expected to carry out their regular infantry duties when their medical expertise was not needed. Furthermore, it appears that the stretcher bearers in divisional stretcher bearer companies were genuine noncombatant medical attendants, not specialised infantry soldiers.

The Hakuaisha, simply translating to 'Benevolence Society' or 'Humane Society,' was a relief organisation founded by Sano Tsunetami to care for the displaced, wounded, and bereaved of the 1877 Satsuma Rebellion. In 1887, the Hakuaisha was admitted to the International Committee of the Red Cross and thereupon renamed the Japanese Red Cross Society. The Japanese Red Cross was able to engage in its first disaster relief effort with the eruption of the volcano Mount Bandai in 1888. During the Sino-Japanese War, the Japanese Red Cross collected donations of food, supplies, and winter clothing for the soldiers as well as providing medical care to both Chinese and Japanese wounded. This humane treatment of Chinese soldiers won Japan great praise from the rest of the world, but unfortunately much of it was a manufactured public relations campaign.[35] When journalists were not around, Chinese wounded often had their throats slit or were shot. The Japanese blamed this on Chinese soldiers pretending to be injured to either sneak attack medical staff or to ransack the Red Cross hospitals.

34　Heath, *Japan*, p.48.
35　Paine, *The Sino-Japanese War*, pp.176–177.

The Kempeitai

The Kempeitai was the military police of the Imperial Japanese Army. Originally the Kempeitai was going to be called the 'Keipeitai' (literally translating to Police Soldier Detachment), but this did not carry through because previous government documents had used the wording 'Kempeitai' (lit. Law Soldier Detachment) to refer to the general task of military policing.[36]

Formed in 1881 as a response to the 1878 Imperial Guard uprising and other disturbances within the army, the Kempeitai was based on the French Gendarmerie and focused on overseeing the conscription process, enforcing discipline within the army and repressing political dissent in the military and later in occupied territories. The Kempeitai was initially staffed with police officers from the Tokyo Metropolitan Police Department who had previous experience in fighting and repressing riots and rebellions. Kempeitai who were stationed in the Japanese home islands were prefixed as 'Imperial Decree' Kempeitai, while those overseas were called 'Military Decree' Kempeitai. This was because those at home were under civilian authority, while those overseas were under military authority.

The Kempeitai rank system was virtually identical to that of the Line army, but the highest rank was that of colonel and there was only one class of private. After Imperial Decree 111 on 15th July 1895 (Meiji 28), the rank of Kempeitai privates was changed to that of Kempeitai superior privates and these superior privates were treated as officers.[37]

The Tondenhei

The Tondenhei, also called the 'Hokkaido Militia,' were colonial militia units composed of former samurai sent to Hokkaido (and eventually other Northern frontier regions) as part of the Tonden system. The Japanese Tonden System, taken from the Chinese 'tuntian' system, translating literally to 'soldiers stationed in fields,' was a form of settler-colonialism in which the Tondenhei and their families would relocate to Hokkaido and develop self-sustaining agricultural colonies that were capable of militarily defending themselves. The purpose of the Tondenhei was twofold: first, to serve as soldiers to deter potential invasion from the indigenous Ainu people or foreign powers like Russia; and second, to serve as farmers to cultivate and settle the land, contributing to the expansion and stabilisation of Japanese territory.[38] Initially, the Tondenhei was exclusive to the samurai class to provide them an honourable means for subsistence, but beginning in 1891, commoners were able to apply.

Upon joining, Tondenhei soldiers and their families were awarded a plot of land, a house, agricultural equipment, household goods, weapons, and three years' supplies. Transported to Hokkaido gratis by the Japanese government, Tondenhei soldiers established village 'colonies,' which were

---

36 'Kempei', Weblio, <https://www.weblio.jp/wkpja/content/%E6%86%B2%E5%85%B5+%28%E6%97%A5%E6%9C%AC%E8%BB%8D%29_%E6%86%B2%E5%85%B5+%28%E6%97%A5%E6%9C%AC%E8%BB%8D%29%E3%81%AE%E6%A6%82%E8%A6%81>, accessed 7 Feb 2024.
37 Kokuritsu Kobunshokan, Naikaku Sorifu, Ref.A15112957900.
38 Heath, *Japan*, pp.48–49.

governed locally by a military council elected by the soldiery. Furthermore, Tondenhei soldiers received special tax exemption and property right privileges. Unsurprisingly, the Tondenhei had a stricter set of criteria for joining compared to the regular army; approximately 33% of all Tondenhei applicants were accepted. As they had a dual role as both farmers and soldiers, Tondenhei soldiers had to have two or more family members willing to join them in Hokkaido.[39] Debtors, those with criminal records, those who lived in the area of recruitment for less than a year, and those whose children were below one year old were turned away. The ages of service for Tondenhei soldiers was initially from 18 to 35, but in 1885 this was changed to 17 to 30, and finally in 1890 to 17 to 25. In reality, the informality of Tondenhei colonies meant that soldiers might be well below or above these ages. The official term of service for a Tondenhei soldier was 40 years in 1885, and 20 in 1890. If a Tondenhei soldier died or was unable to serve, a substitute was to be found to complete his term. Additionally, the Tondenhei also maintained its own first and second Reserve, which was part of soldiers' terms of service.[40] In 1890, soldiers had to serve three years in the regular Tondenhei, four in the Tondenhei first Reserve and their remaining thirteen in the second. After these twenty years, Tondenhei soldiers were supposed to serve another 10 years in the supplementary service (see Conscription) by being on call for emergencies in the case of war.

The Tondenhei did not participate in the Sino-Japanese War. For most of the war they remained in Hokkaido as a reserve, but in March 1895 some Tondenhei units were mobilised as the temporarily formed 7th Division and called up to the front.[41] They reached Aomori in April via steamship and then Tokyo by train. They were officially incorporated into the 1st Army on 30 April, but the war ended before they arrived in mainland Asia. The Tondenhei were sent home having seen no action in June, and the 7th Division disbanded on 22 June 1895. But by the end of the Sino-Japanese War, Hokkaido was no longer a sparsely populated border region and now could raise its own regular army through conscription, which it did. The permanent Seventh Division was formed in 1896 and began to gradually augment and absorb the Tondenhei garrison until the abolishment of the entire Tondenhei System in 1904, followed by the abolition of the exclusive land rights and tax exemptions held by Tondenhei soldiers in 1906.

The Tondenhei rank system was essentially a parallel of the Line Army's, with the only real difference being that Tondenhei unit ranks were prefixed with 'Tonden' (e.g. Rikugun Tonden Hohei Shosa, meaning 'Army Tondenhei Infantry Major'), up to the rank of colonel. All five branches except the commissariat of the Line IJA had their Tondenhei counterparts, but some of the ranks did not carry over. For example, the Tondenhei did not have engineering or artillery supervisors, nor did they have dedicated

---

39 'Tondenhei,' Tonden, <https://tonden.org/wiki/index.php?title=%E5%B1%AF%E7%94%B0%E5%85%B5>, accessed 23 March 2024.
40 Heath, *Japan*, p.49.
41 'Tondenhei Seido,' Tonden, <https://tonden.org/wiki/index.php?title=%E5%B1%AF%E7%94%B0%E5%85%B5%E5%88%B6%E5%BA%A6>, accessed 23 March 2024.

cobblers, metal casters, or tailors (probably because these positions could be easily fulfilled by soldiers' families or colonist civilians). The Tondenhei did have legal provisions for their own military police, uncreatively called the 'Tondenhei Kempeitai.' However, given the general informality and lax enforcement of regulations within Tondenhei colonies, military police duties were carried out according to the wishes of local officials, and there was no specialised Tondenhei Kempeitai service branch.

In 1891, the Tondenhei in total had four infantry battalions, one artillery company of six guns, one company of engineers, and one squad of cavalry. Because of their numerical inferiority, Tondenhei unit organisation was quite different from Line Army organisation. Given the different needs of each Tondenhei village, infantry battalions could consist of anywhere from two to eight companies. Furthermore, their artillery, engineer and cavalry units were referred to as 'corps' in English due to there only being one of each.

Total strength

Fortunately, the IJA was much more organised than their Chinese counterpart, so total estimates of pre-war IJA strength are far more accurate (and easier) to compile.[42] In December 1893, the regular IJA had about 63,000 men, but on the eve of the war in 1894 this was increased to 67,000 men, and then 90,000 upon mobilisation[43]. At its peak, the IJA reached some 161,000 men during the First Sino-Japanese War, mostly reservists being called up to perform garrison duty in the absence of the regular army.

Organisation of the Imperial Japanese Army in December 1893

Division	Brigade and headquarters	Infantry	Artillery	Fortress Artillery	Engineers	Commissariat	Cavalry
Imperial Guard	None	Four regiments	One regiment	None	One company	One battalion	One battalion
1st Division (Tokyo)	1st Brigade (Tokyo); 2nd Brigade (Sakura)	1st (Tokyo) and 15th (Takasaki) Regiments; 2nd (Sakura) and 3rd (Tokyo) Regiments	One regiment	Two battalions	One battalion	One battalion	One battalion
2nd Division (Sendai)	3rd Brigade (Sendai); 4th Brigade (Aomori)	4th (Sendai) and 16th (Shibata) Regiments; 5th (Aomori) and 17th (Sendai) Regiments	One regiment	None	One battalion	One battalion	One company, two platoons
3rd Division (Nagoya)	5th Brigade (Nagoya); 6th Brigade (Kanazawa)	6th (Nagoya) and 18th (Toyohashi) Regiments; 7th (Kanazawa) and 19th (Nagoya) Regiments	One regiment	None	One battalion	One battalion	One company, two platoons

---

42 Inouye Jukichi, *The Japan-China War : on the Regent's Sword : Kinchow, Port Arthur, and Talienwan* (Yokohama : Kelly & Walsh, 1895), pp.26–32. All total strength tables here are from this source, but with arithmetic errors corrected.
43 Heath, *Japan*, p.41.

Division	Brigade and headquarters	Infantry	Artillery	Fortress Artillery	Engineers	Commissariat	Cavalry
4th Division (Osaka)	7th Brigade (Osaka); 8th Brigade (Himeji)	8th (Osaka) and 9th (Otsu) Regiments; 10th (Himeji) and 20th (Osaka) Regiments	One regiment	None	One battalion	One battalion	Two companies
5th Division (Hiroshima)	9th Brigade (Hiroshima); 10th Brigade (Matsuyama)	11th (Hiroshima) and 21st (Hiroshima) Regiments; 12th (Marugame) and 22nd (Matsuyama) Regiments	One regiment	None	One battalion	One battalion	One company, two platoons
6th Division (Kumamoto)	11th Brigade (Kumamoto); 12th Brigade (Kokura)	13th (Kumamoto) and 23rd Regiments (Kumamoto); 14th (Kokura) and 24th Regiments (Fukuoka)	One regiment	One battalion	One battalion	One battalion	Two companies

Imperial Guard strength, as of 31st December 1893

Type	General and Field Officers	Officers	Cadets	Non-commissioned Officers	Enlisted	Total men
Infantry	20	165	47	426	5,655	6,313
Cavalry	1	14	6	33	288	342
Artillery	3	26	9	53	377	468
Engineers	1	10	6	25	192	234
Commissariat	1	15	0	38	174	228
Military Band	0	1	0	12	39	52
Total	26	231	68	587	6,725	7,637

1st Division strength, as of 31st December 1893

Type	General and Field Officers	Officers	Cadets	Non-commissioned Officers	Enlisted	Total men
Infantry (Tokyo)	12	113	28	254	2,785	3,192
Cavalry (Tokyo)	1	12	6	33	258	310
Artillery (Tokyo)	4	36	6	63	556	665
Engineers (Tokyo)	1	14	7	34	313	369
Commis-sariat (Tokyo)	1	18	0	40	301	360
Infantry (Takasaki)	6	59	13	142	1,371	1,591
Infantry (Sakura)	6	55	15	137	1,379	1,592
Fortress Artillery (Yokosuka)	4	32	18	80	917	1,051
Total	35	339	93	783	7,880	9,130

2nd Division strength, as of 31st December 1893

Type	General and Field Officers	Officers	Cadets	Non-commissioned Officers	Enlisted	Total men
Infantry (Sendai)	12	120	24	289	2,753	3,198
Cavalry (Sendai)	1	15	3	28	265	312
Artillery (Sendai)	4	37	6	69	566	682
Engineers (Sendai)	1	15	6	36	315	373
Commissariat (Sendai)	1	18	0	46	300	365
Infantry (Shibata)	6	57	11	147	1,382	1,603
Infantry (Aomori)	6	55	11	136	1,382	1,590
Total	31	317	61	751	6,963	8,123

THE ARMY OF THE EMPIRE OF JAPAN

3rd Division strength, as of 31st December 1893

Type	General and Field Officers	Officers	Cadets	Non-commissioned Officers	Enlisted	Total men
Infantry (Nagoya)	12	111	25	303	2,773	3,224
Cavalry (Nagoya)	1	14	4	32	265	316
Artillery (Nagoya)	4	33	5	74	564	680
Engineers (Nagoya)	1	13	6	35	315	370
Commissariat (Nagoya)	1	18	0	41	301	361
Infantry (Toyohashi)	6	55	13	144	1,391	1,609
Infantry (Kanazawa)	6	56	12	149	1,376	1,599
Total	31	300	65	778	6,985	8,159

4th Division strength, as of 31st December 1893

Type	General and Field Officers	Officers	Cadets	Non-commissioned Officers	Enlisted	Total men
Infantry (Osaka)	12	116	22	283	2,774	3,207
Cavalry (Osaka)	1	15	5	37	265	323
Artillery (Osaka)	4	35	6	68	561	674
Commissariat (Osaka)	1	19	0	43	301	364
Military band (Osaka)	0	0	0	13	37	50
Infantry (Otsu)	6	62	11	130	1,383	1,592
Infantry (Himeji)	6	59	10	146	1,381	1,602
Engineers (Fushimi)	1	16	7	36	318	378
Total	31	322	61	756	7,020	8,190

5th Division strength, as of 31st December 1893

Type	General and Field Officers	Officers	Cadets	Non-commissioned Officers	Enlisted	Total men
Infantry (Hiroshima)	12	117	19	289	2,770	3,207
Cavalry (Hiroshima)	1	14	4	35	262	316
Artillery (Hiroshima)	4	35	6	75	562	682
Engineers (Hiroshima)	1	13	7	36	317	374
Commissariat (Hiroshima)	1	19	0	41	297	358
Infantry (Marugame)	6	57	10	146	1,398	1,617
Infantry (Matsuyama)	6	61	9	145	1,392	1,613
Total	31	316	55	767	6,998	8,167

6th Division strength, as of 31st December 1893

Types	General and Field Officers	Officers	Cadets	Non-commissioned Officers	Enlisted	Total men
Infantry (Kumamoto)	12	105	25	277	2,657	3,076
Cavalry (Kumamoto)	1	13	4	30	264	312
Artillery (Kumamoto)	4	35	6	67	556	668
Engineers	1	15	4	35	317	372
Commissariat (Kumamoto)	1	17		46	299	363
Infantry (Kokura)	6	55	13	145	1,381	1,600
Infantry (Fukuoka)	6	57	12	144	1,379	1,598
Infantry (Okinawa)	0	5	0	12	112	129
Fortress Artillery (Akamagaseki)	1	15	17	55	463	551
Infantry (Tsushima)	1	12	0	31	189	233
Total	33	329	81	842	7,617	8,902

Kempeitai strength, as of 31st December 1893

Type	Field Officers	Officers	Non-commissioned Officers	Enlisted	Total men
Kempeitai (Tokyo)	1	10	78	175	264
Kempeitai (Sendai)	1	6	39	91	137
Kempeitai (Nagoya)	1	7	45	104	157
Kempeitai (Osaka)	1	9	54	155	219
Kempeitai (Hiroshima)	1	6	42	87	136
Kempeitai (Kumamoto)	1	6	40	89	136
Total:	6	44	298	701	1,049

Tondenhei strength, as of 31st December 1893

Types	General and Field Officers	Officers	Non-commissioned officers	Enlisted	Total men
Infantry	4	59	244	3,381	3,688
Cavalry	0	4	8	117	129
Artillery	0	3	10	85	98
Engineers	0	3	11	83	97
Total	4	69	273	3,666	4,012

Total Imperial Japanese Army strength, as of 31st December 1893

	General and Field Officers	Officers	Cadets	Non-commissioned Officers	Enlisted	Total men
Infantry	168	1599	330	4088	42255	48,440
Cavalry	7	101	32	236	1984	2,360
Artillery	32	287	79	614	5207	6,219
Engineers	7	99	43	248	2170	2,567
Commissariat	7	124	0	295	1973	2,399
Infantry (Tsushima)	1	12	0	31	189	233
Military band	0	1	0	25	76	102
Kempeitai	6	44	0	298	701	1,049
Total	228	2,267	484	5,835	54,555	63,369

1st Reserve strength, as of 31st December 1893

Division	General Officers	Field Officers	Officers	Non-commissioned Officers	Infantry	Cavalry	Artillery	Engineers	Commissariat	Other	Total men
1st Division	12	23	89	670	9,625	423	1,319	549	258	3,175	16,143
2nd Division	2	5	63	955	12,116	152	878	375	193	3,181	17,920
3rd Division	3	17	89	460	9,474	129	816	402	219	3,030	14,639
4th Division	1	23	64	610	9,785	213	876	489	313	3,008	15,382
5th Division	4	24	87	788	9,220	141	829	389	222	2,916	14,620
6th Division	1	12	68	571	10,071	205	1,494	478	260	2,866	16,026
Total	23	104	460	4,054	60,291	1,263	6,212	2,682	1,465	18,176	94,730

2nd Reserve strength, as of 31st December 1893

Division	Field Officers	Officers	Non commissioned Officers	Infantry	Cavalry	Artillery	Engineers	Commissariat	Other	Total men
1st Division	14	71	397	9,215	517	805	426	164	8,820	20,429
2nd Division	5	35	283	8,385	53	600	186	102	10,576	20,225
3rd Division	10	53	294	7,722	37	551	180	75	7,326	16,248
4th Division	6	53	225	8,278	18	759	365	109	6,567	16,380
5th Division	12	48	253	6,594	21	506	146	89	8,934	16,603
6th Division	10	40	330	6,737	14	749	388	85	7,815	16,168
Total	57	300	1,782	46,931	660	3,970	1,691	624	50,038	106,053

Military culture

Frequently, the average Japanese soldier of this period is depicted as a patriotic, stalwart individual with a near suicidal devotion to his Emperor. These qualities are customarily credited to Japan's samurai 'Bushido' tradition; public adoration of the samurai values of courage, honesty, and loyalty remain unceasing even today. Cinematic portrayals of samurai stabbing themselves in the gut as a preferable alternative to 'dishonour' or throwing away obvious advantages in battle for being too sneaky are good fun, but in reality 'Bushido' never existed as a universally followed code of honour, and was not even in vogue as a phrase until after the Meiji period.[44] The commendable ardour of the Japanese soldier did not occur naturally; in reality, the Imperial Japanese Army's starting situation was just as divided and disjointed as that of the Chinese armies. The unity and esprit de corps of the Imperial Japanese Army was the result of decades of carefully constructed social engineering and propaganda, not some omnipresent Oriental mysticism or inscrutable 'warrior spirit.'

Clans, Classes and Cleavages

For hundreds of years, the population of Japan had been strictly segregated into feudal classes. The samurai acted as the professional warrior class, but after the end of the Sengoku period in 1615, the samurai began to ease into peaceable work as scholars, bureaucrats, and government officials.[45] Regardless, they retained their special status and enjoyed numerous social privileges in Japanese society, although accomplished officials or civil servants could be awarded the honorary title of 'samurai.' Nevertheless, for the most part non-samurai remained disenfranchised, as they could not bear surnames, ride horses or carry swords in public. This strict class system did not benefit all samurai. Less wealthy samurai sometimes even renounced their status to become farmers, craftsmen or artisans. Their elite

---

[44] Rich, Bushido: Way of Total Bullshit, Tofugu (2014), <https://www.tofugu.com/japan/bushido/>, accessed 24 March 2024.

[45] Nick Komiya, 'Imperial Rescript to Soldiers and Sailors', War Relics (2017), <https://www.warrelics.eu/forum/japanese-militaria/imperial-rescript-soldiers-sailors-687558/>, accessed 12 Feb. 2024.

warrior status returned during the Boshin War, where they formed the bulk of the professional soldiers, though augmented by peasant conscript armies. In 1871, the nascent Imperial Japanese Army continued to draw recruits exclusively from the samurai class, even though the samurai made up less than 10% of the entire Japanese population, which was problematic. Also problematic was the enduring legacy of the Japanese feudal domains and their social influence. Japanese samurai retained strong ties to their domain or clan, many of which had actually opposed the Meiji Emperor and were only half-heartedly obeying his edicts. Their loyalty was so distrusted that the Imperial Guard, a force consisting of domains loyal to the Emperor independent of the army, was formed.

Similarly to the Qing, these significant cleavages in the Imperial Japanese Army proved a formidable obstacle to its successful operation. The departure of feudalism in Japan began to erode the samurai's monopoly over the wealth and prestige in society. Now that class mobility was possible, the samurai saw their dominant position being threatened by wealthy merchants and farmers, who could also purchase or gain the honorary title of samurai. Furthermore, the injection of Western philosophy and institutions into Japan seemed to many samurai to be a betrayal of the 'sonno joi' policy that had attracted them to the Imperial cause in the first place.

The Meiji began to slowly undermine the samurai's feudal and economic privileges in society. In 1870 the introduction of the rising sun flag as a standard issue military banner was meant to be a symbolic act of unity, and the samurai who had proudly carried their domain or family crests into battle for the past hundred years grumbled. An attempt was made at universal conscription in 1870, but after near-universal opposition from all classes it was scrapped. A year later the traditional samurai haircut was also banned, leading to violent riots in which six men were executed. These symbolic gestures were already appalling enough, but the Meiji government was far from finished in its reforms. In 1869 the Satsuma and Choshu domains willingly ceded their property and population to the control of the national government, and in 1871 all other domains were expected to follow suit to centralise Japanese administration. Landowning samurai lost all of their feudal estates and traditional incomes. The government offered some consolation prizes; the establishment of the Tondenhei colonial militia in Northern Hokkaido (and later Karafuto) to defend against Russian aggression served a dual purpose of employing disgruntled samurai who had lost their social status and livelihoods.[46] The Meiji government also provided the disgruntled samurai with a meagre stipend (and later government bonds) and the class label of 'shizoku' (warrior families). These did not solve the disaffection of the samurai; not all of them wanted to move to Hokkaido, the stipends could not compare to the vast wealth of their ancestors, and shizoku was simply a demographic classification and possessed no special prerogative. To add insult to injury, in 1876 samurai were barred from wearing swords in public. Some samurai, especially those of the Meiji political elite or

---

46 Heath, *Japan*, p.106.

those in commerce, were perfectly fine with this and integrated themselves into modern society. Many others were not, and the intensification of anti-government sentiment among samurai was inevitable.

In late 1872, the infamous Conscription Edict required that all men in their twenties, regardless of feudal class, be responsible for the defence of the nation and thus serve a three year military service, with the first draft in 1873. The eradication of the samurai's privilege as an elite warrior class was the final straw. The samurai took issue with the fact that their special status as warriors was being infringed upon by dirty commoners, and likewise the dirty commoners did not want to lose their strong and healthy young men who formed the direly needed labour force in Japanese agricultural and artisan communities. And, of course, the commoners did not want to fight to begin with; the rich could literally buy their way out of being conscripted, which led to class tensions. Other concurrent social reformations helped fan these flames. The imposition of mandatory schooling for all children in 1872 was intended to create a patriotic and literate population, but Japanese families were again uncomfortable with losing farm or home labour. The emancipation of the Confucianist 'untouchable' class (burakumin) in 1871 also did not sit well with a society that had relied on these divisions for hundreds of years. Finally, in the Conscription Edict of 1872, some enthusiastic Francophile had used the gnomic aphorism 'blood tax' as an allegory for the national duty of each and every Japanese to fight for the Emperor. This rhetorical flourish was lost on the majority of the Japanese public and interpreted as a literal extraction of Japanese blood to sell to foreign barbarians.

This culminated in the so-called Blood Tax Riots, in which hundreds of rioters were brutally killed by the Japanese government. This shameful display would be only the first of many, as the samurai attempted to restore their ruling position. The samurai had hoped that an invasion of Korea would bring back their traditional privileges, but when this idea was completely shut down in 1874, numerous samurai of the former Saga Domain rose up and attempted to incite a popular uprising and restore the Shogunate. This failed completely, and although the Saga rebels were butchered by Imperial troops, their deaths did not succeed in enacting any conciliatory measures for reactionaries. The Saga Rebellion would be followed by almost 30 others with similar cause and result. The most substantial and final samurai insurrection was the Satsuma Rebellion of 1877, led by the famous Saigo Takamori. The Satsuma Domain had been one of the most ardent supporters of the Meiji Restoration, but even they were upset by the sweeping changes to Japanese society and culture. Takamori was a strong proponent of invading Korea, even offering to be assassinated in Korea as an excuse for war, but when this was rejected, he resigned from all government positions along with some 600 samurai. These frustrated samurai found home and employment in the Satsuma Domain, where Takamori was publicly supported by the samurai-dominated government. By 1876, the Satsuma had its own de facto private army and government, which caused consternation in the Imperial government. Confessions (extracted by torture) regarding a potential assassination of Takamori and a botched attempt by Imperial authorities to confiscate Satsuma weapons escalated the affair into open warfare. Saigo

A follicularly gifted officer posing with his wife at a wedding. He wears the double-breasted full dress jacket and pants, plus a decorative sash and a sabre. His ceremonial Type One kepi is adorned with a plume. (Public domain)

Takamori was hesitant to contest the Emperor's authority, but after some rebel successes in raiding Imperial armouries, he was persuaded to come out of his retirement.

The successful, though expensive and difficult, crushing of the Satsuma Rebellion proved that a conscript-based army was a worthy fighting force and continued the Westernisation of Japanese society. But even with the pacification of the samurai feudal class, the loyalty and devotion of the Imperial Army was extremely suspect. Though the Imperial Army had beaten the Satsuma rebels, they had done so with much unnecessary loss of life and numerous tactical blunders. The situation was so bad that in 1878 the Imperial Guard rose up in revolt after controversy over payments for service in the Satsuma Rebellion. The Imperial Guard uprising was crushed but given that they were specifically handpicked from the most fanatically loyal of the fanatically loyal, the fact that the rebellion had happened at all was telling of the Empire's unpopularity. The incident was covered up and heavily censored until the end of World War Two.

After the 1878 revolt, the Imperial Army was a burlap doll stitched together from various levels of Japanese society, from lowly farmers to haughty former samurai. Even if they were not actively mutinying, loyalty among the ranks was extremely lacking. Esprit de corps was even worse, as centuries of feudal divisions had led to the quasi-speciation of the samurai and the commoners. For the IJA to become a reliable and effective fighting force, massive amounts of indoctrination were required. The primary architect of this was Lieutenant General Yamagata Aritomo, a Choshu native, who issued a propaganda pamphlet called the 'Lesson to Soldiers and Sailors' (Gunjin Kunkai) mere months after the 1878 revolt. In it, he compared the IJA to a young boy: strong and healthy, but lacking in maturity, discipline, and wisdom. The pamphlet emphasised three core values of loyalty, courage and obedience (chujitsu, yukan, and fukuju) to be followed by all. Furthermore, the IJA had seen the effects of charismatic military leadership with Saigo Takamori, and Yamagata included a lengthy oration in his pamphlet laying the foundation for the Emperor Meiji's cult of personality. A simple pamphlet was but the first engagement in the war for the hearts and minds of the IJA, and in 1882 Emperor Meiji officially issued the famous 'Rescript to Soldiers and Sailors' (Gunjun Chokuyu). The Rescript was ghostwritten by Nishi Amane, a scholar of both Eastern and Western political philosophy who had served as advisor to the previous Shogun. The Rescript instructed the IJA (and IJN) to live their lives by five main principles: loyalty, respect, courage, righteousness, and frugality. In its emphasis on loyalty to the Emperor, the Rescript also contained the famous quotation 'duty is heavier than a mountain, whilst death is lighter than a feather.' Much of this propaganda was reprinted in the paybook of IJA regulars, such that only the last few pages contained the soldier's personal information. Japanese soldiers were required to memorise every single word of the entire Rescript and be able to recite any precept at any time, essentially making it the Little Red Book of the Meiji military. This, along with the invention of the so-called 'Bushido', began to foster loyalty, patriotism, and pride within the Imperial Japanese Army.

The political indoctrination in the military was not enough. Unlike the Qing, the Meiji government saw the need to alter all of Japanese society, not just the army. The mandatory schooling instituted by the government meant that young men and women were swayed by patriotic propaganda embedded within textbooks, teachers, and the curriculum. Popular media promoted loyalty to the government above personal interests, and dissenting opinions were censored. Emperor Meiji himself travelled around Japan and made sure to make as many public appearances as possible in both military and civil ceremonies to cultivate his cult of personality as a living god. Taking heed of class tensions that had arisen because of the rich's ability to escape conscription through payment or education, the IJA abolished exemptions for the draft for all cases besides total mental or physical incapability. Additionally, the IJA began to attract a steady stream of volunteers from agricultural communities. Japanese farmers had to work backbreaking hours in the sun and could only afford to eat brown rice and sleep on hay. Army life was infinitely easier, and there was an infinite supply of luxurious white rice to eat and beds to sleep on, to the point where Japanese farmers began to look upon soldiers as spoiled brats. These material benefits, along with the constant ideological and nationalist propaganda being dished out at every possible opportunity, gradually constructed a unified, faithful, and well-motivated Japanese army, just in time for the Sino-Japanese War.

Conscription

The first modern conscription act was issued in 1870, calling for feudal lords to raise five soldiers per 10,000 koku (the amount of rice one man consumed per year). These men initially were to be recruited from both samurai and commoners, but after unanimous opposition from both groups, only samurai were to be recruited.[47]

Japanese social reformers did not wait long, however, and in 1873 the Conscription Edict was promulgated throughout Japan, calling for universal conscription of all men aged between 20 and 40 to serve in either the army or navy. First, they would serve three years in the active army (jobigun), then two in the First Reserve (yobigun), and finally another two in the Second Reserve (kobigun), also called the territorial army. The First Reserve was to be called up in times of war to bring the active army up to full strength, while the Second Reserve was only reserved for emergencies. NCOs, however, served their entire term of seven years in the active army, and thus did not need to join the reserves. Active army conscripts were divided into the branches of service by their height and strength; the strongest and tallest became artillerymen, followed by cavalrymen, infantrymen, engineers, and commissariat personnel. Some soldiers drew special lots of 'supplementary service' and did not have to join the active army but were to remain on call at any time for one year and were not exempt from their four years in the reserves after supplementary service ended.

---

47   Heath, *Japan*, pp.36–39.

Initially, the unpopularity of the 1873 Conscription Edict meant that it was very loosely enforced. Potential conscripts who were heads of families, acting heads of families, oldest sons, only sons, only grandsons, the brother of a wounded or killed, teachers, priests, and so on were exempt from service. Until 1883, wealthier conscripts could pay a commutation fee of 270 yen to avoid being drafted. Additionally, in certain territories conscription was enforced much later than in mainland Japan; for example, Okinawa did not have to fear the draft until 1898, Hokkaido and the Bonin Islands until 1887, and the Sakishima Islands until 1902. Some Japanese fled to these regions to draft-dodge, while others injured themselves intentionally or simply refused to attend the drawing of lots. Consequently, conscription was not very effective in building an army, and up to 53 percent of a year's potential recruitment could be jettisoned due to exemptions, malingering, or other excuses. For example, in 1887 out of 777,972 available conscripts there were 303,948 exemptions.

As the financial situation of the IJA improved, they could afford to feed, train, and equip more soldiers. Subsequently, enforcement of the Conscription Edict became stricter and most exemption requests based on the family system were denied. In 1879 the period of a conscript's service was extended from seven years to ten, comprising three years in the active army, three in the First Reserve and four in the second. Supplementary service was briefly changed to a period of 90 days in 1875, but this was changed back to one year in 1879. Additionally, the Kokumin Gun, translating roughly to 'National People's Army' or 'National Militia,' was established in the 1870s for those who were otherwise healthy mentally and physically but still found reasons for exemption. In theory, the Kokumin Gun was to be a kind of national guard militia and a third reserve force if both the active army and the first two reserves failed. However, in practice, the Kokumin Gun contributed little to the military establishment other than existing and drilling infrequently.

In 1883, the period of conscripts' service was finally changed to 23 years. Men who drew active service numbers and were not exempt would serve in the Kokumin Gun from ages 17 to 20 for three years, then three years in the active army, then four in the First Reserve, five in the second, and finally eight again in the Kokumin Gun. Men who drew supplementary service lots would serve again in the Kokumin Gun for three years from 17–20, one year in supplementary service, six in the First Reserve, five in the second, and then eight in the Kokumin Gun. Finally, those who were exempted from active service but were otherwise mentally and physically suitable would serve in the Kokumin Gun for three years, in the Second Reserve for 12 years, and then return to the Kokumin Gun for eight years. Students aged 17–26 who had graduated government schools or had passed military examinations only had to serve one year in the active army, two years in the First Reserve and five in the second. Students from non-government schools who had studied either law or political economy served six years in the active army, seven in the First Reserve, and three in the second. Reservists also had to attend sixty days at most (usually half that) of training, plus one day of inspection if in the First Reserve. The number of supplementary servicemen was also required to

A Japanese sentry looks pensively at the camera while on duty at the port of Busan after the conclusion of the Korea campaign. His rifle appears to be a Snider-Enfield, identifying him as a member of the reserves, left behind in Korea to pacify the civilian population and the Donghak Rebellion. His summer uniform is characteristically austere in terms of detail and decoration. The man next to him is a Korean civilian. Photographed by Georges Ferdinand Bigot. (Public domain)

be 40 percent of active army manpower. Finally, in 1889, the exemption rules were reduced to virtually nothing except physical or mental disability, and with much less complaint because by this time the institution of mandatory military service had been firmly implanted with Japanese society.

Interservice rivalry

The infamous interservice rivalry between the Imperial Japanese Army and Imperial Japanese Navy was initially due to tensions between former feudal domains, especially the Choshu Domain and the Satsuma Domain. Both domains had a sour relationship, despite their alliance of necessity during the Boshin War. This originated at the decisive Battle of Sekigahara in 1600, when the Tokugawa Clan secured a victory against an enemy alliance which included Choshu and Satsuma. The two clans cast the blame on each other, but their dislike of the Shogunate status quo superseded their feudal tensions enough for them to fight together in the Boshin War. After the Meiji Restoration, IJA officers were mainly recruited from Choshu men, while the IJN was dominated by those from the Satsuma Domain.[48] The two domains retained their grudges, and many officers only recruited those who were from their own feudal domain and rejected those who were not, regardless of qualification. These feudal tensions, called 'hanbatsu' (meaning 'domainism' or 'domain cliques'), were intense in the early years of the Meiji military but gradually lost their fire. Eventually, graduates of the Japanese Army War

---

48 'Hanbatsu', Japanese Wiki, <https://www.japanesewiki.com/history/Hanbatsu%20(domain%20clique).html>, accessed 24 March 2024.

Colleges and Naval Academies, regardless of former feudal allegiances, began to be welcomed in both branches as their educational experience was direly needed. For example, famous IJA generals from the Satsuma Domain, like Oyama Iwao and Nozu Michitsura, gained positive reputations even among Choshu colleagues for their efforts. Thus, by the time of the Sino-Japanese War, hanbatsu was steadily diminishing as a factor in the interservice rivalry.

The interservice rivalry found other reasons to continue. Japan, though spending a majority of her gross domestic product on the military, never had enough funds to satisfy both branches.[49] Inevitably, this led to omnipresent battles over budgetary allocations. The army believed itself to be the face of the Imperial Japanese military and the most popular and well-known defenders of the Emperor, but the navy worked hard to improve its public image as well as stress the strategic importance of a strong navy. Moreover, many IJA leaders like Yamagata Aritomo had a distrust of politicians and democratic institutions for their corruption and perfidy, and as a result those involved in party politics were barred from holding high positions in the Army. In contrast, the navy formed alliances with civilian politicians to secure funding and support. Additionally, the Army primarily recruited from rural or agricultural communities, while the Navy targeted urban populations, thus bringing in all the prejudices associated with rural bumpkins and city slickers.

Finally, the Meiji Constitution had stipulated that the Emperor was to have paramount authority in all affairs of war, while being counselled by the Army and the Navy. Both branches had a General Staff which could bypass civilian governmental organs and directly report to the Emperor and, in theory, any disagreements between the two were to be mediated by the Emperor himself. No other laws or procedures existed for interservice conflict resolution beyond that. During the Sino-Japanese War, Emperor Meiji and other powerful statesmen managed to keep a relatively firm grip over the IJA and IJN. Regrettably, they were not immortal, and subsequent emperors were reduced to the position of figureheads. Thus, before and during the Sino-Japanese War, the IJA and IJN, besides exchanging a bit of sarcastic persiflage, had a generally functional relationship, but afterwards the IJA and IJN began to operate as independent political entities, allowing the interservice rivalry to metastasise.

Luckily, this did not happen during the First Sino-Japanese War – for the most part. The IJA and IJN clashed on a variety of minor issues; for example, they refused to share the same names for ranks or departments. The IJA medical service was named the 'Sanitation Department' (Eisei Bu) to set itself apart from the IJN's 'Military Medicine Department' (Gun-i Bu), and IJA paymasters were called 'auditors' (kantoku) to avoid being called 'paymasters' (shukei) like in the navy. An amusing trade of snarky remarks occurred at an interservice conference held right before the Sino-Japanese War discussing potential troubles in the Korean campaign.[50] The IJA General

---

49   Ernest May (ed.) et. al, *History and Neorealism* (Cambridge: Cambridge University Press, 2010), pp. 187–188.
50   David Evans et al., *Kaigun: Strategy, Tactics, and Technology in the Imperial Japanese Navy, 1887–1941* (Annapolis: Naval Institute Press, 1997), p.25.

Kawakami Soroku was elaborating passionately on how the IJA would be the deciding factor in the war when Captain Yamamoto Gombei, then the chief of the IJN Ministry secretariat, interrupted to ask about the IJA's engineer corps. General Kawakami responded that they were first rate and then asked why in the seven hells was this relevant. Yamamoto smugly replied that if the IJA were planning to get to Korea without the navy, they would have to build quite a long bridge.

These petty name changes and exchanges of witty banter were innocuous, but the interservice rivalry showed its true destructive potential with the handling of the beriberi disease. Beriberi, also known as thiamine or vitamin B1 deficiency, can be caused by a consistent diet of white rice or other refined carbohydrates. Unfortunately, a white-rice based diet was common to the rank and file of both the Japanese army and navy before the 1880s, and beriberi ravaged the ranks.[51] The most common illness suffered by IJA soldiers during the Sino-Japanese War was beriberi, followed by dysentery, gastric catarrh and cholera. Cholera had the highest mortality rate (58.5 percent) by far, compared to beriberi (11.3 percent). However, beriberi deaths must have been much higher since they were frequently mislabelled as gastric catarrh or other gastrointestinal or nutritional diseases, which had similar symptoms. The number of beriberi deaths alone, even discounting the other possible diagnoses, exceeded the total number of Japanese combat deaths more than two times over. On average, it took 43.5 days for a beriberi patient to recover fully if they did at all. Clearly, beriberi was a crippling obstacle to the execution of military operations. Yet during the war, the disease was limited to the army and virtually unknown in the navy.

Numerous unsuccessful explanations and treatments were proposed, ranging from traditional Chinese methods like moxibustion to avoiding supposedly unhealthy soil of certain regions of Japan. By the 1870s, the publicly accepted explanation was that beriberi was a contagious bacterial infection. Before the Sino-Japanese War, the English-trained navy doctor Takagi Kanehiro noticed that beriberi was completely absent from Western navies. Takagi theorised (incorrectly) that this was because Western navies fed their men lots of protein. After some experimentation, he discovered that feeding sailors with protein-rich barley mixed with rice completely solved the issue. Barley, in point of fact, is very rich in both protein and thiamine, and the true cause of beriberi would not be discovered until the 1900s. Regardless, Takagi completely eradicated the plague of beriberi from the navy within a few years, becoming Surgeon General of the IJN in 1885.

This was a tremendous achievement for the Japanese navy, but unfortunately its success was tempered by the arrogance and ignorance of Imperial Japanese Army leaders. Ishiguro Tadanori, who became the Surgeon General of the army in 1890, continued to perpetuate the belief that beriberi was an infectious disease and not a nutritional affliction. Other well-respected army doctors like Mori Ogai, a colonel at the time of the Sino-Japanese

---

51 Anne Ewbank, 'How Killer Rice Crippled Tokyo and the Japanese Navy', Atlas Obscura (2018), <https://www.atlasobscura.com/articles/rice-disease-mystery-edo-tokyo-navy-beriberi>, accessed 2 March 2024.

War, also refused to budge. This was not a simple scientific disagreement. The army doctors had conducted their own research and determined the superiority of white rice, and to have their results be challenged by a navy doctor would constitute a humiliating loss of 'face.' Barley rations had been introduced in the Japanese army around 1884, and by 1891 beriberi cases had almost become extinct, but despite these clear results Tadayoshi banned the issuing of barley as a riposte to Takagi's solution. Instead, Tadayoshi forced the IJA Sanitation Department to try to improve their sanitation standards to impossible levels to combat a non-existent bacteria. Consequently, during the Sino-Japanese War, thousands of Japanese soldiers were sacrificed to save the army's 'face.' Ironically, Japanese soldiers suffering from starvation and inadequate food supply who had to make do with brown rice, millet, or other unrefined carbohydrates did not have to deal with beriberi, while well-fed units with steady supply lines to mainland Japan died in droves from the disease. Imperial army leaders tried to cover up these inconvenient statistics through both subtle misdirection and blatant censorship. After some 27,000 men perished from beriberi in the Russo-Japanese War, the IJA finally began to issue barley rations. This travesty would serve as a mortifying first symptom of the destructive interservice rivalry between the Imperial Japanese army and navy.

Modernisation

Like the Chinese, the Japanese believed in their own cultural superiority as a people descended from the Sun God Amaterasu.[52] These beliefs allowed the Japanese to mobilise nationalism and bolster the Emperor's legitimacy as that of a living god but did not give them the hubristic sense of overconfidence that the Middle Kingdom possessed. A significant proportion of Japanese culture was heavily derived from Chinese civilisational influence, including but not limited to their traditional writing system, social structure, ethical scruples, and so on. Even the national flower of Japan was originally not native to the home islands and was brought from China. The Japanese therefore had a well-established history of contact with other civilisations, and picking and choosing the best to adapt into their own nation. The Japanese therefore did not have as strong an instinctual aversion to learning from inferior 'barbarians' as did the Chinese. This historical continuity is given a handy symbol with the Westernisation slogan 'Japanese spirit, Western technique' (wakon yosai), which had in fact been modified from the older 'Japanese spirit, Chinese technique' (wakon kansai).[53] In addition to this history of cross-cultural learning, the Japanese nation had a profound sense of vulnerability that led them to take threats seriously.[54] The Japanese home islands were and are prone to earthquakes, tsunamis and other deadly natural disasters, so the faith in omnipotent cultural superiority was exclusively Chinese.

---

52 Paine, *The Sino-Japanese War*, p.339.
53 Paine, *The Sino-Japanese War*, p.81.
54 Paine, *The Sino-Japanese War*, p.339.

Imperial Japanese Army hospitalisation statistics for disease (6th June 1894 to 31st December 1895)

Disease name	Number of patients	Number of fully recovered patients	Full recovery rate	Average number of days of treatment for full recovery	Number of deaths from disease	Mortality rate
Dysentery	12,205	7,028	57.6%	34.8	1,964	16.1%
Malaria	11,214	5,509	49.1%	26.5	665	5.9%
Cholera	9,753	2,906	29.8%	12.6	5,709	58.5%
Typhoid	5,248	2,567	48.9%	43.1	1,493	28.4%
Beriberi	34,783	15,874	45.6%	43.5	3,944	11.3%
Other nervous system diseases	1,492	782	52.4%	31.4	135	9.0%
Gastric catarrh	13,138	6,594	50.2%	20.7	1,703	13.0%
Other gastro-intestinal diseases	11,102	5,944	53.5%	32.1	381	3.4%
Other nutritional diseases	2,601	1,719	66.1%	33.1	23	0.9%
Respiratory disease	7,929					
Cardiovascular disease	1,253					
Beriberi, gastric catarrh, other gastro-intestinal diseases and other nutritional diseases	61,624	30,131	48.9%		6,051	9.8

Training and military academies

The Shogunate had made numerous attempts to reform its armies, and after its total defeat against its own vassal of Choshu in 1866, it was decided that self-studying Western texts would not do. A French military expedition was requested and arrived in 1867, intending to train a Japanese new model army. They established three separate officer schools and ended up training an elite force called the Denshutai. The Denshutai responded to and gave orders in French, used French rifles and artillery, and even rode imported French horses. The outbreak of the Boshin War forced this first French military expedition to return home to respect the neutrality of their nation, but nearly half of the advisors, including the famous Jules Brunet, chose to participate in the war on the side of the Shogunate. Many of them chose to stay to the bitter end with their former students.

Although the French had, even if informally, opposed the Meiji government during the Boshin War, the new Imperial Japanese Army swallowed old grudges and chose the French army as its model again. Although many senior Japanese officers preferred other national systems, the Japanese army was already heavily French-inspired in organisation, form, and drill. Likewise, many pro-Shogunate officials and statesmen were offered positions in the new Meiji administration for their expertise and experience in dealing with Western affairs. In 1868, a military academy was established at Kyoto, mainly taught by former pupils of the French. French language academies were also founded at Kyoto and Yokohama. Another military academy was created at Osaka, but by the end of 1871 both this and the Kyoto academy were relocated to Tokyo. At first, the young Meiji government had trouble reigning in its new subjects, and many of them pursued routes of military modernisation independently, which were based on various European models. In 1870, the military quotas for all the feudal domains were standardised and set, later that year all feudal domains were required to organise their forces based on the French system. During this time, the Japanese top brass sent numerous promising students to study overseas. The Iwakura Mission of 1871 to 1873 endeavoured to study not only Western military techniques, but also the underlying philosophical, cultural, technological and intellectual principles behind them. General Oyama Iwao studied in France starting from 1870 and observed the French during the Franco-Prussian War before staying in Geneva for three years and finally returning to Japan in 1875; General Nozu Michitsura visited the United States in 1876 to attend the Centennial International Exhibition of American arts, manufactures and other technology; and in 1884 General Miura Goro (with Oyama again) travelled to France to study their army. In 1872, another French military expedition was invited to Japan, which stayed for eight years. During this period, the French military advisors contributed greatly to the construction of various coastal fortresses and arsenals. Furthermore, the (in)famous conscription law of the IJA was heavily inspired by French concepts of the citizen-soldier, as was the unfortunate 'blood tax' allegory.

This second French military expedition established the Toyama Military Academy for non-commissioned officers in 1873 and the simply named Army Military Academy (Rikugun Shikan Gakko) for officers in 1874, with the latter's first class a year later. Located in Ichigaya in eastern Tokyo, the Military Academy initially had infantry and cavalry cadets study for two years before graduation and engineering and artillery cadets three, but in 1876 this was changed to three and four years, respectively. In 1881 engineering and artillery student terms were increased to five years, and after graduation they were expected to remain for a while longer for field practice and to teach their younger counterparts. At that time, the French military did not require officers to gain experience as enlisted men or as non-commissioned officers and instead recruited officers directly from military academies. This was ideal for the IJA, as they needed a well-educated officer corps as soon as possible, but there were definitely major downsides. Being cloistered from the churlish ranks of the enlisted, officers became excessively elitist and effete, and even after being commissioned they remained aloof from the men they were supposed to lead. This led to a poor retention rate of officers, as they were unable to properly command and communicate with their men and thus had to retire mid-career. Additionally, many officer cadets lacked discipline and behaved very poorly in class, forming gangs and brawling with one another. Several were court-martialled and subsequently expelled from the Military Academy. This lacklustre officer training would be a major reason for the later switch to Prussian models.

The French loss of the Franco-Prussian War of 1870 caused some consternation among IJA leaders, but due to feelings of sunk cost and familiarity, French influence continued to dominate. However, the difficulty of putting down the Satsuma Rebellion of 1877 exposed many of the shortcomings of the primarily defensive French military organisation. This was the last straw and from then on, the French gradually lost their monopoly on influencing IJA affairs. After the French expedition left Japan in 1880, some pro-French hardliners remained, such as General Miura Goro, but they were overshadowed by the Prussian lobby. Major General Katsura Taro, having watched the French defeat with his own eyes as a military attaché with the Germans, spearheaded the pro-Prussian faction. In 1885, he invited General Klemens Wilhelm Jacob Meckel of the Prussian military to serve as an instructor. A true Prussian patriot, Meckel was initially hesitant to go on the tongue-in-cheek rationale that Japan had no Moselle wine.[55] After being persuaded by the entire German general staff (and learning that all varieties of European alcohol could be readily purchased at Yokohama), Meckel relented, but only on the condition that he return home in one year. He would end up staying three years. Prussian influence would certainly be substantial, but not to the point of monopoly; for example, the IJA artillery arm of service took great inspiration from Royal Italian Army methods, a third French military mission arrived in 1884, and officers of all nationalities assisted with Japan's military industry.

The Army War College, founded in 1882, had originally taught a French-style curriculum, but by 1887 Meckel had completely replaced them with his own, far more challenging edition; only half of his first class managed to graduate. Under his guidance, the Japanese army was changed from a defensive army to an offensive one. The 1891 IJA infantry training manual was basically a direct copy of the Prussian one, with heavy emphasis on infantry assault tactics coupled with decentralised battlefield command. Meckel drummed into the Japanese the German military traditions of learning from military history as opposed to pure theory, training trips to imitate real command and control, and war games to simulate manoeuvres. Meckel also placed heavy emphasis on the importance of logistics in warfare, something that had been a massive issue during the Satsuma Rebellion. The old system of organisation had been based on French-style stationary garrisons (chindai), but in 1888 they were switched to mobile all-arms divisions (shidan) capable of mobilising quickly and taking the fight to the enemy. Likewise, the German officer system supplanted the French one in 1887 and produced officers of far superior qualifications. The new system required officers first rise through the ranks from enlisted private to a non-commissioned officer before enrolling in an officer cadet military academy.

At one point, Meckel boasted that he could conquer all of Japan with one division of the German army.[56] Although intended to motivate the Japanese, this poorly considered remark was objected to as being demeaning and offensive by officer cadet Nezu Hajimi, who was not alone in believing the Japanese to be equals of the Europeans. The lecture quickly turned into

---

55 'Klemens W. J. Meckel', Weblio, <https://www.weblio.jp/content/%E3%82%AF%E3%83%AC%E3%83%A1%E3%83%B3%E3%82%B9%E3%83%BB%E3%83%B4%E3%82%A3%E3%83%AB%E3%83%98%E3%83%AB%E3%83%A0%E3%83%BB%E3%83%A4%E3%83%BC%E3%82%B3%E3%83%97%E3%83%BB%E3%83%A1%E3%83%83%E3%82%B1%E3%83%AB>, accessed 7 Feb 2024.

56 'Klemens W. J. Meckel', Weblio, <https://www.weblio.jp/content/%E3%82%AF%E3%83%AC%E3%83%A1%E3%83%B3%E3%82%B9%E3%83%BB%E3%83%B4%E3%82%A3%E3%83%AB%E3%83%98%E3%83%AB%E3%83%A0%E3%83%BB%E3%83%A4%E3%83%BC%E3%82%B3%E3%83%97%E3%83%BB%E3%83%A1%E3%83%83%E3%82%B1%E3%83%AB>, accessed 7 Feb 2024.

an exchange of insults, and Meckel threatened to leave Japan entirely. Nezu was expelled from the War College and confined to being a Major in the reserves, and although he wrote several articles criticising the overemphasis on technical as opposed to moral education in the Japanese government, the former cadet later praised Meckel and credited him with the decisive victory over China in the Sino-Japanese War. Meckel himself would leave Japan in 1888 but would continue to teach Japanese cadets in Berlin privately. His successor, Major Heinrich Emin von Wildenbruch, arrived in Japan in 1888 and continued Meckel's legacy in the Japanese military. Von Wildenbruch left in April 1890 and was replaced by Major Alexander von Grutschreiber, who himself left in July 1894.

Military industry

The Meiji government believed that meeting the military challenge of the West was the highest priority, so the Japanese industrial revolution's humble beginnings are virtually inextricable with the development of military industry. Thus, Japan's path to industrialisation was heavily lopsided, such that by the late 1890s the Japanese armament industry was world class, while basic civilian industries, such as the textile and machine tools industries, were outmoded, inefficient, and totally dependent on foreign imports.[57]

The Shogunate (and other feudal domains) had established a handful of armament factories with foreign help, and when the Shogunate was deposed, the Meiji government quickly brought them back to working condition.[58] In the 1880s, many civilian factories and mines were practically given gratis to what would become the Zaibatsu cliques, but the military industry (besides a few shipyards) were exempt from this policy.[59] Rather, they remained under centralised government management, nurtured with protective subsidies, and state capital. Two main arsenals and their associated subsidiaries dominated this period: the Tokyo Arsenal, which mainly produced small arms; and the Osaka Arsenal, which focused mostly on artillery. Additionally, military clothing and a number of accoutrements such as horse saddles, backpacks and other such miscellany were manufactured in both of the aforementioned arsenals as well as in dedicated factories such as the Senju Woolen Cloth Factory.

---

57 Tohata Seiichi (ed.), *The Modernization of Japan* (Tokyo: Institute of Asian Economic Affairs, 1966), p.454.
58 Ushisaburo Kobayashi, *Military Industries of Japan* (Oxford: Oxford University Press, 1922), p.29.
59 Tohata, *Modernization*, p.451.

Notable Japanese Arsenals

Factory name	Establishment	Remarks
Tokyo Arsenal	Confiscated from the Shogunate's Sekiguchi Arsenal in 1868[60]	
Osaka Arsenal	Confiscated from the Shogunate's Nagasaki Arsenal in 1870	
Kagoshima Arsenal	Established in 1875	Under the Osaka Arsenal
Wakayama Arsenal	Established in 1875	Under the Osaka Arsenal
Hagi Arsenal	Unknown	Originally under the Tokyo Arsenal; transferred to the Osaka Arsenal in 1877
Itabashi Powder Mill	Established as part of the Tokyo Arsenal in 1875; began production in 1876[61]	Under the Tokyo Arsenal
Takinogawa Powder Mill	Established as a branch of the Itabashi Powder Mill in 1878; began production in 1879[62]	Under the Tokyo Arsenal
Takinokami Powder Mill	Confiscated from the Kagoshima Domain in 1870	Under the Tokyo Arsenal
Senju Woolen Cloth Factory	Established in 1877; began production in 1879	Originally a civilian factory; transferred to military control in 1888
Iwabana Powder Mill	Established in 1879; began production in 1882[63]	Under the Tokyo Arsenal
Meguro Powder Mill	Established in 1885[64]	Originally owned by the Imperial Japanese Navy; transferred to the Tokyo Arsenal on paper in 1885 and in practice in 1893.

The Tokyo Arsenal

Soon after the Meiji Restoration, the Shogunate's old Sekiguchi Arsenal in Koishikawa, Tokyo, was quickly brought under Imperial control and renamed the Tokyo Arsenal.[65] The Tokyo Arsenal was officially established in 1870 and quickly began to use the old Shogunate workshops to repair and manufacture weapons, mainly Enfield muzzle loaders. Ammunition for the assortment of other rifles in use by the forces of the Emperor were also made on an ad-hoc basis, but this was mostly terminated after the standardisation of the Enfield rifle in 1870. The quality and quantity of these products were dubious, so foreign experts were invited to Japan. In 1870, French Colonel Margritte and his entourage were tasked with not only training the military but also reforming the military industry. In 1871 Phillipe Jauly, a Belgian engineer, found employment at the Tokyo Arsenal, and directed the expansion of the

---

60 Tohata, *Modernization*, p.452.
61 Kobayashi, *Military Industries*, pp.31–32.
62 Kobayashi, *Military Industries*, p.32.
63 Kobayashi, *Military Industries*, p.33.
64 Tohata, *Modernization*, p.452.
65 Kobayashi, *Military Industries*, pp.30–36.

small arms machinery there until his contract expired in 1875. Under his instruction, construction began for a new small arms factory in 1872. In 1873, the Tokyo Arsenal began to convert the outdated Enfield muzzle loaders into 'Allumettes,' possibly referring to either Enfield-Albini-Braendlin or Enfield-Terssen rifles.[66] The Japanese got lots of mileage out of their Enfields, which were first converted to the oddly termed Allumettes, these then being converted to Sniders in 1875. In 1874 plans were drawn up for the construction of the Itabashi Powder Mill which was formally established in 1875 and finished in 1876. The construction process was greatly aided by the 1875 installation of hydraulic sawing and lathing machines for the Tokyo Arsenal's woodworking mill, powered by steam. Other improvements included a drying place for mercuric fulminate in 1875; a small arms forge, an ammunition factory, and a fire arrow factory built in 1876; numerous high explosive mill machines installed in 1877; and smelting furnaces and machine fans fitted in 1877. The Tokyo Arsenal's small arms factory produced rifles for the first time in 1876.

The outbreak of the Satsuma Rebellion, among others, forced the Tokyo Arsenal to workday and night to fulfil demand, and existing facilities were greatly expanded. Additionally, due to labour shortages, a number of young women were hired at the Tokyo Arsenal as an auxiliary to its main force of over 500 workmen. The quantity of ammunition manufactured was so great that new magazines had to be built at Aoyama and Izumishinden. Likewise, a temporary high explosive mill was established in 1877 in what today is Kanda-Misakicho. The Itabashi Powder Mill also saw numerous expansions, and in 1878 a regional branch aptly called the Takinogawa Branch Bureau was created and started production in 1879. That same year planning began for the establishment of the Iwabana Powder Mill; construction began in 1880, finished in 1881 and production began in 1882.

The conclusion of the Satsuma Rebellion also introduced numerous reforms in the armament of the Japanese military, which then necessitated changes in the Tokyo Arsenal. The Tokyo Arsenal continued to convert both Enfields and Alumettes into Sniders and standardised the stock wood as either beech or walnut. In 1880, the Type 13 Murata rifle was adopted as the standard issue rifle of the IJA, and the Tokyo Arsenal set to work right away first converting existing stocks of Chassepots into Murata rifles and then manufacturing their own from scratch. A German engineer named Heer was brought over in 1880 to assist in the production of the Type 13 ammunition; trials began in 1881 and production commenced for good in 1882. The introduction of the Type 18 Murata rifle demanded an expensive modification of Type 13 machinery. The first prototypes of the Murata magazine rifle were tested in 1886, and after satisfactorily passing all fields, began production in 1889 and was thus designated the Type 22 after the year. Production of the Type 18 for military use was then discontinued in 1888, but apparently limited numbers were manufactured for civilian hunting or export purposes, and the Type 18 was fully discontinued in 1889. However, sufficient quantities of the Type 22 were not produced in time to arm the

---

66 Anon. 'Pre-Murata Japanese Military Rifles,' Military Rifles (2023), <https://www.militaryrifles.com/japan/premurata>, accessed 12 Feb. 2024.

whole army by the time of the Sino-Japanese War, and the vast majority of soldiers had to make do with the Type 18. The Tokyo Arsenal began producing ammunition for the Osaka-designed Model 1882 cannons in 1885, and in the same year the Itabashi Powder Mill began to manufacture suitable gunpowder for them, followed by the Iwabana Powder Mill in 1886. In 1887, the Tokyo Arsenal installed steam engines and boilers, greatly increasing the rate of production. In 1893, the Itabashi Powder Mill installed machinery for producing gun cotton and smokeless powder. That same year, the Imperial Japanese Navy also turned over the Meguro Powder Mill to the Army's hands, placing it under the Tokyo Arsenal's authority.

Foreign experts to the Japanese military industry

Name	Nationality	Specialty	Term of service
Colonel Margritte[67]	France	General arms manufacturing	1870 to unknown
Philippe Jauly[68]	Belgium	Small arms manufacturing	1871 to 1875
Captain Lebon and four non-commissioned officers	France	General arms manufacturing	1872 to unknown
Mr Pironnet	Belgium	Engineering	1872 to unknown
Second French Military Mission	France	General arms manufacturing	1872 to 1880
Mr Lemoine	France	Casting	1875 to 1877
Mr Bacquet	France	Engineering	1875 to 1877
Mr Partray	France	Stuffing gun powder	1875 to unknown
Mr Heer	Germany	Manufacturing rifle cartridges	1880 to unknown
Major Pompeio Grillo	Italy	Artillery manufacturing	1884 to 1888
Antonio Fornelis and Giacomo Hisso	Italy	Engineering	1884 to 1888
Major Alexandro Quaratezi	Italy	Artillery manufacturing	1888 to 1889
Major Scipione Braccialini	Italy	Artillery and precision instrument manufacturing	1892 to late 1893 or 1894

The Osaka Arsenal

The Osaka Arsenal originated from the Nagasaki Arsenal that had been installed by the old Shogunate and was officially established upon its seizure by the Meiji government in 1870.[69]

At this stage, the Osaka Arsenal was only able to carry out patchwork repairs of existing weaponry. Fuel was purchased from the Navy and most of the raw materials had to be expensively imported from abroad. After the arrival of Colonel Margritte in 1870, the Osaka Arsenal began to purchase the machinery and train the workmen necessary for the foundation of a successful military industry. Initially, there was only an iron foundry left over from the Shogunate, but by 1875 there was a copper gun foundry, several explosive mills, saddle works, woodworking mills, and a forge. In 1872, a 4 pound French style mountain gun was produced for the first time. This gun was made of French-style steel bronze, as the Japanese did not have a thriving domestic steel

---

67 Kobayashi, *Military Industries*, p.39–40.
68 Kobayashi, *Military Industries*, p.40.
69 Kobayashi, *Military Industries*, pp.36–53.

industry until the 1900s, so they took the comparatively plentiful copper as an economical substitute. This was followed by the forging of modern field guns of the same pattern and material one year later. Like the Tokyo Arsenal, the Osaka Arsenal worked overtime to quell the Satsuma Rebellion. In 1877, a small arms factory at Hagi, which had previously been under the Tokyo Arsenal, was transferred to the jurisdiction of the Osaka Arsenal to more efficiently produce arms and ammunition to combat the rebels. In 1882, the Japanese began to design French-inspired bronze guns and howitzers, and in early 1882 the Osaka Arsenal completed Japan's first domestically produced breech loading howitzer, of 150 millimetre calibre and of the now standardised hardened copper material. Although production and design began in 1882, the 70 millimetre bronze mountain guns began only in 1883, followed by the field guns two months after. Larger pieces of the same design intended for coastal defence or siege battles also began manufacture in the same year, of 120 millimetre calibre.

However, the Japanese had trouble with making anything larger than 150 millimetres and to further improve upon the quality of the hardened copper and to streamline the process of production, Italian artillery experts were invited starting from 1884. The first to come was Major Pompeio Grillo, a seasoned veteran of the Royal Italian Army, soon followed by an engineer of the same nationality, Antonio Fornelis and his assistant Giacomo Hisso. Having enrolled in a military academy in his teens, Major Grillo proved himself a courageous and capable artillery officer during the Wars of Italian Independence, and the Japanese considered his unique expertise to be highly comparable to their own situation: both Italy and Japan lacked a functional steel industry at the time, so Major Grillo brought new techniques for producing hardened steel bronze cannon barrels to Japan. He also personally designed the 280 millimetre cast iron howitzer, which he based on the Krupp system.[70] This weapon was installed in strategic coastal fortresses and was not used during the Sino-Japanese War, but would distinguish itself during the Russo-Japanese War, albeit in siege warfare instead of coastal defence. With Grillo's help, the Osaka Arsenal expanded rapidly. The gun factory building began construction in 1875 and finished in 1884, where a month later production began. In 1884, the gun and vehicle works were substantially expanded and the shell lathing works completed; from 1885 to 1889 railways were built leading to the Osaka Arsenal, greatly improving the delivery time of raw materials and finished goods both to and from the Arsenal; and in 1886 manufacture of coastal defence gun carriages began. In 1887 large numbers of large calibre coastal defence guns were produced with the Italians' help, as well as pivoting mounts made of cast iron. Grillo's contract expired in 1888, and he and his two engineer friends were replaced by Major Alexandro Quaratezi, another Italian artillery expert. For reasons unknown, Quaratezi returned to Italy after barely a year, but fortunately the Japanese had learned more than enough about steel bronze guns from Grillo. 'Short firing guns' of 190 millimetres began production in 1890, followed by those of 240 and 280 millimetre calibres in 1891. Just a year afterward, 90 millimetre quick

---

70 At that time, the Italian 280mm howitzer was actually based on the Armstrong system; Grillo did not want the Japanese to have an exact copy of Italian military equipment.

firing guns were cast in the Osaka Arsenal. These were of wholly Japanese design and manufacture, clearly showing the Japanese effort to become self-sufficient in military industry. In 1892, yet another Italian artillerist, Major Scipione Bracialini, was invited to Japan. Major Braccialini was universally recognised as an expert in ballistics and range finding, and his most well-known contribution to the field was a double-entry table that compiled angle and distance data together, greatly simplifying the arithmetical grunt work of artillerymen worldwide. His own range finding device, the Italian Model 1886 Rangefinder, had been adopted by the Royal Italian Army and found its way into the hands of the IJA during a tour in Europe. Upon his arrival, Braccialini designed a similar, but not identical, rangefinder for the Japanese so as to not betray the confidentiality of the Italian Army's intellectual property. He also helped establish a factory for manufacturing rangefinders, field glasses, and other precision instruments. Due to health issues Bracialini left Japan in 1894, before the end of his contract, but Japanese soldiers continued to use his advanced artillery techniques and technology for years to come.

Osaka Arsenal total production, as of November 1890

Name	Number produced
Coast guns; all calibres	114
Coast gun ammunition; all calibres	2,248
Coast gun carriages; all calibres	76
Siege and garrison guns	2
Siege and garrison gun ammunition	875
Siege and garrison gun carriages	2
Model 1882 70mm mountain guns	251
Model 1882 70mm mountain gun carriages	277
Model 1882 70mm field guns	255
Model 1882 70mm field gun carriages	278
Model 1882 70mm ammunition	370,756
Fuses of all kinds	300,238

The Senju Woolen Cloth Factory

The Senju Woolen Cloth Factory began as a civilian affair under the direct authority of the Ministry of Civil Affairs, before being transferred to the Ministry of Agriculture and Commerce upon the latter's founding.[71] It started construction in 1877 and commenced operations in 1879; before 1879, Japanese clothing was exclusively made of hemp instead of wool, and all wool was imported at exorbitant prices from overseas. Thus, the Senju Factory acted as a kind of trailblazer in the Japanese industrialization process as a whole and was accordingly used as a public relations tool. Before 1888, the factory was open to curious visitors and locals, who could receive a tour and explanation of the machines at work. This helped ease Japanese society into their own industrial revolution, as well as diffusing general technical knowledge into the population.

---

71 Kobayashi, *Military Industries*, pp.103–105.

With the promulgation of the Model 1886 (Meiji 19) Uniform Regulations, Japanese soldiers began to wear all wool jackets, trousers and hats. The Senju Factory had previously manufactured woollen articles mostly for civilian consumption, but this new jump in demand led to its transfer to the Ministry of the IJA in 1888. New machinery was installed to process the waste products of the wool making process to create artificial cloth, which were used to make the lighter summer uniforms.

Uniforms

This section describes the uniforms of the Imperial Japanese Army from 1894–1895. Although some information outside of this period will be given, the descriptions are all specifically written for the Sino-Japanese War. See Appendix III for a thorough list of uniform colours for every rank and occupation.

The Model 1886 (Meiji 19) Uniform regulations
At the time of the Sino-Japanese War, the uniforms in use followed the Model 1886 Uniform (Meiji 19) Regulations. The Model 1886 Regulations for enlisted men were formally issued in Cabinet Notice 14[72] on 1st March while the regulations for officers came as Imperial Decree 48 on July 7th.[73] The Model 1886 Regulations divided uniforms into two categories: Type One (isshu), or 'full dress' (sei) was the formal or parade variant, while the second (nishu), or 'field dress' (gun), was service wear. The Model 1886 Regulations also came in two colours: dark blue (sometimes described as black) for winter and white for summer. During its lifetime, the Model 1886 saw a few notable but overall minor changes, many of them concerning rank insignia to match the ever-changing army rank system. The Model 1886 uniforms continued to be worn all the way until they were formally replaced with the near-identical Model 1900 (Meiji 33) in 1900. The Model 1900 underwent massive changes in 1905 during the Russo-Japanese War and was finally discontinued and replaced with the Model 1911 (Meiji 45).

Additionally, a moderate number of hats, jackets, pants, and such from earlier French-inspired Model 1875 (Meiji 8) and 1873 (Meiji 6) Uniforms were altered to fit the 1886 insignia and used simultaneously. In the field, elements of both winter and summer dress were worn simultaneously, sometimes intentionally and sometimes because of necessity or availability. For example, a unit might wear their white cap covers while dressed in dark blue winter jackets and white summer pants.[74] Wealthy officers also sometimes privately commissioned uniforms that were fancier and flashier than what the regulations would have liked, and of course there were differences in the manufacture and specific measurements of caps, jackets, trousers and boots between regions and factories. This is particularly obvious in the highly varying crown and brim sizes of Model 1886 forage caps.

---

72 Kokuritsu Kobunshokan, Naikaku Sorifu, 10.11502/2944008.
73 Kokuritsu Kobunshokan, Naikaku Sorifu, 10.11501/2944008.
74 Heath, *Japan*, p.96.

Headwear

The Model 1886 Type One formal hat was a French-style shako for enlisted men and a dark blue kepi for officers. The Type One hat had a silver 'rising sun' badge (nichisho) attached to the front, an embroidered star in the centre of the crown and white plumes would be attached during ceremonial occasions or while on parade. These plumes (maetate) varied in size for general officers, field officers and enlisted men respectively. For enlisted men, the Type One service cap was only used as a parade dress uniform, but officers sometimes wore their kepi in the field. The Type Two service cap was a dark blue German-inspired peaked forage cap with a coloured band and seam piping based on the service branch. On the front was a silver five pointed star badge. The Type Two service caps of officers would have a varying number of horizontal black stripes around the band indicating rank: general officers (generals, lieutenant generals, and major generals) and their rank equivalents had three stripes, field officers (colonels, lieutenant colonels, and majors) and their equivalents two, and junior officers (captains, lieutenants, and second lieutenants) and their equivalents only had one. Adjutants and warrant officers had no stripes. The hat band was either red for Guard units or yellow for Line units, with exceptions for specific noncombatant or civilian personnel. In summer, a white cover (ni oi) for both field kepis and forage caps was also provided; the entire crown of the kepi would be covered while only the coloured band of the forage cap would be left exposed. The summer hats were also modified to include havelocks; during the Sino-Japanese War, this was of two overlapping nap flaps but afterwards it was of two smaller flaps on either side and a larger one on the back.

Earlier prototypes of the Type Two peaked caps had been issued during the early 1870s, a few were seen mixed in with the Model 1886 during the Sino-Japanese War. The Model 1873 forage cap had a much smaller crown, apparently a shorter peak and came in a peak less version. The Model 1873 cap badge was of a bronze five-pointed star in a roundel, but this might have been replaced or abandoned altogether by the time of the Sino-Japanese since according to contemporary illustrations the cap badge is missing.[75]

A more mysterious piece of summer headgear was the Japanese pith helmet. Officially, the IJA did not have a pith helmet until much after 1895, but several photographs and contemporary illustrations show its use during the war in Taiwan. The IJA sun helmet was apparently used on a very limited scale, suggesting that soldiers may have purchased or acquired them individually. Given the highly variant colours of this sun helmet in contemporary depictions, a khaki or grey cover may have also been issued. The Imperial Japanese Navy did have an official sun helmet which was put in service in 1887,[76] and the ones worn by their army counterparts appear to be visually identical.

---

75 Heath, *Japan*, p.47.
76 Nick Komiya, 'The Evolution of the Japanese Imperial Army Sun Helmet: Part I (1887–1921)', Military Sun Helmets, <https://www.militarysunhelmets.com/2016/part-i-1887-1921#more-18688>, accessed 12 Feb. 2024.

History of Model 1886 Uniform Regulations

Date	Decree number	Changes
1 March 1886 (Meiji 19)	Cabinet Notice 14	Model 1886 Regulation enlisted men and NCO uniforms introduced
7 July 1886 (Meiji 19)	Imperial Decree 48	Model 1886 Regulation officer uniforms introduced
2 July 1888 (Meiji 21)	Imperial Decree 51	Kempeitai trousers changed from blue with red stripe to red with black stripe
27 December 1888 (Meiji 21)	Imperial Decree 96	Pharmaceutical prescriptionist uniforms updated to be identical to those of chief medical attendants and enlisted medical attendants' cuff insignia changed to that of three stripes in dark green to reflect the fact that the positions of medical attendants first, second and third class were reduced to one position
4 June 1889 (Meiji 22)	Imperial Decree 77	Proportions of summer uniform and greatcoat cuff insignia changed slightly. One year volunteer epaulette borders applied to support staff
22 May 1890 (Meiji 23)	Imperial Decree 83	Fortress artillerymen epaulette numerals changed to red cloth
28 December 1890 (Meiji 23)	Imperial Decree 287	Paymaster uniform facing colours changed from blue to 'silver brown' (portrayed as gold in contemporary illustrations)
28 December 1890 (Meiji 23)	Imperial Decree 291	One year volunteer epaulette borders removed from Sanitation Department staff uniforms
31 March 1891 (Meiji 24)	Imperial Decree 29	Tondenhei uniforms changed from red to service branch coloured collars, epaulettes, cuff insignia and trouser stripes. Tondenhei cavalry swords, scabbards and uniforms also standardised to be identical with those of the Line army
24 April 1893 (Meiji 26)	Imperial Decree 25	Officer summer uniforms changed from Attila jackets to plain military jackets with three pockets. Summer uniform insignia changed from trefoils to stars and stripes for officers but completely removed for enlisted men and NCOs
17 July 1894 (Meiji 27)	Imperial Decree 111	Fabric type of officer summer uniforms changed
1 September 1894 (Meiji 27)	Imperial Decree 159	Officer greatcoats and raincoats issued to officer cadets and adjutants
26 November 1894 (Meiji 27)	Imperial Decree 191	Model 1886 Regulations updated to reflect that the Imperial Guard had its own service branches (no changes to uniforms, only terminology)
30 September 1895 (Meiji 28)	Imperial Decree 134	Tondenhei pants changed from frost blue to regular dark blue
30 September 1895 (Meiji 28)	Imperial Decree 135	Tondenhei received new collar badges
23 March 1896 (Meiji 29)	Imperial Decree 32	Added four-petaled flower collar badge to Taiwan garrison troops; officers wore it on both collars
9 June 1896 (Meiji 29)	Imperial Decree 247	Officer and Sanitation Department cadet uniforms changed to be identical with enlisted men uniforms besides rank insignia
3 December 1896 (Meiji 29)	Imperial Decree 380	New epaulette insignia added for enlisted men and NCOs in the railway corps
5 March 1897 (Meiji 30)	Imperial Decree 23	Accountant officer cadet uniforms changed to be identical with accountant first class uniforms
24 March 1897 (Meiji 30)	Imperial Decree 38	Changed uniforms of auditor superintendent general and medical superintendent general to match rank insignia of major general uniform insignia besides service colours
22 June 1897 (Meiji 30)	Imperial Decree 217	Regional military academy cadet uniforms changed to be identical with central military academy cadet uniforms, except the cuff insignia, epaulettes and trouser stripes of regional cadets were red
8 February 1899 (Meiji 32)	Imperial Decree 33	Specified placement of four-petaled flower collar badge for Taiwan garrison troops; officers wore it on both collars while NCOs wore it on the left collar only unless not assigned to a particular unit
9 October 1899 (Meiji 32)	Imperial Decree 399	Medical attendant cuff insignia system changed to reflect the new 'kango sotsu' added to the original position of 'kango te.' Additionally, medical attendants were no longer required to wear Type One shakos on parade
30 November 1899 (Meiji 32)	Imperial Decree 441	Model 1886 Regulations updated to reflect name changes of certain ranks and positions (no changes to uniforms, only terminology).
30 November 1899 (Meiji 32)	Imperial Decree 442	Cuff insignia of support forces changed to reflect new ranks and positions added. The Rod of Asclepius was also removed from medical attendant uniforms
10 September 1900 (Meiji 33)	Imperial Decree 364	Model 1886 Uniform Regulations discontinued and replaced with Model 1900 Uniform Regulations

Military Jackets

IJA military jackets could be divided into three types: regular jackets, officer parade jackets, and Attila jackets. Regular jackets were worn by all non-cavalry enlisted men and NCOs, officer parade jackets, unsurprisingly, by officers on parade, and Attila jackets by officers and cavalrymen in the field.

For non-cavalry enlisted men, winter military jackets consisted of a dark blue single-breasted jacket and paired with trousers of European proportions. The jacket had coloured collars, cloth epaulettes, and cuff insignia to denote rank and service branch, while the trousers had a coloured stripe running down the seam of either side. Only Guard units had service branch coloured edging on their jackets; Line units made do without. On the epaulettes were brass numerals indicating battalion number. Cuff insignia consisted of a series of bars around the sleeve which were coloured according to the service branch. However, for NCOs there was always a thin gold line before the thickest bar, regardless of service branch, a feature that is sometimes incorrectly interpreted.[77] In 1886, these cuff bars appear to have gone all the way around a soldier's sleeve, but by 1894 apparently, they only encircled the outer side. In summertime, the uniform was white with no coloured collars, edging or cuff insignia; only officers had cuff insignia. Parade jackets for enlisted men were identical to their service jackets.

Officer parade jackets were double-breasted with 14 gold or brass buttons, arranged seven per column. The edging, cuffs, and collar borders were the colour of the wearer's arm of service, while the collar itself was gold and lavishly decorated with various patterns. The cuff insignia was of golden 'Austrian trefoils' (also called Austrian knotting) of varying complexity and number. Below the Austrian trefoils design, the cuff was coloured the service branch of the wearer or left uncoloured for general officers and certain support functions. Officer parade jackets had woven epaulettes of three different possible sizes to denote rank, with one to three stars on them. Additionally, the parade jackets of non-combatant branches like the military band and Sanitation Department had special epaulette badges.

The officer Attila jacket was short-skirted, had five braided 'Hungarian knot' loops across the chest, was dark blue edged in black in winter, and was worn by both cavalrymen and officers in the field. Excepting general and cavalry officers, officer jackets had two lower pockets edged in black. All officer and cavalry jackets had woven knot buttons except for those of cavalry officers, who had brass buttons. Officer field dress cuff insignia was identical to the officer parade dress except that the Austrian trefoils were in black instead of gold, and there was no special colouring to indicate service branch. Officer jacket Hungarian knotting and edging was in black, but otherwise without any special collar insignia or colouring. Particularly rakish officers could afford to disobey regulations and pay for specially tailored field dress uniforms with the trefoils in gold or silver or with service branch coloured cuffs. Only cavalry officers wore woven epaulettes; all other service branch officers did not wear any at all. The original 1886 summer officer jackets were

---

77 The extremely talented Ritta Nakanishi's work unfortunately misinterprets the thickest coloured cuff bar as being non-existent, although he correctly illustrated the golden line.

essentially a white version of the winter Atilla jacket with the same cuff insignia and all, but in 1893 the officer summer jacket was changed to a plain jacket that more closely resembled those issued to enlisted men. The 1893 plain jacket had three pockets (two upper breast pockets and one lower pocket on the left), no decorative edging, and a new set of cuff insignia of stars and stripes.

Cavalry jackets were much more colourful than officer jackets. Their Hungarian knots, edging and cuff insignia were coloured either yellow for Line cavalry or red for Imperial Guard cavalry. Cavalry jacket collars were always light green regardless of Line or Guard affiliation. Epaulettes on cavalry jackets were woven unlike the flat cloth ones present on non-cavalry enlisted men jackets. Cavalrymen did not have any special cuff insignia and simply followed the same rules as enlisted men and NCOs of other service branches.

The Model 1886 Regulations also introduced new greatcoats (gai to) for Japanese soldiery; for officers they were double-breasted, while for enlisted men they were single-breasted. Both types of 1886 greatcoats had detachable hoods, two pockets as well as unique cuff insignia that were simplified from the military jacket designs. Regulation books show these greatcoats as being black, indicating that they were meant to be the same dark blue colour as the winter dress, but it was apparently a much duller colour and closer to grey. The Model 1886 raincoat (ama o) was the same for both enlisted men and officers, though it was apparently mostly, if not exclusively, issued to officers. Likewise, a summer coat (natsu gai to) was issued for officers stationed in tropical regions. Finally, a number of non-regulation fur coats and vests were acquired by the men, either through local purchase or through the generous donations of their civilian friends and family back home.

A handsome young Japanese soldier of unknown rank wearing the Type One ceremonial shako, without the chinstrap. The brass numbers on his epaulettes indicate he is of the 3rd Battalion. (Public domain)

Military trousers and footwear

Military trousers were dark blue in winter with a service-coloured stripe and completely white in summer. Officer boots were high-topped and supposedly easy to put on and kick off to fit the Japanese custom of removing shoes before entering indoors. Enlisted men and NCOs were issued with Western-style boots and white gaiters, although they might ditch these for more comfortable Japanese footwear. Parade and field dress pants and shoes were identical.

Early on in the Sino-Japanese War, most Japanese soldiers preferred traditional Japanese socks (tabi) and straw sandals (waraji) to uncomfortable and heavy Western-style boots. Dating back to the Boshin War, this practice was a mark of traditional Japanese military spirit, but it proved impractical in the cold weather of northern China. Frostbite was first seen to be an issue in late 1894 and to combat this Imperial Japanese authorities tried to procure adequate winter boots for the soldiers.[78] One attempt took the form of requesting the residents of Akita Prefecture to donate 10,000 civilian snow boots of all shapes and sizes within 60 days to the troops. These likely took the form of traditional fukagutsu or yukigutsu straw boots used in snowy northeast Japan. This inconsistent and unsystematic method apparently only saw limited success, as cold weather remained a significant issue for Japanese soldiers until the end of the war. The high incidence of frostbite among Japanese soldiers during the Battle of Weihaiwei indicates that the proper winter gear was not supplied. In early 1895, a Major Saito led his men out on a one-day long reconnaissance march through 0.60 metres of snow while wearing straw sandals.[79] After returning, over 1,500 men suffered severe frostbite and had to be removed from active combat. Many had to have extremities amputated and were crippled for life.

Enlisted Men and NCO uniforms
The uniforms of non-cavalry Line enlisted men and NCOs consisted of the Type Two forage cap in the field and the Type One shako while on parade, the regular military jacket, and a pair of trousers. The jacket and pants were dark blue in winter with a service coloured collar, cuff insignia, and trouser stripe, but completely white in summer without any service branch colouring or cuff insignia. Non-cavalry enlisted men and NCOs had cloth epaulettes while cavalrymen had woven ones.

Each of the five main service branches had a unique service colour: red for infantry, yellow for artillery, brown/rust for engineers, blue for commissariat, and light green for cavalry. Non-combatant support forces had identical uniforms to the rest of the Line army except their cuff insignia, which took the form of an inverted chevron with the point facing away from the sleeve opening. Farriers were considered cavalrymen even though they did not wear cavalry uniforms, so they had light green as their service colour. Likewise, cobblers and tailors were officially part of the accounting department, so they used medium blue facings. The other support forces of metal caster, blacksmith, carpenter, gunsmith, saddler, and demolitions expert were all classified as part of the artillery branch and therefore shared artillery's service colour of yellow.

Cavalry uniforms for enlisted men and NCOs comprised a Type Two forage cap in the field and the Type One shako while on parade, a dark blue Attila jacket, and a pair of red trousers with a light green stripe and riding boots. Although farriers were technically considered cavalrymen, they did not wear cavalry uniforms.

Officer uniforms
By the time of the Sino-Japanese War officers wore dark blue Attila jackets edged in black in winter and plain white service jackets with three pockets in summer. Officers were supposed to wear the Type One kepi exclusively on

---
78 Kokuritsu Kobunshokan, Naikaku Sorifu, C05121576400.
79 Nathan Chaikin, First Sino-Japanese War, page 38.

parade, but many chose to wear it in the field instead of the recommended Type Two forage cap. Officer trousers had a coloured stripe in winter but no colour at all in winter. The field dress of officers were split into three categories: general officers (sho) which included generals, lieutenant generals, and major generals; field officers (sa) which included colonels, lieutenant colonels, and majors; and company officers (i) which included captains, lieutenants, and second lieutenants. General officers had three horizontal black bands around the Type Two forage cap, field officers two, and company officers one. Likewise, general officers' winter trouser stripe insignia was of two thick stripes with one thin line between them; field officers had one thick stripe and company officers one thin stripe. Non-combatant military personnel with rank equivalents typically had identical rank insignia except for the colours; for example, the Medical Superintendent General, equivalent to the rank of Major General, had the same kepi insignia (except for a silver star), the same Type Two forage cap (though with dark green cap band), the same cuff insignia (except in silver and gold), and the same trouser stripe configuration (in dark green again) as an army Major General. For full dress, officers (except cavalry ones) wore the double-breasted parade jackets. These always had woven epaulettes; gold, silver or both cuff trefoils; golden collars with meander patterns, and service coloured edging and cuffs. While on parade officers had to wear special sashes (kazari tai) that were striped in different sizes and colours and had two tassels at the ends. These were worn over the sword belt instead of across the chest.

Officers did not have regulations dictating the specific placement or carrying of personal items like water bottles, spectacles or pistols, so each essentially did as he liked. Officers usually did not wear gaiters. Officers were issued Western-styled swords that were either curved or straight (see section on Cold Weapons), but officers could feel free to use non-regulation antique swords of traditional Japanese provenance to use in battle. Although regulation officer jackets were dark blue edged in black without any service branch coloured insignia, this was not always the case in contemporary prints and depictions. If not simply an error, a possible explanation would be that many officers were rich enough to commission new custom-made uniforms or modifications with flashier colours.

Imperial Guard uniforms
Imperial Guard enlisted men uniforms were fundamentally the same as their line counterparts, with only a few notable differences. First, their Type One shakos had red bands and their Type Two forage caps had a red band instead of yellow. Second, Imperial Guard military jackets were edged in their service branch colour (red for infantry, yellow for artillery, brown for engineers, and blue for commissariat). The only exception to this rule was the cavalry, whose jackets were piped in red. As medical staff, administrative staff, military band personnel, and support force staff did not have their Imperial Guard counterparts, they had no special uniforms even when serving Imperial Guard units. Finally, Imperial Guard cuff insignia were red, except for the golden line of sergeants first and second class and sergeant majors. Imperial Guard officers had identical uniforms to their line counterparts, except for their red Type One kepis and the red band on their Type Two forage caps.

Wounded and ill Japanese line up at Busan, waiting to be invalided home. Quite evidently, Japanese military uniforms were not as perfectly standardised as would be expected. Of the 14 men clearly shown, one has half boots, another has knee boots, and the rest have shoes or straw waraji sandals; three have dark blue or black winter trousers with grey gaiters while the rest wear white summer trousers without any gaiters; the cut of the trousers range from being close fitting to being baggy; two do not wear jackets; eight wear either gassai bukuro tube packs or rolled up greatcoats of various colours over their left or right shoulders; three men have forgotten their white cloth cap covers; only six have havelocks on their caps; and the proportion of the caps themselves appear to vary greatly as well. Photographed by Georges Ferdinand Bigot. (Public domain)

Kempeitai uniforms

Like other branches of the IJA, Kempeitai enlisted men and NCOs wore regular jackets and striped trousers with boots while officers wore either Attila jackets or double-breasted parade jackets. The Kempeitai did not wear Type Two forage caps at all. The Kempeitai, being a special branch of the IJA, had both red and black as their service colours, red for their facings, kepi and trousers with a black kepi band and trouser stripe. The iconic white armband with the characters 'Kempei' in bright red began its service only in 1923 and was not worn during this period.

Military band uniforms

Military band personnel at and below the rank of assistant bandmaster wore regular military jackets while first and second class bandmasters wore only double-breasted officer parade jackets. Military band regular jackets had red cuffs with blue rank bars, and their epaulettes were red edged in blue. However, officer parade jackets did not have any blue and instead had red edges, cuffs, and collars. Military band members of all ranks also had a special gold badge of a stylised harp on both collars, and on woven epaulettes for first and second class bandmasters. Military band personnel only wore Type One kepis and did not have forage caps, nor did they wear gaiters.

Tondenhei uniforms

The Model 1886 Regulations initially assigned the same uniform to all Tondenhei soldiers regardless of service branch, which was identical to Line infantry except with 'frost blue' coloured trousers with red stripes. These specially coloured trousers would become an enduring symbol of the Tondenhei, and at times attracted envy from Line and even Imperial Guard units. As the colonisation of Hokkaido progressed, the Tondenhei expanded to include other service branches, and so in 1891 service branch coloured facings were applied to all Tondenhei uniforms. In 1895, the Tondenhei was forced to eschew their precious frost blue trousers in favour of the standard dark blue ones, but NCOs and enlisted men received new silver badges. These were worn symmetrically (i.e. with the points facing one another) on both collars to form the shape of the character for 'north.' Finally, in 1904, when the Tondenhei system was abolished and all units absorbed into the Hokkaido Division, the Tondenhei uniform was changed to be identical to that of other Line units.

Sanitation Department uniforms

The IJA Sanitation Department considered all military doctors, veterinarians and pharmacists officers, chief medical attendants and pharmaceutical prescriptionists NCOs, and medical attendants enlisted men. Therefore, Sanitation Department officers wore the officer Attila jacket with Hungarian knotting, a kepi or forage cap, and striped trousers while NCOs and enlisted men wore regular jackets. The service colour of the Sanitation Department was dark green, so all Type Two forage cap bands, trouser stripes and cuff bars were in dark green. Those in the military medicine and pharmaceutical branches had a silver Rod of Asclepius badge on their epaulettes, while those in the veterinary branch had a crossed leaf design.

Accountant and Paymaster uniforms

During the Sino-Japanese War the IJA had separate departments for accountants and paymasters: the Accounting Department (Gunri Bu) and the Auditing Department (Kantoku Bu). Later on in 1902, these two were merged into the Administration Department (Keiri Bu).[80] Paymasters were called 'kantoku' (auditor) until 1903, when their title was changed to 'shukei' (paymaster) to better fit their actual job.[81] Much of this peculiar terminology revolved around the IJA's obdurate refusal to share names with the Imperial Japanese Navy, who had their own accounting functions. For example, the Auditing Department (Kantoku Bu) was called the 'Auditing Department' instead of the 'Paymaster Department (Shukei Bu)' because the 'Paymaster Department' already existed in the navy.

As for uniforms, the NCOs of the Accounting Department wore regular uniforms identical to other Line units, but with medium blue as their service colour. Paymasters were all considered officers and therefore wore Attila jackets while working and double-breasted officer parade jackets for full

---

80 Kokuritsu Kobunshokan, Naikaku Sorifu, Ref.A15113419600.
81 Kokuritsu Kobunshokan, Naikaku Sorifu, Ref.A15113460500.

dress. After 1890, paymasters had 'silvery brown' or 'silver tea' (gincha) as their service colour, which was often portrayed as a bronze or dark yellow in contemporary illustrations.

Equipment

The Murata rifles

Major Murata Tsuneyoshi, the eponymous inventor of the Murata rifle, had studied traditional Japanese swordsmanship and gunnery in his youth. During the Boshin War, he quickly made his way up the IJA hierarchy with his excellent marksmanship skills. In 1875, he travelled to various European countries including France and Germany to study modern weaponry and tactics. Although what he saw was greatly limited due to fears of reverse-engineering, he still managed to get his hands on both a Gras and a Beaumont rifle. Drawing inspiration from the M1874 Gras, M1871 Beaumont, and possibly also the M1871 Mauser, Murata's new design was finally adopted in 1880 (Meiji 13) and named the Type 13 Murata rifle for the year of Emperor Meiji's reign.[82] The Type 13 was a single-shot breech loading rifle that fired 11 millimetre black powder paper cartridges. A shortened, but otherwise identical, version of the Type 13, known colloquially as the Type 16 carbine, was developed in 1883. Around 8,000 French Chassepot rifles were also remodelled to include Type 13 style actions.[83]

Murata Type 13 production numbers

Year	Number produced
1880	Less than 7,800
1881	Less than 7,800
1882	7,800–8,000
1883	7,800–8,000
1884	30,000
1885	Unknown; all production of Type 13 stopped and replaced with Type 18

In 1885 the Type 18 rifle was introduced. Being an aggregate of various modifications to the Type 13, the Type 18 fired metal cartridges, had a shorter gun and bayonet length, and had some ergonomic improvements, such as the removal of an extraneous barrel band. Approximately 80,000 Type 18 rifles were manufactured from 1885–1889.[84] The Type 18 also had an obscure cavalry carbine variant, of which only around 10,000 were manufactured.[85] Then in 1889 came Japan's first magazine rifle, the Type 22 Murata rifle. With a reduced calibre of 8 mm, the Type 22 drew inspiration from the Kropatschek, Mauser, and Lebel series. It fired smokeless ammunition and had an eight round tubular magazine, but could hold 10 rounds in total, with

---

82   Heath, *Japan*, p.71.
83   Stanley Zielinski, *Japanese Murata rifles 1880–1897* (Online: Z&Z Publishing, 2023), p.492.
84   Zielinski, *Murata*, p.740.
85   Zielinski, *Murata*, p.802.

one in the feed chamber and another in the breech.[86] The Type 27 Murata carbine, issued in 1894, was a shortened version of the Type 22 intended for cavalry use, and held only five rounds in its magazine.[87] Around 160,000 Type 22 rifles and carbines were produced in total from 1889 to 1898. In 1897 the Arisaka Type 30 (also known as the Meiji rifle), designed by Murata's student and de facto successor Arisaka Nariakira, took the Type 22's place.

Murata Type 18 production numbers

Year	Number produced
1885	10,000
1886	30,000
1887	30,000
1888	20,000; production of Type 18 for 'military purposes' stopped
1889	Unknown; all production of Type 18 stopped and replaced with Type 22

Murata Type 22 production numbers

Year	Number produced
1889	10,000
1890	15,000
1891	20,000
1892	20,000
1893	20,000
1894	25,000
1895	25,000
1896	15,000
1897	Unknown
1898	Unknown
1899	Unknown; Type 22 officially replaced with Type 30

Designing the rifle was one thing but producing it was another. Even though the Type 13 had been adopted in 1880, it took six years for just the Imperial Guard to be uniformly issued with the Murata rifles, while the rest of the army retained their Snider-Enfields. It was claimed that by the end of 1887 the entire army would be armed with the Type 13, but this did not happen. By 1892, the IJA was at least armed with Type 13s, with a good number of Type 18s thrown in, but by that time the Type 18 was already outdated and Imperial authorities were working hard to produce sufficient quantities of the Type 22. Apparently, this did not succeed, as during the Sino-Japanese War the Type 18 Murata rifle (and its carbine variant) was the standard-issue arm to frontline troops, with the Type 13 and Snider-Enfields for reserve units. By 1894 only the 4th Line Division and Imperial Guard had received the Type 22, but they did not see combat until the Yiwei War in Taiwan.[88]

---

86 Heath, *Japan*, p.71.
87 Zielinski, *Murata*, p.1174.
88 Xu, *Jundui Tonglan*, p.271.

Murata rifles specifications

Specification	Type 13 rifle	Chassepot Type 13 conversion	Type 13 carbine (Type 16 carbine)	Type 18 rifle	Type 18 carbine	Type 22 rifle	Type 22 carbine (Type 27 carbine)
Type	Breech loading single shot	Breech loading single shot	Breech loading single shot	Breech loading single shot	Breech loading single shot	Breech loading eight round magazine	Breech loading five round magazine
Cartridge	11x60 mmR	11x60 mmR	11x60 mmR	11x60 mmR	11x60 mmR	8x53 mmR (also called 8x52 mmR)	8x53 mmR (also called 8x52 mm)
Cartridge type	Paper	Paper	Paper	Metal	Metal	Metal	Metal
Approximate total length	129 cm	131 cm	117 cm (?)	127 cm	117 cm	121 cm	96 cm
Approximate barrel length	79 cm	80 cm	74 cm (?)	79 cm	68 cm	75 cm	50 cm
Approximate bayonet length	71 cm	70 cm; same as Chassepot bayonet	No bayonet	58 cm	No bayonet	28 cm (first model); 37 cm (second model)	No bayonet

Handguns

During the Boshin War, imported foreign handguns included Smith and Wesson, Lefaucheux, and Colt Navy revolvers. In 1877, the Smith and Wesson Type One revolver was designated the official regulation sidearm of officers. Developed at the Koishikawa Arsenal, the six-shot nine millimetre calibre Type 26 revolver replaced the Type One in 1893 and began to be issued to cavalrymen and officers a year later.[89] The Type 26 used a top break mechanism but only allowed for double action use. This latter feature was unpopular, and consequently some officers continued to carry imported foreign revolvers acquired privately. Also available was the Kuwabara pistol, a six shot 7.65 millimetre revolver made at the eponymous workshop in Tokyo.[90] Though weaker than the Type 26, the Kuwabara pistol used the same top break mechanism but could be used with both single and double action. The Kuwabara pistol saw limited official issue in the Imperial Guard only but was mostly purchased privately by those with the means.

Cold Weapons

The Japanese were very fond of their bayonets (juken), so every single model of the Murata rifle had an accompanying bayonet (except the carbines) with an identical designation. The Murata Type 13 bayonet was a sword bayonet and around 0.71 metres in total length with a 0.57 metre blade.[91] Chassepot Murata Type 13 conversions used the standard Chassepot bayonet.[92] The

---

89 Heath, *Japan*, p.73.
90 Shiraishi Hikaru, 'Kuwabara Seikeiben Kenjū', *Rekishijin* (2024), <https://www.rekishijin.com/39487>, accessed 4 January 2025.
91 Heath, *Japan*, p.71.
92 Zielinski, *Murata*, p.1244.

Type 18 bayonet was 0.58 metres in total length with a 0.46 metre blade. Type 18 bayonets had the Japanese chrysanthemum symbol stamped on their crossguard and were angled slightly downward to not block the rifle's barrel.[93] The Type 22's bayonet had two different variations: one with shorter grips that apparently came earlier and one with longer grips.[94] The shorter version was slightly less than 0.37 metres in length with a 0.28 metre blade. The longer grip version came at the very latest in 1897 and was slightly longer in length at about 0.38 metres but with a 0.30 metre blade. Type 22 bayonets were attached to the nose cap of the rifle instead of the barrel like the Type 13 and 18 bayonets.

Japanese officers received their first regulation sword around 1871, and another of either French or American inspiration between 1873 and 1875.[95] In 1886, however, official regulations for officer swords were finally set in stone, which would remain until 1900. Funnily enough, the same Murata Tsuneyoshi who had designed the rifles was also responsible for the design of the Japanese sabres, and they were nicknamed 'Murata to,' or 'Murata sabres.' According to the Model 1886 Regulations, swords were differentiated between double-edged, straight back (ken) and single-edged, curved back (to). 'Ken' and 'to' referred to specific types of swords in antiquity, but by this period they were more generic labels applied similarly to the Chinese 'jian' and 'dao.' Regardless of rank or service branch, all officers in the field used curved to-style sabres with long Western handguards for two-handed use, with varying amounts of ornamentation based on rank. Only general officers, Sanitation Department officers (military doctors, pharmacists and veterinarians), accountant officers and paymasters carried ken-style swords, and even then, only on parade. The field to swords had silver scabbards while those of parade ken swords were black with brass fittings. However, non-regulation scabbards might be custom-made of any material. Speaking of disobeying regulations, many officers bought traditional Japanese swords and scabbards from artisans.[96] This practice was far from discouraged and was even promoted in propaganda woodblock prints as a symbol of Japanese martial spirit.

The IJA Line cavalry had abandoned the lance by the Sino-Japanese War, though some Imperial Guard units retained it.[97] Cavalry sabres were initially European imports from France and then Germany, but eventually Japan began to manufacture their own copies, including the Type 7 of 1874 and the Type 25 of 1892. The Type 7 had a pierced guard and a long hilt with a bulged centre while the Type 25 had a solid brass guard and shorter hilt. Artillerymen and engineers were armed with the simply named 'artillery sword' (hohei to), which was sometimes described as a sword-bayonet but was basically a short sword that doubled as a tool. It had a straight blade of about 0.52 metres and a 0.13 metre hilt and was worn on a frog like an infantry bayonet.

---

93   Zielinski, *Murata*, p.1254.
94   Zielinski, *Murata*, pp.1263–1271.
95   Heath, *Japan*, p.73.
96   Heath, *Japan*, p.99.
97   Heath, *Japan*, p.72.

A Japanese second lieutenant (left) standing to attention with his guard, photographed shortly before deployment in the Sino-Japanese War. The second lieutenant seems to be quite well-off, as he holds a non-regulation Kuwabara pistol in his right hand and wears a custom tailored jacket with army branch coloured cuffs under the rank trefoils. His backpack is probably also a custom item. At this left hip is a binoculars case and at his right is the holster for his handgun. His guard wears his gaiters under his pants. (Public domain)

Artillery

The main Japanese breech loading gun used in the Sino-Japanese War was a slightly modified copper copy of the Krupp that began manufacture in 1882.[98] After the Franco-Prussian War, the Japanese purchased 24 Krupp field guns to use as models for their own domestic artillery production. Although the Model 1882 guns were based on the Krupp, at that time the Japanese steel industry was virtually non-existent so they were produced in steel bronze, a process brought over by visiting French engineers and later refined by Italian artillery experts. Produced under licence at the Osaka Arsenal, the Model 1882 had both a field and a mountain variant. They fired the same 75 millimetre shells, but the mountain gun had a shorter barrel and was mounted on a smaller carriage. The mountain gun could be disassembled easily and transported by five horses, with one carrying the barrel, another the wheels, two for each carriage wheel, and the last the ammunition cases.[99] By 1886, the Japanese had completely standardised the use of the Model 1882 in the military, so they constituted the majority of the models used in the Sino-Japanese War. The Model 1882 proved in combat to be only mediocre in accuracy and mobility but was generally far superior (if in consistency) to whatever the Chinese had in stock. Regardless, the Model 1882 was quickly replaced after the Sino-Japanese War ended.

Model 1882 mountain gun specifications

Specification	Details
Production	Began in 1882; first model produced in 1883
Calibre	75 millimetres
Barrel length	1 metre
Elevation	10 degrees down to 21 degrees up
Initial speed of projectile	255 metres per second
Maximum range	3,000 metres

Model 1882 field gun specifications

Specification	Details
Production	Began in 1882; first model produced in 1883
Calibre	75 millimetres
Barrel length	1.78 metres
Elevation	7 degrees down to 19 degrees up
Initial speed of projectile	422 metres per second
Maximum range	5,000 metres

In 1891, the Osaka Arsenal began producing a custom-designed 90 millimetre bronze mortar. This mortar could be slung from bamboo poles carried by two coolies,[100] and was first used at the Battle of Jiuliancheng.[101] Given its difficult transportation, it was used on a far smaller scale than the Model 1882 guns, but notably it was present during the Battles of Haicheng,

---

98 Xu, *Jundui Tonglan*, pp.275–276.
99 Heath, *Japan*, p.75.
100 Heath, *Japan*, p.75.
101 Xu, *Jundui Tonglan*, p.278.

Niuzhuang, Tianzhuangtai and Lushunkou. The Model 1891 mortar would see a long service life, poetically beginning in the First Sino-Japanese War and concluding at the end of the Second Sino-Japanese War in 1945.[102] Less commonly fielded was the Model 1893 150 millimetre mortar, which was essentially an enlarged version of the Model 1891 90 millimetre mortar, also designed and produced in Osaka.[103] The Model 1893 was only used during the Battle of Weihaiwei.[104]

Model 1891 mortar specifications

Specification	Details
Production	Began in 1891
Calibre	90 millimetres
Barrel length	850 millimetres
Elevation	8 degrees down to 68 degrees up
Initial speed of projectile	245 metres per second
Maximum range	4,150 metres

Model 1893 mortar specifications

Specification	Details
Production	Began in 1893
Calibre	149.1 millimetres
Barrel length	1,100 millimetres
Elevation	0 degrees down to 66 degrees up
Initial speed of projectile	242 metres per second
Maximum range	4,750 metres

Starting in 1887, the Japanese designed and manufactured bronze siege guns based on the Model 1882 in 120, 150, 240, and 280 millimetre calibres.[105] Designed for static batteries in coastal fortresses, these were only used once during the Sino-Japanese War, where a siege train consisting of four 120 mm guns, 12 90 mm guns, eight Model 1893 150 mm mortars and 12 Model 1891 90 mm mortars was fielded against the defences of Weihaiwei in early 1895.[106] Not used during the Sino-Japanese War were massive cast iron howitzers of 90, 150, 240, and 280 millimetre calibres designed, again, for coastal forts, but they would get their chance to shine during the Russo-Japanese War. Machine guns were only used during the invasion of Taiwan in 1895, and these were Osaka Arsenal copies of Maxim guns.

Accoutrements
Full IJA campaign kit consisted of a backpack or tube pack, a haversack, a canteen, a spare pair of shoes, a greatcoat, and a blanket.[107] Sources generally

---

102 By that point, they had of course switched to a steel version of the Model 1891.
103 Xu, *Jundui Tonglan*, p.278.
104 Heath, *Japan*, p.75.
105 Xu, *Jundui Tonglan*, p.277.
106 Heath, *Japan*, p.75.
107 Heath, *Japan*, p.96.

agree that the full kit weighed about 19 to 21 kilograms, though one source claims a measly 16 kilograms; this was much lighter than the standard 27 to 30 kilograms of most European army kits at the time. Japanese military belts were made of leather and had two black or dark brown leather cartridge boxes on the front and one on the back. These Type 13 and 18 cartridge boxes had round edges and did not resemble the more iconic rectangular boxes for the Type 22 Murata magazine rifle. The two front boxes could hold 20 rounds each, while the back box could hold 40; another 20 was stored in the backpack drawer (see below). The back box was considerably bulkier, and on its left side was a pocket for a bottle of gun oil and on the right a pocket for a combination tool (called 'kairaki' or 'tenraki') consisting of two pieces joined together at a rotatable pivot: a screwdriver for the screws on the rifle, and a wrench for the square headed screw that attached the trigger flat spring to the receiver.[108] The screwdriver had a thick end and a thin end; the former was for the bolt handle plug screw, and the latter for the remaining small screws. The wrench was about half the length of the screwdriver, and both pieces were about 0.45 centimetres thick. Cavalry cartridge boxes were carried on a sling and did not have the small tool pockets; instead, these small tools, along with extra ammunition, were stored on cartridge boxes attached to the saddle.

Entrenching and basic demolition tools were issued to infantry squads as a collectively owned set and not to any single soldier, so each soldier took turns carrying specific tools.[109] Even numbered squads received five shovels and one pickaxe while odd number squads had five shovels, one pickaxe, and one of either a hand axe or a folding saw. These would be held in a leather case strapped to the left back side of the backpack, or at the belt with the bayonet. The infantry M1887 shovels were of a German feldspaten shape (rectangular and blocky), while engineer M1888 shovels were of a more conventional curved spade design. Axes, saws and pickaxes were strapped horizontally at the top of the backpack, in front of the greatcoat/blanket roll; the axe might be hung from the belt by the blade cover, but the pickaxe and saw apparently were too cumbersome for this arrangement.

The Japanese Model 1887[110] backpacks drew heavy inspiration from French models and consisted of an inner wooden frame that was ergonomically curved instead of being perfectly cubical, covered with cloth and lacquered over, and waterproofed on the outside with cowhide.[111] This cowhide was prone to harbouring insects and emanated ghastly smells when wet. The canteen would be strapped to the backpack flap while a blanket roll, with a greatcoat inside, could be arranged in a horseshoe shape on top.

---

108 The author expresses his sincere gratitude to Stanley Zielinski for providing information on this rare piece of equipment.
109 Nick Komiya, 'The Evolution of the Japanese Infantryman's Entrenching Tool: 1887–1945', War Relics (2019), <https://www.warrelics.eu/forum/japanese-militaria/evolution-japanese-infantrymana-s-entrenching-tool-1887-1945-a-753444/>, accessed 12 Feb. 2024.
110 Prototypes were first drawn up in 1884, and field testing commenced in 1886.
111 Nick Komiya, 'The Evolution of the Japanese Imperial Army Backpacks (1874–1945)', War Relics (2018), <https://www.warrelics.eu/forum/japanese-militaria/evolution-japanese-imperial-army-backpacks-1874-1945-a-695642/>, accessed 12 Feb. 2024.

Inside the backpack was spare ammunition (for infantrymen and engineers), a mess kit, a medicine case, a tin of insect power, a water filter, two pairs of underwear, two shirts, two handkerchiefs, two pairs of socks, four pairs of straw sandals (waraji), and emergency rations.[112] These emergency rations were either canned foods or cooked rice foods like onigiri, giving Japanese soldiers a mobility advantage over the Chinese, who carried their rations and rice raw.[113] Infantrymen, artillerymen and engineers each had their own special backpack variants, while commissariat personnel were not issued backpacks at all. Engineer backpacks had longer straps than artillery and infantry backpacks, and only infantry and engineer backpacks had a tin drawer accessible from one side for storing ammunition. Artillery backpacks had two straps securing the horseshoe-shaped blanket roll on top of the backpack; however, for infantrymen and engineers the blanket would block access to the ammunition side drawer, so their backpacks only had one strap for the drawer side for easier opening but two on the other. Artillery backpacks also did not have side holding straps for other equipment.

An alternative to the backpack was the gassai bukuro ('travelling bag'), which was a dark blue tubular cloth sack that was worn diagonally around the body like a banderole.[114] These tube packs were theoretically meant to be carried empty inside the backpack and then used in combat when the unwieldy backpack was inappropriate, but in practice many soldiers simply did not wear backpacks at all and only used tube packs.[115] For example, soldiers of the 5th Division did not wear backpacks at all and instead only used tube packs. Meanwhile, soldiers who were not issued backpacks at all like commissariat personnel could only use tube packs. Sometimes Japanese soldiers might wear both the tube pack along with their blanket and a greatcoat roll diagonally across their body. In addition to both the backpack and tube pack was the Model 1892 haversack made of thick hemp and designed to carry 30 rounds of ammunition, rations for one meal, some personal items, and a canteen (which was later removed). This bag was issued to all soldiers with rifles, so artillerymen, commissariat personnel, and Kempeitai officers were excluded. Artillery and commissariat soldiers had to make do with only a backpack or tube pack, while the Kempeitai received their own special leather haversacks.

The Model 1892 IJA canteens were based on the Prussian Model 1867 canteen and made of glass since early metal prototypes rusted easily or were potentially toxic to their users.[116] The Model 1892 canteen was to be slung on a hook inside the haversack of the same designation. During the Sino-Japanese War, soldiers found that the canteen inside the bag would smack

---

112 Heath, *Japan*, p.96.
113 Junshi Jilu, Weiguan Zhanchang: Jiawu Zhanzheng, Jinlu Zhizhan, CCTV, (2012).
114 Heath, *Japan*, p.96.
115 Komiya, 'Backpacks', War Relics (2018), <https://www.warrelics.eu/forum/japanese-militaria/evolution-japanese-imperial-army-backpacks-1874-1945-a-695642/>, accessed 12 Feb. 2024.
116 Nick Komiya, 'The Evolution of IJA Canteens (1889–1945) Expanded Version', War Relics (2015), <Nick Komiya, 'The Evolution of IJA Canteens (1889-1945) Expanded Version', War Relics (2015)>, <https://www.warrelics.eu/forum/japanese-militaria/evolution-ija-canteens-1889-1945-expanded-version-586153/>, accessed 12 Feb. 2024.

A Japanese soldier guarding Chinese prisoners. The stubby handle of a German style army shovel can be seen attached to the other side of his backpack, while at his hip is the Model 1892 leather-clad glass canteen, apparently the version with a shoulder strap issued in early 1895. He appears to have a pair of traditional straw waraji shoes strapped to the top of his backpack. Additionally, note the fact that his cartridge box has a small pocket with a bottle of gun oil clearly visible; this indicates that he has taken off his two front cartridge boxes and replaced them with his rear box. Photographed by Georges Ferdinand Bigot. (Public domain)

against the wearer's leg, which impeded kneeling and prone firing. As such, in early 1895, the 1892 canteen was removed from the haversack and given a strap to be worn around the shoulder. More problems followed. The glass canteens would shatter if the water inside froze and expanded, which proved devastating for soldiers stationed in the freezing temperatures of China. Metal canteens were tested, but they released toxins if the inside was not properly sealed, so in late 1894 the IJA instead issued two piece leather covers that would insulate and prevent the glass canteen from freezing. The bottom piece would also serve as a drinking cup. In theory, soldiers were to prevent water from touching the leather covers, but as they were difficult and cumbersome to remove, the covers frequently got wet. When exposed to the cold, these wet covers would actually expedite the bursting of the glass canteens, and in hotter temperatures the leather cover would shrink and harden around the canteen and create a most unpleasant odour. One proposed solution to these problems was to replace the bottom leather cover with a wicker basket for drinking, while some units experimented with using lacquered wooden drinking cups. Prototype nontoxic metal canteens were researched heavily during the Sino-Japanese War, but the IJA would not get their first standard issue aluminium canteen until 1898.

Japanese mess kits used in the Sino-Japanese War were of the Model 1883 variety, a lacquered tin container with up to six cooked onigiri rice balls stored inside.[117] The tin containers did not have handles as they were not supposed to be used to cook foods, only store them. Instead, the commissariat branch was responsible for carrying large circular bowls for cooking rice for entire units, and in the field individual soldiers had to rely on bringing pre-cooked rations. This proved to be an issue, and after the Sino-Japanese War in 1898, IJA soldiers were issued individual copper cooking pots in addition to their tin mess kits.

Some sources depict Japanese infantry kit during the Sino-Japanese War as having a white 'tent section' bundled up and attached on the top of the backpack. This is incorrect; this piece of equipment refers to the M1903 'portable shelter' (keitai tenmaku), which was developed much after the Sino-Japanese War, but saw service during the Russo-Japanese War. The M1903 could be carried on the backpack in the aforementioned fashion but also worn as a rain poncho. Each man carried a square shaped (1.5 metres on each side) hemp/cotton cloth, two tent poles, two tent pegs, and two metres of hemp rope. A single M1903 could be used individually or joined together with others in various permutations to provide shelter for a varying number of men. The necessity for such a useful piece of equipment was no doubt inspired by the lacklustre commissariat arrangements during the Sino-Japanese War, when soldiers often had to sleep in the open during heavy rain and snow.

In the field, Japanese soldiers used bugles and visual signals to communicate; Japanese bugles had red tassels and were of a Western style.

---

117 Nick Komiya, 'The Evolution of the IJA Mess Kit 1874–1945', War Relics (2022), <https://www.warrelics.eu/forum/japanese-militaria/evolution-ija-mess-kit-1874-19-a-816235/>, accessed 12 Feb. 2024.

Drums, fifes, whistles or any other instruments were totally absent, excepting of course military bands.

Flags

The (in)famous Japanese rising sun flag consisting of a red ball with a varying number of rays on a white background was formally adopted as the war flag of the IJA in 1870, where it was called the '16 rayed rising sun flag' (juroku jo kyokujitsu ki).[118] The IJA flag theoretically had the sun centred while the navy had their sun slightly to the direction of the hoist. Regimental flags were initially identical to the army war flag, but in 1874 a new design was presented to the two infantry regiments of the Imperial Guard. This 1874 design had the original centred rising sun flag design with (theoretically) 16 rays with a gold border and purple fringes. At the bottom near the hoist was a blank white panel with the regiment's number written in Chinese characters by the Emperor himself as 'hohei dai (regiment number) rentai.' These infantry regimental flags were 100 by 80 centimetres. Later that same year regulations were set for Line infantry, cavalry and artillery regimental flags. The Line infantry regimental flags were identical to the ones unveiled to the Imperial Guard, except of course for the text on the white panel. Cavalry and artillery regimental flags had the same 16 rayed rising sun design and purple frills, but in square proportions of 82 by 82 centimetres. However, since in 1874 the highest unit of organisation of cavalry and artillery was a battalion, these regimental flags were only issued to Line infantry regiments. Flagpoles were finished in black lacquer and had gold Japanese chrysanthemum symbol discs at the tip. Unfortunately, the cavalry and artillery regimental flags would not see use in the Sino-Japanese War; the artillery flag was completely scrapped in 1885 while the cavalry version was truncated down to 64 by 64 centimetres and only issued in 1896 once the IJA cavalry organisation was finally expanded to true regiment strength. Starting in 1885, the infantry Second Reserve were issued regimental flags identical to their active army counterparts but with red instead of purple fringes.

Also introduced in 1874 alongside the Line army regimental colours were infantry battalion flags that differentiated each of the three battalions in every infantry regiment.[119] These had multicoloured zig zag lines on them, used to represent the mountainous terrain of Japan. The first infantry battalion of a regiment had one set of thick zig zag lines in red; the second had two thin sets with the red above the black; and the third had three sets with the black set in between the two reds. Infantry battalions without a specific regimental affiliation used the same design as the first infantry battalion, but with Chinese characters below bearing unit designation: 'dai (battalion number) daitai.' Those in the Second Reserve were very similar but with a palette swap: the first battalion had one set of thick zig zags but in black; the

---

118 Nick Komiya, 'The Banner of Golden Brocade', War Relics (2016), <https://www.warrelics.eu/forum/japanese-militaria/banner-golden-brocade-647336/>, accessed 12 Feb. 2024.
119 Heath *Japan*, pp.100–101

second battalion had two set of zig zags with the black over the red; and the third battalion had the same three sets of zig zags but with the red in between the black. Finally, the Kokumin Gun had a single set of thick zig zags in light purple for the first battalion; two sets of thin zig zags in light purple for the second; and one set of thick zig zags in a slightly darker purple for the third. Military academy battalions used identical flags to Line army first battalion insignia, but with a special 10-pointed star design bottom centre. Cavalry, artillery and the First Reserve did not use battalion flags. Lances were phased out of Line cavalry units by the Sino-Japanese War, but cavalry lances in the Imperial Guard were not and had a special red and white pennant for ceremonial use.

Like in Western armies, the Japanese associated great pride and spirit with their regimental banners, which were presented to them by the Emperor himself in ostentatious military ceremonies. These regimental banners were considered sacred objects, and they were passed down from year to year. This was pushed to such an extreme that in the 1940s some regimental banners were so old and worn-out from decades of service that nothing remained except the purple fringes. Regimental standard bearers held their position for one year and were usually first and second lieutenants, although the former was rarer. As the symbolic representation of the Japanese military and the Emperor's blessings, only the most courageous, intelligent and physically attractive Japanese soldiers could become regimental standard bearers. Regimental standard bearers were also meant to be virgins, a rule that was informal and unwritten but still firmly adhered to. Despite all this pomp and circumstance, eyewitnesses record that the Japanese resisted the temptation and did not often carry their flags into active combat like the Chinese did and brought them on campaign mostly for ceremonial occasions.[120]

---

120 Heath, *Japan*, p.101.

Chapter 4

The Navy of the Empire of Japan

Introduction

The Japanese had never had an illustrious and well-developed military naval tradition. Japan was not a maritime nation; they did not need to openly contest sea power, nor did they heavily rely on overseas trade. What they did have was more related to piracy and even then, those pirates liked to fight on foot and on land. Even Toyotomi Hideyoshi's invasion of Korea in the 1590s prioritised the navy as a form of transportation for his land troops, leading to the navy's ignominious thrashing by the Koreans and Chinese.[1]

The defeat of the great and respected Qing Empire in the Opium Wars was the first alarm bell for the Japanese regarding the importance of naval strength in the defence of the nation. The arrival of Commodore Matthew Perry to Japan in 1853 and the total Japanese helplessness to foreign aggression convinced the Shogunate to study the barbarian ways. At first, the existing Dutch enclave in Deijima was the first source of Western learning. Dutch naval experts were invited to establish a naval training centre at Nagasaki in the late 1850s, while open-minded men of the samurai class were sent abroad to Holland.[2] Japan's first steamship, the *Kanko Maru*, was acquired in 1855 as a gift from the King of Holland.[3] Later on in 1865, the French built a shipyard at Yokosuka. By the mid-1860s, the Shogunate had collected a ragtag band of eight Western warships, most of which were used for generic transportation purposes. The Domains each had their own independent fleets as well.

Emboldened by the 1863 edict from the Emperor ordering the expulsion of the foreign barbarians, the highly anti-foreign Choshu Domain felt confident enough to challenge the British barbarians and their guns at

---

1 David Evans et al., Kaigun: Strategy, Tactics, and Technology in the Imperial Japanese Navy, 1887–1941 (Annapolis: Naval Institute Press, 1997), pp.2–4.
2 Evans, *Kaigun*, p.5.
3 Dieter Jung et al., *Warships of the Imperial Japanese Navy, 1869–1945* (Annapolis: Naval Institute Press, 1976), p.88.

Shimonoseki began to shoot at any foreign ship in range.[4] Unfortunately, the aforementioned edict was not seriously enforced and no one really listened to it except the Choshu, whose coastal forts were shelled by the Americans and later demolished by the French. A few more examples were needed for the Japanese to fully digest the lesson. The Satsuma Domain had been one of the first to recognise the importance of modern naval power, as they had built a naval centre at Kagoshima and sent students abroad. By 1862 the Satsuma had acquired a few small lots of foreign weaponry and vessels through haphazard purchase and attempted to challenge British sea power by firing at all the foreign ships they could see. In 1863, the British sailed into Kagoshima Bay to correct this belief, seizing and burning all Satsuma vessels and laying waste to the city and the nearby coastal batteries. The Choshu Domain tried their hand again in 1864 with the same irritating modus operandi as last time, until 17 warships from Britain, France, Holland, and America bombed Shimonoseki and British, French, and Dutch landing parties destroyed the rebuilt coastal forts.

The Boshin War did not involve any major improvements to the Japanese navy, as maritime conflicts were restricted to boarding actions or basic support actions instead of long-range gun duels.[5] Afterward, the young Meiji government was more than aware of Japan's naval weakness but had to first deal with the various domestic reforms and later rebellions so important to the very survival of the government. The military nonetheless paid lip service to the navy's importance and always put 'navy' (kaigun) before 'army' (rikugun) in official notices. In 1872, the Imperial Japanese Navy (IJN) was officially born, as a ministry separate from the army.[6]

Even after the basic security of the Imperial government had been secured, the navy had to take a backseat. The Japanese at this stage had no intent to project power and consequently the navy remained a small coast guard force. Not that it could have been anything else either, as upon the founding of the Empire, Japan had a ramshackle gaggle of wooden steamboats, sailboats, and paddle boats. Even after steel gunboats and ironclads were slowly acquired in the 1870s and 1880s the IJN continued to patrol local waters only. In 1870, the IJN began to base their modernisation on the British Royal Navy instead of the Dutch, and likewise the first few IJN steamships were all British.[7] The 3,800 ton wrought iron frigate *Fuso* was completed in 1878 and was the first armoured ship to be built for Japan in England. Following the *Fuso* were the *Kongo* and *Hiei* in the same year, both of which were armoured corvettes.[8] Japanese engineers were sent to watch and learn from the construction of these ships. Although the IJN had no qualified sailors to deliver these three from England to Japan, a number of Japanese officers were present with the British crews; among them was future Admiral Togo Heihachiro. The first steel cruisers in the Japanese navy came in 1886 in the form of the *Naniwa*

---

4 Heath, *Japan*, p.10.
5 Evans, *Kaigun*, p.7.
6 Evans, *Kaigun*, p.7.
7 Evans, *Kaigun*, p.12.
8 Jung, *Warships*, p.13.

and *Takachiho*.⁹ Though based on the British Elswick protected cruisers, they were in fact superior and considered the best of their kind in the entire world.

The Japanese also began to make efforts at self-sufficiency. Navy yards based on Dutch examples had been established at Tokyo, Nagasaki, Ishikawajima, Uraga, and Yokosuka by the Shogunate, and the Imperial government took them over.¹⁰ In 1882, the IJN discontinued domestic production of wooden vessels, and two years later, the Yokosuka Dockyard, with French and British help, was able to produce small ironclad warships. The Tokyo Dockyard was able to repair modern ships and machinery by 1874 and began to turn out miniscule amounts of Western steel by 1882. This time was also the beginning of the famous shipbuilding firms of Ishikawajima and Kawasaki, who made their bones churning out torpedoes, cannons, and smaller warships on contract with the IJN. The Japanese were less successful with regards to coal production; a nationwide coal mine survey conducted in 1886 found that the vast majority of Japanese coal was the poor quality bituminous coal, which produced excessive amounts of black smoke whenever burned and was not energetically efficient. Bituminous coal could be converted to the far superior coke, but Japan lacked the industrial capacity to do so on a large scale; therefore, 25 percent of the IJN's fuel was imported Cardiff coal from Britain. When the Sino-Japanese War broke out, the Japanese were forced to rely on their own lower quality domestic deposits, much of which was rationed for other military purposes and unavailable to the Japanese navy; only 60 percent of daily consumption could be covered by domestic coal.

The British-built ships were delightful, but the Japanese also sought French assistance. The French had provided much aid since the days of the Shogunate but had lost much of their influence in the IJA after their defeat by the Germans. However, the French navy's prestige had remained generally unscathed, especially after their effortless thrashing of the Chinese navy during the Sino-French War. Furthermore, French naval doctrine of the 'Young School' (Jeune Ecole) at that time emphasised a fleet of small but numerous warships and torpedo boats that could outmanoeuvre larger vessels.¹¹ This was the perfect doctrine for the Japanese, mainly for economic reasons. Accordingly, the first naval expansion bill of 1882 issued government bonds worth over 17 million yen for the construction of 48 ships (later reduced to 46 in 1889) over an eight year period; 22 were torpedo boats and the rest were small cruisers. Additionally, new naval bases would be constructed at Kure and Sasebo to house, repair and maintain the new navy, along with the previously established facility at Yokosuka. An overwhelming majority of the 1882 torpedo boats were built in France with great success. Soon afterwards, the famous French naval architect Emile Bertin was invited to Japan on a two year contract (later expanded to three) to act as the helmsman of the IJN's expansion. Bertin designed the three *Sankeikan* class cruisers: the *Matsushima,* the *Hashidate*, and the *Itsukushima*, each named after one

---

9   Evans, *Kaigun*, p.14.
10 Evans, *Kaigun*, p.14.
11 Evans, *Kaigun*, pp.15–17.

of the three most celebrated Japanese scenic sights, called the 'sankei.'[12] The *Itsukushima* and *Matsushima* were both built in France, but the *Hashidate* was built in nearly six and a half years at the Yokosuka Dockyard, making her the first armoured ship to be built in Japan. The *Sankeikan* class, however, left much to be desired. Designed to be a cheaper counter to the terrifying Chinese *Dingyuan* and *Zhenyuan*, the *Sankeikan* class cruisers were poorly balanced, failed to reach design speeds, had unreliable boilers, and their singular large gun, although among the strongest in the world, was unwieldy and caused the ship to tip over clumsily. Fortunately, the *Sankeikan* class ships were saved from being totally useless with the installation of quick-firing guns onto each vessel. Some of the French-built cruisers also suffered poor fortune; the 741 ton *Chishima*, an unprotected cruiser, was sunk in a collision in 1892[13] while the 3,615 ton *Unebi* was lost by foundering in 1887 while travelling from Singapore back to Japan.[14] The Japanese returned to their old friends, the British, and purchased the *Yoshino* in 1892. At 4,150 tons and with a top speed of 23 knots, she was the fastest cruiser in the world at the time.[15] She was also the eighth ship in the world to be equipped with the vaunted Barr & Stroud Rangefinder.

On the eve of the Sino-Japanese War, the IJN carefully studied their own advantages and disadvantages against the Chinese Beiyang Navy. The Chinese fleet had superiority in weight of guns, overall ship tonnage, and numbers, as well as a number of foreign advisors serving on board their vessels. The Japanese had smaller, quicker guns, but no foreign experts on their ships in combat. The Japanese ships were also much faster, as the *Sankeikan* class cruisers were speedier than anything in the entire Beiyang Navy. However, the IJN high command believed that ultimately the outcome of the naval showdown would be decided by the naval tactics and actual execution of the battle, not by conjectural number-crunching of theoretical ship capabilities.[16]

Naval Academies and Training

The IJN's humble beginnings were similar to that of the Beiyang Navy, and yet there could have been no greater contrast by 1894. At its beginning, the IJN was dominated by men of the former Satsuma Domain. Most of these had received their positions due to nepotism and feudal factionalism as opposed to experience or competence. The navy minister from 1873 to 1878, Katsu Awa, had never even been to sea before.

To rectify this, the first IJN naval academy was established in Tokyo in 1869 and later moved to Etajima in 1888.[17] Initially, the academy was dominated by cadets from Satsuma families, but in 1871, the naval academy began to accept students based on exams that measured merit as opposed to feudal networking. Although Satsuma ascendancy over the navy persisted

---

12 Jung, *Warships*, p.96.
13 Jung, *Warships*, p.93.
14 Jung, *Warships*, p.96.
15 Jung, *Warships*, p.98.
16 Evans, *Kaigun*, p.41.
17 Evans, *Kaigun*, pp.10–13.

THE NAVY OF THE EMPIRE OF JAPAN

Imperial Japanese Navy officers and sailors pose in front of a Chinese government office after the capture of Dalian. The officers wear the austere service dress; the jackets decorated only with two lower pockets and edging in black. The sailors behind wear the formal sailor uniform in dark blue, and some of them wear their trousers over their gaiters. The man in the bowler hat on the bottom right is probably a war correspondent. Photographed by Ogawa Kazumasa. (Public domain)

well into the 1920s, they had lost their total monopoly. The Satsuma swallowed their old grudges, and in 1870 the British navy was chosen as the model for the IJN's modernisation. In 1873, a British naval mission led by Lieutenant Commodore Archibald Douglas was invited to teach at the Tokyo Naval Academy for several years, giving IJN maritime tradition a very British foundation. At the end of the 1870s, the IJN began to rely more heavily upon individual foreign advisors and Japanese students who had returned from abroad as opposed to direct government assistance, but British influence continued to dominate.

Japanese students sent abroad returned home in 1886 with knowledge of the new self-propelled Whitehead torpedo in development by the Royal Navy, and established the Yokosuka Torpedo Training Academy.[18] In 1887, Captain John Ingles of the Royal Navy was hired as a teacher at the Tokyo Naval Academy, but also provided a much broader range of services advising and mentoring the young IJN.[19] Ingles found the IJN's discipline and esprit de corps was second to none, but its officers lacked understanding of tactics, strategy, and deeper technical understanding of the scientific principles behind the operation of a modern fleet. Ingles urged the IJN to dispense with their sail and oar powered ships and to replace them with steamships. The captain also pushed for the additional criterion of mastery of Western science and engineering for the selection of IJN officers. In the same year that Ingles arrived in Japan, a new academy for the IJN's best and brightest was

---

18   Evans, *Kaigun*, p.18.
19   Evans, *Kaigun*, pp.12–13.

opened, called the Navy Officer Higher Education Academy (Koto Shikan Gakko) and was later renamed the Navy Staff College (Kaigun Daigakko). During his tenure at the Staff College from 1887 to 1893, Ingles gave a series of lectures on modern naval tactics that would form the foundation of Japanese war philosophy during the Sino-Japanese War. Furthermore, upon Ingles' request, scientific knowledge was also added to the curriculum, though specialised engineering officers attended a separate engineering school. Moreover, Lieutenant Commodore L.P. Willan, a veteran of the Royal Navy, was appointed to teach gunnery and navigation at the Tokyo naval academy in 1879 while serving as a gunnery instructor with the screw corvette *Tsukuba*. Willan's contributions expanded much beyond his job description, and his written work on modern naval tactics became the IJN's first taste of modern naval tactics, organisation, and manoeuvres.

The IJA had the Franco-Prussian War to use as a reference for their organisation and tactics, but unfortunately, the IJN had no such luxury. The only "modern" naval engagement they could reference was the Battle of Lissa in 1866; out of the two ships lost, one had been rammed and the other set on fire.[20] A desperate scramble to equip ships with ram bows ensued afterwards, but the Battle of Lissa had taken place during a unique time period where the gunnery of both sides left much to be desired, so the importance of the ram was much debated. The ram was far from the only controversial technology available. Japanese naval tacticians reached no definitive consensus on the distribution of armour, placement of guns, number of guns, weight and size of guns, incidence of torpedo tubes and torpedo boats, and so on. The French 'Young School' of naval thought championed using smaller fleets of smaller torpedo ships to outmanoeuvre larger warship fleets, which the Japanese liked mainly due to its economic viability.[21]

When the Japanese navy was still small, naval tactics were irrelevant and not even possible to apply, as the navy focused entirely on simple guard and patrol manoeuvres. But after the 1882 shipbuilding frenzy, the IJN devoted more time to first studying Western naval tactics and innovating on them. Although some translated works were available beforehand, in 1887 a young navy Lieutenant Shimamura Hayao compiled a comprehensive overview of British and American naval tactics that was the most detailed of its time.[22] Following Shimamura's suggestions, the Japanese began to innovate, design and adapt their own tactics with small committees of ship captains, staff officers and other technical specialists. First, tactics, formations, and movements were proposed on paper, and their merits and drawbacks debated. Next, the ship captains would put them into practice on the high seas. Finally, the captains would make corrections and modifications based on their experiences. Through this method, the Japanese navy settled on a column arrangement with the flagship leading as their go-to formation. Moreover, the Japanese torpedo boats were found to be generally unseaworthy and had

---

20 Evans, *Kaigun*, p.32.
21 Evans, *Kaigun*, p.15.
22 Evans, *Kaigun*, pp.34–37.

poor aim and manoeuvrability, so IJN doctrine restricted their use to night attacks and against ships in harbour.

Admiral Ding Ruchang of the Beiyang Navy had been appointed based on loyalty and trustworthiness as judged by Li Hongzhang. Ding was indeed worthy of this appraisal but knew little of naval tactics given his background as a cavalryman and also failed to manage and inspire his subordinates. On the other hand, the IJN was led by Vice Admiral Ito Sukeyuki, who was highly knowledgeable in tactics and had studied abroad previously. The Fujianese clique of the Beiyang Navy had no counterpart in the IJN; although the Satsuma coterie was still prominent, their officers were still competently trained and cooperated effectively with non-Satsuma officers. Likewise, the IJN maintained high standards of discipline both within its officers and sailors, so feudal factionalism did not really impact the navy's performance and function. Finally, unlike the Chinese Beiyang Navy, whose state of the art ships were squandered by the poor discipline and infrequent training of their crews, the Japanese made it a priority to drill regularly.

Total strength

Japan was divided into the five naval districts of Yokosuka, Kure, Sasebo, Maizuru and Muroran.[23] By the Sino-Japanese War, only the first three districts were functional with the latter two still lacking suitable bases. During the war, the Maizuru district was placed under the control of the Kure and Yokosuka districts, while Muroran fell under the jurisdiction of Yokosuka alone. In peacetime, the IJN was split into three sections among the naval bases at Yokosuka, Kure, and Sasebo. Not all of these were frontline ships ready to do battle; some of the ships, like the *Kasuga*, *Kanju*, and *Manju* were sail ships used for despatch for the former and training for the latter two. In wartime, these outmoded ships were not mobilised at all and remained in reserve or assigned for patrol and training duties. The wartime organisation divided the IJN's 26 frontline ships into four divisions, plus a 'Flying Squadron' and a de facto reserve division. The torpedo boats were organised into three fleets, with a fourth still being formed during the war and a fifth of older vessels for coastal defence. Lastly, some 288 merchant steamships belonging to various civilian companies were able to be requisitioned and called up for transport duty.

---

23 Olender, *Sino-Japanese*, p.52.

Imperial Japanese Navy Ships, 1894[24]

Name	Type	Tonnage	Horse-power	Maximum speed (knots)	Complement	Construction information
Naniwa	Protected Cruiser	4,150	7,500	18	338	1884–1886; Armstrong, Mitchell & Company, England
Takachiho	Protected Cruiser	4,150	7,500	18	338	1884–1886; Armstrong, Mitchell & Company, England
Takao	Cruiser	1,927	2,332	15	222	1886–1889; Yokosuka Dockyard, Japan
Fuso	Battle cruiser	3,800	3,932	13	250	1876–1878; Samuda Brothers, England
Yaeyama	Cruiser	1,584	5,400	21	217	1887–1892; Yokosuka Dockyard, Japan
Amagi	Cruiser	1,030	720	11	159	1875–1878; Yokosuka Dockyard, Japan
Tsukuba (ex-*Malacca*)	Cruiser	1,978	526	10	275	1851–1855; Mould, Burma (built as HMS *Malacca*, sold to Japan in 1870)
Chiyoda	Armoured cruiser	2,400	5,600	18	350	1888–1890; John Brown & Company, England
Yoshino	Protected Cruiser	4,150	15,750	23	360	1892–1893; Armstrong, Mitchell & Company, England
Kongo	Battle cruiser	3,718	2,450	13.75	314	1875–1878; Earle's Shipbuilding & Engineering Company, England
Hiei	Battle cruiser	2,248	2,490	14	314	1875–1878; Milford Haven Shipbuilding & Engineering Company, England
Tsukushi (ex-*Arturo Prat*)	Cruiser	1,542	2,600	16	177	1879–1883; Armstrong, Mitchell & Company, England (built as *Arturo Prat* for the Chilean navy, sold to Japan in 1885)
Atago	Gunboat	612	963	12	104	1886–1889; Yokosuka Dockyard, Japan
Maya	Gunboat	612	963	12	104	1885–1887; Onohama Dockyard, Japan
Akagi	Gunboat	612	963	12	104	1886–1890; Onohama Dockyard, Japan
Chokai	Gunboat	612	963	12	104	1885–1888; Ishikawajima Dockyard, Japan
Tenryu	Cruiser	1,525	1,267	12	214	1878–1885; Yokosuka Dockyard, Japan
Hosho	Gunboat	316	217	10	65	1868–1869; Alexander Hall & Sons, England
Tateyama	Sail Training Ship	543	None	Unknown	51	1879–1880; Kobe Dockyard, Japan
Hashidate	Protected Cruiser	4,217	5,400	16.5	360	1888–1894; Yokosuka Dockyard, Japan
Itsukushima	Protected Cruiser	4,217	5,400	16.5	360	1888–1891; Societe des Forges et Chantiers, France
Matsushima	Protected Cruiser	4,217	5,400	16.5	360	1888–1891; Societe des Forges et Chantiers, France
Akitsushima	Protected Cruiser	3,100	8,516	19	330	1890–1894; Yokosuka Dockyard, Japan
Musashi	Cruiser	1,478	1,622	13	231	1884–1888; Yokosuka Dockyard, Japan
Yamato	Cruiser	1,478	1,622	13	231	1883–1887; Onohama Dockyard, Japan
Katsuragi	Cruiser	1,478	1,622	13	231	1882–1887; Yokosuka Dockyard, Japan
Oshima	Gunboat	630	1,216	16	130	1889–1892; Onohama Dockyard, Japan
Banjo	Gunboat	708	659	10	112	1877–1880; Yokosuka Dockyard
Kaimon	Cruiser	1,429	1,267	12	210	1877–1884; Yokosuka Dockyard, Japan
Kanju	Sail Training Ship	877	None	Unknown	102	1886–1888; Onohama Dockyard, Japan
Manju	Sail Training Ship	877	None	Unknown	102	1886–1888; Onohama Dockyard, Japan
Kasuga	Cruiser	1,289	1,217	9	138	1863; J.S. White, England
Ryujo (ex-*Ihosho Maru*)	Ironclad	1,864	800	9	275	1864–1869; Alexander Hall & Sons, England

---

24 Jung, *Warships*.

THE NAVY OF THE EMPIRE OF JAPAN

Name	Type	Tonnage	Horse-power	Maximum speed (knots)	Complement	Construction information
Azuma (ex-*Kotetsu*, ex-*Staerkodder*, ex-*Stonewall*, ex-*Sphinx*)	Ironclad	1,560	1,300	9	135	1863–1865; L'Arman Brothers, France
Tatsuta	Cruiser	830	5,000	21	107	1893–1894; Armstrong, Mitchell & Company, England
Izumi (ex-*Esmeralda*)	Cruiser	2,920	5,500	18	300	1881–1884; Armstrong, Mitchell & Company, England (built for Chilean navy as the *Esmeralda*, sold to Japan in 1894)
Iwaki	Gunboat	656	590	10.5	112	1877–1880; Yokosuka Dockyard

Imperial Japanese Navy Armament

Name	Armament	Torpedoes
Naniwa	Two 259 mm 35 cal Krupp guns, six 150 mm 35 cal Krupp guns, six 47 mm guns, 14 machine guns	Four 381mm torpedo tubes
Takachiho	Two 259mm 35 cal Krupp guns, six 150mm 35 cal Krupp guns, six 47mm guns, 14 machine guns	Four 381mm torpedo tubes
Takao	Four 152 mm quick firing guns, one 119 mm quick firing gun, one 57 mm gun, 2 machine guns	Two 381 mm torpedo tubes
Fuso	Four 239 mm Krupp breech loading guns, two 170 mm Krupp breech loading guns, six small guns, 5 machine guns. In 1894 the Fuso was rearmed with: eight 152 mm 50 cal quick firing guns, seven machine guns.	Two 457 mm torpedo tubes added in 1894
Yaeyama	Three 119 mm quick firing Krupp guns, eight 47 mm guns	Two 381 mm torpedo tubes
Amagi	One 170 mm Krupp breech loading gun, four 119 mm breech loading guns, three 79 mm breech loading guns, 3 machine guns	None
Tsukuba	Six 114 mm breechloading rifled guns, two 30 pounder guns, two 24 pounder guns. In 1892 four 152 mm quick firing guns were added	None
Chiyoda	Ten 119 mm 40 cal quick firing guns, fifteen 47 mm breechloading guns	Three 457 mm torpedo tubes
Yoshino	Four 152 mm 40 cal quick firing guns, eight 119 mm 40 cal quick firing guns, twenty two 47 mm guns	Five 356 mm torpedo tubes
Kongo	Three 172 mm Krupp breech loading guns, six 147 mm Krupp breech loading guns, four 1 pounder guns, seven machine guns. In 1895 a single 25 mm quick firing gun was added	Two 356 mm torpedo tubes
Hiei	Three 172 mm Krupp breech loading guns, six 147 mm Krupp breech loading guns, four 1 pounder guns, seven machine guns. In 1895 a single 25mm quick firing gun was added	Two 356 mm torpedo tubes
Atago	One 211 mm 22 cal breech loading Krupp gun, one 4.7 25 cal breech loading Krupp gun, 2 machine guns	None
Maya	Two 150 mm 25 cal Krupp guns, two 57 mm Nordenfelt guns, 2 machine guns	None
Akagi	Four 119 mm 40 cal quick firing guns, six 47 mm Hotchkiss guns	None

SUNSTRUCK GIANT VOLUME 1

Name	Armament	Torpedoes
Chokai	One 211 mm 22 cal breech loading Krupp gun, one 4.7 25 cal breech loading Krupp gun, 2 machine guns	None
Iwaki	One 150 mm Krupp gun, One 120 mm Krupp gun, two 80 mm Krupp guns, three Nordenfelt machine guns	None
Tsukushi (ex-*Arturo Prat*)	Two 254 mm breech loading guns, four 119 mm breech loading guns, two 76 mm guns, four machine guns	Two 381 mm torpedo tubes
Tenryu	One 170 mm breech loading Krupp gun, six 4.7 breech loading Krupp guns, four machine guns, one 76 mm breech loading Krupp gun	None
Hosho	One 178 mm breech loading Armstrong gun, one 5.5 breech loading Armstrong gun, two smaller guns	None
Tateyama	Two 57 mm 40 cal guns	None
Hashidate	One 12.152 mm 38 cal Canet gun, eleven 119 mm 40 cal quick firing guns, five 57 mm guns, eleven 47 mm guns	Four 127 mm torpedo tubes
Itsukushima	One 12.152 mm 38 cal Canet gun, eleven 119 mm 40 cal quick firing guns, five 57 mm guns, eleven 47 mm guns	Four 127 mm torpedo tubes
Matsushima	One 12.152 mm 38 cal Canet gun, eleven 119 mm 40 cal quick firing guns, five 57 mm guns, eleven 47 mm guns	Four 127 mm torpedo tubes
Akitsushima	One 12.152 mm 38 cal Canet gun, twelve 119 mm 42 cal quick firing guns, eight 47 mm guns Rearmed in 1894–1895: four 152 mm 40cal quick firing guns, six 119 mm 50 cal quick firing guns, eighteen 47 mm guns	Four 381 mm torpedo tubes Rearmed in 1894–1895: four 457 mm torpedo tubes
Musashi	Two 170 mm breech loading Krupp guns, five 119 mm breech loading Krupp guns, one 76 mm quick firing Krupp gun, four machine guns	Two 381 mm torpedo tubes
Yamato	Two 170mm breech loading Krupp guns, five 119mm breech loading Krupp guns, one 76mm quick firing Krupp gun, four machine guns	Two 381 mm torpedo tubes
Katsuragi	Two 170 mm breech loading Krupp guns, five 119 mm breech loading Krupp guns, one 76 mm quick firing Krupp gun, four machine guns	Two 381 mm torpedo tubes
Oshima	Four 119 mm 40 cal guns, five 47 mm Hotchkiss guns	None
Banjo	One 150 mm 22 cal breech loading Krupp gun, one 119 mm 25 cal breech loading Krupp gun, two 79 mm breech loading Krupp guns, three machine guns	None
Kaimon	One 170 mm breech loading Krupp gun, six 114 mm breech loading Krupp guns, one 76 mm breech loading gun, 4 machine guns	None
Kanju	Two 20 pounder guns, two 17 pounder guns	None
Manju	Unknown, probably same as *Kanju*	None
Kasuga	One 178 mm muzzle loading Forbes gun, four 114 mm breech loading gun, two 30 pounder muzzle loading guns	None

THE NAVY OF THE EMPIRE OF JAPAN

Name	Armament	Torpedoes
Ryujo	Two 165 mm breech loading guns, ten 140 mm breech loading guns	None
Azuma	One 228 mm breech loading gun, two 172 mm breech loading Armstrong guns	None
Tatsuta	Two 119 mm quick firing guns, four 47 mm guns, five 37 mm guns	Five 381 mm torpedo tubes
Izumi	Two 254 mm 30 cal guns, six 152 mm 26 cal breech loading guns, two 57 mm guns, 7 machine guns	Three 381 mm torpedo tubes

Imperial Japanese Navy Peacetime Organisation

District	Active duty ships	Reserve ships	Guard ships	Training ships	Despatch ships
Yokosuka	*Naniwa, Takao*	*Fuso, Hashidate, Yaeyama*	*Musashi, Atago*	*Amagi, Tsukuba, Kanju*	None
Kure	*Itsukushima, Chiyoda*	*Yoshino, Hiei, Maya*	*Tsukushi, Yamato, Akagi*	*Kongo, Tenryu, Hosho, Tateyama*	None
Sasebo	*Matsushima, Takachiho*	*Akitsushima, Katsuragi*	*Oshima, Chokai, Banjo*	*Kaimon, Manju*	*Kasuga*

Imperial Japanese Navy Torpedo Boats

Name	Tonnage	Horse-power	Maximum speed (knots)	Armament	Torpedoes	Complement	Construction information
Boat One to *Boat Four*	40	430	22	Two 37 mm guns	Three 356 mm torpedo tubes	Unknown	1878–1880; Yarrow & Company, England
Boat Five to *Boat Fourteen*, *Boat Sixteen* to *Boat Nineteen*	54	525	19	Two 37 mm guns	Two 381 mm torpedo tubes	16	1890–1894; Ch. de Chalons-sur-Saone, France
Boat Fifteen to *Boat Twenty*	53	657	20	Two 37 mm guns	Two 381 mm torpedo tubes	20	1891–1893; Normand, France
Boat Twenty One	80	1,121	20.7	Two 37 mm guns	Two 381 mm torpedo tubes	21	1891–1892; Normand, France
Boat Twenty Two to *Boat Twenty Three*	85	990	19	Two 37 mm guns	Three 356 mm torpedo tubes	20	1891–1893; Schichau, Germany
Boat Twenty Four	80	1,121	20.7	Two 37 mm guns	Two 381 mm torpedo tubes	21	1895; Kure Dockyard, Japan
Boat Twenty Five	Unknown	904	Unknown	Unknown	Unknown	Unknown	1894–1895; Onohama Dockyard, Japan
Kotaka	203	1217	19	Four 37 mm guns	Six 381 mm torpedo tubes	Unknown	1885–1886; Yarrow & Company, England

Uniforms

During the Sino-Japanese War, the IJN used the Model 1883 (Meiji 16) set of uniform regulations with a few modifications mainly pertaining to the unnecessarily convoluted system of naming orders of dress and insignia. While the IJA's Model 1886 was indubitably German, the Model 1883 was based on British naval dress and stressed a simple, utilitarian design.[25]

For officers and NCOs, there were three orders of dress: full dress (seifuku), military dress (gunfuku), and service dress (tsujo gunfuku). Full dress was worn during ceremonial events; military dress was for semi-formal events and service dress was, unsurprisingly, the everyday dress of IJN officers. This system was implemented in 1893 and lasted until 1904. IJN formal dress consisted of a black bicorne hat with a slightly lighter black cockade underneath a golden laced strap, a double breasted navy blue jacket and trousers of the same colour, and a sword belt. Epaulettes, collar insignia, buttons, trouser stripes and belt buckles were gold, and the coat did not have coloured piping. Underneath the jacket, a Western collared shirt and bow tie were worn. Military dress was a plain navy blue double-breasted jacket with gold cuff insignia and buttons, but no other decorations like epaulettes or piping. The coat had seven pairs of buttons, with the upper two pairs hidden in the jacket lapel. Underneath, the standard collared shirt and bow tie were worn along with a peaked cap. The service dress was worn with the peaked cap and a single-breasted jacket with two lower pockets. The pockets and opening were both edged in black, which was also the colour of the cuff insignia. A navy blue mantle was provided to officers starting from 1884, with a collar and six ribboned buttons; a pocketless raincoat with detachable hood and a similarly featureless poncho were also issued. Officer greatcoats were double-breasted and had six rows of gold buttons and special cuff insignia consisting of one line with two, three or four buttons for junior, senior and admiral officers, respectively. The officer summer uniform was a simple five-buttoned jacket with two pockets on the left; a pith helmet and white cover for the peaked cap could also be worn.

For sailors, formal dress was a navy blue sailor shirt and branch distinction denoted via shoulder patches. The sailors' working uniform (jigyofuku) was a plain white shirt with a Western-style collar (changed from the sailor square collar in 1890). Underneath the uniform was a short-sleeved undershirt with the neckline piped in navy blue; soldiers who prioritised comfort over smartness ditched the other layers and only wore the undershirt. Sailors typically wore Western style shoes on formal occasions, but in action they were more likely to go either barefoot or wear special reinforced tabis that did not slip. Winter gear like traditional Japanese sashes, sweaters, scarves and cotton wraps were provided by the IJN.

The IJN had their own military band, and at the time of the Sino-Japanese War they wore red seven-buttoned jackets with black cuffs and gold cuff insignia, gold epaulettes, black collars, and special collar badges. IJN military band trousers were navy blue with one red stripe. Rear echelon personnel

---
25 Etsuko Yagyu, *Nihon Kaigun Gunsou Zukan* (Tokyo: Namiki Shobou, 2014), pp.32–33.

THE NAVY OF THE EMPIRE OF JAPAN

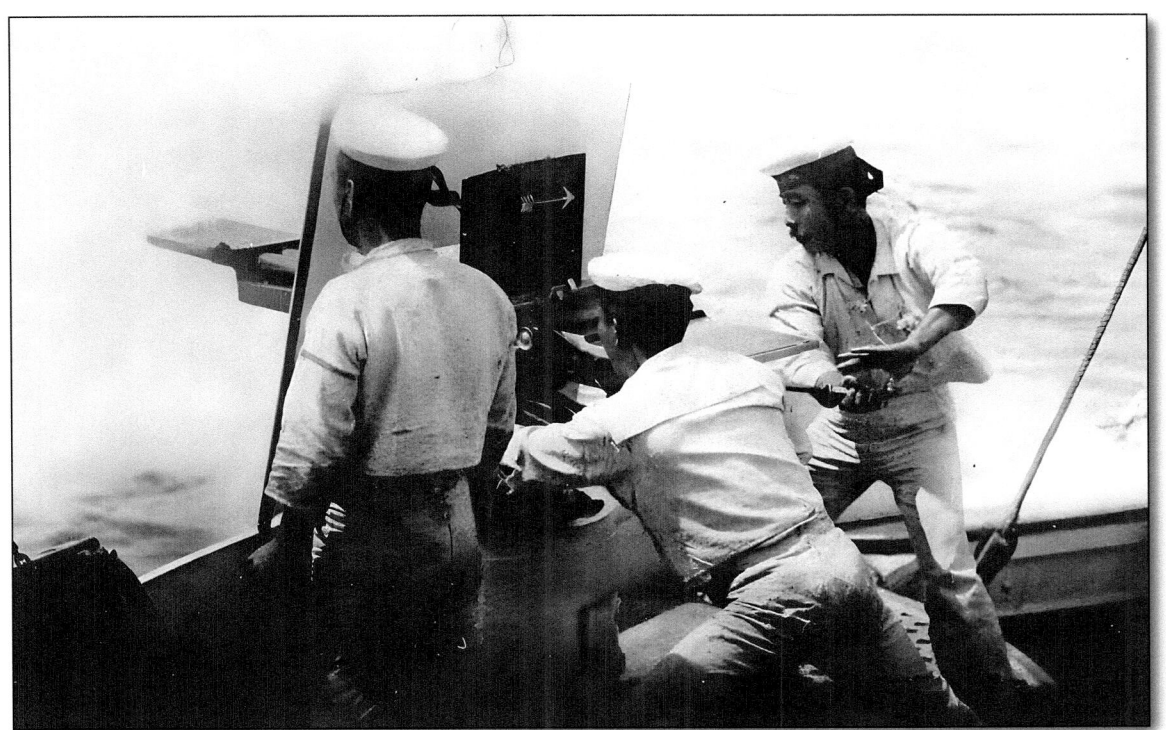

Three Japanese sailors operating a Nordenfeldt gun fitted with a shield. They are dressed in simple working uniforms, although the man on the left has apparently chosen to wear formal navy blue trousers instead of the white working ones. Photographed by Ogawa Kazumasa. (Public domain)

like clerks, nurses, and technicians wore seven-buttoned uniforms similar to that of military band musicians.

Flags

Unsurprisingly, most IJN flags were based on the rising sun design. The naval ensign had sixteen rays, while the commissioning pennant had the same design limited to the widest area of the pennant closest to the flagpole.[26] Rank flags were hoisted according to the rank of the most senior officer on board. In use from 1889 to 1945, the Navy Minister's flag was of two 'mountain line' designs with an anchor topped with a stylised cherry blossom and exceptionally did not feature the rising sun. Initially, this anchor flag was the naval ensign of the IJN but was relegated to the Minister's flag in 1871. Admirals used an eight rayed rising sun flag from 1871 until 1897; vice and rear admirals used admiral flags with a circle on the top left quadrant and both left quadrants respectively until 1896 when distinct designs were introduced for their ranks. Senior and junior officers used similar rank flags of a forked pennant with the eight rayed rising sun design; senior officer rank flags had a red sun on a white background but junior officer rank flags had the colours inverted.

---

26 Xu, *Jundui Tonglan*, pp.343–344.

Chapter 5

Colour Plate Commentaries

Chinese military uniforms of the Sino-Japanese War

Please note that since many of these illustrations are based on real artifacts, some of the Chinese names on the identification discs have been changed or removed, according to the wishes of the owner.

A1. Ren Army Auxiliary Battalion Tiger Brave

This uniform belonged to 'Tiger Brave' Jin Taiyu of the Second Squad of the Centre Company of the Auxiliary Battalion of the Ren Army of the Huai Army. On the identification patch, the rank of the soldier (Hu Yong) is in the centre, the name of the soldier (Jin Taiyu) is at the bottom left, the company (Zhong Shao) and squad (Er Dui) designations are to the bottom right, the army name (Renzi) and battalion designation (Fu Ying) are directly above the rank, and the army affiliation (Huai Jun) is directly above the army division and battalion designation. The Ren Army Auxiliary Battalion in particular was commanded by General Tan Qingyuan and was stationed at Asan during the Battle of Seonghwan.

    The physical uniform, along with B1, B2, and C5, and possibly A2 and A4, were brought back to Japan after being captured during the Korea campaign and displayed publicly at Yasukuni Shrine. After 1945 these war trophies were turned over to the occupation government and probably destroyed as part of the de-militarisation programme, so only a handful of Japanese prints and written descriptions exist today to confirm their existence. Photographs were taken of the flags captured in Korea (see plate D), but apparently none of the uniforms. Some of the printed depictions are contradictory with one another, but all agree that the Ren Army uniform had red edging. The rest of the jacket was some shade of blue, most commonly the turquoise shown here, but sometimes a grey blue or medium blue. The zhan qun is confirmed by a written description to be deep purple edged in red, but is often depicted inaccurately in prints as being dark blue edged in red. The white piping on both the jacket and zhan qun is sometimes shown and sometimes not. Japanese prints almost always show this uniform being paired with a wide-brimmed paper or straw hat that is either black or red. Prints also show the company designation to be on the bottom right and the squad designation on the bottom left, but here I have moved them to their more likely position on the bottom right with the name on the bottom left, in accordance with Huai Army regulations. The aforementioned written description also mentions that the pants (not shown here) were light blue.

Note that A1, A2, A4, A6, C1, and C8 all have narrow sleeves compared to the other uniforms; as the 19th century went on, cutting down the size of sleeves became increasingly popular in order to better facilitate the handling of rifles, but clearly this modernisation was not universally implemented.

It is unclear if 'Hu Yong' refers to an abbreviated location of the unit's provenance (i.e. Huai Yong for Anhui troops, Lu Yong for Lutai troops) or the nickname of the unit, meaning 'Tiger Brave'. I have decided to interpret it as the latter, since to my knowledge the Ren Army was never stationed anywhere with the abbreviation 'Hu.'

A2. Sheng Army Left Army Right Battalion Huai Brave

This uniform belonged to a 'Huai Brave' of an unknown squad and company of the Right Battalion of the Left Army of the Sheng Army. On the identification patch, the rank of the soldier (Huai Yong) is in the centre, the squad and company on the bottom right, the battalion (You Ying) and army designation (Left Army) are directly above the rank, and the army name (Shengzi) is directly above the battalion and army designation. The soldier's name, squad and company have not been filled out on the patch (see below). The Sheng Army Left Army Right Battalion was one of the units that entered Korea after the Battle of Seonghwan and fought at the Battle of Pyongyang under General Wei Rugui; A4 and C1 also belong to this same battalion.

This illustration is taken from two photographs of a Korean civilian posing in a captured Chinese uniform, taken by Georges Ferdinand Bigot shortly after the Battle of Pyongyang. The uniform is paired with a straw boater hat with a plain band. Since the photograph is black and white, the colours of A2 are entirely conjectural; red edged in black was one of the most common combinations, and in the photographs the uniform appears to have very dark edging. The colour of the jacket piping is certainly not white, since the colour is completely different from the second set of piping on the zhan qun, which are a far lighter colour; here I have shown it as yellow, as that was the next most common choice of piping colour. The buttons appear to be metal beads instead of Chinese knot buttons. Given the lack of detail in the photographs, the only text clearly visible are the army, battalion, and rank designations; besides that, I have given the illustration a Chinese meander pattern border like the other Sheng Army uniform C1. The name, company and squad designation are illegible in the original photograph, so I have left them blank; in theory, every identification patch was supposed to include the name, company, and squad designation, but in practice this was not always carried out, as is the case for A4, A5, B1, B4, B5, B8, B13, C1, C3, C5, C10, and C11.

The design on the zhan qun is called a 'pingsheng sanji' symbol; in the Chinese language, the phrase 'promoted three levels' is a homonym for 'three halberds emerging from a vase.' The latter image soon became a symbol of good luck for government officials and soldiers and can also be seen on

A6 and A6a. The red design in the middle of the vase is called a 'tongqian' pattern, intended to represent the shape of a traditional Chinese copper coin and therefore serve as another good luck symbol; this motif can also be found on the zhan qun of A3, A6, C5, and C11, and on the flags D11 and D13.

Note that the soldier's rank is 'Huai Yong,' or 'Huai Brave.' This terminology refers to a soldier from Anhui Province and is also used in B12 and C3.

An illustration by war correspondent Frederick Villiers records soldiers wearing identical uniforms to A2 attempting to shoot their rifles with one hand while holding their umbrellas in the other; given the corrupt and undisciplined nature of the Sheng Army, this kind of behaviour is not entirely unexpected.

A3. Zhao Huaiye's Army Auxiliary Battalion Bodyguard

This uniform belonged to Bodyguard Zhang Guotao of the Second Squad of the Centre Company of the Auxiliary Battalion of Zhao Huaiye's Army (a division of Li Hongzhang's Huai Army). On the identification patch, the rank (Qin Bing) is on the centre, the name (Zhang Guotao) on the bottom left, the company (Zhong Shao) and squad (Er Dui) designation on the bottom right, the battalion (Fu Ying) designation and army (Huaizi) name above the rank, and the army affiliation (Huai Jun) directly above the rank. Zhao Huaiye's Army fought at (or rather, deserted from) Jinzhou, Dalian and Lushunkou during the Liaodong Peninsula campaign. After the Battle of Lushunkou, Zhao himself was heavily punished, as he sold off government property to turn a profit and deserted his own men.

This illustration is taken from the China's Hidden Century exhibition held in the British Museum in 2023; the exhibition displayed both the jacket and the zhan qun, along with a conical cool hat made of bamboo. The cool hat does not belong with the uniform at all and was acquired by the museum separately; by this time most northern Chinese armies solely wore turbans. The jacket and zhan qun were loaned to the British Museum by The Box (formerly Plymouth Museum), which received them from a donation from one Mrs Curtis in 1912, along with B10 and C9. Since Zhao Huaiye's Army deserted in large numbers and abandoned their uniforms, it is possible that Mr Curtis, a British naval officer during the war, simply picked an unused set off the ground. Three other artifacts of Zhao Huaiye's Army are known to exist. A jacket belonging to a Regular Brave of the Right Battalion is in possession of the National Taiwan Museum, another jacket belonging to a Regular Brave of the Rear Battalion is in a private collection and is recreated in B14, and finally another Regular Brave of the Right Battalion jacket is on display at the Jinzhou Deputy Governor's Office (Jinzhou Fu Dutong Yamen) museum.

Note the unusual orange cloth neck guard, sewn directly to the opening of the jacket and closed with another button. An identical neck guard appears on the jacket in the Jinzhou Deputy Governor's Office museum, but these are the only two examples that the author has ever seen with such neck guards.

Compare A3 with B14, another jacket of Zhao Huaiye's army. Both of these jacket identification patches use regular Chinese numerals instead of the more complex formal versions, unlike every single other uniform shown in this book. However, both the National Taiwan Museum jacket and the Jinzhou Deputy Governor's Office jacket use formal characters.

A4. Sheng Army Left Army Right Battalion Bodyguard
This uniform belonged to a Bodyguard of an unknown squad and company of the Right Battalion of the Left Army of the Sheng Army. On the identification patch, the rank (Qin Bing) is displayed in the centre, the squad and company designation on the bottom right, the battalion (You Ying) and army (Left Army) designation above the rank, and the army name (Shengzi) above the battalion and army designation. The space for the soldier's name on the bottom left and the soldier's company and squad on the bottom right have not been filled out.

This uniform comes from a single Japanese print depicting captured Chinese and Korean objects after the Battle of Pyongyang. As a rule, Japanese prints depicting scenes of battle are usually inaccurate with regards to Chinese military uniforms, as they were made by artists who were thousands of miles away from the war. Contrariwise, Japanese prints specifically depicting captured items are reasonably accurate, as these are based off real artifacts brought back to Japan to be publicly displayed. Here, I have faithfully reproduced all elements of the original print as much as possible, even if some elements may be inaccurate; for example, note that the Chinese meander pattern often seen on the border of the identification patch is missing; the other two Sheng Army uniforms A2 and C1 do have this border.

A5. Ming Army Centre Army Right Battalion Regular Brave
This uniform belonged to a Regular Brave of the First Squad of the Centre Company of the Right Battalion of the Centre Army of the Ming Army. On the identification patch the rank (Zheng Yong) is placed in the centre, the squad (Yi Dui) and company (Zhong Shao) designations in the bottom right, the battalion (You Ying) and army (Zhong Jun) designations above the rank and the army name (Mingzi) above the battalion and army designations. The bottom left space reserved for the soldier's name is not filled out. The Ming Army fought in the northern China campaigns, starting from Jiuliancheng and ending with a rearguard action at Tianzhuangtai. Even after General Liu Shengxiu handed over control of the Ming Army to General Jiang Guiti, the Ming Army continued to wear identical uniforms. Additionally, during the Battle of Keelung (Jilong) in the Yiwei War, the Ming Army was recorded as wearing identical uniforms to this one, along with white uniforms similar to B12 and B13.

The illustration of the jacket is taken from an existing uniform from the Hong Kong Museum of Coastal Defence, as well as another exactly identical artifact from the First Sino-Japanese War Museum on Liugongdao. The illustration of the zhan qun is taken from a contemporary Chinese documentary reconstruction of the entire Ming Army uniform; in this reconstruction, the jacket and zhan qun are paired with purple pants, black Tartar boots edged in yellow, and a dark blue turban. In the Hong Kong Museum of Coastal Defence, the jacket is displayed with a Manchu warm hat, though it is uncertain whether this hat actually belonged to the same uniform.

This is one of the most well-known uniforms of the Sino-Japanese War, being illustrated in Osprey Publishing's *Armies of the First Sino-Japanese War (1894–1895)* and *Imperial Chinese Armies (1840–1911)*, albeit without the zhan qun, with an improbable Manchu hat (a turban would have been more likely), and with completely nonsensical identification patches.

A6. Sui Army Left Battalion Squad Leader

This uniform belonged to a Squad Leader of the First Squad of the Left Company of the Left Battalion of the Sui Army. On the embroidered text, the rank (Shichang) is in the centre, the squad designation (Yi Dui) on the bottom left, the company designation (Zuo Shao) on the bottom right, and the battalion designation (Zuo Ying) and army name (Sui Jun) on the top.

The Sui Army Left Battalion was stationed at the north gate of Weihaiwei before the Sino-Japanese War and was disbanded due to desertion and losses incurred during the ensuing fighting there.

This illustration is taken from a jacket and a zhan qun captured by the Japanese and now in a private collection. Another highly similar uniform also exists in another private collection; this example is almost entirely identical but the embroidered text instead reads 'Bodyguard Long Ming of the Second Squad of the Left Battalion of the Sui Army;' this uniform is shown in Figure Four of the colour illustrations (see below). The placement of the text on the bodyguard jacket is identical, except that instead of the company designation on the bottom right and the squad designation on the bottom left like in A6, this bodyguard uniform has squad designation on the bottom right and the soldier's name on the bottom left. Additionally, the pingsheng sanji design on the bodyguard zhan qun, shown in A6a, has handles and a more detailed bottom than the A6 one. As Chinese military uniforms of this time were still handmade, slight variations like so were highly common. Also see the description of C8 for an almost exactly identical jacket of the Gong Army, the sister unit of the Sui Army.

Note the white string loops attached to the sleeves; these could be fastened to a button on the other side of the sleeve to fold and reduce the length of the sleeves for convenience; C1 also has this feature.

B1. Tenacious Army Veteran Front Battalion Bodyguard

This uniform belonged to a Bodyguard of the First Squad of the Front Squad of the Veteran Front Battalion of the Tenacious Army. On the identification patch, the rank (Qin Bing) is in the centre, the squad (Yi Dui) and company (Qian Shao) designations on the bottom right, the battalion designation (Lao Qian Ying), and the army name (Wuyi) above the battalion designation. The soldier's name on the bottom left is not written in. The Veteran Front Battalion, numbering 200 men, arrived in Korea on 8 June, being among the first batch of troops to do so. They fought at Seonghwan, Pyongyang, and tagged along with General Nie until his departure, and after that they remained at Motianling until the end of the war.

This uniform has the same provenance as A1 and is commonly depicted in Japanese prints. These of course do not always agree with one another, so the white piping, the Chinese meander border on the identification plates, and the colour are all conjectural. However, all prints show blue grey zhan qun being worn. The shape of this zhan qun is sometimes portrayed in prints as completely rectangular, but this is probably a mistake as zhan qun were made to resemble Manchu armour leg coverings, which had curved sides.

Note that the vest has two wide cloud head patterns on it, one above the identification patch and the other below. This is an extremely unusual decision since Chinese military jackets typically only had one, and those with two cloud head patterns usually did not have an identification patch at all. The author has only seen two other examples of this unique design: one, a picture of Chinese troop manoeuvres in Zhili Province; and two, a crude Japanese drawing of a Chinese uniform captured from Seonghwan. The latter two jacket designs are incredibly similar to B1 and are recreated in C5 as a potential uniform of the Tenacious Army.

B2. Ren Army Auxiliary Battalion Military Labourer

This uniform belonged to Military Labourer Lin Ruizhi of the Third Squad of the Front Company of the Auxiliary Battalion of the Ren Army of the Huai Army. On the identification patch, the rank of 'military labourer' (Changfu) is in the centre, the soldier name (Lin Ruizhi) on the bottom left, the squad (San Dui) and company (Qian Shao) on the bottom right, the battalion designation (Fu Ying) and army name (Renzi) above the rank, and the army affiliation (Huai Jun) above the battalion and army designations. This uniform belonged to the same battalion as A1.

This uniform is taken from a written description and a Japanese print depicting items captured from the Korea campaign. The illustrations of this uniform are exceptionally basic and substitute the name, squad, company and army affiliation with dots; therefore, these have been added conjecturally to the illustration, along with a Chinese meander border. The illustrations appear to show metal ball buttons instead of knot buttons, but this is uncertain. What is knowable is that the uniform was blue edged in red, as confirmed by the very austere written description.

B3. Sui, Gong and Other Armies Battalion Office Bodyguard

This uniform belonged to a Bodyguard of the Sui, Gong and Other Armies Battalion Administration. From top to bottom, the embroidered characters read: Sui Gong, Deng, Jun, Yingwuchu, Qin, and Bing. 'Sui Gong' obviously refers to the Sui and Gong Armies, but 'Deng' literally means 'et cetera' or 'other,' so the soldier's unit name was literally called the Sui, Gong and Other Armies Battalion Administration Office. Since this was a rear echelon unit, the men who wore this uniform probably were stationed at the Chinese headquarters at Weihaiwei.

This illustration is taken from an existing uniform in the Motianling Museum in Weihai, China.

B4. Gui Army Centre Battalion

This uniform belonged to a soldier of the Centre Battalion of the Gui Army of the Huai Army; the identification patch reads, from top to bottom: Huai Jun, Gui, Zi, Zhong, and Ying. When the majority of the Resolute Army left Lushunkou for Manchuria to prepare for a potential Japanese invasion, General Jiang Guiti stayed behind and was ordered to raise the Gui Army to garrison the city. Being new recruits and plagued with poor leadership, much of the Gui Army deserted before the Battle of Lushunkou. After the battle, they followed General Jiang Guiti out of the Liaodong Peninsula and linked up with General Song Qing's forces in the north.

Three uniforms of this type are known to exist; B4 is based on one in a private collection; B5 is based on one in possession of the National Taiwan Museum since 1933, and the final one is in another private collection. Note the minor differences between B4 and B5: the cloud head shape on the bottom has different proportions, the identification patch of B5 includes text for company and squad designation while B4 does not, the buttons are placed differently, and the interior of the vests are different colours. Additionally, the privately owned uniform that is not depicted has an illegible identification patch, but it overall more closely resembles B4, as its interior is blue and its lowest button is in the middle of the cloud head design. Again, Chinese uniforms were all handmade items, so such variation is expected.

According to photographs, Resolute Army soldiers wore similar uniforms to B4 and B5; see Figure Two.

B5. Gui Army Left Battalion

This uniform belonged to a soldier of an unknown squad and company of the Left Battalion of the Gui Army of the Huai Army. The patch reads, from top to bottom: Huai Jun, Gui, Zi, Zuo, and Ying; the rightmost two characters read shao and dui respectively, referring to company and squad designations. No squad or company designations are actually written in.

This uniform was originally captured and brought home as a souvenir by Japanese soldier Hirose Sugi of Nishioka, Saga Prefecture, but in 1933 one Mitani Chiyu of Saga Prefecture donated the uniform to the Taiwan Governor-General Museum, the Japanese colonial predecessor to the National Taiwan Museum.

See commentary for B4 for more information about the features of the Gui Army uniform.

B6. Jiuliancheng Uniform

This uniform is taken from a photograph by Ogawa Kazumasa of a prisoner posing in front of abandoned Chinese trenches after the Battle of Jiuliancheng. Not much is known about the uniform, as no unit details are inscribed on it. As blue edged in red was the most popular colour combination for Chinese military clothing, I have chosen it for this illustration. The photograph does show that the edges were also highlighted in a darker colour. Unusually, this vest does not have a cloud head pattern at the bottom and instead has a simpler sword head (jian tou) motif.

COLOUR PLATE COMMENTARIES

B7. Tianjin Trained Army Auxiliary Battalion Lu Brave

This uniform belonged to Lu Brave Li Jiebao of the Eighth Squad of the Centre Company of the Auxiliary Battalion of the Trained Army of Tianjin. On the identification patch, the rank (Lu Yong) is positioned in the centre, the name (Li Jiebao) on the bottom left, the squad (Ba Dui) and company (Zhong Shao) designations on the bottom right, the battalion designation (Fu Ying) and army type (Lian Jun) above the rank, and the location stationed (Tianjin) above the battalion designation and army type. The presence of 'Lu Yong' denotes that this unit was from Lutai and therefore part of the Luyu Defence Army, commanded by General Nie Shicheng. 200 men of the Luyu Defence Army arrived in Korea on 24 July, where they were promptly merged with the Tenacious Army battalions. The Japanese specifically praised the Lu Braves for their valour during the Battle of Jiuliancheng.

Two examples of this uniform exist; both held in the Hefei Zimuyuan Museum. Both are completely identical except of course for the soldier's name, squad, company, and battalion; this other identical uniform belonged to the Regular Battalion instead of the Auxiliary Battalion. Interestingly, B16 also belonged to a soldier of the Regular Battalion of the Luyu Defence Army but is completely different from B7.

Note that the soldier's rank is 'Lu Yong,' or 'Lu Brave.' This terminology refers to a soldier from Lutai, Tianjin, and is also used in B16.

B8. Cheng Army Centre Battalion

This uniform belonged to an Artillery Officer of the Front Company of the Centre Battalion of the Cheng Army of the Huai Army. In the identification patch, the rank (Pao Tong) is in the centre; the company designation (Qian Shao) is on the bottom right, and the battalion designation (Zhong Ying) and army name (Chengzi) are above the rank, and the army affiliation (Huai Jun) is above the battalion designation and army name. The Cheng Army participated in the Battles of Tuchengzi and Lushunkou, and in the latter they were abandoned by their commanding officer, General Wei Rucheng, before fleeing themselves. Wei Rucheng was the brother of Wei Rugui, who was beheaded for cowardice in early 1895.

Along with several other weapons and flags from the Sino-Japanese War, this uniform is currently on display in the Konnoh Hachimanga Shrine in Shibuya, Tokyo. Unfortunately, the shrine owners refused to show the author the entire uniform, so only a portion of the back is visible. Hence, the shape, size, and existence of the cloud head motif are conjectural. The uniform appears to have a double lapel (dui jin), as no side opening or side buttons are present. The back identification patch is visible, but much of the text, on the bottom left and centre are illegible. The uppermost character in the centre easily reads 'pao,' or 'cannon,' but the bottommost character is in very tired condition and appears to read 'tong,' meaning 'general;' in other words, the identification patch may mean 'artillery officer.' This is an unusual designation, but the author was not able to find any other plausible interpretation.

The author expresses his sincerest gratitude to Briana Lopez for taking excellent photos of the uniform.

B9. Jinsheng Army Centre Army Centre Battalion Regular Brave

This uniform belonged to Regular Brave Lu Henqing of the Eighth Squad of the Rear Company of the Centre Battalion of the Centre Army of the Jinsheng Army. On the patch, the name (Lu Henqing) is on the bottom left; the squad (Ba Dui) and company (Hou Shao) are on the bottom left; the rank (Zheng Yong) in the centre; the battalion (Zhong Ying), army designation (Zhong Jun), and army name (Jinsheng Jun) above the rank. Finally, the uppermost two characters read 'Jin Yong,' meaning a brave from Tianjin.

General Cao Kezhong's Jinsheng Army was stationed at Tianjin and Beijing for the entirety of the war and did not participate; however, Admiral Ding Ruchang did request their help during the Siege of Liugongdao. Jinsheng Army translates to 'Tianjin Victorious Army.'

This illustration is taken from an artifact in a private collection; according to photographic evidence, the Jinsheng Army did participate during the Battle of Tianjin during the Boxer Rebellion, so this uniform was probably captured then.

B10. Ye Zhichao's Bodyguard Cavalryman

This uniform belonged to a cavalryman of Ye Zhichao's bodyguard. The top line reads 'Zhili,' and the second line 'Juegedu Butang,' referring to a type of supervisory government office intended to deal with corruption. The bottom four characters read 'Qin Jun Ma Dui,' meaning 'Bodyguard Cavalry Detachment.' A number of mounted bodyguards accompanied General Ye Zhichao to Korea; the uniform of a bodyguard artilleryman is depicted in B17. Ye Zhichao's Bodyguard, predictably, fought with him during the entirety of the Korea campaign and comprised 80 men at full strength.

B10 is a rare example of a uniform with a one lapel (yizi jin); see also C6.

This uniform is from the Box museum; it is part of the same collection as A3 and C9.

B11. Jiesheng Trained Army Jingal Squad

This uniform most likely belonged to a jingal gunner of the Jiesheng Trained Army; it is unique for being the only physical uniform that the author has ever seen with Manchu text on its identification patch. On the front, the Manchu reads 'Sunjaci Meyen,' meaning 'Fifth Squad.' The Chinese characters on the right read 'Liushijiu Hao,' meaning 'Number 69,' while those on the right comprise the soldiers' name 'Zhao Yongqian.' On the back, the Manchu reads 'Aisin Jeo-i Meihereme Miyoocan-i Meyen.' 'Aisin' means 'gold' in Manchu, and 'jeo' is a transliteration of the Chinese 'zhou,' so 'Aisin Jeo' refers to the city of Jinzhou on the Liaodong Peninsula. 'Meihereme' is a verb meaning 'carried over the shoulder,' while 'miyoocan' refers to a musket; therefore, 'meihereme miyoocan' refers to a jingal.

The Jiesheng Trained Army was a force of reorganised Manchu Bannermen led by General Irgen Gioro Lianshun and was stationed in Jinzhou and its environs. Photographic and written evidence confirms that they did indeed use jingals during the Battle of Jinzhou, so it is most probable that this uniform belonged to a soldier of that unit. It is unclear why this identification patch uses Manchu script, when by 1894 very few Manchus could write or even read it fluently. Indeed, there is an orthographic error in the writing of 'sunjaci,' and 'Aisin Jeo' is a rather clumsy conversion of 'Jinzhou' to Manchu, as the direct transliteration 'Gin Jeo' would have been more common in everyday speech.

This uniform is taken from an existing artifact from the Sugino Costume Museum in Tokyo, along with C10.

The author expresses his sincere gratitude to Professor Mark Elliott for the incredibly valuable Manchu language translations, as well as the linguistic nuances surrounding them.

B12. *Ming Army Right Rear Battalion Huai Brave*

This uniform belonged to a Huai Brave Niu Tingzhi of the First Squad of the Rear Company of the 'Right Rear Battalion' of the Ming Army. On the patch, the rank (Huai Brave) is in the centre, the name (Niu Tingzhi) on the bottom left, the squad (Yi Dui) and company (Hou Shao) on the bottom right, the battalion designation (You Hou Ying) above the rank, and the army name (Ming Jun) above the battalion designation. 'Right Rear Battalion' is an odd designation and may refer to the Rear Battalion of the Right Army; a uniform of a Huai Brave of the 'Right Left Battalion' exists today in the Shogenji Shrine of Minokamo in Gifu Prefecture. Since 'Right Left Battalion' does not make sense as a unit, it is likely that the uniform actually belonged to the 'Left Battalion of the Right Army,' as the name of the army was usually given before the battalion (i.e. A2, A4, A5, B9, and C1). This naming convention is also followed in B13.

An original example of this uniform exists at the Minsu Museum in Sanhe, Hebei in China; a recreation exists in the museum at Li Hongzhang's former residence in Hefei, China. I have chosen to copy the proportions and shape of the jacket from the original while using the identification patch from the recreation, as the patch in the original is slightly illegible.

Note the red stamp on the bottom left of the identification patch; traces of a similar red stamp also appear in many other uniforms such as the originals of B13, B14, and B15, but I did not include the stamp in other illustrations because they were so faded that it was impossible to recover their original form. However, these stamps typically were to signify that the identification disc in question was legitimate, and that its creation was sanctioned by the local commander and battalion administration office. The text of these stamps was usually in small seal script.

Also note the more complex identification patch meander border of B12 and B13, and compare with the simpler designs of A1, A2, A5, B1, B2, and so on. Apparently, the Ming Army Huai Braves were entitled to a fancier patch, as no other units possess this more detailed meander pattern. Additionally, B12 and B13 use the term 'Ming Jun' to refer to the Ming Army, while A5 uses the more conventional 'Mingzi.' 'Ming Jun' simply means Ming Army, while Mingzi literally translates to 'Chinese character Ming.' Finally, an identification patch of a Ming Army Centre Army Regular Battalion Huai Brave also exists in another private collection. This identification patch is odd, as no company is listed but rather a 'Left Eighth Squad' is. Additionally, it uses the phrase 'Mingzi' instead of 'Ming Jun,' and also has the same complex meander border as B12 and B13. This patch was probably captured during the Battle of Keelung in the Yiwei War, where some units of the Ming Army fought.

Two other white and red uniforms similar to B12, B13, and B14 are kept today in the Shogenji Shrine of Minokamo in Gifu Prefecture; unfortunately, these two specimens do not have their identification patches remaining, and thus their units cannot be properly identified.

B13. Ming Army Right Auxiliary Battalion Squad Leader

This uniform belonged to a Squad Leader of an unknown squad and company of the Right Auxiliary Battalion of the Ming Army. On the identification patch, the rank (Shichang) is shown in the centre, the unfilled company and squad designations on the left, the battalion designation (You Fu Ying) above the rank, and the army name (Ming Jun) above the rank. 'Right Auxiliary Battalion' may actually refer to the 'Right Army Auxiliary Battalion,' as described above in B12. The name space in the bottom left and the company and squad designations on the bottom right are left empty.

This illustration is taken from a private collection. Compare B13 with B12; note the differences in the shape of the cloud head pattern, the proportions of the sleeves, the colour of the buttons and identification patch and so on.

B14. Zhao Huaiye's Army Rear Battalion Regular Brave

This uniform belonged to Regular Brave Chen Yongli of the First Squad of the Rear Company of the Rear Battalion of Zhao Huaiye's Army of the Huai Army. On the identification patch, the soldier's name (Chen Yongli) is listed on the bottom left, the soldier's rank (Zheng Yong) in the centre, the soldier's squad (Yi Dui) and company (Hou Shao) designations on the bottom right, the soldier's battalion (Hou Ying) designation and army name (Huaizi) above the rank, and the soldier's army affiliation (Huai Jun) above the battalion designation and army name.

This uniform is taken from a private collection; see A3 for more information.

B15. Ming Army Bodyguard Regular Battalion Bodyguard

This uniform belonged to Bodyguard Li Jinyuan of the Fourth Squad of the Left Company of the Bodyguard Regular Battalion of the Ming Army. On the identification patch, the name (Li Jinyuan) is on the bottom left, the rank (Qin Bing) is in the centre, the squad (Si Dui) and company (Zuo Shao) designations are on the bottom right, the battalion designation (Qin Bing Zheng Ying) above the rank, and the army name (Mingzi) above the battalion designation. The identification patch of this uniform is incredibly strange, being octagonal and far more detailed than any other example the author has ever seen.

This uniform comes from the Baqi (Eight Banners) Museum in Yuexiu, Guangdong, China. How it got there is a mystery. There is another similar military jacket currently on display at the Sanhe Guzhen Huai Army Museum; however, the shape of the cloud head is different and there is an additional embroidered lining on all of the orange-red edging, in the same colour. A third example of this kind of jacket exists in the Shogenji Shrine of Minakomo City of Gifu Prefecture in Japan, without any particularly unique features from B15 besides a differently shaped cloud head. In the Hefei Zimuyuan Museum, there exists only an identification patch of the same kind, albeit not cut out from its original cloth stencil. This latter identification patch was captured by the Japanese during the Battle of Dalian and later donated to the museum by posterity.

B16. Tianjin Trained Army Regular Battalion Lu Yong

This uniform belonged to Lu Brave Li Jiale of the Fifth Squad of the Rear Company of the Regular Battalion of the Trained Army of Tianjin. On the patch, the soldier's name (Li Jiale) is on the bottom left, the squad (Wu Dui) and company (Hou Shao) designations on the bottom right, the soldier's rank (Lu Yong) in the centre, the soldier's battalion (Zheng Ying) and army type (Lian Jun) above the rank, and the soldier's location (Tianjin) above the battalion and army type. See B7 for details regarding the Luyu Defence Army.

This illustration is taken from an artifact in a private collection.

B17. Ye Zhichao's Bodyguard Artilleryman

This uniform belonged to artilleryman Wang Fengming of the Artillery of the Fifth Squad of the Left Company of General Ye Zhichao's Bodyguard. On the identification patch, the soldier's position (Pao Dui) is in the centre, the soldier's name (Wang Fengming) on the bottom left, and the soldier's company (Zuo Shao) and squad (Wu Dui) designations on the bottom left. The uppermost section of the identification patch reads 'Zhili Tidu Junmen,' which translates roughly to 'Commander in Chief of Zhili Province.' The section below reads 'Zongtong Huai Lian Ma Bu Shuilei Deng Yingqi,' which means 'Commander in Chief of the Huai and Trained Armies Cavalry, Infantry, Torpedo, and Other Battalions Banner;' this is just a very fancy way of referring to Ye Zhichao's Bodyguard.

The identification patch on the uniform itself lacks the centre two characters, as the ink or embroidering has peeled off, but from the light spots remaining one can still ascertain that it used to read 'Pao Dui,' or 'artillery.' The colour of these two characters are conjectural.

This uniform, along with C6 and C6a, was captured by the Captain of the 3rd Company of the 18th Infantry Regiment, and his descendants donated them to the Oiso Town Local History Museum in Kanagawa Prefecture, Japan. The author expresses his sincere gratitude to Misako Tomita for showing both artifacts.

C1. Sheng Army Left Army Right Battalion Squad Leader

This uniform belonged to a Squad Leader of an unknown squad and company of the Right Battalion of the Left Army of the Sheng Army. On the patch, the rank (Shichang) is positioned in the centre, the unfilled squad and company designations on the bottom right, the battalion (You Ying) and army (Zuo Jun) designations above the rank, and the army name (Shengzi) above the battalion and army designations.

This uniform is taken from an existing artifact from the Minsu Museum in Sanhe, Hebei in China.

C2. Fubiao Bodyguard Army Centre Battalion Bodyguard
This uniform belonged to a Bodyguard of the Centre Battalion of the Fubiao Bodyguard Army. On the patch, the soldier's position (Qin Bing) is in the centre, the battalion designation (Zhong Ying) above the position to the left of the opening, and the army name (Fubiao Qin Jun) divided between the area to the right of the battalion designation and the uppermost two characters. The Fubiao Bodyguard Army refers to the force led by General Liu Shuyuan, which numbered 3,000 men from six battalions and fought during the last two counterattacks on Haicheng. The name itself deserves some explanation: the 'fu' in 'fubiao' refers to the Qing name for a governor of a province, or 'xunfu.' A 'biao' was a specific type of Green Standard Army unit, so 'fubiao' would mean a unit of soldiers directly under the command of the governor. This would mean that the Fubiao Bodyguard Army was the bodyguard of Hunan Governor Wu Dacheng.

Two of these uniforms exist, both in private collections. Both examples are completely identical except for the state of preservation of the identification patch.

C3. New Qing Army Auxiliary Battalion Huai Brave
This uniform belonged to Huai Brave Yu Kaiqi of the Ninth Squad of the Right Company of the Auxiliary Battalion of the Qing Army (Zhang Guangqian's New Qing Army). On the identification patch, the rank (Huai Yong) is in the centre, the soldier's name (Yu Kaiqi) on the bottom right, the soldiers' company (You Shao) and squad (Jiu Dui) on the bottom right, and directly above it is the battalion designation (Fu Ying) and army name (Qingzi). Above the battalion designation and army name reads 'Juegedu Butang,' which refers to a government office responsible for curtailing corruption.

As for the military unit, the Qing Army was named after General Wu Changqing and uses a different Chinese character than the Qing Dynasty. Wu had his military beginnings in 1853, after joining his father Wu Tingxiang's Lujiang militia to combat the Taiping rebels. After the elder Wu's death in combat in 1854, Wu Changqing continued the suppression efforts, eventually racking up enough victories to be noticed by Zeng Guofan. In 1862, Wu was given the honour of being one of the first 13 battalions of the Huai Army, with Zeng's auspices. He continued annihilating the rebel forces, rising through the ranks of the civil and military service. In 1882, he led six battalions of his Qing Army to Korea to suppress the Imo Mutiny, and later also played a great role in training the Korean Singeon Chingunyeong (often translated as 'Capital Guards Command,' but literally translated as 'Newly Formed Bodyguard Army'). In 1884, on the eve of the Sino-French War, he led the Front, Centre, and Regular Battalions of the Qing Army back to China while leaving behind the Left, Rear, and Auxiliary Battalions in Korea. Unfortunately, Wu was getting on in years and died of illness in 1884. The three battalions in Korea were handed over to General Zhang Guangqian as the New Qing Army, and the three that had made it to China were given to General Huang Shilin as the Qing Bodyguard Army. Despite the differentiation between the New Qing and the Qing Bodyguard Armies, both were still considered part of the 'Qing Army' and contemporary photographs show that they were still brigaded in barracks that simply read the latter label. This confusing practice seems to have carried over on the identification patch of this uniform, which reads only 'Qing Army'. Fortunately, the designation of 'Auxiliary Battalion' indicates that this uniform belonged to one of the three battalions left behind to garrison Korea in 1884, and therefore part of General Zhang Guangqian's New Qing Army.

This illustration is taken from an existing artifact in the National Taiwan Museum; the name and squad designation on the original are completely illegible, so those on the illustration are embellishments.

All the buttons on this jacket are within the jacket and are thus not visible from without. Very oddly, the sleeves do not have coloured borders. This may have been to shorten the sleeve length.

C4. Zhejiang Chu Army

This uniform belonged to a soldier of the Second Squad of the Left Company of the Front Battalion of the Zhejiang Chu Army. On the identification patch, the squad designation (Er Dui) is listed on the bottom left, the company designation (Zuo Shao) is on the bottom right, the battalion designation (Qian Ying) in the centre, and the army name (Zhejiang Chu Jun) above the battalion designation. The author believes some elements of the Zhejiang Chu Army had merged with the Guangwu Army and therefore fought with them at the Battle of Gaiping (see below).

This illustration is based on several photographs taken by Isabella Bishop Bird in 1894 while traveling in Fengtian. The identification patch is mostly visible (if contrast is increased), except for the squad designation and the space above the army name. In this illustration, the former has been given a random designation while the latter has been left blank.

In the photograph, the identification patch lists them as soldiers of an unknown squad of the Left Company of the Front Battalion of the Zhejiang Chu Army. The term 'Chu Army' typically refers to the Hunanese army of General Zuo Zongtang, yet little is known about the 'Zhejiang Chu Army.' Records state it was once commanded by Li Xihu, a Hunan native and (younger) uncle of Li Guangjiu. Li Xihu did serve in the Sino-Japanese War, but as an officer in the Centre Battalion of the Old Xiang Army (see Chapter Six of Volume Two), not with the Zhejiang Chu Army. Another known commander, He Shaocai, also from Hunan, died in 1892. However, the author believes that some, if not all, of the Zhejiang Chu Army was absorbed into the Guangwu Army sometime before the Sino-Japanese War. This is because the Guangwu Army was an offshoot of Zuo Zongtang's original Chu Army, and many of its units were still referred to as 'Chu Braves.' Likewise, the founder of the Guangwu Army, General Chen Shijie, was a Hunanese and had also served previously as the Governor of Zhejiang. The Guangwu Army's deployment from Shandong to Manchuria (See Chapter Four of Volume Two) aligns with the photograph's purported provenance of Fengtian. Therefore, the most likely explanation is that the Zhejiang Chu Army was brigaded with the Guangwu Army and merged into its organisation and happened to be en route to Manchuria when the photograph was taken. See Chapter One of Volume One and Chapter Four of Volume Two for more information on the Guangwu Army.

C5. Tenacious Army Auxiliary Front Battalion

This uniform belonged to a Squad Leader of an unknown squad and company of the Auxiliary Front Battalion of the Tenacious Army. On the identification patch, the unfilled squad and company designations are on the bottom right, the rank (Shichang) is in the centre, the battalion designation (Fu Qian Ying) above the rank, and the army name (Wuyi) above the battalion designation. 500 men of the Tenacious Army Auxiliary Front Battalion arrived in Korea along with the Veteran Front Battalion (see B1) as part of the Donghak suppression force.

This illustration is highly speculative; it is based on a poor quality illustration of captured Chinese uniforms from Seonghwan and a single photograph. Regarding the illustration, it leaves much to be desired in terms of detail, and only shows the rank of 'Shichang,' or 'Squad Leader,' on the identification patch. It does state that the uniform was blue edged in red, and the drawing implies white piping. Most importantly however, the illustration clearly and unambiguously shows the wide cloud head pattern above the identification patch and another below. This is a very rarely observed feature, unique to the Tenacious Army (B1), so it may be readily assumed that C5 belonged to the Tenacious Army. The rest of the identification patch is conjectural, while the rest of the uniform and zhan qun are based on a photograph of Chinese military exercises in Zhili Province; the soldiers in this photograph wear jackets with the aforementioned rare wide cloud head design. Since General Nie Shicheng's Tenacious Army was stationed in Tianjin in Zhili Province, it is highly possible that the photograph and therefore the illustration depicts their uniform. The zhan qun is shown to be a lighter colour than the jacket in the photograph, but unlikely to have been coloured white.

C6. Yingkou Daobiao Army Regular Soldier

This uniform belonged to a Regular Soldier of the First Squad of the Centre Company of the Yingkou Daobiao Trained Army Infantry. On the identification patch, the rank (Zheng Bing) is in the centre, the squad designation (Yi Dui) on the bottom left, the company designation (Zhong Shao) on the bottom right, the army name (Daobiao Lian Jun Budui) above the rank, and the location stationed (Yingkou) above the army type. Led by General Wang Deyi, one battalion of the Yingkou Daobiao Army participated in the Sino-Japanese War; 'participate' might be too generous a word, as they fled immediately upon sight of the Japanese. The 'dao' in 'daobiao' refers to the position of Circuit Intendant (daotai), while biao, as mentioned in C2, was a type of Green Standard Army unit. Since Yingkou belonged to the Shanhaiguan Circuit, the Yingkou Daobiao Army would have been commanded by the Circuit Intendant of Shanhaiguan, which at the time was Foimo Shanlian of the Manchu Bordered Red Banner.

C6a is a detailed view of the button, depicting a boatman on his sampan next to a palm tree.

Note the use of the phrase 'Zheng Bing,' or 'Regular Soldier.' This refers to a soldier of a government-controlled Trained Army as opposed to a private Brave Army, which would have had the inscription 'Zheng Yong,' or 'Regular Brave.' Uniforms of 'Regular Soldiers' are more common amongst Boxer Rebellion examples, such as the two identification patches held in the Australian War Memorial and the military jacket owned by the Museum of Military History of Vienna, Austria.

As an anecdote, the Yingkou historical site called Lianjunying today was originally named Daobiaoying after the Daobiao Army, which was stationed there.

C7. Gubeikou Trained Army Right Battalion dogtag

This dogtag comes from the same print as A4. The top line reads 'Zhili Tidu Gubeikou Lian Jun,' meaning 'Gubeikou Trained Army under the authority of the Commander in Chief of Zhili.' The four centre characters read 'Lian Jun You Ying,' meaning 'Trained Army Right Battalion.' To the left reads 'Hu Bing Fang,' meaning 'Guard Sector,' referring to the soldier's role as a guard, messenger, and/or runner. The text to the right of the centre reads 'Zuo Shao Jiu Dui,' or 'Left Company, Ninth Squad.' Finally, the bottom right boxed characters read 'You Ying,' or 'Right Battalion.' The soldier's name is probably written on the other side of the dogtag.

500 men of the Gubeikou Trained Army Right Battalion arrived in Korea on 8 June to quell the Donghak Rebellion; they fought at the Battles of Seonghwan and Pyongyang, and after that followed General Nie Shicheng to Motianling.

C8. Gong Army New Left Battalion Squad Leader

This uniform belonged to a Squad Leader of the Third Squad of the Front Company of the New Left Battalion of the Gong Army. On the embroidered text, the rank (Shichang) is placed in the centre, the squad (San Dui) designation on the bottom left, company (Qian Shao) designation on the bottom right, the battalion designation (Xin Zuo Ying) above the rank, and the army name (Gong Army) above the battalion designation. The Gong Army Left Battalion was stationed at Haobudongkuang near the Longmiaozui Fort before the war, and during the Battle of Weihaiwei they participated in the Battle of the Southern Forts. However, no 'New Left Battalion' appears in records (see below).

This illustration was taken from a photograph of dead Chinese soldiers at the Longmiaozui Fort, taken by Ogawa Kazumasa. In the photo, all the text is clearly visible except for the character in front of 'Zuo Ying,' or 'Left Battalion.' It appears to be 'xin', meaning 'new', but no 'New Left Battalion' of the Gong Army ever existed. It is possible that it simply refers to a newly raised portion of the Left Battalion; since numerous new troops were indeed recruited at the time, this is the most plausible explanation. Since the photograph is in black and white, the colours and some features are conjectural. Again, red edged in black was the most probable combination for a light colour edged in a very dark colour, so it is employed here. The photograph appears to show white piping and another white outline around the edging, and also clearly shows knot buttons in use.

Another jacket of the Gong Army exists in the collection of the Box Museum in Plymouth (from the same collection as A3, B10, and C9). It is almost entirely identical to the jacket of A6, except that it reads 'Gong Jun You Ying' (Gong Army Right Battalion) and 'Qin Bing' (Bodyguard) and is without any squad or company designation. Furthermore, the colour of the strings used for the buttons is an orange or tan colour, while that in A6 is white. Despite this difference, the shape of the cloud head is incredibly similar.

C9. Gongbei Fort Deputy Commander Bodyguard

This uniform belonged to a bodyguard of the Deputy Commander of the Gongbei Fort, the largest coastal defence battery on Penghudao (today Magongdao) of the Penghu Archipelago (often called the Pescadores). The top two characters read 'Bang Dai' (Deputy Commander), the second line reads 'Gongbei Paotai' (Gongbei Fort), and the bottom two read 'Qin Bing' (Bodyguard). Although the Gongbei Fort garrison was apparently poorly trained in the use of their coastal guns, some elements did put up a stubborn, heroic, but ultimately fruitless resistance to the Japanese infantry on land.

This uniform is currently kept in the Box museum; it is part of the same collection as A3 and B10.

C10. Jiesheng Trained Army Infantry

This uniform possibly belonged to a soldier of the Jiesheng Trained Army; the top line reads 'Jiesheng,' the second 'Lian Jun Qian Ying' (Trained Army Front Battalion), the bottom right 'Zhong Shao' (Centre Company), and the bottom centre 'Bu Dui' (Infantry Detachment). The identification patch of this uniform is almost completely conjectural; the ink of the original is nearly illegible, with only 'Bu Dui' (Infantry Detachment) and 'Zhong' (Centre) clearly visible on the backside. However, given the fact that 'Bu Dui' was a term typically used by Manchu Banner units and that this uniform is from the same collection in the Sugino Costume Museum as B11, it is likely that this uniform was captured at the Battle of Jinzhou and belonged to an infantryman of the Jiesheng Trained Army. Two other forces fought at the Battle of Jinzhou, Zhao Huaiye's Army (of which multiple uniforms exist and look nothing like C10), and General Xu Bangdao's Gongwei Army. However, the Gongwei Army was known to have identification patches reading 'Zheng Yong' (Regular Brave), and a single photograph by Ogawa Kazumasa showing a dead Chinese soldier south of Jinzhou with such a patch confirms that C10 could not have been the uniform of the Gongwei Army; thus, C10 most likely belonged to the Jiesheng Trained Army. Again, this cannot be ascertained for sure but given the lack of any other relevant information this seems to be one of the only viable conclusions.

C11. Resolute Brave

This exceptionally jaunty uniform was most likely only worn by standard bearers, and even then, perhaps only on parade; photographic evidence (see below) suggests that the majority of rank and file soldiers of the Resolute Army wore more practical uniforms like in Figure Two.

This uniform is taken from two sources: a contemporary Chinese print and a photograph of the Resolute Army on parade at Lushunkou. The print shows a soldier with a black turban, a red and yellow jacket, black plain zhan qun, blue trousers, white puttees, light blue socks, and blue shoes with 'Yi Yong' (Resolute Brave) written on the identification patch. Though Chinese prints were typically inaccurate with regards to the specifics of military uniforms, those shown in this particular series of prints, now in a private collection, are corroborated by other pictorial and written evidence (i.e. the uniform of a soldier of the Gansu Braves wearing a white uniform with a blue turban matches perfectly a description given by a Westerner in 1900, and the uniform of a Manchu matchlockman is nearly identical to a Western engraving and another Western illustration). The photograph on the other hand only shows the Resolute Army from the back, and while the enlisted men appear to be dressed like Figure Two, a number of noncommissioned officers and standard bearers in the front are dressed in colourful jackets and zhan qun. Therefore, the colour of the jacket (and its buttons) and the rank designation 'Yi Yong' (Resolute Brave) on the identification patch in C11 comes from the print, while the zhan qun is copied from the photograph with conjectural colours. However, the extra set of red lining on the jacket is taken from the photograph, and the identification disc has been modified to be a more conventional colour and format. The zhan qun has five bat shaped good luck symbols around the central tongqian pattern; in the original photograph, it is difficult to tell how many bats there are and how specifically they are arranged, since every single zhan qun has a different orientation and number.

Chinese military flags of the Sino-Japanese War

D1–3. Seonghwan surname flags

These three flags captured from Seonghwan all bear the surname of a Chinese commander: D1 reads 'Nie,' D2 'Feng,' and D3 'Hu.' The colours of all three are taken from various Japanese prints, which surprisingly remain mostly consistent. D1 is probably the personal flag of General Nie Shicheng, while another flag identical to D3 but bearing the surname 'Li' was also captured at Seonghwan. D3 appears to be made of three separate strips of cloth stitched together horizontally. These three are referred to as personal standards of Chinese generals, to be flown outside their official quarters and carried by their bodyguards.

After the Battle of Seonghwan, over 50 Chinese flags were captured and brought to Japan to be displayed publicly. Most regrettably, none exist today. At least five Qing dragon flags appear in the most detailed photograph the author has found but are not illustrated in this book due to being too unclear to properly reproduce. The five coloured 'Five Races Under One Union' flag is shown in the same photograph, as is a six-striped flag that alternates red and white and an oblong flag bearing the words 'Tianshang Shengmu.' This latter flag is a Beiyang Navy flag, and reconstructions can be easily found online. A red and yellow flag 'without any markings' is mentioned in Japanese records; it may refer to the aforementioned alternating red and white flag.

D4–7. Seonghwan signal flags

These flags are smaller in proportion to the other examples and are used for various kinds of signalling. D4 reads 'Xun Shi,' meaning 'Military Inspection,' and was placed in front of General Ye Zhichao's headquarters to mark his location, as well as raised during military inspections alongside a yellow dragon flag. D6 and D7 are apparently handheld semaphore flags, but without clear meaning. However, according to Tenacious Army and Self-Strengthening Army military manuals published after the Sino-Japanese War, pairs of handheld flags identical to D6 were used to communicate numerals over long distances. Whether or not D6 served this same purpose during the Sino-Japanese War is anyone's guess. D6 and D7 are consistently coloured as shown, but D4 is sometimes shown as red with black text.

The smaller flag D5 reads 'shuai,' or 'general.' It was probably flown for General Ye Zhichao as a symbol of his authority. Colours are conjectural, since the photograph is monochrome, but the vast majority of such flags were yellow. The print mentioned in C11 shows a triangular 'shuai' flag in black text with orange scalloped bordering; additionally, there are blue and white cloud designs surrounding the 'shuai' character.

Not shown in these illustrations is a plain turquoise flag with the character 'ling,' or 'command,' in red text. This command flag and its colours were depicted consistently in a few Japanese prints.

D8. Resolute Army Command flag

This flag comes from a photograph of a Resolute Army parade at Lushunkou in the late 1880s or early 1890s. The flag is extremely dark in colour and has a stylised character for 'ling,' or 'command,' written on it. Such flags were used to signal troop movements. Colours are conjectural. Also seen in the photograph is a flag similar to D1 and D2, except with the character 'Ma' for General Ma Yukun. In other photographs depicting the same parade, the Resolute Army is seen flying another 'Command' flag but this time much larger and with the text in a darker colour, plus a striped five coloured flag with a smaller version attached above it on a flagpole with three tufts of red horsehair.

D9. Resolute Second Company flag

This flag comes from the same photograph as D8. The colours here are conjectural, as the photograph is monochrome; all that is known is that the flag reads 'Er Shao,' or 'Second Company.' In the photograph other company flags of identical design but probably different base colours can be seen for other companies.

D10. General Zhou's flag
This is a flag reading 'Zhou' that was captured after the Battle of Pyongyang and photographed by Georges Ferdinand Bigot. The flag appears to have white text on a dark base and has a smaller flag of indeterminate design (possibly plain?) above it on the flagpole. Nothing is known about General Zhou, and colours are conjectural.

D11–13. Seonghwan battalion flags
These three flags were for battalion commanders; one was given to each battalion and hoisted by a squad leader in the bodyguard company. D11 is the flag of a bodyguard battalion, D12 reads the surname 'Wei,' and D13 reads 'Su.' D11 is sometimes mistaken for a flag of the Chingunyeong, a modernised unit of the Korean military formed in 1882 and extant until 1895. The source of this error lies in the use of Chinese characters in documents regarding the captured flags: D11 is referred to with the Chinese characters 'Qin Bing Ying,' or 'Bodyguard Battalion,' which is similar enough to the Chinese characters for 'Qin Jun Ying,' or 'Chingunyeong.' This has led some sources to confuse the two. No Korean troops are known to have fought alongside the Chinese at Seonghwan, although some soldiers of the Chingun Jangwiyeong (a unit of the palace guard based in Seoul) fought on the Japanese side. According to photographs, D12 lacks the decorative edges of D11 and D13, or it is edged in such a similar color to be invisible; however, some Japanese prints show otherwise. According to Japanese prints, General Nie Shicheng flew a flag similar or identical to D13, except of course with his own surname. Additionally, when he was called back to defend Beijing in the later stages of the war, he was confirmed by Western artist Charles Edwin Fripp to have flown such a flag.

D14. General Zheng's flag
This flag appears in a single Japanese print depicting spoils of war from the Battle of Pyongyang, the same one as A4. The large character reads 'Zheng,' while the smaller characters read: 'Pige Jianfang Tidu Guandai Shengzi Zhong Jun You Ying Tiyong Batulu Jun Gongjia Yi Ji' roughing meaning 'under the authority of the Commander in Chief, the General is appointed to the position of Commander of the Sheng Army Centre Army Right Battalion, awarded the title of Tiyong Batulu for military merit, and promoted by one rank.' 'Tiyong' appears to be a solely Chinese word meaning 'elevated courage', while 'Batulu' is a Manchu military honour meaning 'warrior,' so 'Tiyong Batulu' means 'Warrior of Elevated Courage.' Regrettably, nothing is known about General Zheng.

D15. Liu Hanfang's Flag
This flag belonged to General Liu Hanfang during the Sino-Japanese War and was captured by the Japanese after the Battle of Lushunkou. The flag is around three metres tall and bears the Chinese character for 'Liu' and in smaller text to its left a description of Liu's rank, reading 'Qinchai Beiyang Dachen Yanhai Shui Lu Yingwuchu Haifang Ying Hualing Zhili Ji Bu Douguan Fu.' This is roughly translated as 'Imperial Commissioner to the Beiyang Minister,

responsible for all naval, coastal, and land military operations, in charge of coastal defence garrisons, decorated with a peacock feather for meritorious service, stationed in Zhili Province, and immediately appointed to the central customs office.' The two smaller, horizontal characters above read 'Guan Dai,' a type of military officer equivalent roughly to a fourth rank mandarin, also used as a generic term for a commander.

This illustration is based on an artifact donated to the National Taiwan Museum in 1933, where it was initially misidentified as a flag of former Governor of Taiwan Liu Mingchuan.

D16. Ye Zhichao's command banner
This command banner, belonging to General Ye Zhichao, was captured by the Japanese at the Battle of Seonghwan and listed as a large flag (dao qi). A triangular version of the large flag is mentioned in Japanese documents, but no visual source corroborates it; it is possible that the triangular large flag refers to the company flag with the surname 'Ye' on it (C10). The colour of the flag borders is usually shown as a green or turquoise in prints.

The two small characters above the rest read 'Qin Ming,' or 'by Imperial Decree.' The text below reads 'Zhili Tidu Junmen Jiezhi Gezhen Etuhun Batulu Ye,' approximately meaning 'Commander in Chief of Zhili Province; responsible for the military command of all garrisons; awarded the title of Etuhun Batulu; who bears the name Ye.' 'Etuhun' likely refers to the Manchu word 'eten,' meaning victory, so the title translates to 'Victorious Warrior.' This flag would have been hung in Ye's headquarters.

D17. Xu Bangdao's flag
General Xu Bangdao was reported to have flown white and red flags at the Battles of Jinzhou and Tuchengzi; a single photograph of the Zhongjiashan Fort taken by Ogawa Kazumasa at Jinzhou shows such a flag in a dark colour edged by a lighter one and with the character 'Xu' in black on it.

D18–21. Seonghwan company flags
Five triangular company flags with rhombi-shaped serrations were captured from Seonghwan, four of them bearing surnames Ye, Zhong, Wei, and Gao, and the final one with a yin and yang symbol. Only four are illustrated here: the Gao, Ye, Zhong, and yin and yang flags. Note that the exact same surname Wei also appears on the much larger battalion flag (D12); it is unclear if they refer to the same General Wei, or if General Wei simply had a relative with him (a not uncommon practice in Chinese armies).

According to the testimony of prisoners who fought at Seonghwan, each company commander was given two company flags, which were carried by the soldiers of the first squad of the company. Company flags were triangular and were differently coloured to suit the specific unit they were signalling, although the borders always remained green. The front company had red, the rear company had green (shade not specified; probably a darker green), the centre company had yellow, the left company had blue, the right company had red-brown and artillery companies had black. The bodyguard company had 'blue-green on top and red on bottom,' which might refer to the colours of the border and interior, respectively. Despite this apparently clear cut colouring system, Japanese prints of the era show a diverse assortment of colour palettes, including red edged in green, blue edged in red, red edged in blue, red edged in yellow, yellow edged in dark blue/purple, and purple edged in green. Two different written sources reported seeing red and green or red and blue flags, and an eyewitness artist drew flags that were red edged in green, red edged in white, white edged in green, plainly red, plainly white, white edged in red, white edged in black, yellow edged in red, yellow edged in green and red edged in black. Many of these are probably random colours chosen for the sake of convenience or limited palette as opposed to genuine observations.

As for the illustrations, D18 reads 'Gao,' D19 reads 'Zhong,' and D20 reads 'Ye.' D21 is another company flag with unknown designation. Unfortunately, no colour combination is given for each flag, so in the illustrations colours have been randomly assigned: D18 is the left company, D19 is the front company, and D20 is the bodyguard company. D21 consistently appears red with a black and white yin yang and serrated border across most prints. Although according to photographs the other company flags have quadrilaterally shaped serrations, it is not confirmed whether or not D21 has these, so it is portrayed with rounder serrations for sake of variety. D21 is most likely not a company flag, and, although it has similar proportions and design, may be what the Chinese called a 'headquarters flag,' or 'ben qi.' This vaguely described headquarters flag was attached to a polearm with a red tuft of horsehair and planted in the ground before a battle to boost morale.

Colour Figures

Figure One: Sheng Trained Army Cavalryman
This plump fellow is a horseman of the Right Wing of the Sheng Trained Army, a force formed from the Manchu Bannermen of Fengtian (Shengjing) and under the command of General Gobulo Fengsheng'a of the Plain White Banner. Shortly after the Battle of Seonghwan, the Sheng Trained Army were sent to Pyongyang from Fengtian; many Westerners witnessed them on the march and recorded them as carrying bayonets attached to red poles, their pet birds on perches, rusty muskets, and smoothbore jingals. An especially unruly group of them even attempted to rob the local governor's office, and, when confronted by guards, claimed that it was better to be shot in China than in Korea. Nicknamed 'duck egg soldiers' by Chinese civilians for their inability to withstand even the slightest pressure, the Sheng Trained Army first fought at Pyongyang, where they led a failed cavalry charge against Japanese infantry and artillery. They then spent the remainder of the war either continuously on the retreat from the enemy or participating in half-hearted counterattacks.

The top line of this soldier's jacket reads 'Feng Jun' (Feng Army), the second 'Shengzi You Yi' (Sheng Trained Army Right Wing), and the bottom two characters 'Ma Dui' (Cavalry Detachment). His jacket comes from a Japanese woodblock print depicting a battle in Fengtian; although woodblock prints generally cannot be considered authoritative sources for uniforms of both sides, this particular depiction of the jacket unit insignia is accurate enough to merit some credence. His zhan qun is conjectural. Dangling below his jacket on his traditional xingfu dai belt are several purses, a pipe pouch, a fan case, and a chopsticks case. He amateurishly holds his old smoothbore flintlock, a weapon that may not even be in working condition. On the other hand, he holds a cage with his beloved pet crested myna (Chinese starling).

By the time of the First Sino-Japanese War, the Army of the Eight Banners had declined to the point of being useless in warfare. After the mid-century rebellions, the Brave Armies and relative peace of the metropolitan areas had made the Banner garrisons essentially redundant, and these superfluous Bannermen continued to live off a fixed military stipend, often whittled down to a bare minimum by corruption. The families of invalided, elderly, or even dead Bannermen continued to collect their salaries, and when called up to parade or pass a military examination, simply hired substitutes. Unable or unwilling to train for war and prevented by law from taking up trades, many Bannermen spent their time meticulously cultivating extravagant but useless hobbies, most commonly rearing pet birds, training fighting crickets, watching opera, and raising goldfish. Opium and gambling were also favoured pastimes. In modern China, the 'Baqi zidi' (descendants of the Eight Banners) is a well-known stereotype of the indolent, prodigious dandies whose forefathers had conquered all of China. Therefore, the figure illustrated here is a painful symbol of the social and military decline of the Eight Banners institution.

The Manchu author Lao She put it best himself in his semi-autobiographical work *Under the Plain Red Banner*:

> The grime accumulated during two hundred years of history made most Bannermen abandon all semblance of self-discipline and self-improvement. Instead, he [the Bannermen] evolved a unique lifestyle: the haves attempted to refine extravagance to perfection, while the have-nots refined as much as their poverty allowed. Life bobbed up and down in this stagnant puddle of refined hedonism. For example, my elder sister's father-in-law set no value on carrying out his official duties or charging into the enemy lines on horseback. Instead, he and his peers only expected him to draw his stipend, recite opera ditties, and feed his four songbirds. Likewise, my brother-in-law not only took pride in his 'flying sycees,' but would have given his life for a single one of his pet pigeons. Whenever walking outside, his eyes were always glued to the skies, regardless of the importance of whatever personal or official duty he was attending to … He did this for the off chance that a tired pigeon was flying low and looking for a place to rest. If such a blessing occurred, it did not matter if he were carrying the most critical of military dispatches; he would rush home and send several of his own trained pigeons to catch the 'sycee' sent from Heaven itself … Should another man attempt to take the pigeon for himself, he was fully ready to take up arms and place his own life on the line for that pigeon … Both father and son were intelligent, vigorous, and precise, but applied these talents to squeeze pleasure out of trivialities. They finely cultivated the arts of the cricket cage, the pigeon whistle, the deep-fried meatball, etc., but knew nothing about the major events

of the world. Their lives were like a delicate, clear, yet confused dream. It is only natural that such people would bungle things if given high positions in the army.

Figure Two: Resolute Army soldier

This is a Regular Brave of the Left Battalion of the Front Army of the Resolute Army; this particular unit first participated at the Battle of Pyongyang, where their well-aimed rifle, artillery, and Gatling gun fire decisively turned back the Japanese attacking the south part of the city. They were not alone in this regard, as the Resolute Army was one of the finest units China had during the Sino-Japanese War. At the Battle of Hushan near Jiuliancheng, a troop of Resolute Army soldiers under General Ma Jinxu, held on against vastly overwhelming numbers of Japanese until it became impossible to do so any longer. At the Battle of Ganwangzhai, the Resolute Army succeeded in inflicting the highest percentage of casualties onto the Japanese out of any battle in the war; a similar feat was achieved at Dapingshan.

This soldier is taken from a series of photographs of the Resolute Army out on parade near Lushunkou. Dressed smartly, in a loose but relatively form fitting jacket, trousers, and vest, he has his queue coiled inside his simple black turban. Though the cut of his jacket and trousers indubitably betray Western influence, his brightly coloured vest and traditional Chinese boots are clear concessions to Chinese tastes. His accoutrements are of secondhand German origin; note the new dragon design stamped onto the buckle. He carries a Mauser M1871/1884 repeating rifle, a weapon which he has been trained to handle well, as the Japanese attested to on multiple occasions. His vest is nearly identical to that of the Gui Army (see B4 and B5), itself an extension of the Resolute Army. However, the identification patch for this figure is conjectural; following Beiyang Army regulations, the top section reads 'Yi Jun' (Resolute Army), the band below 'Qian Jun Zuo Ying' (Front Army Left Battalion), the bottom right 'Qian Shao Er Dui' (Front Company Second Squad), the bottom centre 'Zheng Yong' (Regular Brave), and the bottom left 'Li Douhuang' (the soldier's name).

Figure Three: Baoding Trained Army Bodyguard

This is a soldier of the Left Battalion of the Baoding Trained Army, one of the first six units formed in 1865 for the new Trained Army military system. The jacket of this Baoding Trained Army is taken from an artifact currently in possession of the Art Gallery of Greater Victoria, with the claim that the item was used in the Sino-Japanese War. The author has not seen any records that corroborate this claim; more likely would be the fact that the Baoding Trained Army was mobilised to defend Tianjin and Beijing from attack but did not actually participate in the war. The jacket may have been abandoned by deserting Chinese troops or taken during the later Boxer Rebellion, but this is pure conjecture. Nevertheless, this figure may be taken as representative of many of the modernised units that participated during the Sino-Japanese War: equipped with excellent weaponry but still dressed in a semi-archaic fashion.

Unfortunately, the existing jacket which this figure is based on is in poor condition, as only one half of the front remains. Thankfully, the identification patch on the back is still in good condition, allowing us to make out that the top line reads 'Baoding Lian Jun Zuo Ying' (Baoding Trained Army Left Battalion), the bottom centre reads 'Qin Bing' (Bodyguard), the bottom right reads 'Dui' (Squad), and the bottom left reads 'Zhang Shoutang.' Aside from the jacket, this soldier wears a Western style straw 'boater' hat, trousers, puttees, and Chinese slippers. His rifle is the M1891 Kuaili 'Jiangnan' rifle, a domestically designed modification of the Mannlicher that was considered by the Japanese to be superior to the Type 22 Murata (see Chapter One). His ammunition bandolier may contain several different types of cartridges, as the ignorance of many Chinese officials meant that ammunition was often distributed without regard for type, age, or size.

Figure Four: Sui Army bodyguard

This is a bodyguard of the Second Squad of the Bodyguard Company of the Left Battalion of the Sui Army. The Sui Army Left Battalion fought at the Battle of Weihaiwei, where they deserted in large numbers before, during, and after the fighting. The Sui Army was an example of a Chinese force modernised in armament and equipment, but not in training and attitude (see Chapter One). This, then, accounts for this man's excellent Mannlicher rifle, and also for his unenthusiastic bearing.

This uniform comes from an existing artifact now in a private collection; see A6 for more information on Sui Army uniforms. The top line reads 'Sui Jun Zuo Ying' (Sui Army Left Battalion), the bottom centre 'Qin Bing' (Bodyguard), the bottom right 'Er Dui' (Second Squad), and the bottom left 'Long Ming.' Unlike A6, the soldier's company is not included explicitly, since the implication is that because the soldier is a bodyguard, his company is the centre bodyguard company.

Figure Five: Japanese infantryman (front)

This is a Japanese sergeant first class of the infantry. He wears a typical M1886 or Meiji 19 hat, jacket, and trousers, with yellow hat piping, hat band, and cuff insignia. The collars, trouser stripes, and epaulettes are all red for the infantry. The cuff insignia consists of a fat bar with a thin gold thread to indicate noncommissioned officer status, plus two rank stripes. The brass numeral on his epaulette, though not visible here, indicates his battalion number.

He has chosen to leave behind his heavy backpack and uncomfortable western boots; therefore, this figure represents a Japanese infantryman as he would appear in battle, as opposed to on the march or presenting for review. He has his accoutrements stored in a cloth gassai-bukuro slung over his right shoulder (the viewer's left), his greatcoat wrapped over his left shoulder, and his feet protected by a set of traditional tabi socks and waraji sandals. Usually the gassai-bukuro was dark blue, but sometimes was a lighter blue or red. His weapon is the Type 18 Murata single shot rifle, the standard issue for all Japanese soldiers during the Sino-Japanese War. The M1892 hemp haversack at the soldier's right (viewer's left) has his M1892 canteen stored inside, in the pre-1895 fashion.

COLOUR PLATE COMMENTARIES

Figure Six: Japanese infantryman (back)

This is a Japanese private second class, viewed from the back. Though his weapon and uniform are basically identical to that of Figure Five, his cuff insignia, a single yellow stripe, shows that he is a private second class. Additionally, unlike Figure Five, he wears Western boots and full kit. In the centre and strapped onto the brown cowhide M1887 backpack flap is the M1883 lacquered tin mess kit. Wrapped around the backpack in a 'horseshoe' shape is the soldier's blanket roll and greatcoat; according to regulations the greatcoat was to be placed on the interior (behind the blanket roll and invisible to the viewer), while the blanket roll was on the outside. On either side of the backpack are two spare Western style shoes; if a soldier wished to do so, he might also strap a pair of traditional straw waraji sandals on top of the blanket roll. Note that the right side of the backpack has two straps securing the shoe, greatcoat, and blanket roll, while the left side only has one, to allow easier access to the ammunition drawer. However, contemporary pictures show that sometimes soldiers would only tie the bottom two straps, such that the upper right strap was unused.

Attached to the soldier's belt on his left is his Type 18 bayonet in his scabbard, and directly below the backpack is another ammunition box containing spare cartridges. This rear box has a compartment for a bottle of gun oil on the left side and a combination screwdriver/wrench on the other. On the soldier's right is his M1892 hemp haversack, and on top is his M1892 glass canteen fitted with the late 1894 two piece leather coverings, and with the strap introduced in 1895 that allowed it to hang outside on the haversack. Note that the Japanese would only receive a standard issue aluminium canteen in 1898, after the Sino-Japanese War.

Figure Seven: Japanese infantry captain

This stalwart figure is a captain of the infantry; the single line on his hat band indicates that he is a company officer, and the French-inspired black trefoil design on his cuffs gives his specific rank. For service jackets, the space underneath the trefoils remained the base colour of the jacket, although wealthy dandies could choose to have custom tailored service jackets with service branch coloured under spaces and other embellishments. This captain's standard issue Western style sabre hangs from a belt underneath his jacket and hanging from slings at his side are a holster for his privately purchased Kuwabara pistol, a M1892 haversack, and a binocular case. Officers were free to wear these items as they saw fit, since there were no regulations dictating otherwise. Some photographs also show the wearing of backpacks or knapsacks, but these were certainly privately acquired items and not issued officially.

Figure Eight: Japanese cavalryman

This man is a sergeant second class of the Japanese cavalry. Wearing a dashing Attila jacket with yellow coloured Hungarian knotting and piping, his striking red riding breeches brings to mind the 'cherrybums' of Lord Cardigan's 11th Hussars. The inner parts of these breeches were given an extra piece of fabric for increased durability and protection against rubbing.

His collars and trouser stripes are the light green of the cavalry; note that only the bottom of the collars are piped with yellow, and the rest of the collar is plain light green. Note the unique woven epaulette, which was the same for all enlisted men and noncommissioned officers. His Murata Type 18 carbine is slung over his shoulder, and his cartridge box hangs at his side from a sling. Sometimes this single box was also worn on the belt, either on one side on the front or in the centre of the back. More ammunition, as well as personal effects, were stored on other compartments on the horse saddle. Although cavalrymen could also wear any combination of the M1892 haversack, the post-1895 canteen with strap, and a binocular case on their persons, the pictured trooper has apparently elected to leave these behind on his horse.

Appendix I

Chinese military ranks

Chinese officer and non-commissioned officer ranks[1]

Mandarin grade	Sanguan rank (nominal titles for officers who did not hold a fixed position)	Imperial Guard rank	Eight Banners Army rank	Green Standard Army rank	Brave Army rank (no mandarin grade equivalence)
Upper First Rank	Jianwei Jiangjun	Ling Shiwei Nei Dachen	None	None	None
Lower First Rank	Zhenwei Jiangjun	Nei Dachen	Jiangjun, Dutong	Tidu	Zongtong (Army Commander)
Upper Second Rank	Wuxian Jiangjun	None	Fu Dutong	Zongbing	Tongling (Brigade Commander)
Lower Second Rank	Wugong Jiangjun	Sanzhi Dachen	None	Fujiang	None
Upper Third Rank	Wuyi Duwei (Wuyi meaning 'Tenacious')	Yideng Shiwei, Suiyin Xieli Shiwu Shiwei Banling	Canling	Canjiang	Yingguan (Battalion Commander)
Lower Third Rank	Wuyi Duwei (Wuyi meaning 'Martial Wing')	None	Xieling	Youji	Fu Yingguan (Assistant Battalion Commander)
Upper Fourth Rank	Zhaowu Duwei	Erdeng Shiwei, Shiwei Banling	Zuoling	Dusi	None
Lower Fourth Rank	Xuanwu Duwei	None	None	None	None
Upper Fifth Rank	Wude Qiwei	Sandeng Shiwei	Fangyu	Shoubei	None
Lower Fifth Rank	Wude Zuo Qiwei	Sideng Shiwei	None	None	None
Upper Sixth Rank	Wulue Qiwei	Qinjun Xiao, Zhushi, Lanling Shiwei	Qianzong	Qianzong	Shaoguan (Company Commander)
Lower Sixth Rank	Wulue Zuo Qiwei	None	None	None	Fu Shaoguan (Deputy Company Commander)

---

1 Brave Army ranks have no clear-cut equivalence to either Japanese military ranks or to the other Chinese systems. Those ranked 'zongtong' (commander of an entire army) were typically 'tidu' (commander in chief of a province), while those ranked 'tongling' (commander of several battalions) were typically 'zongbing' (commander in chief of a town/city), but beyond these two examples the remainder of the Brave Army ranks are listed according to responsibility (i.e. a yingguan and a Japanese major would both command a battalion, a shichang and a sergeant major would both lead a squad, etc.).

SUNSTRUCK GIANT VOLUME 1

Mandarin grade	Sanguan rank (nominal titles for officers who did not hold a fixed position)	Imperial Guard rank	Eight Banners Army rank	Green Standard Army rank	Brave Army rank (no mandarin grade equivalence)
Upper Seventh Rank	Wuxin Qiwei	None	Xiao Qixiao	Bazong	None
Lower Seventh Rank	Wuxin Zuo Qiwei	None	None	None	None
Upper Eighth Rank	Fenwu Xiaowei	None	None	Waiwei Qianzong	Shichang (Squad Commander)
Lower Eighth Rank	Fenwu Zuo Xiaowei	Shu Qin Junxiao	None	None	None
Upper Ninth Rank	Xiuwu Xiaowei	None	Lingcui	Waiwei Bazong	None
Lower Ninth Rank	Xiuwu Zuo Xiaowei	None	None	Ewai Waiwei	Wuchang (Deputy Squad Commander)

Beiyang Navy officer ranks

Mandarin Grade	Beiyang Navy rank (equivalent to Green Standard Army ranks)	Western equivalent	Responsibilities
Lower First Rank	Tidu	Admiral	Admiral of the Beiyang Navy
Upper Second Rank	Zongbing	Rear Admiral	Captain of an ironclad
Lower Second Rank	Fujiang	Captain	Captain of a cruiser
Upper Third Rank	Canjiang		
Lower Third Rank	Youji	Commander	Captain of a training ship
Upper Fourth Rank	Dusi (Guandai)	Lieutenant Commander	Captain of a torpedo boat or gunboat
Upper Fifth Rank	Shoubei	Lieutenant	Captain of a torpedo boat
Upper Sixth Rank	Qianzong	Second Lieutenant	Subordinate to Captain (rank)
Upper Seventh Rank	Bazong		
Upper Eighth	Jingshi Waiwei		

Beiyang Navy enlisted ranks

Rank name	Romanisation
Gunner	Zheng Paomu
Deputy Gunner	Fu Paomu
Head Seaman	Shuishou Zheng Toumu
Deputy Head Seaman	Shuishou Fu Toumu
Seaman First Class	Yideng Shuishou
Seaman Second Class	Erdeng Shuishou
Seaman Third Class	Sandeng Shuishou
Trainee First Class	Yideng Lianyong
Trainee Second Class	Erdeng Lianyong
Trainee Third Class	Sandeng Lianyong
Head Torpedo Operator	Yulei Toumu
Torpedo Operator First Class	Yideng Yulei Bing
Torpedo Operator Second Class	Erdeng Yulei Bing
Head Torpedo Engineer	Yulei Jiang
Rudder and Torpedo Engineer First Class	Yulei Yideng Duogong
Rudder and Torpedo Engineer Second Class	Yulei Erdeng Guogong
Lamplighter	Dianhuo Jiang
Gunsmith	Yangqiang Jiang
Head Flag Signaller	Guanqi Toumu
Flag Signaller First Class	Yideng Guanqi
Flag Signaller Second Class	Erdeng Guanqi
Head Carpenter	Mujiang Toumu

APPENDIX I

Rank name	Romanisation
Carpenter First Class	Yideng Mujiang
Carpenter Second Class	Erdeng Mujiang
Propeller Mechanic First Class	Yideng Guanlun
Propeller Mechanic Second Class	Erdeng Guanlun
Propeller Mechanic Third Class	Sandeng Guanlun
Boiler Engineer	Guolu Jiang
Blacksmith	Tiejiang
Coppersmith	Tongjiang
Sail Engineer	Fanjiang
Painter	Youqi Jiang
Steward	Guan Jiaju
Cabin Attendant First Class	Yideng Guancang
Cabin Attendant Second Class	Erdeng Guancang
Head Stoker	Yideng Shenghuo Toumu
Deputy Head Stoker	Erdeng Shenghuo Toumu
Stoker First Class	Yideng Shenghuo
Stoker Second Class	Erdeng Shenghuo
Stoker Third Class	Sandeng Shenghuo

Appendix II

Imperial Japanese Army and Navy Ranks

Imperial Japanese Army Ranks

Category	Rank name	Rank equivalent	Japanese Romaji
General Officers	General (no branch)	N/A	Taisho
	Lieutenant General (no branch)	N/A	Chujo
	Major General (no branch)	N/A	Shosho
Field Officers	Colonel (all five branches)	N/A	Taisa
	Lieutenant Colonel (all five branches)	N/A	Chusa
	Major (all five branches)	N/A	Shosa
Company Officers	Captain (all five branches)	N/A	Tai-i
	Lieutenant (all five branches)	N/A	Chu-i
	Second Lieutenant (all five branches)	N/A	Sho-i
Warrant Officers	Special Sergeant (all five branches)	N/A	Tokumu Socho
Non-commissioned Officers	Sergeant Major (all five branches)	N/A	Socho
	Sergeant First Class (all five branches)	N/A	I-to Gunso
	Sergeant Second Class (all five branches)	N/A	Ni-to Gunso
Enlisted Men	Superior Private (all five branches)	N/A	Jo-to Hei
	Private First Class (all five branches)	N/A	I-to Sotsu
	Private Second Class (all five branches)	N/A	Ni-to Sotsu

APPENDIX II

Imperial Japanese Army Rear Echelon Ranks

Category	Rank name	Rank equivalent	Japanese Romaji
Warrant Officers	Superior Supervisor (engineers and artillery)	Special Sergeant	Jo-to Kango
Non-commissioned Officers	Supervisor (artillery, fortress artillery, engineers)	Sergeant Major	Kango
	Demolitions Expert Sergeant Major (artillery)	Sergeant Major	Kako Socho
	Chief Metal Caster (artillery)	Sergeant First Class	Iko Cho
	Chief Blacksmith (artillery)	Sergeant First Class	Tanko Cho
	Chief Carpenter (artillery)	Sergeant First Class	Mokko Cho
	Chief Gunsmith (artillery)	Sergeant First Class	Juko Cho
	Chief Saddler (artillery)	Sergeant First Class	Kurako Cho
	Chief Cobbler (all five branches)	Sergeant First Class	Kutsuko Cho
	Chief Tailor (all five branches)	Sergeant First Class	Nuiko Cho
	Chief Farrier (artillery, transportation, and cavalry)	Sergeant First Class	Teitetsuko Cho
	Demolitions Expert Sergeant First Class (artillery)	Sergeant First Class	Kako I-to Gunso
	Assistant Chief Metal Caster (artillery)	Sergeant Second Class	Iko Kacho
	Assistant Chief Blacksmith (artillery)	Sergeant Second Class	Tanko Kacho
	Assistant Chief Carpenter (artillery)	Sergeant Second Class	Mokko Kacho
	Assistant Chief Gunsmith (artillery)	Sergeant Second Class	Juko Kacho
	Assistant Chief Saddler (artillery)	Sergeant Second Class	Kurako Kacho
	Assistant Chief Cobbler (all five branches)	Sergeant Second Class	Kutsuko Kacho
	Assistant Chief Tailor (all five branches)	Sergeant Second Class	Nuiko Kacho
	Assistant Chief Farrier (artillery, transportation, and cavalry)	Sergeant Second Class	Teitetsuko Kacho
	Demolitions Expert Sergeant Second Class (artillery)	Sergeant Second Class	Kako Ni-to Gunso
Enlisted Men	Metal Caster (artillery)	Private	Iko
	Blacksmith (artillery)	Private	Tanko
	Carpenter (artillery)	Private	Mokko
	Gunsmith (artillery)	Private	Juko
	Saddler (artillery)	Private	Kurako

Category	Rank name	Rank equivalent	Japanese Romaji
	Cobbler (all five branches)	Private	Kutsuko
	Tailor (all five branches)	Private	Nuiko
	Farrier First Class (artillery, transportation, and cavalry)	Private	I-to Teitetsuko
	Farrier Second Class (artillery, transportation, and cavalry)	Private	Ni-to Teitetsuko
	Demolitions Expert (artillery)	Private	Kako Sotsu

Imperial Japanese Army Sanitation Department Ranks

Category	Rank name	Rank equivalent	Japanese romaji
General Officers	Medical Superintendent General	Major General	Gun-i Soukan
Officers	Medical Superintendent	Colonel	Gun-i Kan
	Medical Officer First Class	Lieutenant Colonel	I-to Gun-i Sei
	Medical Officer Second Class	Major	I-to Gun-i Sei
	Military Doctor First Class	Captain	I-to Gun-i
	Military Doctor Second Class	Lieutenant	Ni-to Gun-i
	Military Doctor Third Class	Second Lieutenant	San-to Gun-i
	Veterinarian Superintendent	Major	Jui Kan
	Veterinarian First Class	Captain	I-to Jui
	Veterinarian Second Class	Lieutenant	Ni-to Jui
	Veterinarian Third Class	Second Lieutenant	San-to Jui
	Pharmaceutical Superintendent	Major	Yakuzai Kan
	Pharmacist First Class	Captain	I-to Yakuzai
	Pharmacist Second Class	Lieutenant	Ni-to Yakuzai
	Pharmacist Third Class	Second Lieutenant	San-to Yakuzai
Non-commissioned Officers	Chief Medical Attendant First Class	Sergeant Major	I-to Kango Cho
	Chief Medical Attendant Second Class	Sergeant First Class	Ni-to Kango Cho
	Chief Medical Attendant Third Class	Sergeant Second Class	San-to Kango Cho
	Pharmaceutical Prescriptionist First Class	Sergeant Major	I-to Chozai Te
	Pharmaceutical Prescriptionist Second Class	Sergeant First Class	Ni-to Chozai Te
	Pharmaceutical Prescriptionist Third Class	Sergeant Second Class	San-to Chozai Te
Enlisted Men	Medical Attendant	Private	Kango Te

Imperial Japanese Army Kempeitai Ranks

Category	Rank name	Rank equivalent	Japanese Romaji
Officers	Military Police Colonel	Colonel	Kempei Taisa
	Military Police Lieutenant Colonel	Lieutenant Colonel	Kempei Chusa
	Military Police Major	Major	Kempei Shosa
	Military Police Captain	Captain	Kempei Tai-i
	Military Police Lieutenant	Lieutenant	Kempei Chu-i
	Military Police Second Lieutenant	Second Lieutenant	Kempei Sho-i
Non-commissioned Officers	Military Police Sergeant Major	Sergeant Major	Kempei Socho
	Military Police Sergeant First Class	Sergeant First Class	Kempei I-to Gunso
	Military Police Sergeant Second Class	Sergeant Second Class	Kempei Ni-to Gunso
Enlisted Men	Military Police Superior Private	Superior Private	Kempei Jo-to Hei

APPENDIX II

Imperial Japanese Army Military Band Ranks

Category	Rank name	Rank equivalent	Japanese Romaji
Officers	Military Bandmaster First Class	Second Lieutenant	I-to Gunka Cho
Warrant Officers	Military Bandmaster Second Class	Special Sergeant	Ni-to Gunka Cho
Non-commissioned Officers	Assistant Military Bandmaster	Sergeant Major	Gunka Jicho
	Military Band Musician First Class	Sergeant First Class	I-to Gunka Te
	Military Band Musician Second Class	Sergeant Second Class	Ni-to Gunka Te
Enlisted Men	Military Band Assistant Musician	Superior Private	Gunka Te Ho
	Military Band Student	Private	Ka Sei

Imperial Japanese Army Tondenhei Ranks

Category	Rank name	Rank equivalent	Japanese Romaji
Field Officers	Colonel (all four branches)	N/A	Taisa
	Lieutenant Colonel (all four branches)	N/A	Chusa
	Major (all four branches)	N/A	Shosa
Company Officers	Captain (all four branches)	N/A	Tai-i
	Lieutenant (all four branches)	N/A	Chu-i
	Second Lieutenant (all four branches)	N/A	Sho-i
Non-commissioned Officers	Sergeant Major (all four branches)	N/A	Socho
	Sergeant First Class (all four branches)	N/A	I-to Gunso
	Sergeant Second Class (all four branches)	N/A	Ni-to Gunso
	Demolitions Expert Sergeant Major (artillery)	Sergeant Major	Kako Socho
	Chief Blacksmith (artillery)	Sergeant First Class	Tanko Cho
	Chief Carpenter (artillery)	Sergeant First Class	Mokko Cho
	Chief Gunsmith (artillery)	Sergeant First Class	Juko Cho
	Chief Saddler (artillery)	Sergeant First Class	Kurako Cho
	Chief Farrier (artillery, transportation, and cavalry)	Sergeant First Class	Teitetsuko Cho
	Demolitions Expert Sergeant First Class (artillery)	Sergeant First Class	Kako I-to Gunso
	Assistant Chief Blacksmith (artillery)	Sergeant Second Class	Tanko Kacho
	Assistant Chief Carpenter (artillery)	Sergeant Second Class	Mokko Kacho
	Assistant Chief Gunsmith (artillery)	Sergeant Second Class	Juko Kacho

Category	Rank name	Rank equivalent	Japanese Romaji
	Assistant Chief Saddler (artillery)	Sergeant Second Class	Kurako Kacho
	Assistant Chief Farrier (artillery and cavalry)	Sergeant Second Class	Teitetsuko Kacho
	Demolitions Expert Sergeant Second Class (artillery)	Sergeant Second Class	Kako Ni-to Gunso
Enlisted Men	Superior Private (all four branches)	N/A	Jo-to Hei
	Private First Class (all four branches)	N/A	I-to Sotsu
	Private Second Class (all four branches)	N/A	Ni-to Sotsu
	Blacksmith (artillery)	Private	Tanko
	Carpenter (artillery)	Private	Mokko
	Gunsmith (artillery)	Private	Juko
	Saddler (artillery)	Private	Kurako
	Farrier (artillery and cavalry)	Private	Teitetsuko
	Demolitions Expert (artillery)	Private	Kako

Imperial Japanese Army Accounting Department Ranks

Category	Rank name	Rank equivalent	Japanese Romaji
Officers	Accountant Officer First Class	Captain	I-to Gunri
	Accountant Officer Second Class	Lieutenant	Ni-to Gunri
	Accountant Officer Third Class	Second Lieutenant	San-to Gunri
Non-commissioned Officers	Accountant First Class	Sergeant Major	I-to Shoki
	Accountant Second Class	Sergeant First Class	Ni-to Shoki
	Accountant Third Class	Sergeant Second Class	San-to Shoki

Imperial Japanese Army Auditing (Paymaster) Department Ranks

Category	Rank name	Rank equivalent	Japanese Romaji
General Officers	Chief Paymaster	Major General	Kantoku Cho
Officers	Paymaster First Class	Colonel	I-to Kantoku
	Paymaster Second Class	Lieutenant Colonel	Ni-to Kantoku
	Paymaster Third Class	Major	San-to Kantoku
Non-commissioned Officers	Assistant Paymaster	Captain	Kantoku Ho

APPENDIX II

Imperial Japanese Navy Ranks

Category	Rank name	Rank equivalent	Japanese Romaji
Flag Officers	Admiral	N/A	Taisho
	Vice Admiral	N/A	Chujo
	Rear Admiral	N/A	Shosho
Senior Officers	Captain	N/A	Taisa
	Lieutenant Captain	N/A	Shosa
Junior Officers	Lieutenant	N/A	Tai-i
	Ensign	N/A	Sho-i
Warrant Officers	Chief Petty Officer	N/A	Joto Heiso
	Military Bandmaster	Chief Petty Officer	Gunka Shi
Non-commissioned Officers	Petty Officer First Class	N/A	Ito Heiso
	Petty Officer Second Class	N/A	Nito Heiso
	Petty Officer Third Class	N/A	Santo Heiso
	Chief Signalman First class	Petty Officer First Class	Ito Shingo Te
	Chief Signalman Second Class	Petty Officer Second Class	Nito Shingo Te
	Chief Signalman Third Class	Petty Officer Third Class	Santo Shingo Te
	Military Musician First Class	Petty Officer First Class	Ito Gunka Te
	Military Musician Second Class	Petty Officer Second Class	Nito Gunka Te
	Military Musician Third Class	Petty Officer Third Class	Santo Gunka Te
Seamen	Seaman First Class	N/A	Ito Suihei
	Seaman Second Class	N/A	Nito Suihei
	Seaman Third Class	N/A	Santo Suihei
	Seaman Fourth Class	N/A	Yonto Suihei
	Seaman Fifth Class	N/A	Goto Suihei
	Signalman First Class	Seaman First Class	Ito Shingo Hei
	Signalman Second Class	Seaman Second Class	Nito Shingo Hei
	Signalman Third Class	Seaman Third Class	Santo Shingo Hei
	Signalman Fourth Class	Seaman Fourth Class	Yonto Shingo Hei
	Signalman Fifth Class	Seaman Fifth Class	Goto Shingo Hei
	Military Musician Student First Class	Seaman First Class	Ito Gunka Sei
	Military Musician Student Second Class	Seaman Second Class	Nito Gunka Sei
	Military Musician Student Third Class	Seaman Third Class	Santo Gunka Sei
	Military Musician Student Fourth Class	Seaman Fourth Class	Yonto Gunka Sei
	Military Musician Student Fifth Class	Seaman Fifth Class	Goto Gunka Sei

Imperial Japanese Navy Machinery and Engineering Department Ranks

Category	Rank name	Rank equivalent	Japanese Romaji
Flag Officers	Machinery and Engineering Superintendent General	Major General	Ki Waza Soukan
Senior Officers	Machinery Superior Supervisor	Colonel	Kikan Daikan
	Machinery Supervisor	Major	Kikan Shokan
	Engineering Superior Supervisor	Colonel	Waza Daikan
	Engineering Supervisor	Major	Waza Shokan
Junior Officers	Superior Machinist Officer	Captain	Dai Kikan Shi
	Machinist Officer	Lieutenant	Sho Kikan Shi
	Superior Engineer Officer	Captain	Dai Waza Shi
	Engineer Officer	Lieutenant	Sho Waza Shi

Category	Rank name	Rank equivalent	Japanese Romaji
Warrant Officers	Chief Machinist	Superior Petty Officer	Kikan Shi
	Chief Shipbuilder	Superior Petty Officer	Sensho Shi
Non-commissioned Officers	Machinist First Class	Petty Officer First Class	Ito Kikan Te
	Machinist Second Class	Petty Officer Second Class	Nito Kikan Te
	Machinist Third Class	Petty Officer Third Class	Santo Kikan Te
	Shipbuilder First class	Petty Officer First Class	Ito Sensho Te
	Shipbuilder Second Class	Petty Officer Second Class	Nito Sensho Te
	Shipbuilder Third Class	Petty Officer Third Class	Santo Sensho Te
	Chief Blacksmith First Class	Petty Officer First Class	Ito Kaji Te
	Chief Blacksmith Second Class	Petty Officer Second Class	Nito Kaji Te
	Chief Blacksmith Third Class	Petty Officer Third Class	Santo Kaji Te
Seamen	Stoker First Class	Seaman First Class	Ito Kafu
	Stoker Second Class	Seaman Second Class	Nito Kafu
	Stoker Third Class	Seaman Third Class	Santo Kafu
	Stoker Fourth Class	Seaman Fourth Class	Yonto Kafu
	Stoker Fifth Class	Seaman Fifth Class	Goto Kafu
	Carpenter First Class	Seaman First Class	Ito Mokko
	Carpenter Second Class	Seaman Second Class	Nito Mokko
	Carpenter Third Class	Seaman Third Class	Santo Mokko
	Carpenter Fourth Class	Seaman Fourth Class	Yonto Mokko
	Carpenter Fifth Class	Seaman Fifth Class	Goto Mokko
	Shipbuilder First Class	Seaman First Class	Ito Sensho
	Shipbuilder Second Class	Seaman Second Class	Nito Sensho
	Shipbuilder Third Class	Seaman Third Class	Santo Sensho
	Shipbuilder Fourth Class	Seaman Fourth Class	Yonto Sensho
	Shipbuilder Fifth Class	Seaman Fifth Class	Goto Sensho

Imperial Japanese Navy Military Medicine Department Ranks

Category	Rank name	Rank equivalent	Japanese Romaji
Flag Officers	Medical Superintendent General	Major General	Gun-i Soukan
Senior Officers	Superior Medical Superintendent	Colonel	Gun-i Daikan
	Medical Superintendent	Major	Gun-i Shokan
	Pharmaceutical Superintendent	Major	Yakuzai Shokan
Junior Officers	Superior Military Doctor	Captain	Dai Gun-i
	Military Doctor	Lieutenant	Sho Gun-i
	Superior Pharmacist	Captain	Dai Yakuzai
	Pharmacist	Lieutenant	Sho Yakuzai
Warrant Officers	Superior Chief Medical Attendant	Superior Petty Officer	Joto Kango Te
Non-commissioned Officers	Chief Medical Attendant First Class	Petty Officer First Class	Ito Kango Te
	Chief Medical Attendant Second Class	Petty Officer Second Class	Nito Kango Te
	Chief Medical Attendant Third Class	Petty Officer Third Class	Santo Kango Te
Seamen	Medical Attendant First Class	Seaman First Class	Ito Kanbyo
	Medical Attendant Second Class	Seaman Second Class	Nito Kanbyo
	Medical Attendant Third Class	Seaman Third Class	Santo Kanbyo
	Medical Attendant Fourth Class	Seaman Fourth Class	Yonto Kanbyo
	Medical Attendant Fifth Class	Seaman Fifth Class	Goto Kanbyo

APPENDIX II

Imperial Japanese Navy Accounting Department Ranks

Category	Rank name	Rank equivalent	Japanese Romaji
Flag Officers	Paymaster Superintendent General	Major General	Shukei Soukan
Senior Officers	Superior Paymaster Superintendent	Colonel	Shukei Daikan
	Paymaster Superintendent	Major	Shukei Shokan
Junior Officers	Superior Paymaster	Captain	Dai Shukei
	Paymaster	Lieutenant	Sho Shukei
Warrant Officers	Superior Chief Accountant	Superior Petty Officer	Joto Omo Cho
Non-commissioned Officers	Chief Accountant First Class	Petty Officer First Class	Ito Omo Cho
	Chief Accountant Second Class	Petty Officer Second Class	Nito Omo Cho
	Chief Accountant Third Class	Petty Officer Third Class	Santo Omo Cho
Seamen	Food Worker First Class	Seaman First Class	Ito Chiyufu
	Food Worker Second Class	Seaman Second Class	Nito Chiyufu
	Food Worker Third Class	Seaman Third Class	Santo Chiyufu
	Food Worker Fourth Class	Seaman Fourth Class	Yonto Chiyufu
	Food Worker Fifth Class	Seaman Fifth Class	Goto Chiyufu

Appendix III

Imperial Japanese Army Uniform Colours

Enlisted Man Winter Uniform Colours

Service Branch	Type One Shako	Type Two Forage Cap	Collar	Epaulettes	Hungarian Knotting	Cuff Insignia	Jacket Edging	Trousers	Remarks
Line Infantry	Dark blue	Dark blue with yellow band	Red	Red cloth with brass numerals	None	Yellow	None	Dark blue with red stripe	
Line Artillery	Dark blue	Dark blue with yellow band	Yellow	Yellow cloth with brass numerals	None	Yellow	None	Dark blue with yellow stripe	
Line Fortress Artillery	Dark blue	Dark blue with yellow band	Yellow	Yellow cloth with red cloth numerals	None	Yellow	None	Dark blue with yellow stripe	
Line Engineers	Dark blue	Dark blue with yellow band	Brown	Brown cloth with brass numerals	None	Yellow	None	Dark blue with brown stripe	
Line Commissariat	Dark blue	Dark blue with yellow band	Blue	Blue cloth with brass numerals	None	Yellow	None	Dark blue with blue stripe	
Line Cavalry	Dark blue	Dark blue with yellow band	Light green	Yellow woven	Yellow	Yellow	Yellow	Red with light green stripe	Attila jacket
Cobblers and Tailors	Dark blue	Dark blue with medium blue band	Dark blue (no coloured collar)	Medium blue cloth with brass numerals	None	Medium blue	None	Dark blue with medium blue stripe	Cuff insignia in inverted chevron shape
Farriers	Dark blue	Dark blue with yellow band	Light green	Light green cloth with brass numerals	None	Yellow	None	Dark blue with light green stripe	Cuff insignia in inverted chevron shape
All other support functions (Metal Casters Blacksmiths Carpenters Gunsmiths Saddlers and Demolition Experts)	Dark blue	Dark blue with yellow band	Yellow	Yellow cloth with brass numerals	None	Yellow	None	Dark blue with yellow stripe	Cuff insignia in inverted chevron shape

APPENDIX III

Officer Winter Field Uniform Colours

Service Branch	Type Two Forage Cap	Collar	Epaulettes	Hungarian Knotting	Cuff Insignia	Jacket Edging	Trouser	Remarks
Line Infantry Officers	Dark blue with yellow band	Dark blue edged in black	None	Black	Black	Black	Dark blue with red stripe	
Line Artillery Officers	Dark blue with yellow band	Dark blue edged in black	None	Black	Black	Black	Dark blue with yellow stripe	
Line Engineers Officers	Dark blue with yellow band	Dark blue edged in black	None	Black	Black	Black	Dark blue with brown stripe	
Line Commissariat Officers	Dark blue with yellow band	Dark blue edged in black	None	Black	Black	Black	Dark blue with blue stripe	
Line Cavalry Officers	Dark blue with yellow band	Dark blue edged in black	Gold woven	Black	Black	Black	Red with light green stripe	Brass buttons instead of woven ones

Officer Parade Colours

Service Branch	Type One Kepi	Inner Collar	Epaulettes	Hungarian Knotting	Cuff Insignia	Jacket Edging	Trouser	Remarks
General Officers	Dark blue with gold lining; gold star	Gold	Gold woven	None	Gold trefoils with dark blue (uncoloured) cuff	Black	Dark blue with red stripe	
Line Infantry Officers	Dark blue with gold lining; gold star	Red	Gold woven	None	Gold trefoils with red cuff	Red	Dark blue with red stripe	
Line Artillery Officers	Dark blue with gold lining; gold star	Yellow	Gold woven	None	Gold trefoils with yellow cuff	Yellow	Dark blue with yellow stripe	
Line Engineer Officers	Dark blue with gold lining; gold star	Brown	Gold woven	None	Gold trefoils with brown cuff	Brown	Dark blue with brown stripe	
Line Commissariat Officers	Dark blue with gold lining; gold star	Blue	Gold woven	None	Gold trefoils with blue cuff	Blue	Dark blue with blue stripe	
Line Cavalry Officers (Attila Jacket)	Dark blue with gold lining; gold star	Light green	Gold woven	Black	Gold trefoils with light green cuff	Black	Red with light green stripe	Attila jacket; brass buttons instead of woven ones

Officer Parade Sash Colours

Rank	Sash	Tassel Head	Tassels
Generals	Red and gold stripes	Gold with three silver stars	Gold
Lieutenant Generals	Red and gold stripes	Gold with two silver stars	Gold
Major Generals	Red and gold stripes	Gold with one star	Gold
Field Officers	Red and white stripes	Gold	Gold
Company Officers	Bright red and white stripes	Red	Red

Imperial Guard Enlisted Man Winter Uniform Colours

Service Branch	Type One Shako	Type Two Forage Cap	Collar	Epaulettes	Hungarian Knotting	Cuff Insignia	Jacket Edging	Trouser	Remarks
Imperial Guard Infantry	Red	Dark blue with red band	Red	Red cloth with brass numerals	None	Red	Red	Dark blue with red stripe	
Imperial Guard Artillery	Red	Dark blue with red band	Yellow	Yellow cloth with brass numerals	None	Red	Yellow	Dark blue with yellow stripe	
Imperial Guard Engineers	Red	Dark blue with red band	Brown	Yellow cloth with red cloth numerals[1]	None	Red	Brown	Dark blue with brown stripe	
Imperial Guard Commissariat	Red	Dark blue with red band	Blue	Brown cloth with brass numerals	None	Red	Blue	Dark blue with blue stripe	
Imperial Guard Cavalry	Red	Dark blue with red band	Light green	Red woven	Red	Red	Red	Red with light green stripe	

Imperial Guard Officer Winter Uniform Colours

Service Branch	Type One Kepi	Type Two Forage Cap	Collar	Epaulettes	Hungarian Knotting	Cuff Insignia	Jacket Edging	Trouser	Remarks
Imperial Guard Infantry Officers	Red with gold lining; gold star	Dark blue with red band	Dark blue edged in black	None	Black	Black	Black	Dark blue with red stripe	
Imperial Guard Artillery Officers	Red with gold lining; gold star	Dark blue with red band	Dark blue edged in black	None	Black	Black	Black	Dark blue with yellow stripe	
Imperial Guard Engineer Officers	Red with gold lining; gold star	Dark blue with red band	Dark blue edged in black	None	Black	Black	Black	Dark blue with brown stripe	
Imperial Guard Commissariat Officers	Red with gold lining; gold star	Dark blue with red band	Dark blue edged in black	None	Black	Black	Black	Dark blue with blue stripe	
Imperial Guard Cavalry Officers	Red kepi	Dark blue with red band	Light green	Gold woven	Black	Black	Black	Red with light green stripe	Brass buttons instead of woven ones

1　Changed to red cloth numerals in 1890.

APPENDIX III

Kempeitai Winter Uniform Colours

Service Branch	Type One Kepi	Type Two Forage Cap	Collar	Epaulettes	Hungarian Knotting	Cuff Insignia	Jacket Edging	Trouser	Remarks
Kempeitai Officers Parade Dress	Red, black band with gold lining; gold star	None	Red (inner)	Gold woven	None	Gold trefoils with red cuff	Red	Blue with red stripe, changed to red with black stripe in 1888	Double-breasted parade jacket
Kempeitai Officers	Red, black band with gold lining; gold star	None	Red	Gold woven	Black	Red	Black	Blue with red stripe; changed to red with black stripe in 1888	Attila jacket
Kempeitai Enlisted Men and Non-commissioned Officers	Red, black band with gold lining; gold star	None	Red	Red cloth	None	Red	None	Blue with red stripe; changed to red with black stripe in 1888	Single-breasted regular jacket

Tondenhei Enlisted Man Winter Uniform Colours

Service Branch	Type One Shako	Type Two Forage Cap	Collar	Epaulettes	Hungarian Knotting	Cuff Insignia	Jacket Edging	Trousers	Remarks
Tondenhei Infantry	Dark blue	Dark blue with yellow band	Red; special badge added in 1895	Red cloth with brass numerals	None	Yellow	None	Frost blue with red stripe; replaced with dark blue in red stripe in 1895	
Tondenhei Artillery	Dark blue	Dark blue with yellow band	Yellow; special badge added in 1895	Yellow cloth with brass numerals	None	Yellow	None	Frost blue with yellow stripe; replaced with dark blue in yellow stripe in 1895	
Tondenhei Engineers	Dark blue	Dark blue with yellow band	Brown; special badge added in 1895	Brown cloth with brass numerals	None	Yellow	None	Frost blue with brown stripe; replaced with dark blue in brown stripe in 1895	
Tondenhei Commissariat	Dark blue	Dark blue with yellow band	Blue; special badge added in 1895	Blue cloth with brass numerals	None	Yellow	None	Frost blue with blue stripe; replaced with dark blue in blue stripe in 1895	
Tondenhei Cavalry	Dark blue	Dark blue with yellow band	Light green; special badge added in 1895	Yellow woven	Yellow	Yellow	Yellow	Frost blue with light green stripe; replaced with red with light green stripe in 1895	
Tondenhei Farriers	Dark blue	Dark blue with yellow band	Light green; special badge added in 1895	Light green cloth with brass numerals	None	Yellow	None	Frost blue with light green stripe; replaced with dark blue in light green stripe in 1895	Cuff insignia in inverted chevron shape
All other Tondenhei support functions (Blacksmiths Carpenters Gunsmiths Saddlers and Demolitions Experts)	Dark blue	Dark blue with yellow band	Yellow; special badge added in 1895	Yellow cloth with brass numerals	None	Yellow	None	Frost blue with yellow stripe; replaced with dark blue in yellow stripe in 1895	Cuff insignia in inverted chevron shape

Tondenhei Officer Winter Uniform Colours

Service Branch	Type Two Forage Cap	Collar	Epaulettes	Hungarian Knotting	Cuff Insignia	Jacket Edging	Trouser	Remarks
Tondenhei Infantry Officers	Dark blue with yellow band	Dark blue edged in black	None	Black	Black	Black	Frost blue with red stripe; replaced with dark blue in red stripe in 1895	
Tondenhei Artillery Officers	Dark blue with yellow band	Dark blue edged in black	None	Black	Black	Black	Frost blue with yellow stripe; replaced with dark blue in yellow stripe in 1895	
Tondenhei Engineer Officer	Dark blue with yellow band	Dark blue edged in black	None	Black	Black	Black	Frost blue with brown stripe; replaced with dark blue in brown stripe in 1895	
Tondenhei Commissariat Officers	Dark blue with yellow band	Dark blue edged in black	None	Black	Black	Black	Frost blue with blue stripe; replaced with dark blue in blue stripe in 1895	
Tondenhei Cavalry Officers	Dark blue with yellow band	Dark blue edged in black	Gold woven	Black	Black	Black	Frost blue with light green stripe; replaced with red with light green stripe in 1895	Brass buttons instead of woven ones

Military Band Uniform Colours

Rank	Type One Kepi	Collar	Epaulettes	Cuff Insignia	Jacket Edging	Sash	Trouser	Remarks
Military Bandmasters First Class	Red with gold lining; gold star	Red with brass harp badge	Gold woven with brass harp badge	Gold trefoils with red cuffs	Red	Red and blue stripes with red tassel head and tassels	Red with blue stripe	Double-breasted officer parade jacket
Military Bandmasters Second Class	Red with gold lining; gold star	Red with brass harp badge	Yellow woven with brass harp badge	Gold chevron with red cuffs	Red	Red and blue stripes with red tassel head and tassels	Red with blue stripe	Double-breasted officer parade jacket
Assistant Military Bandmasters and below	Red with gold lining; gold star	Red with brass harp badge	Red cloth edged in blue	Blue with red cuff	None	None	Red with blue stripe	Single-breasted regular jacket

Sanitation Department Officer Field Uniform Colours

Service Branch	Type One Kepi	Type Two Forage Cap	Collar	Woven Epaulettes	Hungarian Knotting	Cuff Insignia	Jacket Edging	Trouser	Remarks
Military Doctors	Black with gold lining; silver star	Dark blue with dark green band	Black	None	Black	Black	Black	Dark blue with dark green stripe	Red cross armband on left upper arm
Veterinarians	Black with gold lining; silver star	Dark blue with dark green band	Black	None	Black	Black	Black	Dark blue with dark green stripe	Red cross armband on left upper arm
Pharmacists	Black with gold lining; silver star	Dark blue with dark green band	Black	None	Black	Black	Black	Dark blue with dark green stripe	Red cross armband on left upper arm

APPENDIX III

Sanitation Department Officer Parade Uniform Colours

Rank	Type One Kepi	Collar	Epaulettes	Cuff Insignia	Jacket Edging	Sash	Trouser	Remarks
Medical super-intendent generals	Dark blue with gold lining; silver star	Dark green	Gold and silver woven with Rod of Asclepius	Gold and silver trefoils with dark blue (uncoloured) cuffs	Black	Dark green and silver stripes with silver tassel head and tassels; one brass star	Dark blue with dark green stripe	
Medical Super-intendents	Dark blue with gold lining; silver star	Dark green	Gold and silver woven with silver Rod of Asclepius badge	Gold and silver trefoils with dark blue (uncoloured) cuffs	Black	Dark green and silver stripes with silver tassel head and tassels	Dark blue with dark green stripe	
Veterinary Super-intendents	Dark blue with gold lining; silver star	Dark green	Gold and silver woven with silver crossed leaves badge	Gold and silver trefoils with dark blue (uncoloured) cuffs	Black	Dark green and silver stripes with silver tassel head and tassels	Dark blue with dark green stripe	
Pharma-ceutical Super-intendents	Dark blue with gold lining; silver star	Dark green	Gold and silver woven with silver Rod of Asclepius badge	Gold and silver trefoils with dark blue (uncoloured) cuffs	Black	Dark green and silver stripes with silver tassel head and tassels	Dark blue with dark green stripe	
Medical Officers First Second and Third Class	Dark blue with gold lining; silver star	Dark green	Gold and silver woven with silver Rod of Asclepius badge	Gold and silver trefoils with dark blue (uncoloured) cuffs	Black	Dark green and silver stripes with silver tassel head and tassels	Dark blue with dark green stripe	
Military Doctors First Second and Third Class	Dark blue with gold lining; silver star	Dark green	Gold and silver woven with silver Rod of Asclepius badge	Gold and silver trefoils with dark blue (uncoloured) cuffs	Black	Dark green and white stripes with dark green tassel head and tassels	Dark blue with dark green stripe	
Veterinar-ians First Second and Third Class	Dark blue with gold lining; silver star	Dark green	Gold and silver woven with silver crossed leaves badge	Gold and silver trefoils with dark blue (uncoloured) cuffs	Black	Dark green and white stripes with dark green tassel head and tassels	Dark blue with dark green stripe	
Pharmacists First Second and Third Class	Dark blue with gold lining; silver star	Dark green	Gold and silver woven with silver Rod of Asclepius badge	Gold and silver trefoils with dark blue (uncoloured) cuffs	Black	Dark green and white stripes with dark green tassel head and tassels	Dark blue with dark green stripe	

Sanitation Department Enlisted Man Uniform Colours

Service Branch	Type One Shako	Type Two Forage Cap	Collar	Cloth Epaulettes	Cuff Insignia	Jacket Edging	Trouser	Remarks
Chief Medical Attendant First Second and Third Class	Black	Dark blue with dark green band	Dark green	Dark green with Rod of Asclepius badge	Dark green	None	Dark blue with dark green stripe	Red cross armband on left upper arm
Medical Attendant	Black	Dark blue with dark green band	Dark green	Dark green with Rod of Asclepius badge	Dark green	None	Dark blue with dark green stripe	Red cross armband on left upper arm
Pharmaceutical Prescriptionist	Black	Dark blue with dark green band	Dark green	Dark green with Rod of Asclepius badge	Dark green	None	Dark blue with dark green stripe	Red cross armband on left upper arm

Accountant and Auditing Department Enlisted Field Uniform Colours

Service Branch	Type Two Forage Cap	Collar	Epaulettes	Hungarian Knotting	Cuff Insignia	Jacket Edging	Trouser	Remarks
Accountant Officers	Dark blue with medium blue band	Medium blue	Medium blue cloth	Black	Black	Black	Dark blue with medium blue stripe	Attila jacket
Accountants (Non-commissioned Officers)	Dark blue with medium blue band	Medium blue	Medium blue cloth	None	Medium blue	None	Dark blue with medium blue stripe	Regular jacket
Paymasters	Dark blue with silver brown band	Black	Gold and silver woven	Black	Black	Black	Dark blue with silver brown stripe	Attila jacket

Accountant and Auditing Department Parade Uniform Colours

Rank/Service Branch	Type One Kepi	Inner Collar	Woven Epaulettes	Cuff Insignia	Jacket Edging	Sash	Trouser	Remarks
Accountant Officers	Dark blue with gold lining; silver star	Black	Gold and silver	Gold and silver trefoils with dark blue (uncoloured) cuff	Black	Medium blue and white stripes with medium blue tassel head and tassels	Dark blue with medium blue stripe	
Chief Paymasters	Dark blue with gold lining; silver star	Black	Gold and silver	Gold and silver trefoils with dark blue (uncoloured) cuff	Black	Silver brown and white stripes with silver tassel head and tassels; one brass star	Dark blue with silver brown stripe	
Paymasters First Class	Dark blue with gold lining; silver star	Black	Gold and silver	Gold and silver trefoils with dark blue (uncoloured) cuff	Black	Silver brown and white stripes with silver tassel head and tassels	Dark blue with silver brown stripe	Dark blue with silver brown stripe
Assistant Paymasters, Paymasters Second and Third Class	Dark blue with gold lining; silver star	Black	Gold and silver	Gold and silver trefoils with dark blue (uncoloured) cuff	Black	Silver brown and white stripes with silver brown tassel head and tassels	Dark blue with silver brown stripe	

Bibliography

Chinese Sources

Anon., *Shenyang Xianzhi* (Shenyang: Chengwen Chubanshe, 1974).
Anon., 'Daodi Shi Shui Nuoyong Le Beiyang Jiandui Junfei? Weng Tonghe Zhishi Diaonan, Zuikui Huoshou Lingyou Qiren,' *Redian Xinjian* (2024) <https://kan.china.com/qd/mkan/article/1170376_4.html?qudao=mkan>, accessed 6 February 2024.
Anon., 'Jilinshi Faxian "Hujiangjun" Yiktang'a Mudi,' *Jiangcheng Wanbao* (2014), <https://www.sssc.cn/a/20120629/134093472973328.shtml>, accessed 4 February2024.
Anon., 'Long Qi Piaoyang de Jiandui Jiexuan – Cong Lang Weili Kan Yang Guwen,' *Jianchuan Zhishi Wangluo Ban* (2003), <https://mil.news.sina.com.cn/2003-01-14/102544.html>, accessed 6 February 2024.
Anon., 'Tuchengzi Zhizhan: Rijun Beida De Luohua Liushui,' *Sohu* (2019), <https://www.sohu.com/a/309339284_120044586>, accessed 2 March 2024.
Buchende Jingyuan, 'Jiawu Zhanzhengshi, Qingjunde Zhuangbei Zongti Shangruoyu Rijun, Dui Zhanzheng Jieguo Youbuxiaode Yingxiang,' *Toutiao* (2019), <https://www.toutiao.com/article/6770525340583330311/>, accessed 7 February 2024.
Cai Erkang, *Zhongdong Zhanji Benmo* (Shanghai: Guangwenhui, 1896).
Changge Kanyu, 'Ta shi diyi ge bei jibi de Rijun Shaojiang, Yisheng Taoguo Liang ci Danan, Zuizhong Mingsang Motianling,' *Changge Kanyu* (2024), <https://www.163.com/dy/article/IUG55J4E05564UD9.html>, accessed 3 March 2024.
Chen Kegang and Chen Xinkui, 'Qingdai Huaijun Jiangling Chen Fenglou Shiji Gouchen,' *Zhonghua Wenshi* (2006), <http://www.historychina.net/qsyj/ztyj/ztyjzz/2006-05-30/24388.shtml>, accessed 2 March 2024.
Chen Mingfu, 'Shimenzi Zujizhan,' *Kangri Zhanzheng Jinian* (2018), <https://www.krzzjn.com/show-1820-73336.html>, accessed 1 March 2024.
Chen Xulu (ed.) et al., *Sheng Dang: Jiawu Zhongri Zhanzheng* (Shanghai: Shanghai Renmin Chubanshe, 2016).
Chen Yue, *Zhongguo Junjian Tuzhi* (Shanghai: Shanghai Shudian Chubanshe, 2015).
Du Li, Chen Yan and Zhang Jingqiong, 'Jindai Fuzhuangmen Jinyukou Pande Xingzhi Zuhe Yu Shenmei Biaoda,' *Zhuangshi*, 12:6 (2012).
Fenghuo Tai Chunqiu, 'Zhongri Lushun Jinzhou Zhizhan,' *Fenghuo Tai Chunqiu* (2007), <https://blog.wenxuecity.com/myblog/22960/200708/42787.html>, accessed 27 February 2024.
Gu Tinglong (ed.) and Ye Yalian(ed.), *Li Hongzhang Quanji* (Shanghai: Shanghai Renmin Chubanshe, 1987).
Guan Jie, *Xin Bian Jiawu Zhongri Zhanzheng Shi* (Taipei: Zhonghua, 2022).
Han Yongfu, 'Qingmo Jiangling Ye Zhichao Bing Sixing Bu Jianyu Kao,' *Lishi Dang'an* (2017), <https://xueshu.baidu.com/usercenter/paper/show?paperid=1s5j0jj0gb1e0a30su160pg0jx122428&tn=SE_baiduxueshu_c1gjeupa&ie=utf-8&site=baike>, accessed 7 February 2024.
Junshi Jilu, Weiguan Zhanchang: Jiawu Zhanzheng, Jinlu Zhizhan, CCTV, (2012).
Junshi Jilu, Weiguan Zhanchang: Jiawu Zhanzheng, Liaoyang Donglu, CCTV, (2012).
Junshi Jilu, Weiguan Zhanchang: Jiawu Zhanzheng, Liaoyang Nanlu, CCTV, (2012).
Junshi Jilu, Weiguan Zhanchang: Jiawu Zhanzheng, Liugongdao Zhizhan, CCTV, (2012).
Junshi Jilu, Weiguan Zhanchang: Jiawu Zhanzheng, Pingrang Zhizhan, CCTV, (2012).

Kuai Zaifeng, 'Beiyang Shuishi De Zuida Chiru: Yi Zheng Zhi Yulei Jiandui Jiti Taopao,' *NetEase* (2017), <https://www.163.com/dy/article/CKG18O0S0523D5D7.html>, accessed 2 March 2024.

Lan Tai, 'Mingzhi Weixin Qian: Riben Nongmin Tudi Zhanyou Zhidu Yuan Luohou Qingchao,' *Fenghuang Lishi* (2014), <https://news.ifeng.com/history/zhongguojindaishi/special/minzhongfudan/>, accessed 4 February 2024.

Lan Tai, 'Zouxiang Jindai Hua: Taipingtianguo Zhanzheng Hou Qing Lujun Jiji Xuexi Xifang,' *Fenghuang Lishi* (2014), <https://news.ifeng.com/history/zhongguojindaishi/special/wuqizhuangbei/>, accessed 28 February 2024.

Liugongdao, '1895 Liugongdao Shang Naxie Yangyuan', *Liugongdao* (Unknown), <http://www.liugongdao.com.cn/index.php?m=content&c=index&a=show&catid=34&id=673>, accessed 2 March 2024.

Lu Chaoying, 'Tianjin Wubei Xuetang,' *Tianjin Dang'an* (2004), <https://xueshu.baidu.com/usercenter/paper/show?paperid=82f07a5e1a032b73e9c0657b5b6f0d00&tn=SE_baiduxueshu_c1gjeupa&ie=utf-8&site=baike>, accessed 7 February 2024.

Munemitsu Mutsu, *Jianjianlu* (Beijing: Xinzhi Sanlian Shudian, 2018).

Ping Xu, *Jiawu Zhanzheng Zhongri Jundui Tonglan 1894–1895* (Beijing: Zhongguo Renmin Jiefangjun Chubanshe, 2014).

Qi Qizhang, *Jiawu Zhanzheng Shi* (Shanghai: Shanghai Renmin Chubanshe, 2014),

Qihao Shuo Sanguo, 'Jiawu Haizhan shi, weihe Nanyang Shuishi kanzhe Beiyang Shuishi quanjun fumie, ye bu beishang bangzhu ta?' *Qihao Shuo Sanguo* (2020), <https://www.sohu.com/a/399050670_120174872#:~:text=%E7%94%B2%E5%8D%88%E4%B8%AD%E6%97%A5%E6%88%98%E4%BA%89%E7%88%86%E5%8F%91,%E6%89%80%E4%BB%A5%E5%8E%8B%E6%A0%B9%E4%B8%8D%E6%95%A2%E5%8C%97%E4%B8%8A%E3%80%82>, accessed29 February 2024.

Qingfeng Wenshi, 'Jiawu zhanzheng zhong, Nanyang shuishi weihe bu beishang canzhan? Qishi shi bu xiang qu "song rentou"', *Qingfeng Wenshi* (2022), <https://www.163.com/dy/article/HINND4040552XHZR.html>, accessed 29 February 2024.

Renmin Zhengxie Bao, 'Jiawu Zhanzheng Shiqi De Kuandian Dajie,' *Zhongguo Gongchandang Xinjian* (2014), <http://dangshi.people.com.cn/n/2014/0828/c85037-25559380.html>, accessed 2 March 2024.

Shen Zuxian, *Yang Shouyuan Zouyi* (Taipei City: Wenhai Chubanshe, 1966).

Tang Bo, '"Cheqi Shijian" yu Beiyang Jiandui Zhihui Quan Zhizheng,' *HistoryChina.net* (2019), <http://www.qinghistory.cn/qsjj/qsjj_dwgx/387856.shtml>, accessed 29 February 2024.

Wang Kan, 'Wan Qing Zuihou de Mingjiang Nie Shicheng', *Lishi Dang'an* (2022), <http://www.ifengweekly.com/detil.php?id=17777>, accessed 27 February 2024.

Xiaodu Xushi, 'Jiawu Zhanzheng Zhong, Xu Bangdao Zai Tuchengzi Zhizhan Zhiqian de Shimenzi Zuji Zhanzong, Biaoxian Ruhe?', *Xiaodu Xushi* (2022), <https://www.sohu.com/a/529388822_120935290>, accessed 1 March 2024.

Xiong Songce, 'Qingmo "Changqi Shijian" Shimo,' *Gejie* (2012), volume 180.

Yingxiongaixizao, 'Lushunkou Da Chuan – Lushun Da Tusha,' *ACFUN* (2021), <https://www.acfun.cn/a/ac30168985?from=video>, accessed 2 March 2024.

Yongge Dushi, 'Jiawu Zhanzheng Dao Le Guanjian Shike, Ci Qingjun Jiangling Mangzhe Yunzou Zijia Caiwu,' *Yongge Dushi* (2019), <https://www.sohu.com/a/289729114_129546>, accessed 2 March 2024.

Zeng Guofan, 'Bing,' in anon. (ed.), *Zeng Guofan Quanji* (Beijing: Zhongguo Zhigong Chubanshe, 2001), vol. 16.

Zeng Guofan, 'Ying Gui,' in anon. (ed.), *Zeng Guofan Quanji* (Beijing: Zhongguo Zhigong Chubanshe, 2001), vol. 16.

Zhao Erxun et al., *Qing Shigao* (Beijing: National History Museum of the Republic of China, 1929).

Zhongguo Diyi Lishi Dang'an Guan, Haishi.

Zhongguo Diyi Lishi Dang'an Guan, Qingshi Yanjiu Zhuanti Yanjiu Junshi.

Zhongguo Diyi Lishi Dang'an Guan, Shandong Xunfu Yamen Dang.

Zhu Chengru, 'Qing Tong Guang Chao Bingdu Zougao Hanzha Xu,' *Zhonghua Wenshi* (2006), <http://www.historychina.net/magazinefree/html/15/88/content/168.shtml>, accessed 2 March 2024.

'Guangwu Jun Jianshi,' Guiyang County People's Government, <http://www.hngy.gov.cn/zwgk/zwdt/7478/7493/content_1443719.html>, accessed 12 November 2024.

'Lian Jun,' Qingshi Baike, <http://www.historychina.net/qsbk/bz/389134.shtml>, accessed 4 February 2024.

'Tai Qiang,' Wuqi Daquan, <http://www.wuqidaquan.com/index.php?doc-view-14932>, accessed 7 February 2024.
'Xu Zhen,' Liaoyang County People's Government, http://www.liaoyangxian.gov.cn/mlly/001011/20150805/152617461233549.html, accessed 12 November 2024.

Japanese Sources

Hikaru Shiraishi, 'Kuwabara Seikeiben Kenjū,' *Rekishijin* (2024), <https://www.rekishijin.com/39487>, accessed 2 March 2024.
Imperial Japanese Navy (ed.), *Meiji Niju Nana Hachi Toshi Kaishin Fumito* (Tokyo, Shunyodo, 1905)
Kokuritsu Kobunshokan (National Archives of Japan), Naikaku Sorifu.
Masanori Tsujida, *Nihon no Gunka: Kokumin Teki Ongaku no Rekishi* (Tokyo: Gentosha, 2014).
Shunyodo, *Nisshin Kosen Roku* (Tokyo: Shunyodo, 1894).
Ue Kawamura et al., *Nisshin Senso Jikki* (Tokyo: Hakubunkan, 1894–1896),
Yagyu Etsuko, *Nihon Kaigun Gunsou Zukan* (Tokyo: Namiki Shobou, 2014).
'Hanbatsu,' Japanese Wiki, <https://www.japanesewiki.com/history/Hanbatsu%20(domain%20clique).html>, accessed 24 March 2024.
Hatta Kinnosuke, *Sasanami to densetsu no Pyonyan* (Tokyo: Pyonyan Kenkyukai, 1934).
'Kempei,' Weblio, <https://www.weblio.jp/wkpja/content/%E6%86%B2%E5%85%B5+%28%E6%97%A5%E6%9C%AC%E8%BB%8D_29_%E6%86%B2%E5%85%B5+%28%E6%97%A5%E6%9C%AC%E8%BB%8D%29%E3%81%AE%E6%A6%82%E8%A6%81>, accessed 7 February 2024.
'Klemens W. J. Meckel,' Weblio, <https://www.weblio.jp/content/%E3%82%AF%E3%83%AC%E3%83%A1%E3%83%B3%E3%82%B9%E3%83%BB%E3%83%B4%E3%82%A3%E3%83%AB%E3%83%98%E3%83%AB%E3%83%A0%E3%83%BB%E3%83%A4%E3%83%BC%E3%82%B3%E3%83%97%E3%83%BB%E3%83%A1%E3%83%83%E3%82%B1%E3%83%AB>, accessed 7 February 2024.
'Konoe Shidan,' Weblio, <https://www.weblio.jp/wkpja/content/%E8%BF%91%E8%A1%9B%E5%B8%AB%E5%9B%A3_%E8%BF%91%E8%A1%9B%E5%B8%AB%E5%9B%A3%E3%81%AE%E6%A6%82%E8%A6%81>, accessed 7 February 2024.
'Tondenhei Seido,' Tonden, <https://tonden.org/wiki/index.php?title=%E5%B1%AF%E7%94%B0%E5%85%B5%E5%88%B6%E5%BA%A6>, accessed 23 March 2024.
'Tondenhei,' Tonden, <https://tonden.org/wiki/index.php?title=%E5%B1%AF%E7%94%B0%E5%85%B5>, accessed 23 March 2024.

English Sources

'A Divided House,' The North-China Herald (Shanghai), 29 March 1895.
'Says Chinese Don't Care,' The New York Times (New York), 16 May 1895.
Liu Kwang-Ching, 'The Military Challenge,' in Albert E. Dien and Keith N. Knapp (eds.), *The Cambridge History of China* (Cambridge: Cambridge University Press, 2019).
'The China-Japanese War,' The Pall Mall Gazette (London), 4 September 1894.
'The China-Japanese War,' The Pall Mall Gazette (London), 4 September 1894.
Allan James, *Under the Dragon Flag: My Experiences in the Chino-Japanese War* (London: W. Heinemann, 1898).
Anon. 'Pre-Murata Japanese Military Rifles,' *Military Rifles* (2023), <https://www.militaryrifles.com/japan/premurata>, accessed 12 Feb 2024.
Atteridge Andrew, *The Wars Of The Nineties: A History Of The Warfare Of The Last Ten Years Of The Nineteenth Century* (London: Cassell and Company Limited, 1899).
Bishop Isabella, *Korea, and Her Neighbors* (New York: F.H. Revell Company, 1898).
Boulais Guy, *Manuel du Code Chinois* (Shanghai: Imprimerie de la Mission Catholique, 1924).
Cavendish Alfred, 'The Armed Strength (?) Of China,' *Journal of the Royal United Services Institution*, 42:244 (1898).
Chang Chun-ming, 'The Chinese Standards of Good Government: Being a Study of the "Biographies of Model Officials" in Dynastic Histories,' *Nankai Social & Economic Quarterly*, 8:2, (1935).
Chunqiu Zhanguo, 'Telling Apart Chinese Polearms: A Quick Visual Guide,' *Great Ming Military* (2019), <https://greatmingmilitary.blogspot.com/2019/03/telling-apart-chinese-polearms-quick.html>, accessed 7 February 2024.
Cunningham Arthur, *The Chinese Soldier and Other Sketches. With A Description of the Capture of Manila* (London: Sampson Low, Marston and Company Ltd, 1899).

Davidson James, *The Island of Formosa, Past and Present: History, People, Resources, and Commercial Prospects. Tea, Camphor, Sugar, Gold, Coal, Sulphur, Economical Plants, and Other Productions* (New York: MacMillan & Co., 1903).

Dekker Peter, 'A Typology of Chinese Sabers,' *Mandarin Mansion* (2016), <https://www.mandarinmansion.com/article/typology-chinese-sabers>, accessed 7 February 2024.

Dekker Peter, 'Chinese Long Sabers of the Qing Dynasty,' *Mandarin Mansion* (2016), <https://www.mandarinmansion.com/article/chinese-long-sabers-qing-dynasty>, accessed 7 February 2024.

Dekker Peter, 'Edged Weapons of the Green Standard Army,' *Mandarin Mansion* (2016), <https://www.mandarinmansion.com/article/edged-weapons-green-standard-army>, accessed 7 February 2024.

Dekker Peter, 'Niaoqiang,' *Mandarin Mansion* (2019), <https://www.mandarinmansion.com/glossary/niaoqiang>, accessed 7 February 2024.

Dekker Peter, 'Qing Dynasty Saber Mounts, Fangshi & Yuanshi,' *Mandarin Mansion* (2016), <https://www.mandarinmansion.com/article/qing-dynasty-saber-mounts-fangshi-yuanshi>, accessed 7 February 2024.

Dekker Peter, 'Spears of the Qing Dynasty,' *Mandarin Mansion* (2016), <https://www.mandarinmansion.com/article/spears-qing-dynasty>, accessed 7 February 2024.

Elleman Bruce, *A History of the Modern Chinese Navy, 1840–2020* (London: Routledge, 2021).

Elliott Jane, *Some Did It for Civilization, Some Did It for Their Country* (Hong Kong: The Chinese University Press, 2002).

Esherick Joseph, *Origins of the Boxer Uprising* (Berkeley: University of California Press, 1988).

Evans David et al., *Kaigun: Strategy, Tactics, and Technology in the Imperial Japanese Navy, 1887-1941* (Annapolis: Naval Institute Press, 1997).

Ewbank Anne, 'How Killer Rice Crippled Tokyo and the Japanese Navy,' *Atlas Obscura* (2018), <https://www.atlasobscura.com/articles/rice-disease-mystery-edo-tokyo-navy-beriberi>, accessed 2 March 2024.

Folsom Kenneth, *Friends, Guests, and Colleagues: The Mu-fu System in the Late Ch'ing Period* (Berkeley: University of California Press, 1968).

Fung Allen, 'Testing the Self-Strengthening: The Chinese Army in the Sino-Japanese War of 1894–1895', *Modern Asian Studies*, 30:1 (1996).

Heath Ian, *Armies of the Nineteenth Century: China* (Nottingham: Foundry Books, 2009).

Heath Ian, *Armies of the Nineteenth Century: Japan and Korea* (Nottingham: Foundry Books, 2009).

Henley David and Porath Nathan, 'Body Modification in East Asia: History and Debates,' *Asian Studies Review*, 45:2.

Hummel Arthur (ed.), *Eminent Chinese of the Ch'ing Period 1644–1912* (Washington: United States Government Printing Office, 1943).

Jukichi Inouye, *A Concise History of the War Between China and Japan* (Osaka: Z. Mayekawa, 1895).

Inouye Jukichi, *The Fall of Wei-hai-wei* (Yokohama: Kelly and Walsh, 1895).

Inouye Jukichi, *The Japan-China War: on the Regent's Sword: Kinchow, Port Arthur, and Talienwan* (Yokohama: Kelly & Walsh, 1895).

Jung Dieter et al., *Warships of the Imperial Japanese Navy, 1869-1945* (Annapolis: Naval Institute Press, 1976).

Kennedy Thomas, *The Arms of Kiangnan: Modernization in the Chinese Ordnance Industry 1860–1895* (Colorado: Westview Press, 1978).

Kobayashi Ushisaburo, *Military Industries of Japan* (Oxford: Oxford University Press, 1922).

Komiya Nick, 'Imperial Rescript to Soldiers and Sailors,' *War Relics* (2017), <https://www.warrelics.eu/forum/japanese-militaria/imperial-rescript-soldiers-sailors-687558/>, accessed 12 February 2024.

Komiya Nick, 'The Banner of Golden Brocade,' *War Relics* (2016), <https://www.warrelics.eu/forum/japanese-militaria/banner-golden-brocade-647336/>, accessed 12 February 2024.

Komiya Nick, 'The Evolution of IJA Canteens (1889-1945) Expanded Version', *War Relics* (2015), <https://www.warrelics.eu/forum/japanese-militaria/evolution-ija-canteens-1889-1945-expanded-version-586153/>, accessed 12 February 2024.

Komiya Nick, 'The Evolution of the IJA Mess Kit 1874-1945', *War Relics* (2022), <https://www.warrelics.eu/forum/japanese-militaria/evolution-ija-mess-kit-1874-19-a-816235/>, accessed 12 February 2024.

Komiya Nick, 'The Evolution of the Japanese Imperial Army Backpacks (1874-1945)', *War Relics* (2018), <https://www.warrelics.eu/forum/japanese-militaria/evolution-japanese-imperial-army-backpacks-1874-1945-a-695642/>, accessed 12 February 2024.

Komiya Nick, 'The Evolution of the Japanese Imperial Army Sun Helmet: Part I (1887–1921)', *Military Sun Helmets*, <https://www.militarysunhelmets.com/2016/part-i-1887-1921#more-18688>, accessed 12 February 2024.
Komiya Nick, 'The Evolution of the Japanese Infantryman's Entrenching Tool: 1887–1945', *War Relics* (2019), <https://www.warrelics.eu/forum/japanese-militaria/evolution-japanese-infantrymana-s-entrenching-tool-1887-1945-a-753444/>, accessed 12 February 2024.
Lamprey John, 'The Economy of the Chinese Army,' *Journal of the Royal United Services Institution*, 11:43 (1867).
Lone Stewart, *Japan's First Modern War: Army and Society in the Conflict with China, 1894–1895* (London: St. Martin's Press, 1994).
May Ernest (ed.) et al., *History and Neorealism* (Cambridge: Cambridge University Press, 2010).
McCord Edward, 'Local Military Power and Elite Formation: The Liu Family of Xingyi County, Guizhou,' in Joseph Esherick and Mary Rankin (eds.), *Chinese Local Elites and Patterns of Dominance* (Berkeley: University of California, 1990).
Miyoshi Sheila, *The Other Great Game: The Opening of Korea and the Birth of Modern East Asia* (Harvard: Belknap Press, 2023).
Moule A.C., 'A List of the Musical & Other Sound-producing Instruments of the Chinese,' *Journal of the North China Branch of the Royal Asiatic Society*, 115:39 (1908).
Neff Robert, 'The secret weapon of the first Sino-Japanese War (1894–1895)', *The Korea Times* (2018), <https://www.koreatimes.co.kr/www/opinion/2024/12/715_252946.html>, accessed 2 March 2024.
Olender Piotr, *Sino-Japanese Naval War 1894–1895* (Sandomierz: Stratus, 2014).
Paine Sarah, *The Sino–Japanese War of 1894–1895: Perceptions, Power, and Primacy* (Cambridge: Cambridge University Press, 2003).
Passman, Joseph, *Schools of Violence: Military Academies in the Fight for Modern China* (Berkeley: University of California at Berkeley, 2024).
Philip Tom, 'Military Sabers of the Qing Dynasty,' *Mandarin Mansion* (2009), <https://www.mandarinmansion.com/article/military-sabers-qing-dynasty>, accessed 7 February 2024.
Powell John, *Who's who in China; containing the pictures and biographies of China's best known political, financial, business and professional men* (Shanghai: The China Weekly Review, 1925).
Rich, Bushido: Way of Total Bullshit, *Tofugu* (2014), <https://www.tofugu.com/japan/bushido/>, accessed 24 March 2024.
Scherer James, *Japan To-day* (Philadelphia: J. B. Lippincott, 1904).
Shih Bin, Xu Lin, Zielinski, 'The Chinese Kuaili Rifle,' *BANZAI: The Japanese Militaria Collector's Bulletin*.
Sin Sun-chol and Yi Chin-Yong, *A Short History of the Donghak Peasant Revolution* (Jeongeup: Donghak Peasant Revolution Memorial Association, 2008).
Sun Lie, 'The Emergence of Appropriate Technology: The Localization of German Krupp Artillery Technology in China (1866–1932)', *Chinese Annals of History of Science and Technology*, 7:1.
Tohata Seiichi (ed.), *The Modernization of Japan* (Tokyo: Institute of Asian Economic Affairs, 1966).
Tyler William, *Pulling Strings In China* (London: Constable, 1929).
Van Aalst Jan, *Chinese Music* (Shanghai: Statistical Dept. of the Inspectorate General of Customs, 1884).
Volpicelli Zenone, *The China-Japan War Compiled from Japanese, Chinese, and Foreign Sources* (London: S. Low, Marston Limited, 1896).
Warrington Eastlake and Yamada Yoshiaki, *Heroic Japan: A History of the War Between China & Japan* (Yokohama: Kelley & Walsh, 1896).
Wright Richard, *The Chinese Steam Navy 1862–1945* (Annapolis: Naval Institute Press, 2001).
Zielinski Stanley, *Japanese Murata Rifles 1880–1897* (Online: Z&Z Publishing, 2023).
'Responsibility,' The North-China Herald (Shanghai), 28 December 1894.
'The Army of the Chinese Troops,' The North-China Herald (Shanghai), 8 February 1895.

Other Sources
Archives Militaires de l'Armee de Terre, Series 7N1664.
Archives Militaires de l'Armee de Terre, Series 7N1666.
Archives Militaires de l'Armee de Terre, Series 7N1679.
Archives Militaires de l'Armee de Terre, Series 7N1665.
Kim Gi-yun et al., *Taimullain M Je 1 Ho* (Seoul: Doseo Chulpan Gilchajgi, 2022).
Kim Gi-yun et al., *Taimullain M Je 2 Ho* (Seoul: Doseo Chulpan Gilchajgi, 2023).

BOOKS IN THIS SERIES:

1. *The Battle of Majuba Hill The Transvaal Campaign 1880–1881* John Laband (ISBN 978-1-911512-38-7)
2. *For Queen and Company Vignettes of the Irish Soldier in the Indian Mutiny* David Truesdale (ISBN 978-1-911512-79-0)
3. *The Furthest Garrison Imperial Regiments in New Zealand 1840–1870* Adam Davis (ISBN 978-1-911628-29-3)
4. *Victory Over Disease Resolving the Medical Crisis in the Crimean War, 1854–1856* Michael Hinton (ISBN 978-1-911628-31-6)
5. *Journey Through the Wilderness Garnet Wolseley's Canadian Red River Expedition of 1870* Paul McNicholls (ISBN 978-1-911628-30-9)
6. *Kitchener The Man Not The Myth* Anne Samson (ISBN 978-1-912866-45-8)
7. *The British and the Sikhs Discovery, Warfare and Friendship c1700–1900* Gurinder Singh Mann (ISBN 978-1-911628-24-8)
8. *Bazaine 1870 Scapegoat for a Nation* Quintin Barry (ISBN 978-1-913336-08-0)
9. *Redcoats in the Classroom The British Army's Schools For Soldiers and Their Children During the 19th Century* Howard R. Clarke (ISBN 978-1-912866-47-2)
10. *The Rescue They Called a Raid The Jameson Raid 1895–96* David Snape (ISBN 978-1-913118-77-8)
11. *Hungary 1848 The Winter Campaign* Christopher Pringle (ISBN 978-1-913118-78-5)
12. *The War of the Two Brothers The Portuguese Civil War 1828-1834* Sérgio Veludo Coelho (ISBN 978-1-914059-26-1)
14. *Forgotten Victorian Generals Studies in the Exercise of Command and Control in the British Army 1837–1901* Christopher Brice (editor) (ISBN 978-1-910777-20-6)
15. *The German War of 1866 The Bohemian and Moravian Campaign* Theodore Fontane (ISBN 978-1-914059-29-2)
16. *Dust of Glory The First Anglo-Afghan War 1839–1842, its Causes and Course* Bill Whitburn (ISBN 978-1-914059-33-9)
17. *Saarbruck to Sedan The Franco-German War 1870–1871 Volume 1* Ralph Weaver (ISBN 978-1-914059-88-9)
18. *The Battle of Lissa 1866 How the Industrial Revolution Changed the Face of Naval Warfare* Quintin Barry (ISBN 978-1-914059-92-6)
19. *The Zulu Kingdom and the Boer Invasion of 1837–1840* John Laband (ISBN 978-1-914059-89-6)
20. *The Fire of Venture Was in His Veins* Major Allan Wilson and the Shangani Patrol 1893 David Snape (ISBN 978-1-914059-90-2)
21. *From the Atacama to the Andes Battles of the War of the Pacific 1879–1883* Alan Curtis (ISBN 978-1-914059-90-2)
22. *The Rise of the Sikh Soldier The Sikh Warrior Through the Ages, c1700–1900* Gurinder Singh Mann (ISBN 978-1-915070-52-4)
23. *Victorian Crusaders British and Irish Volunteers in the Papal Army 1860–70* Nicholas Schofield (ISBN 978-1-915070-53-1)
24. *The Battle for the Swiepwald Austria's Fatal Blunder at Königgrätz, the climactic battle of the Austro-Prussian War, 3 July 1866* Ernst Heidrich (ISBN 978-1-915070-49-4)
25. *British Military Panoramas Battle in The Round, 1800–1914* Ian F.W. Beckett (ISBN 978-1-915113-84-9)
26. *Onwards to Omdurman The Anglo-Egyptian Campaign to Reconquer the Sudan, 1896–1898* Keith Surridge (ISBN 978-1-915070-51-7)
27. *Hungary 1849 The Summer Campaign* Wilhelm Ramming, Christopher Pringle (editor) (ISBN 978-1-915113-80-1)
28. *Line in the Sand French Foreign Legion Forts and Fortifications in Morocco 1900–1926* Richard Jeynes (ISBN 978-1-915113-83-2)
29. *The Republic Fights Back The Franco-German War 1870–1871 Volume 2* Ralph Weaver (ISBN 978-1-915070-50-0)
30. *Controlling the Frontier Southern Africa 1806–1828, The Cape Frontier Wars and The Fetcani Alarm* Hugh Driver (ISBN 978-1-915113-78-8)
31. *The Battle of Magersfontein Victory and defeat on the South African veld, 10–12 December 1899* Garth Benneyworth (ISBN 978-1-915113-79-5)
32. *Too Little Too Late The Campaign in West and South Germany June–July 1866* Michael Embree (ISBN 978-1-804513-77-4)
33. *The Destruction of the Imperial Army* Volume 1: The Opening Engagements of the Franco-German War 1870–71 Grenville Bird (ISBN 978-1-915113-81-8)
34. *Kitchener The Man Not the Myth* Anne Samson (ISBN 978-1-804513-84-2)
35. *From Ironclads to Dreadnoughts* The Development of the German Battleship, 1864–1918 Dirk Nottelmann & David M. Sullivan (ISBN 978-1-804511-84-8)
36. *The Destruction of the Imperial Army* Volume 2: The Battles around Metz Grenville Bird (ISBN 978-1-804511-85-5)
37. *More Work Than Glory* Buffalo Soldiers in the United States Army, 1866–1916 John P Langellier (ISBN 978-1-804513-34-7)
38. *The Spioenkop Campaign* The Battles to Relieve Ladysmith 17–27 January 1900 Robert Davidson (ISBN 978-1-804513-31-6)
39. *The Destruction of the Imperial Army* Volume 3: The Sedan Campaign 1870 Grenville Bird (ISBN 978-1-804513-32-3)
40. *The Destruction of the Imperial Army* Volume 4: Sedan, Strasbourg and Metz 1870 Grenville Bird (ISBN 978-1-804514-59-7)
41. *Memorandum on the Prussian Army in Relation to the Campaign of 1866* Lieutenant Colonel W.E.M Reilly (ISBN 978-1-804516-27-0)
42. *Black Week: The British Army and Defeat in Anglo-Boer War 1899–1900* Quintin Barry (ISBN 978-1-804511-86-2)
43. *War in the East. A Military History of the Russo-Turkish War 1877-78* Quintin Barry (ISBN 978-1-804517-30-7)
44. *The First Schleswig-Holstein War 1848-50* Nick Svendsen (ISBN 978-1-804517-36-9)
45. *The Hundred Thousand Sons of St Louis* Ralph Weaver (ISBN 978-1-804517-37-6)
46. *Bismarck's First War: The Campaign in Schleswig and Jutland 1864* Michael Embree (ISBN 978-1-804517-38-3)
47. *The Honvéd War. Armies of the Hungarian War of Independence 1848-49* Nigel James Smith (ISBN 978-1-804514-60-3)
48. *Radestzky's Marches. The Campaigns of 1848 and 1849 in Upper Italy* Michael Embree (ISBN 978-1-804517-42-0)
49. *The Campaign on the Loire 1870-71: Orléans and Le Mans* Quintin Barry (ISBN 978-1-804517-82-6)
50. *The British Empire's Regulars 1880-1914: Soldiers of Britain, India and Africa* Wendell Scholander (ISBN 978-1-804515-62-4)
51. *The Last Throw of the Dice: Bourbaki and Werder in Eastern France 1870-71* Quintin Barry (ISBN 978-1-804517-78-9)
52. *Three Weeks in November. A Military History of the Swiss Civil War of 1847* Ralph Weaver (ISBN 978-1-804518-49-6)
53. *The Battle of Wörth August 6th 1870* Lieut.-Col. G.F.R. Henderson (ISBN 978-1-804517-90-1)
54. *The Battle of Spicheren August 6th 1870* Lieut.-Col. G.F.R. Henderson (ISBN 978-1-804518-50-2)
55. *The Serbian Army in the Wars for Independence against Turkey 1876-1878* Dusan M. Babac (ISBN 978-1-804518-69-4)
56. *The Campaign in Alsace August 1870* Brigadier-General J.P. Du Cane, C.B. (ISBN 978-1-804518-82-3)
57. *The Franco-Prussian War 1870-71 Volume 1* Quintin Barry (ISBN 978-1-806721-04-7)
58. *The Franco-Prussian War 1870-71 Volume 2* Quintin Barry (ISBN 978-1-806721-05-4)
59. *Sunstruck Giant Volume 1: The Sino-Japanese War of 1894-95 Part 1* John Dong (ISBN 978-1-804518-15-1)